BALANCING ON AN ALP
Ecological change and continuity in a Swiss mountain community

FOR JACQUELINE

Balancing on an Alp

Ecological change and continuity in a Swiss mountain community

ROBERT McC. NETTING

University of Arizona

CAMBRIDGE UNIVERSITY PRESS

Cambridge
London   New York   New Rochelle
Melbourne   Sydney

Published by the Press Syndicate of the University of Cambridge
The Pitt Building, Trumpington Street, Cambridge CB2 1RP
32 East 57th Street, New York, NY 10022, USA
296 Beaconsfield Parade, Middle Park, Melbourne 3206, Australia

© Cambridge University Press 1981

First published 1981

Printed in the United States of America

Library of Congress Cataloging in Publication Data

Netting, Robert McC

Balancing on an Alp.

Includes bibliographical references and index.

1. Human ecology – Switzerland – Törbel.
2. Anthropo-geography – Switzerland – Törbel.
3. Törbel, Switzerland – Social life and customs.
I. Title.
GF632.T63N47   304.2′09494′7   81-358
ISBN 0 521 23743 2 hard covers   AACR1
ISBN 0 521 28197 0 paperback

Contents

Foreword

This is a book about a closed corporate community in Western Europe, a Swiss village situated high up in the mountains, and about the ecological balance between its inhabitants and the environment. The phrase "closed corporate community," made familiar by anthropological authorities on peasant communal life, is deliberately chosen by Robert Netting and recurs throughout his text. So does the word "homeostatic," for population, resources, and environment have been in balance in the village of Törbel because of compensating social mechanisms. ("Negative feedback" would be the phrase that the mechanically minded would be tempted to employ.) Now the concepts of a closed community and of homeostasis, too, are essentially historical. One of the conspicuous virtues of Robert Netting's study – a study of outstanding interest and value from every point of view, or so it seems to me – is that he takes history seriously.

Netting anatomizes Törbel over a period of time, dynamically, and he does so over no less than three hundred years. This enables him to work out the demographic record in detail, using the techniques recently developed for the purpose; and such a record is essential for understanding the perduring balance between the population and its environment. He is well aware that in order to establish the reality and nature of this balance, even greater temporal depth, stretching back into prehistoric times, may be required. Törbel, therefore, may well become the classic example of the small, self-sufficient European community in balanced relation to its environment. Netting is conscious of the possibility that it may persuade people to suppose that all European villages tended to be like this. He repeatedly reminds us, however, that the population studied was, and is, in a highly individual, indeed, an exceptional position. Törbel can hardly be universalized. This is not only because of its remote and mountainous position, in the midst of a continent where a great majority of the people lived in communities set close upon the plains. It is also because the relationship of Törbel as a body of persons with other bodies of persons was decidedly not symmetrical, whatever may have been its relationship with its physical environment.

From the carefully worked out and presented figures that Netting gives – the tables are clear and informative and the discussion of them in the text brief and illuminating – we learn that people were always leaving Törbel but almost never joined it. Over the three hundred years, that is to say, there was a pronounced tendency for out-migration to take place, reaching its height when fertility went up in the nineteenth century, but not for in-migration. Endogamy was at a very high level: At least double the proportion of marriages took place between natives of the village as was usual in England at this time. Most conspicuous of all for me is the unparalleled persistence of family lines.

"Only three men," Netting tells us, "appear to have settled in Törbel, married, and had children there since 1700. One later left with his family, one had living descendants, and a third is currently living." One has to have great confidence in the completeness and reliability of the documentation to make statements of this kind. It is a further mark of the uniqueness of the case, for such circumstances are certainly absent where such things can be studied elsewhere in Northern and Western Europe. In the social and economic core of the community, Netting is able to claim, among the knot of succeeding male holders of citizenship and of the economically crucial right to grazing on the alp, patriline persistence between the early 1700s and the 1950s was markedly superior to the one comparative example he cites, that of the English baronetcies between the 1620s and the 1760s.[1]

Among these peasant farmers in their cramped alpine dwellings, therefore, kinship was better recorded and remembered than it was at Kellynch Hall in Somerset. In that dignified mansion in the early 1800s, as all readers of Jane Austen's *Persuasion* will remember, Sir Walter Elliot, Bart., "never took up any book but the Baronetage . . . there he could read his own history on the page at which his favourite volume always opened . . . Sir Walter had improved it by adding . . 'Heir presumptive, William Walter Elliot, Esq., great grandson of the second Sir Walter.' " This William Walter must have been a fourth, fifth, or even more distant cousin. It is not easy to believe that living together over the generations in the same village did in fact make Törbel peasants better reckoners of their kin, even though it had been held that, on average, succession to English baronetcies did not go much beyond first cousinship. We should not dwell too much on this picturesque point, for it is one element only in Netting's case for solidarity over time and may in any case have a fairly simple statistical or demographic explanation.[2]

Enough has been said in introductory commendation of this book to make it clear how absorbingly interesting are the issues raised by the notion of a community closed and corporate over time, and how crucial this study is to their elucidation. Homeostasis has not been discussed here, though the intricacies of that topic are also surprising. Does ecological homeostasis cease, for example, when the introduction of the potato leads (in Netting's view) to unprecedented fertility and so to even more intense out-migration? Is a population that has to lose people in this way in balance with its resources in any case? And if not, by how much? And if, as our author convincingly claims, this closed population was not conscious of obeying homeostatic rules, how were those rules maintained?

We have also not referred to the residential rules of these people after marriage. Neolocalism was almost universal, and it is firmly laid down that nuclear families were the outcome. This is hardly what we have come to expect of the mountainous areas of Europe; and not far away, on the Italian side of the Alps, the family system was very different. But the readers must be left here with Netting's splendid study to reflect for themselves on these issues and on the many others that Netting raises with such grace and skill.

Peter Laslett

Cambridge
February 1981

Preface

"Why is an anthropologist and an Africanist going to alpine Switzerland?" This question, either directly expressed or implied, was both the first and the most frequent response to my plans in the late 1960s for fieldwork in a Swiss peasant community. Colleagues wondered aloud if I was giving up my concern with farming, household organization, and land tenure among the Kofyar and other Nigerian peoples and forsaking the bush with its tropic sun, thatched roofs, and "tribal" villagers for the coolness of mountains and the comparative ease and safety of civilization. Anthropology, despite its pretensions to comparative studies of cultures, still harbors some suspicion of the scholar who leaves that geographical area where his supposed expertise has been developed and skips from one distinctive type of society to another that appears radically different. Moreover, the folk wisdom of the discipline, passed on in anecdotes of hardship and primitive exotica, betrays a certain pride in the fact that field anthropology is no picnic. The prevailing international image of Switzerland, carefully fostered by a century of travel posters and guided tours, is of a land for vacationing. It was difficult to imagine that serious research might be done when skiing and mountain climbing beckoned from the comfortable resort hotel and where the most familiar national products are cheese, milk chocolate, and wristwatches. On the other hand, the stereotype of the foreign visitor is so pervasive that even after 14 months of data collection in the Swiss village, local residents still politely inquired how I was enjoying my vacation. Swiss social scientists, though uniformly cordial and cooperative, were also mildly astonished at the notion of an anthropologist who was neither folklorist nor linguist coming to study their own rural people.

I cannot say that it was either the visual attractions of the Alps or the sane predictability of Swiss politics, in contrast to recent upheavals in many African nations, that drew me to that small country at the roof of Western Europe. Rather, as I tried to convince my dubious friends, there were a number of problems raised by my earlier research that could be and holds out the possibility of a comprehensive understanding gained directly from conversation, observation, and participation in ongoing daily life. Statistics on mortality, no matter how refined, are difficult for an anthropologist to consider apart from the wakes and funeral processions, the expressions of grief for the dead and condolences for the living, that accompany the physical fact of dying. The comments of friends and consultants on farming practices currently and in the past, on those migrants who had left the village, on wealth and poverty, were needed to flesh out the land registers, the immigrant lists, and the tax accounts. Computations of the frequencies of certain kinds of marriage gained immediacy and meaning from anecdotes of actual courtships and individual disappointments. No conviction is implied here that social interaction as it exists today is a faithful replica of what went on in previous centuries or that past beliefs and values are preserved as if in amber. I am merely pointing out that for a cultural anthropologist interested in the history of certain kinds of activities, the quantitative study of a small range of documented behavior should ideally be interpreted through and supplemented by the unmediated experience of the living society. Such an approach may leave us somewhere between the objective rigor of the physical scientist and the empathetic appreciation of the novelist, but for reasons not altogether clear, this niche is often the one chosen by anthropologists, and they seem to find it congenial.

Granted, then, that to see a human ecosystem in process I required dependable, continuous, and relatively complete records of a localized population and that I preferred to connect these with an existing community whose inhabitants had descended in good part from the documented ancestors. If I wished to learn about population regulation, external influences on the community should be as limited as possible, or at least historically known. By that I mean that I wanted a village with a constant and well-defined natural environment, a fairly static technology of subsistence agriculture, and a recent past relatively undisturbed by economic revolutions, wars, mass migrations, or political transformations.

It would be less than candid to lay before you a series of neatly articulated hypotheses that I wished to test in the fieldwork setting I have outlined. Rather, there were sets of common understandings or premises based on my own studies and on the work of other ecological anthropologists, as well as some persistent questions that none of us seemed able to answer. Our first approximations of local ecosystems had emphasized the complex interactions of variables in relatively isolated, self-sufficient, technologically simple societies. We described the features of climate, precipitation, soils, vegetation, and animal life that seemed relevant to human subsistence, the techniques for gathering or growing food under these circumstances, and the social arrangements and beliefs by which the job was done. Like the biological ecologists, we sought connections in energy flows among factors, timing work effort and counting kilocalories produced and consumed. Such systems models (Rappaport 1971*b*; Little and Morren 1976) are both instructive and aesthetically satisfying, but they necessarily emphasize closure, equilibrium, and mutual adaptations of parts that operate to counteract deviations and insulate the system from environmental perturbations. The articulations of environmental constraints and institutional options that perpetuate a system and allow the human members to fill their physical needs are things of compelling beauty. The theme of balance and the intricate operations of cybernetic regulatory mechanisms were absorbed by all of us from Roy Rappaport's elegant models (1968, 1971*a*) of the Maring. I reasoned that some such ecological equilibrium must also characterize the peasant communities that show such remarkable durability and continuity in so many parts of the world. A situation of long-standing agricultural self-sufficiency, permanent settlement, geographical isolation, and static technological inventory would give me, I hoped, the naturally controlled setting for charting demographic self-regulation.

The tighter the integration of the whole and the more persuasive our models of internal cohesion, the less opportunity there is for us to witness transforming processes or evolutionary change. Without time depth, we cannot explain how the system came to be or what it is likely to become (Vayda and Rappaport 1968). The same criticisms of structural functionalism with its static equilibrium models and organic analogies can be leveled against the "best-of-all-possible-worlds" portrayals of hunter-gatherer seasonality or pig feast cycles (Bayliss-Smith 1977:44). An ecosystem that unaccountably springs full-blown from people-cum-environment will run in its accustomed grooves until derailed by the "initial kick" of declining average temperatures or food-plant mutations or bubonic plague or enemies with cannons. "Equilibria annihilate history. It is the nature of an equilibrium point that all paths in the dynamical space lead to it (at least locally), so that the particular history of change is irrelevant and, once the system is at equilibrium, there is no trace left of historical information" (Lewontin 1974:269).

It seemed to me that the strategy of ecosystem analysis had to be extended, beginning as it always had in a sound appraisal of how people survived in their natural surroundings and how they responded to life-threatening conditions, but going on to those factors that were fundamentally different from one generation to the next, the ways in which people met novel challenges and unprecedented problems that often originated outside their local subsistence system (Cole and Wolf 1974:20). This did not necessarily imply a chameleonlike change in ethnic identities, or a political and economic revolution, or even a discernible change in the existing system of thought and cognition. All that might alter were the proportions of choices from among existing behavioral alternatives. People might do different things in a statistically observable way without intrinsic variation in their traditional mental categories, values, or dominant symbols, without, in effect, experiencing major "cultural" change. Ecological tools are well adapted to exposing those often subtle shifts in behavior that frequently escape ethnography done "from the native's point of view" and that serve both to obscure real change and to promote the conviction of cultural continuity.

I will admit that my plans for approaching such problems in a field study had overambitious aims and a dependence on undemonstrated sources of information, but because these same factors characterize many incipient anthropological enterprises, they were no cause for dismay. The combination of written historical evidence and the continuity of a living community that I sought seemed to recommend a site in Europe. The path from my broad aims to the specific site of Törbel was paved with chance, opportunism, and a measure of serendipity. Switzerland, and particularly its more isolated alpine regions, seemed a good spot to begin the quest. It was reported that peasant agriculture was still practiced there, and the various convulsions that had wracked much of modern Europe had spared neutral Switzerland, at least since 1800. No wars of religion had destroyed the parish archives and filled the towns with refugees. Dairying and crop production had only recently and partially been mechanized, at least in the mountains. I hoped, but did not know with certainty, that villages had retained their boundaries and identities for long periods and that some of them were not yet tourist towns.

A fellow anthropologist, a Swiss, Jean-Claude Muller, whom I met in Nigeria, suggested that Valais Canton in the Rhone drainage of southern Switzerland might afford possibilities for the kind of research that interested me. It was conservative and old-fashioned, with small, stable farming settlements in the side valleys. He mentioned that Gerald Berthoud (1967) had recently completed a study of a French-speaking Valaisan community. From the library and from various advisers I acquired more information on the area, concentrating on the eastern, German-language part of the canton for the simple but regrettable reason that I could speak German but no French. The practical value of choosing a fieldwork site partially on the basis of an already-known language is mentioned by Cole and Wolf (1974:5). It would be more accurate to say that standard German, though an acceptable mode of communication in upper Valais, was by no means the language of daily life. Swiss German (*Schweizerdeutsch*) is a highly distinctive group of regional dialects with a great many lexical and grammatical differences from high German. It remains the first language of children and the colloquial medium of choice when speaking to other Swiss. The upper Valais villagers claim that their own dialect can be unintelligible to Swiss from Zürich or Bern and that there are a number of idiomatic usages found only in their village. Although they refer to it disparagingly as *schlecht Deutsch* (poor German), it is employed not only in private conversation but also on public occasions, such as in humorous plays staged in the village and local town meetings. However, the minutes of all organizations are necessarily kept in standard German, and this so-called *schrift Deutsch* (written German) is learned in school and is the only form found in newspapers and books. An educated individual uses it in public discourse, as for instance the parish priest in his sermons or the speaker on the Swiss national holiday. I was told that, as a professor, it was entirely proper for me to use the standard literary language. For reasons of convenience I did this, and most of my consultants were gracious enough to reply in their second language, but I undoubtedly missed the nuances of overheard dialect speech that convey humor, personal attitudes, and muted hostility. My 6-year-old son, who learned to read German in the village school and to speak dialect on the streets, acquired through his linguistic skills an admiration and affection that I could not match.

The detailed and tremendously informative geography of Gutersohn (1961) suggested several possible field locations. Professor Arnold Niederer, a folklorist at the University of Zürich, concurred in the choice of area and aided us in gaining official permission for our project. John Cole, who already knew the Italian Tyrol well (Cole and Wolf 1974), had been favorably impressed by the Goms valley section. A proposal for ecological research emphasizing the population history of an alpine peasant community in Valais was accepted by the John Simon Guggenheim Memorial Foundation, and this fellowship was supplemented by grants from the University Museum of the University of Pennsylvania and the National Science Foundation (GS-3318). Later funding was provided in 1974–5 by the NICHHD Center for Population Research (HDO 8587-02) and in 1977–78 by the National Science Foundation (BNS-83119). The support of these various agencies is gratefully acknowledged.

One potential site, the formerly very traditional Lötschental, was being studied in 1969–70 by John Friedl of Berkeley. He not only gave us a great deal of background information on the area and living conditions there but also arranged temporary accommodations for me and my family in Kippel while we became acquainted with Oberwallis. Because Valais Canton has had both German- and French-speaking residents since perhaps the ninth century A.D., the ancient geographical and political entity has names in both languages, as do most of its principal towns. French Valais is German Wallis, the capital Sion is also Sitten, Viège is Visp, Val d'Anniviers is Eifischtal, and the Rhone is also the Rotten. I use the French cantonal name because it is more familiar to English-speaking readers, but in line with secondary ethnocentrism that ties me to another linguistic group, I think of the place as Wallis. Friedl also introduced me to the cantonal archive in Sion and to a monograph by Stebler (1922) that lucidly described several villages in Vispertal, the largest of which was Törbel. I was particularly fascinated by an extensive irrigation system timed by the movements of sun and shadow on the slopes and said to be still in operation.

A visit to Törbel confirmed that the village maintained its cow herd and its meadows, that the log chalets were both old and occupied, that there were few summer guests and no winter guests, and that the parish had a promising complement of elderly but well-preserved registers. Herr Otto Karlen, then the president of the community, listened patiently to my halting discussion of our research and offered us every cooperation in pursuing it. The parish priest, Hochwürdiger Herr Pfarrer Markus Jossen, kindly allowed us access to the church records and the trove of parchment rolls that reflected important events in Törbel's history back to the thirteenth century. A local hotel-keeper, Herr Helmut Hosennen, made our entire family, including my wife and three small children, welcome and later helped us to find permanent lodging.

Over the next months, from July 1970 through August 1971, it gradually emerged that Törbel was an exceedingly good place for the work I had in mind and, taken all together, was a lucky choice. Practically every family in the village graciously allowed me to take a household census that included agricultural data and information on migrant kin. With permission from *Gemeinderat* and cantonal authorities, the *Registerhalter*, Herr Roman Wyss, allowed us to consult the large folio volumes of the community real estate registry, and the *Zivilstandsbeamter*, Herr Philemon Seematter, made possible the use of vital statistics that paralleled those of the parish records. Besides those already mentioned, a number of individuals gave generously of their time in sharing with me their knowledge of Törbel past and present. They included Herr Kamil Lorenz and his good wife Hermine Lorenz-Karlen, Herr Siegfried Wyss, Frau Maria Zuber-Lorenz, Herr Werner Juon,

Herr Theodor Seematter, Fräulein Ida Juon, the brothers Heinrich and Ignaz Kalbermatten, Herr Isidor Karlen, Herr Ignaz Ruff, Herr Alois Schaller, and Herr Walter Juon. The unfailing friendship and hospitality of these fine people made us at home in Törbel and their discernment and quick intelligence could be counted on to sharpen and support our inquiries.

Because of the sheer bulk of documentary materials, the task of accurate transcription was possible only because of the dedicated assistance of the university students Christian Lorenz and Ferdinand Schaller (now embarked on careers in the church and in law, respectively) and of Frau Maria Juon-Juon and her son Manfred. Summer residents Frau Marga Furrer of Bern and Dr. Erik Undritz of Basel and Zeneggen discussed the village with me and gave me access to their libraries. Dr. Bernhard Truffer of the *Staatsbibliothek*, Sion, greatly aided me in finding and interpreting materials in the cantonal archives. Historical documents in medieval Latin were translated and usefully commented on by Herr U.-D. Sprenger, and local records of disease were collected by Fräulein Emmy Nussbaumer. Herr Peter Schwendener made us copies of maps and planning surveys of the village. The current *Gemeindepräsident*, Herr Roman Juon, has continued to make community historical resources available to us. Dr. Hanspeter Wagner from Basel kindly provided us with a fine selection of black and white illustrations from among the many photographs and films he has made in Törbel over recent years. It is apparent that research on Törbel has been a communal, cooperative effort in every sense of the word, and I am very grateful to all who participated in it.

Although fieldwork in Switzerland had already covered an initial period of 14 months in 1970–1 and additional 2-month summer stays in 1974 and 1977, the amount of time and effort devoted to analysis of the data was at least as great. One of the painful discoveries of anyone sifting and organizing a large body of quantitative information from disparate historical sources is that the work is necessarily slow, careful, and unbelievably repetitious. One summer spent in a windowless university office went entirely to sorting 3-by-5-inch file cards with names, parents' and spouses' names, birth/marriage/death dates, and family numbers for each of the approximately 5,500 individuals present in the Törbel records. Weeding out duplications, attaching poorly documented death dates to possible candidates, and removing errors of transcription required innumerable small but nerve-racking decisions. Only machine processing of this corpus made sense, but developing a system of keypunched inputs, correcting and updating this file, and producing various outputs for both data retrieval and computation purposes made for an arduous process. A reviewer of one grant application commented that "Netting has become infatuated with computers." On the contrary, I neither liked nor understood this electronic wizardry at the beginning of the project, and even the continual clicking of the key punch machine seemed to me vaguely disturbing. Fortunately, Larry Manire, then head of the Department of Anthropology Research Support Section, University of Arizona, responded with innovative computer programming, tenacity, and sensitivity to the anthropological problems involved. Thanks are also due to Carol Margolis, Jim Mees, Roberta Hagaman, and Susan Ciolek-Torrelo, who aided with the computer work, and to Fran Stier and John Massa, who transcribed and checked demographic data. Walter Elias (Ellis), a physical anthropologist who used some of the Törbel material in his dissertation on inbreeding and isonymy, played an indispensable role in the 3-year task of computerizing the data and applying statistical tests to the results. Walter deftly administered a number of graduate assistants and organized the computer work, planned further research as a co-principal investigator, and published a number of key findings (Elias and Netting 1977; Ellis and Starmer 1978; Hagaman, Elias, and Netting 1978; Netting and Elias 1980). His dedication to the research and his patience over the long haul made his scholarly and personal contributions as a colleague and friend extremely valuable.

In both methods and theory, ecological anthropology is necessarily interdisciplinary. This has been apparent in stimulating overlaps with geography, biology, nutrition, and agricultural economics (Vayda and Rappaport 1968; Netting 1977). In particular, the Törbel study owed much to recent progress in historical demography and economic history. New techniques for reconstructing population parameters and deriving rates from parish registers and household lists had been developed in France and England. Wrigley's exciting summary of this work in his *Population and History* (1969) convinced me of the possibility of deriving dependable demographic indices on a local community through time and comparing that population with other European rural samples from the same period. Moreover, the use of population data in conjunction with documentary evidence of land tenure, village political decisions, climatic fluctuations, and economic conditions in the past was opening the way for what Le Roy Ladurie (1977) has called "an anthropology of history."

Wishing to make contact with some of the most active practitioners in demographic history, I wrote to Tony Wrigley and Peter Laslett, eventually arranging to meet them at a conference in Copenhagen in 1974. We discussed the raw data coming out of Törbel and the difficulties of analyzing the data satisfactorily. Roger Schofield, the other leading member of the Cambridge Group for the History of Population and Social Structure, proposed that I put my reconstituted family data in the form used by the Cambridge computer programs. This would allow tabulations to be performed with sophisticated methods already derived for handling historical materials and would save me having to "reinvent the wheel." I gladly accepted Schofield's offer, and in the next few years the Cambridge Group sent me scores of their standard calculations based on an "English file" of Törbel families that Larry Manire produced. Much of the demography I learned was acquired in interpreting the detailed printouts that arrived from Cambridge, and unexpected break-throughs in our understanding (such as that of changing birth intervals) were directly traceable to these tabulations. The Cambridge Group historians and computer experts have been remarkably generous, supportive of our efforts, and tolerant of our occasional "howlers."

Several American sociological demographers, especially John Knodel and Nancy Howell, have read and commented with considerable insight and restraint on portions of our analyses. There is no doubt, however, that other experts in the study of population will find some of our findings methodologically naive and presumptuous in their suggestions of causation. Anthropologists have been fairly warned that "it is highly dangerous to trespass beyond the limits of one's competence" and that "specialization and keeping to one's last in the social sciences" is required to develop theoretical understanding (Devons and Gluckman 1964:181). Although I cannot claim the specialized training and demonstrated mastery of the demographer or the economic historian, I cannot in all good faith pursue my research goals without benefit of their tools. I would agree with Boissevain (1975:16) that "It may not be possible to stick to your last if the questions asked change. And clearly they have changed. The consequence of this change is that anthropologists must rethink the assumptions, boundaries and techniques of their discipline."

Just as some historians damn the cliometricians in their midst, whereas statisticians condemn the uses historians make of their numbers, so anthropologists accuse each other of giving up on culture in favor of "practical reason" or, on the other hand, of aping the hard sciences in an orgy of quantification. I can only demur that the numbers I use are a kind of shorthand for managing the regularities and more especially the variations observed in some few kinds of human behavior. They reflect something of cultural rules and conscious values but much more of the range of acceptable options people have and the constraints of environment, economics, and status that influence their choices. Shared, conventional understandings may, and I suspect often do, persist while people adapt to their immediate circumstances. Change, as witnessed in process, rather than at the end of a century's continuum, is no more than an alteration in statistical probabilities in certain limited activities. For this reason, people will often deny that anything has happened to significantly change their society, and anthropologists become the high priests of cultural stability. But where series of numbers can be extracted from consistent records of the past, traces of small differences, cycles, cumulative trends emerge, and the workings of an ecosystem can be discerned. Social science becomes at least a possibility.

Because the village universe is not very large, even when extended back for three centuries, and because there have been few other studies of Swiss community populations or of alpine enclaves anywhere, the charge of biased and unrepresentative numbers is easy to make. Anthropologists are by nature (or maybe by culture) blithely unworried by such caveats. Our tribes and kingdoms have characteristically been villages writ large, and without written history or questionnaires we have left many such problems of sampling to the sociologists. A small self-contained unit has its own advantages for study.

> Like the statistical reasoning in small-scale medical research relying on the consistency of findings replicated in different clinics, comparative study in the barnyard and in the small market villages and towns is open to heavy criticism from statisticians whose faith rests on large numbers. Yet to rely exclusively on large numbers automatically eliminates consideration of some of the more important variables that can be observed in play in these small universes. Above all, it obliges one to forego the pleasure of identifying situations in which individuals, in at least some phases of their life cycle, enjoyed and exercised options. This pleasure seems to be considered unscientific, for one hardly ever meets an individual in today's journal articles. [Thrupp 1975:6]

In some parts of the book that follows, graphs and tables litter the pages, and columns of numbers threaten to topple about the ears of the reader. I will not apologize to those who see figures as inherently opposed to humanism or who do not wish to penetrate this variety of "thick description." The numbers are there to support, refine, and qualify arguments about how Swiss peasants survived and even prospered at home in the Alps. This kind of painfully collected evidence may deny a hypothesis as often as it affirms one, and one of my chief joys in this investigation has been to be contradicted by the facts. Quite regularly I have had my first approximations of factors involved in population stability or inheritance and family size or politics and marriage abruptly struck down by the data that we marshaled. Yet, in every case, the failure of a simple model suggested more complex explanations and more satisfyingly inclusive models of human behavior. Falsification is fun, and an arid multivariate analysis may often do more to justify man's way to man than a stack of structuralist volumes. An inductive approach such as this one may be a trifle plodding and piecemeal. Indeed, much of the book took shape as individual papers worked out in terms of single questions and thought through in relative isolation, rather than being fashioned as part of a grand design. But pursuit of this line preserved the delight in the individual-component puzzles to be solved and the possibility of surprise and wonder as new patterns became clear.

The selective use of numbers and the somewhat eclectic choice of topics in the following chapters are not meant to reflect a parochial idea of what anthropology can be or should be. A detailed consideration of family interaction in the kitchen of a farmhouse is just as valuable as, and perhaps a good bit more interesting than, comparisons of household sizes and compositions. The symbolism of every step of a Corpus Christi procession and its implications for village social solidarity are as dramatic and colorful as potato cultivation is dull and prosaic. Nevertheless, the questions I have asked about making a living, balancing population and food supply, and inheriting property have to do with fundamental ecological problems. Trying to answer them in some reasonably comprehensive way has required a focusing of my slender faculties and the development of a few new skills. Other equally legitimate and interesting inquiries await the anthropological observer whose tastes and abilities are different than my own.

Even a semblance of interdisciplinary competence requires a healthy mixture of criticism and encouragement from other fields. I have enjoyed just such contacts with a variety of scholars, especially Professor of Folklore Arnold Niederer, a well-informed and sympathetic interpreter of Wallis, and Professor of History Rudolf Braun, both of Zürich. Professor Niederer was good enough to read and comment on the entire manuscript, saving me from annoying errors of German spelling and a few egregious misinterpretations of fact. Dr. Arthur Imhof of Berlin has maintained a lively interest in the Törbel work. I have benefited greatly from both the exchange of ideas and the hospitality of Dr. Daniela Weinberg and Dr. Ellen Wiegandt, both of whom have done impressive village studies in Valais. Ongoing research on the blood groups of the Törbel population is being conducted by Dr. Wolfgang Scheffrahn and his students in physical anthropology at the University of Zürich. Many of those mentioned earlier, as well as others, including Ester Boserup, Steve Kunitz, Gail Harrison, Donald McCloskey, Aram Yengoyan, Rose Frisch, and William Stini, commented on drafts of articles that have been incorporated into this manuscript. Their suggestions, whether accepted or not, were always appreciated, but the responsibility for the final product is my own.

For preliminary editing, I relied heavily on the skill and discrimination of Carol Gifford. The typists, Barbara Fregoso and Doris Sample, combined prompt efficiency and unfailing good humor. A sabbatical half year from the University of Arizona provided unbroken time for writing and the infinitely more painful task of revision. The Department of Anthropology and its head, Ray Thompson, could always be counted on for research support, from computer time to file cards. Hans Bart of the Arizona State Museum Library was ever willing to aid me with difficult German translations. At Cambridge University Press, editorial director Walter Lippincott encouraged the project and managing editor Rhona Johnson carefully shepherded the manuscript through the publication process. I was fortunate to have such help, and I am grateful for it.

Acknowledgments

Cover photograph and photographs in the text by Dr. Hanspeter Wagner.

Chapter 3 is an expanded revised version of "Of Men and Meadows: Strategies of Alpine Land Use," from *Anthropological Quarterly 45*: 132–44 (1972). Reprinted by permission of The Catholic University of America Press.

Portions of Chapters 3 and 8 are adapted from "What Alpine Peasants have in Common: Observations on Communal Tenure in a Swiss Village," *Human Ecology 4*: 135–46 (1976). Reprinted by permission of Plenum Publishing Corporation.

Chapter 4 is an English adaptation of "Eine lange Ahnenreihe: Die Fortdauer von Patrilinien über mehr als drei Jahrhunderte in einen Schweizerischen Bergdorf," from *Histoire des Alpes, Perspectives nouvelles*, J. F. Bergier, ed. (1979). Basel: Schwabe & Co. [and *Schweizerische Zeitschrift für Geschichte 29*: 194–215 (1979)].

Chapters 5, 6, and 7 are adaptations of "Balancing on an Alp: Population Stability and Change in a Swiss Peasant Village," by Robert McC. Netting and Walter S. Elias from *Village Viability in Contemporary Society*, P. C. Reining and B. Lenkerd, eds. (1980), pp. 69-108, American Association for the Advancement of Science, publication no. 34. Washington: Westview Press. Reprinted with permission.

Chapter 8 is adapted from "Patterns of Marriage in a Swiss Alpine Community," from *Ethnologia Europaea*, vol. XI, 2(1979/80), pp. 139–155. Reprinted by permission of the editor.

Chapter 9 is adapted from "Familienpolitik: Alliance in a Closed Corporate Community," from *The Versatility of Kinship: Essays Presented to Harry W. Basehart*, S. Beckerman and L. S. Cordell, eds. (1980), pp. 251–68. New York: Academic. Reprinted with permission of Academic Press.

Chapter 10 is adapted from "Household Dynamics in a Nineteenth Century Swiss Village, "from *Journal of Family History 4*: 39–58 (1979). Copyrighted 1979 by the National Council on Family Relations. Reprinted by permission.

1

A place in the Alps with a past

Törbel territory centers on a triangle of alpine meadowland pointing due south toward the jagged Mischabel range and the deep Vispertal trench, carved by glaciers through the mountains from the Italian border down into the Swiss canton of Valais. The open, rolling surface of the triangle is canted steeply from its lower tip, just touching the Mattervispa torrent at about 880 meters above sea level, to the irregular edge of a forest around the 1,900-meter mark (Figure 1.1). From the east, two bowed ranks of cliffs shield the village from the eyes of travelers taking the familiar train ride from Visp on the Rhone River north to Zermatt, with the obligatory glimpse of the Matterhorn. A ravine clearly etches the western edge of the point, carrying the brook, Törbelbach, from its source in the tiny lakes of a basin shadowed by the almost 3,000-meter peak of Augstbordhorn. One can step across the stream at many places on its rocky course, but its flow has been sufficient to water the thirsty slopes for centuries and to drive the mills that ground the villagers' grain and sawed their timber. Planted neatly at the triangle's center at 1,500 meters is the nucleated settlement of multistory log houses and barns called Törbel. The road that climbs through eight hairpin turns from Stalden on the valley floor affords no view of the village until one is almost upon it, and the route of the stony mule track that gave grudging way to the road in 1937 is equally hidden. The village core, with its dwellings of blackened larch timbers roofed by orange-lichened slate slabs, faces south toward the winter sun for warmth, and the houses jostle one another along precipitous, twisting paths, peering over the roofs of their downhill neighbors. Even by the standards of mountainous Valais the village of Törbel seems ancient, and the severely rectangular modern concrete church on its lower margin and the new chalets of varnished pine pushing out into the hills above do not really alter that impression. For the romantics who want a view of a *Bauerndorf* (peasant village) as it looked 50 years ago, the hamlet of Feld in the roadless verdant meadows directly below Törbel will certainly do. The surrounding cultivated slopes, unbroken by fence

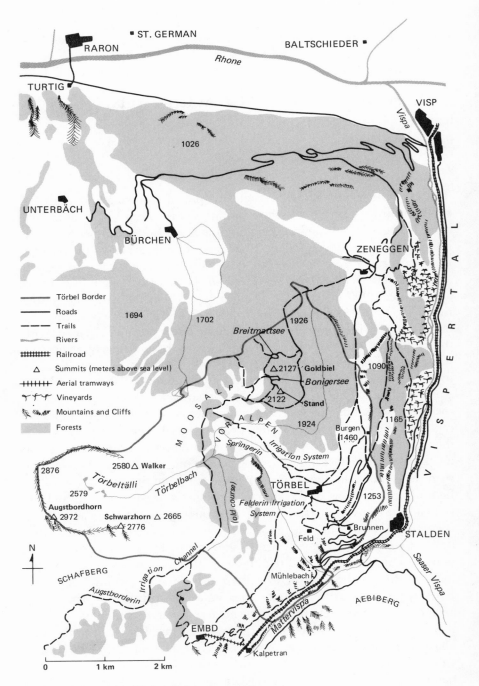

Figure 1.1. *Törbel and the surrounding area.*

lines, are dotted with log barns and occasionally with little clusters of houses. Some of these enclaves, like Feld, Burgen, Brunnen, and Mühlebach, have chapels and a few permanently inhabited dwellings, but most of the houses are used only on a temporary or seasonal basis.

Around the tilted triangular plateau at the heart of Törbel and its hamlet groupings are other contiguous lands. Northeast of the village, forested hillsides interspersed with lateral unfenced hay fields and sheer precipices step down to vineyards terraced along the Vispa banks. The tracks through this area connecting Törbel and the adjacent village of Zeneggen some 4 kilometers away on the north are wider than usual and follow along the contour instead of angling sharply up or down the slopes, as do most of the footpaths. From Törbel proper, the windows overlook another farmed slope to the southwest and some of the outlying buildings of Embd village near the common boundary. The northwest point of the triangle opens near the chapel of Saint Anton into an amphitheater of gentle gradients ringed by forest. These high grasslands with their random scatter of barns and cottages lie just below the summer grazing grounds and are called prosaically the *Voralpen*. The alp itself crowns some knobby hills that command a view east up the long Goms valley toward the source of the Rhone, north to where the mountains wall Valais off from the highlands above Bern, and down along the westward course of the Rhone where it flows past the cathedral towns and vineyards of lower Valais and eventually into Lake Geneva (Figure 1.2).[1] Through grassy bowls and mature woodlands the alp sweeps in a great arc around the cultivated village tract, giving way above to treeless slopes and the barren western watershed of the Törbelbach, where the snows melt late in the mountain folds.

Landscape can be a joy and an inspiration in itself. It was in just this part of Switzerland that tourism in its modern guise began after Whymper scaled the Matterhorn in 1865, and both polyglot visitors and native speakers of the Swiss-German dialect are sensitive to the beauties of an abundant nature. But the village territory that I have crudely sketched is above all a cultural landscape. With the exception of the most dominant of the snow summits, the famous Viertausender, the terrain has been used and modeled for generations by a resident human population. Without the grazing of their livestock and the mowing of the hay, those expansive clearings that so delight the eye would be as forested as the foothills of the Rockies or the Cascades. The parklike stands of larch and fir themselves have been thinned and protected by the hand of man. Waters have been channeled, garden patches retained by terrace walls, soil patiently tilled and fertilized until everything but the cliffs appears ordered and domesticated. The plain solid structures of squared logs, the network of

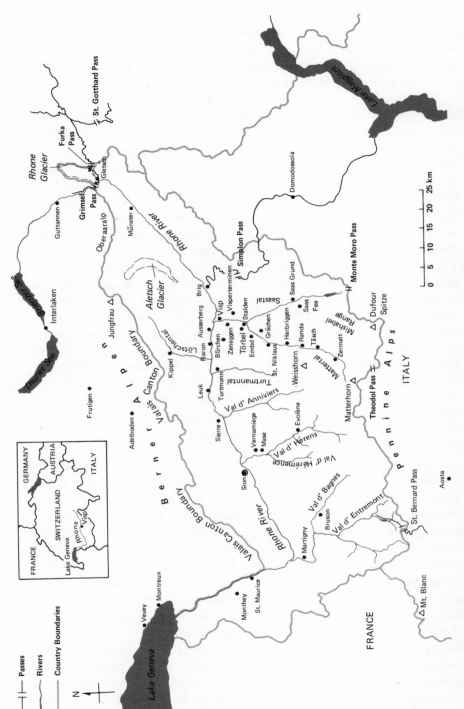

Figure 1.2. Valais and the Rhone valley.

footpaths, and the place-names that distinguish each field and gully and habitation site bespeak a process of settling in, or environmental incorporation, so pervasive that its results appear as enduring and as appropriate as an aspect of untouched wilderness. The landscape of Törbel is an extension of its people, and the possibilities and limitations of their society are in part reflections of their habitat.

The local environment is what people have to work with, and their tools and traditions define the means at their disposal for this task. For a long time, human communities have been able to gain a livelihood, often quite independently, in the mountains. There may well be certain commonalities in both the technological and social adaptations of high-altitude food-producing populations (Burns 1963; Rhoades and Thompson 1975; Brush 1976), but our attention here will be confined to certain features of a particular small bounded ecosystem through only a part of its long history. Although acknowledging specificity and perhaps even uniqueness, the anthropological mode often makes at least covert claims to the representativeness of the community under study. In just this manner we may be inclined to pass rather lightly from snatches of observed behavior in Törbel, circa 1971, to eighteenth-century customs in the same village, thence to Swiss alpine settlements, to north European peasants, and perhaps beyond. A mission of anthropology is to generalize about human culture from an ethnographic case, and at the same time a chief temptation of anthropology is to overgeneralize. I will try to be candid about my evidence and to label my speculations, but the tension between microscopic data and the macrocosmos to which social science aspires will not readily be resolved.

These external forces that have influenced and constrained a cultural group, supporting itself on bread grains and dairy products, are relatively simple and not difficult to perceive in the broad outlines of significant topographic and climatic factors. Altitude and rugged terrain define the area as alpine. The valley of the Rhone is a great trough cleaving the mountain masses that divide northern Europe from the Mediterranean lands (Figure 1.2). The river is not navigable, and although it flows into Lake Geneva, all northern, eastern, and southern exits from the valley require mounting into narrow, high tributary valleys and eventually negotiating passes that are often snowy. The Great Saint Bernard and the Simplon give access to Italy. The Grimsel connects the Valais with Lucerne and eventually Zürich. The Lötschberg tunnel now allows easy movement northward to Bern from the central valley. Although transport and communications into and through the upper Valais have always been possible, they have never until recently been easy or inexpensive. Sheer physical problems of movement discouraged the armies that surged across

across the European plains and also constricted the trade that nourished mercantile centers. Martigny, Sion, Sierre, Visp, and Brig supported modest clerical and administrative establishments in the past and profited from the pass traffic, but there was little in the way of agricultural surplus or mineral wealth to encourage the invader or the foreign immigrant.

The wilderness of mountain peaks north and south of the Rhone both protected its people from outside incursions and cut them off from the winds of economic growth and change that blew more freely into other corners of the Continent. Production for major markets elsewhere was impeded by transport difficulties and limited by the thin soil and short growing season of alpine fields. Broken terrain, gorges, cliffs, and glaciers also separated desirable settlement sites from each other. The Swiss themselves have long regarded the people of Valais as some of the most isolated of all their countrymen. Although the self-sufficiency and traditional independence of the Walliser were lauded, his relative poverty and lack of "progress" give a less favorable aspect to the national stereotype.[2]

The Berner Alpen, with such summits as the Jungfrau north of the Rhone and the Pennine Alps, including Mont Blanc, the Matterhorn, and the 4,634-meter Dufourspitze in the Monte Rosa massif, create climatic divides as well as a set of social barriers. The mountains shelter the valley both from the west winds off the Atlantic and from the air masses moving north from the Mediterranean. Valais is therefore in a rain shadow, with much less moisture than the Berner Oberland or the Italian valleys of Val d'Aosta and Piemonte. Whereas the northern Alps receive 150 to 400 centimeters of precipitation, and 300 to 400 centimeters fall annually on the southern Alps, Valais receives a mere 50 to 80 centimeters. The south wind, known as the *Föhn*, produces higher temperatures on the lee side of the mountains than on the Italian side.[3] Such dryness and the accompanying absence of cloud cover make possible warm Mediterranean summers and extensive wine production in lower Valais. This also means that mountain grasses may require artificial watering if they are to produce abundant hay and pasturage.

These conditions are particularly marked in Törbel. The lower Vispertal has the scantiest rainfall in Switzerland, and the villages of Grächen and Staldenried, both visible from Törbel, record annual precipitation averaging 56 and 53 centimeters, respectively. Törbel itself may have even less moisture, although annual measurements have not been taken there, and geographically it forms part of the *Trockengebiet* or dry zone of Valais. The village's southern exposure and the fact that it faces up the valley of the Mattervispa mean that it has excellent insolation.[4] Zeneggen, Embd, and Törbel make up the Vispertaler

Sonnenberge (the Visp valley sunny mountains), and the village flag blazes with the red and yellow rays of a great orb. Törbel's location gives it a full 7 hours of sunlight, even in midwinter, when its valley neighbor, Stalden, must shiver with only a half hour of direct light. Obviously the agricultural possibilities at this altitude have always been increased by the longer season and exposure to the sun. Today, snow often lies for a month longer in Grächen, which is on a northwest-facing *Schattenseite* (shadow side) and only some 100 meters higher than Törbel. However, what was a handicap in the days of agricultural dependence is now the advantage that has turned Grächen into a booming ski resort, whereas Törbel languished without winter visitors until the Moosalp ski lift was completed in 1980.

The closed-in nature of the valley and its characteristically dry climate produce correspondingly distinctive vegetation. Succulents and other xerophytic plants cling to rocky unirrigated patches. Larches that appear evergreen until their needles turn gold and fall in autumn favor the southern slopes, whereas the somewhat wetter eastern exposures support pine.[5] The timberline reaches as high as 2,200 meters in Törbel, and grass sufficient to support sheep grows to the 2,600-meter mark. An apple tree formerly flourished at an altitude of over 1,700 meters in Törbel (Stebler 1922:90), and across the valley the vineyards of Visper-terminen had the reputation of being perhaps the highest in Europe, with terraces climbing to 1,080 meters (Gutersohn 1961:54). Potato patches in Törbel were planted at the cluster of houses called Bad around 1,900 meters. As throughout the Visp valley, the snow line, the timberline, and the settlement sites are all unusually high.

The village enclaves that took root in these mountains, trading lowland accessibility for sun and pasturage and accommodating to winter snows and summer droughts, convey a remarkable sense of age and permanence to the observer. Given the objective realities of climate, slope, altitude, water, and vegetation, there were few alternatives for producing food and ensuring a peasant livelihood. Decisions on how best to use a piece of land, what hand tool or process is adequate to a task, and what makes for an effective shelter all seem to have been made long ago and continued in force up to a time within living memory. No doubt our view of Törbel antiquity is clouded by the sparseness of historical documentation and the outright lack of an archeological window into the past, but the physical age of buildings like the house dated 1477 in Gothic script, the seasonal round of taking cows to the alp and mowing the meadows with the scythe, and the diet of rye bread and cheese all suggest a life that has changed little in substance or in style.[6] Perhaps the lands of Törbel once afforded grazing to herders coming with their sheep, goats, and cattle from valley settlements to camps on the mountainside. Such summer use would parallel the movements of game. Layers of charcoal found in pollen cores and in road cuts on Moosalp can be interpreted as evidence that these nomads purposely burned the forests to increase their pasturage.[7] The area was a natural choice for permanent settlement.[8] There were unfailing springs as well as the Törbel brook to provide drinking water for people and domestic stock. The southward inclination made the best of the short, high-altitude growing season (Carrier 1932:210). It was also important that the village site be shielded from avalanches and landslides. The fact that the Törbel habitations are built on a slope that goes no higher than 2,122 meters and is forested in its upper reaches means that avalanches are not a danger. Where steeper gradients go up to the barren Törbeltälli and the peaks of Schwarzhorn and Augstbordhorn on the west, the rush of snow can drive uprooted tree trunks right through house roofs, but there is only an occasional hut or stable in its path (Gutersohn 1961:20; Friedl 1976). There are no records of Törbel ever suffering a disastrous rock slide such as those that have often wrecked the church at Saint Niklaus. It is possible that natural clearings encouraged some early settlers to remain through the winter in Törbel and that the existence of terraces with relatively deep soil where grain would grow dependably was a prime attraction. Indeed, Törbel itself is built on an abrupt rocky incline so that the field and garden area just below can be fully devoted to crops.

It is reasonable to believe that the first year-round residents of the Törbel area were Kelts.[9] Keltic settlements are well attested in the Rhone valley, and an Iron Age hill fort commands the height above Zeneggen overlooking the confluence of the Vispa and Rhone.[10] A cemetery in the Sisetsch neighborhood of Zeneggen has produced several La Tène bronze fibulae, bracelets, and metal disks from the first century B.C. (Sauter 1950). The path from Zeneggen to Törbel passes what appears to be a deep mortar cut into a boulder, with hewn steps leading up to it, and several stone-cist graves have been found in Brunnen and on the way to Embd. A relatively easy and possibly very old trail leaves the Rhone valley near Raron, climbs in the direction of Bürchen, and then follows the contours around the headland through Zeneggen, Törbel, and Embd, finally descending again at Saint Niklaus. Such a route was less difficult than following the narrow Vispa defile, and it connected settlements with better farming potential and in less danger of flood and rock slides than the valley towns. Linguistic evidence also suggests that Törbel had a Keltic ancestry. The name is derived from *dorwia*, Gallic for larch or pine forest (Staub 1944; Zimmermann 1968:20). Other traces of the Roman occupation after 25 B.C. are noted in the Latin-derived *Sisetsch* for fence

(Staub 1944) and the field name Barlei related to the word for little barrel (Zimmermann 1968). Since the Allemanic migration in approximately the ninth century A.D., upper Valais has been German-speaking, but it is plausible that a site with the favorable qualities of Törbel would be almost continuously occupied. The first written reference to the village is in a legal document of the eleventh century, and from 1224 (Gremaud 1863) numerous documents mention Törbel unmistakably during every succeeding century.

There is also a sense of continuity with the past in the folk memory and oral tradition of Törbel. People refer to the oldest log structures as *Heidenhäuser* (heathen houses) and point out the archaic elements of split timbers rather than sawn timbers and bowed roof beams supporting ceiling planking. The pre-Christian attribution may well be inaccurate (there was, after all, a Roman Catholic bishop in Octodurum, now Martigny, by 381 A.D.), but the continued existence from perhaps the fifteenth century of wooden houses similar in most respects to those built by the fathers of the current inhabitants rightly conveys an aura of the ancient.[11] Events that threatened the life of the village, such as a bubonic plague epidemic in 1533, are woven into stories anchored by the physical presence of the house of Caspar Dilger, who carried out the corpses, and the round table where the eight survivors gathered. For such comparatively recent events as the miraculous protection given to Captain Peter Wyss when he returned from foreign wars in the 1690s or the manner of coping with Napoleon's troops when they appeared around 1800 on a foraging expedition, the Törbjers can provide details on the parts played by their own forefathers. Indeed, a genealogy book in the church archives definitively links every family of present Törbel citizens to their ancestors living before 1700. One should not stand in awe of such antiquity. The past is not especially venerated in Törbel, nor do people boast of their ancestry. Some individuals even bemoan the lack of progress in the village and the vestiges of isolation: "We are still behind the moon." Yet there is an unstated acceptance of the fact that the generations that came before lived on the same territory and in the same villages and hamlets, that their houses were of the same types, that they shared the same rich lexicon of place-names, and that they sustained themselves by milking cows and reaping grain in the immemorial manner. Törbel is not some Iron Age relic preserved in amber or a living museum of medieval alpine peasantry. But its economic survival, the persistence of its populations, and the social means by which continuity through the centuries was achieved are worthy of our attention in a world where change and disintegration have acquired a contemptuous familiarity.

2

Making a living in the mountains

The probable longevity and stability of land use in Törbel are intimately related to the evident fit between environmental possibilities and a characteristic system of subsistence. Swiss geographers recognize a typical mountain grain-grazing adaptation (*Acker-Alp Betrieb*) whose basic requisites could be completely met within the single village territory. This was a high-altitude variation of the Old World farming pattern combining bread grains and dairy products that swept in a great arc from the Atlantic shores of Ireland to the Indian subcontinent (Arensberg 1963). In the alpine case, winter rye provided a cereal that could flourish despite early snows and short summers. Törbel has several areas of moderate slope and adequate soil depth for plowing. These grainfields or *Acker* are usually in close proximity to the sites of hamlets and other permanent habitations, and they may well have determined the original locations of settlement. Rye and occasionally wheat or barley could be planted below the little enclave of Brunnen at 1,110 meters and similarly just under Feld at 1,310 meters. The broadest single field area, Burgackern, is a natural terrace facing southeast over Stalden (Figure 2.1). It centers at 1,320 meters and shelves off to about 1,140 meters at the crest of the cliffs. Grain was formerly grown in a swath of patchwork fields south of Törbel proper at 1,500 meters and climbing the slopes with inclined, stone-walled plots overlooking the Törbel brook. A final series of fields was maintained along the path to Embd, especially in the 1,300-meter environs of Barlei. Even with the territory's favorable southern exposure, grainfields were not viable much above 1,600 meters.

By far the major part of Törbel's cultivated land was always in hay meadows (*Wiesen*) (Figure 2.1). Grass could be harvested wherever soil and slopes allowed, from the foot of the village territory at 900 meters up to 2,000 meters at Bad and 1,940 meters in the *Voralpen*. Lower-lying or particularly sunny irrigated meadows made possible two successive cuts of hay plus some grazing of tethered animals in spring and fall. Meadowland was never planted or tilled, but the naturally regenerating

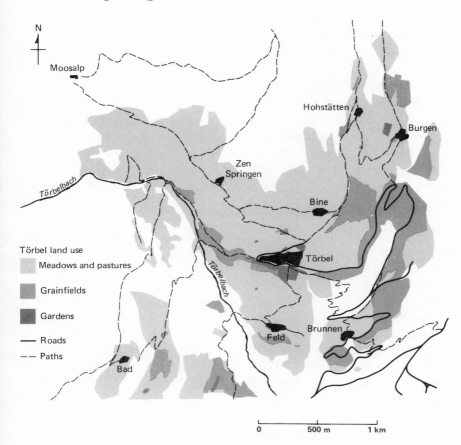

Figure 2.1. Land use in Törbel.

turf was regularly manured with composted cattle dung and watered by a network of irrigation channels. Given the 40 to 50 percent gradient of most grassy slopes, hard labor and the simplest of tools, including the scythe and wood-tooth rake, were used in haying. With no wheeled carts or roads to move them on, hay had to be carried on one's back to a barn actually situated in or near the meadow. The solution to the problem of transporting heavy hay and manure the minimum distance was to build large numbers of barns (*Ställe*) and share their use among the owners of adjacent meadows. Each individual could thus store his fodder in a segmented section of the haymow (*Scheune*), moving his cattle to that stable for a period to consume the hay and then transferring them to another barn in which he also held an interest. The scatter of meadow-lands and fractional ownership rights in barns meant that each cattle owner moved his stock several times during the winter, sometimes living for periods of a month or two in a cabin near the most distant meadows and sometimes commuting twice daily from his permanent residence to tend the animals.

Grasslands too steep or stony or shadowed to afford good vegetative production and those that depended solely on natural precipitation could provide periodic grazing but not hay. Landholders might have such pastures (*Weiden*) interspersed among meadows and around groves of trees. More important, however, were the true alps (*Alpen*), summer grazing grounds that supported the village cow herd plus sheep and goats from June to September. There, on land belonging communally to the entire village, a small group of men could herd the livestock, milk the cows, and make cheese. The rest of the population was freed for intensive haymaking, harvesting, gardening, and irrigating through the long days of the short summer season. The cattle fed on the nutritious forage of Moosalp and Alp Bifigen between 1,950 and 2,200 meters, moving from one pasture area with its stone corrals and forest clearings to another in a regular rotation. Farther up the mountainsides and in the treeless bowl of Törbeltälli, sheep and goats could find more extensive, if scantier, grazing. Certainly the size and productivity of the Törbel alp was a foundation for the community's relative prosperity. Because it directly adjoined the village meadowlands and was easily accessible, it made possible an integrated, self-contained dairy operation without the long journeys to which less well endowed communities were subject. Only by systematic pasturing of livestock could these high-altitude grasslands become an important resource for alpine subsistence farmers.

Although forest clearing must have been a significant part of early settlement in the mountains,[1] there is little sign that pasturage or cultivation has continued to encroach on woodlands. A substantial portion of the alp as well as the more precipitous eastern slopes and the shadier west bank of the Törbelbach have remained in larch or pine and fir. Without this dependable source of firewood, heating of the dwellings and, until recently, cooking over the open hearth would have been uncertain, Logs were also the principal materials for houses, barns, and the special-purpose buildings that every villager needed. Conservation and judicious use of the forest were impressive achievements of the Törbel polity, especially since the trees also served to anchor mountainside soil, protect the watershed, and reduce avalanche danger. The communally controlled forest also gave shelter to livestock on the alp during spring and fall storms, and the shed needles of the conifers were laboriously collected for use in place of straw as bedding for the barns.

To supplement the triumvirate of grass, grain, and wood that supported the local agricultural economy, Törbel had a variety of minor sources of food and drink. The fruits and vegetables were limited to small areas with special growing conditions, and the vagaries of weather could drastically affect yields. Just above the Vispa River, gravelly slopes bear what appear to be very old terraced vineyards (*Reben*). Tiny unfenced plots belong to individuals who tend the grapes and themselves carry out every step of the process leading to casks of wine in the cellars. Such wine is seldom sold; it is consumed in the household. A somewhat larger vineyard is owned and worked corporately by the village, with the wine being dispensed for designated civic purposes. Because of the long walk from the settlement to the grape-growing areas, Törbjers often stayed there overnight in log huts. The various tasks of manuring, pruning, binding the vines to individual stakes, weeding, and harvesting were done at intervals during the late winter, spring, and summer. Usually the whole family participated in the October harvest (*Weinernte*), when the grapes were brought back to the village in oval wooden casks carried by mules. The grapes were processed in cooperatively owned wine presses, and the wine was aged in barrels kept by individuals in their cellars. Altitude limited the extent of Törbel vineyards, and climatic variations gave rise to marked fluctuations in the quantity and quality of annual vintages. Higher terraces and terraces with poorer exposure to the sun produced wine that was less sweet and had a low alcohol content. A frost that interfered with the brief blooming of the grapes could drastically reduce the harvest.

Spring cold spells also endangered the fruit trees that sprinkled the meadows below 1,500 meters and took advantage of protected locations near houses. In good years, small sweet and sour cherries could be gathered in quantity, and there were also orchards of both red and purple plums (Stebler 1922:89–91). These fruits, along with apples, were picked, crushed, and fermented for eventual local distillation into the potent schnapps, valued both as an aperitif and as a medicine for people and cattle. Wild cherries clustered on the terrace borders of the grain-fields, and the grafted varieties of fruits planted in gardens or espaliered on cellar walls had to be carefully guarded from goats. At lower elevations there were formerly some walnut and hazelnut trees, but more important sources of nuts for eating were the stone-pines in the high forest near the timberline. Cones were gathered in quantity in pack baskets in autumn, and the pine nuts were cracked and consumed by convivial groups of young people or families at home (Stebler 1922:92). Wild blueberries, raspberries, and strawberries grew in the forest up onto the alp, and a few currant and elderberry bushes were propagated in gardens. Many varieties of herbs and wildflowers with medicinal uses are known locally, and in the past women and children gathered quantities for sale to Swiss firms producing herbal remedies.

Of all the subsistence techniques indigenous to Törbel, garden cultivation has perhaps the least cultural salience. Garden plots (*Gärten*) are small bits of intensively tilled earth tucked in among houses or in a band just below the village or hamlets. No ceremonial occasions (such as those celebrated when the cattle go up to or leave the alp) mark the calendar of gardening. There was no garden product distributed at communal feasts, whereas bread and wine had their rituals. Vegetables, except for the ubiquitous potato, were not items of daily diet. Potatoes were planted in both gardens and more distant fields (*Aecker*), where they might alternate with grain. They flourished best on dry sunny ground and could be cultivated successfully in terraced spots too small and too steep for the plow. Another garden or field crop was the broad bean (*Grossbohnen, Vicia faba*). After the bean harvest in August, winter rye could be sown in the same soil. Some of the beans were picked and boiled for the table, but most were dried for swine fodder, and the stalks were fed to sheep (Stebler 1922:64–5). The tiny kitchen gardens contained turnips (*Rüben*), which were fed to cattle and pigs, as well as kohlrabi and cabbage for human consumption. Such plants are grown from seeds in the warmer valley towns and set out in Törbel gardens in early June. Today people plant neat rows of onions and lettuce for salad, but it is said that green vegetables were formerly rare and little valued. Before the advent of cheap cotton cloth, hemp and flax were grown locally for homespun textiles.

Although the factors of altitude, slope, exposure to the sun, soil quality, and accessibility largely dictated land use, the distribution of land, its economic significance, and the conditions of its tenure were social and cultural facts, grounded in history and perpetuated by custom and law. Törbel had a quite evident territorial integrity, combining each of the important environmental zones necessary for hay meadows, gardens, orchards, forests, and summer pastures (Netting 1972). Only good vineyard land was lacking within the community boundaries, and this was remedied by the acquisition of plots along the Vispa from Stalden and Zeneggen in the distant past. Because of the rapid ascent of the terrain from the valley bottom to the mountains, all the subsistence niches can be reached on foot in at most a few hours. Törbel is not a "vertical archipelago" (Murra 1972) like those Andean villages that control noncontiguous lowland maize fields, mid-level potato farms, and altiplano grazing grounds. Rather, it is an inclined peninsula with its own range of climates from almost Mediterranean to classic alpine. The prevailing adaptation of peasant settlers to such possibilities has been to span and incorporate them all. Were the transition from lowland to highland more gradual, communities might have specialized in each zone and exchanged their products. As it is, one village can include all the local resources, increasing its self-sufficiency and insulating itself against an unexpected failure of any single food supply. By cutting across the environmental grain, Törbel has the biological advantages of an ecotone. No single support system is highly productive, but all together provide a high degree of security and a hedge against climatic fluctuation. The largely self-contained nature of this ecosystem contributes to a lack of economic dependence on the outside world and sustains a political autonomy that seems to distinguish Törbel from the archetypal peasant community.

The fundamental work of the human community, the basic provision of food and shelter, was carried on in Törbel by the family household. These groups of close kin lived together, produced the necessities of life largely by their own efforts, and consumed these goods together. Such households resembled one another. They were almost without exception headed by subsistence farmers, owning their own land, animals, and tools. Although we cannot be sure, it appears that for at least the last seven centuries there has been no resident aristocracy or landlord class, few full-time artisans or merchants, and no discernible group of landless laborers. This suggests that the economic independence of the village as a whole was repeated in its constituent units. Individual households could maintain a homogeneous and relatively secure peasant livelihood if each of them controlled the same means of production. This meant access to each major type of land: meadows, pastures, grainfields, gardens, forests, and vineyards. Differences in altitude and the broken nature of the terrain decreed that such a goal could not be met in a single enclosed farmstead. On the contrary, a viable household required rights to land in each zone, whether as individually heritable property or as a share in such communally owned resources as the forest and the alp. Within each zone it was also probable that a household would have several parcels at some distance from one another.

The first land record book (*Grundbuch*), based on a survey (*Kataster*) done in the early years of this century and giving the location, size in square meters, use, valuation, and ownership of each piece of farmland, shows that individuals had typically widespread and diverse holdings. Some 235 owners had a total of 4,557 parcels, not including the vineyards that are itemized in the records of other communities. Some households contained several property owners (e.g., several adult celibate siblings, or a widow and one of her married children). But even if the list is limited to the owners who had at least the basic land types of meadow, grainfield, and garden, there are still 181 cases. Table 2.1 indicates that each proprietor had an average of 8.30 separate meadows, 6.25 grainfields, and 3.30 gardens. Woods and wastelands were held by fewer owners, and there were smaller numbers of such parcels in private hands. The total area of individually owned land within the Törbel territory was 438.52 hectares (1,083.14 acres). The largest share of this land (52 percent) was devoted to hay meadows, whereas pasture accounted for 25 percent, grain fields for 15 percent, wasteland for 5 percent, forest for 2 percent, and gardens for 1 percent. An average proprietor held almost 2 hectares (19,961 square meters) of agricultural land exclusive of forest and patches of unproductive wasteland. This was divided into an average of 20.86 plots, with a mean meadow size of 0.123 hectare, grainfields of 0.047 hectare, and gardens of a mere 0.008 hectare (79 square meters). Although a few of these holdings might be concentrated in one locality, as when an outlying house and barn had a pasture, a meadow or two, and a scrap of garden near it, most plots were not adjacent, and it was frequent for an individual to have land in more than 10 different areas (Berthoud 1967). Indeed, one prosperous farmer had title to a total of 123 parcels in 42 distinct named places. It is evident, then, that the average Törbel landholder in the early years of this century maintained a mix of land types, including at least meadows and pastures, grainfields and gardens, that this total property might be approximately 2 hectares, and that it was fragmented into a number of separate plots scattered about the village territory.

To an outsider familiar with larger farms made up of contiguous fields, the parcelization of land in a Swiss alpine village appears grossly uneconomical and irrational. Small plots are difficult to plow efficiently, difficult of access without crossing the land of others, and costly to fence. Travel time to far-flung postage-stamp-size pieces becomes a significant cost added to direct labor on the land. Swiss geographers also write critically of the endless fractionalization of peasant holdings, citing the averages in Ausserberg of 59 plots per owner and in several Goms communities of over 100 (Gutersohn 1961:22, 40). Such division into ever smaller and more dispersed properties supposedly resulted from the tradition of equal inheritance by all children and the great competition for scarce land that allowed tiny plots to come on the market at high prices. Later on we shall consider whether or not partible inheritance

Table 2.1. *Törbel landholdings in 1925*

Land type	Area (ha)	Number of parcels	Average area (m²)	Number of owners	Number of parcels per owner	Average area per owner (m²)
Wiesen	226.0459	1,842	1,227	222	8.30	10,182
Weiden	111.3795	512	2,175	170	3.01	6,551
Acker	63.4792	1,337	475	214	6.25	2,966
Garten	4.8474	613	79	186	3.30	261
Reben[a]	13.6700					
Wald	10.5665	41	2,577	34	1.21	3,108
Wildi	22.1017	211	1,047	102	2.07	2,176
Total	438.5242	4,556				
Average cultivated holding exclusive of *Reben, Wald, Wildi*					20.86	19,961

[a]1929 area from Imboden (1967).

actually did diminish field size in each generation. Here, however, we should look briefly at the ecological rationale for the prevailing Törbel pattern of small, widely distributed farm holdings. Given the great differences that small variations in slope, exposure to sun, soil quality, and moisture can make in eventual yields, a range of characteristics within a single land-use type may be desirable. For instance, a late spring may cut rye production on a partially shaded north-facing terrace, whereas a terrace with a drier southern inclination may allow normal development of the crop. Where the average return on planted seed was not high, as in English medieval arable farming, the peasant protected himself from severe localized fluctuations by cultivating a number of dispersed strips with differing microenvironments (McCloskey 1976). A minimax strategy of this kind reduced the risk of disastrous crop failure and increased access to prime lands, allowing more households to survive the climatic fluctuations that always threatened small-scale agriculture.

By living in a nucleated village or satellite hamlet while maintaining one or more secondary residences in outlying meadow areas, the Törbel landholder could minimize travel time to his far-flung possessions. For many important farming operations he could go to one plot and spend the working day there. The trip to and from the settlement might be long, but it was not complicated by shorter movements from one piece of land to another. Time spent walking to one large consolidated field would probably be little less than that required to go out to a smaller parcel in a different direction every day (McCloskey 1976). For shorter tasks, such as the irrigation of meadows on a regular schedule, a central settlement, as opposed to one on the periphery of the community territory, minimized average travel effort. From Törbel proper, the round trip to the farther *Voralp* meadows in Niwen required 80 minutes, and that to Bad southwest of the village required 125 minutes (Figure 2.2). Märafelli, on the border of Zeneggen, was a 60-minute round-trip journey, and a visit to Walkgraben below Brunnen took 90 minutes. The average round-trip walking time to 85 named cultivated areas was 50 minutes, but the extremities of the Törbel farmlands were 170 minutes apart on a northwest-southeast axis and 185 minutes apart on a southwest-northeast transect.

For tasks that required several days of continuous work or when cows were stabled and tended in distant barns during the winter, travel could be reduced by moving the family temporarily to a hut located in the meadow area. These dwellings, often adjoining or incorporated into the barn structure, may have been smaller and somewhat ruder than the main apartment in the village, but they had the same basic accommodations of living room/bedroom (*Stube*) and kitchen. Those field areas closer to the village could be managed from the main house. They were an average of 38 minutes round trip from Törbel, whereas the places provided with huts required more than an hour's journey (64 minutes). The hay from higher meadows with their own houses was used in the fall and early winter up to Christmastime. As snow made communication with the village difficult, families came back to their main houses for the holidays and used stables there or in nearby areas. Those who owned pastures on the lower slopes would move there with their animals in May to take advantage of the early grazing that appeared at least a month before grass was available in the *Voralpen*.

Scattered land parcels accommodated seasonal scheduling of work (Friedl 1973) and also provided access to varied crops and minimized risks. Because hay for overwintering stock was always in limited supply, a farmer with meadows at various levels could get his cows out of the barn and pasture them at successively higher altitudes as the new spring grass appeared. Each animal was tethered by a rope to a peg, and thus the animals could be shifted frequently from one clearly delimited part of the meadow to another without endangering the regrowth necessary for a later hay harvest (Stebler 1922:53). Today the same purpose is served by temporary electric fences powered by batteries. A gradual up-slope progression also characterized the reaping of grain in the *Aecker* and the

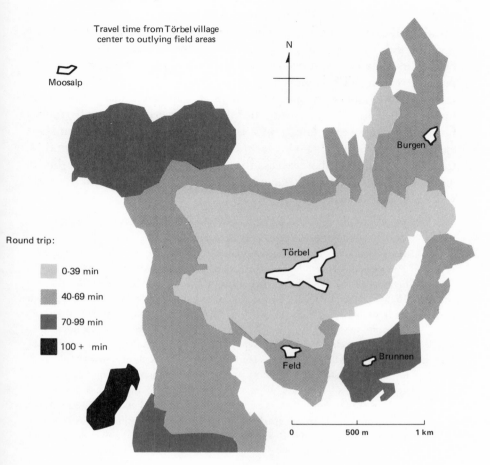

Figure 2.2. Travel time from Törbel village center to outlying fields.

ripening of hay. An observant farmer told me that in Törbel one can distinguish a difference in relative plant growth with every 20 meters of altitude. If a family's land were concentrated in one zone, the highly labor-intensive cutting, raking, drying, and transport of the hay would come all at once, with a long slack interval before the next haymaking. Törbjers did not exchange household labor to any great extent, and the independence of the family unit was enhanced if each could work steadily at haying, moving from lower-lying meadows to upper meadows in the optimum period of July through the beginning of August and then returning to those areas where a second cut (*Emd*) was possible. An efficient allocation of labor allowed maximum growth of the grass and took advantage of the hot days necessary to cure the crop before it could be stored in the barn. To the demands of the weather were added the social pressures of one's neighbors. Once the hay has been cut on the open, fenceless slope, the practiced eye can immediately discern who is behind in his work, and critical comments are freely exchanged on the possible reasons for such delay.

Each household must plan its own work schedule and movements in light of the unique mix of properties that has emerged from inheritance, marriage, trades, and sales. Now that buses and cars make transport easier and agriculture is no longer the principal support of most families, there is less shifting about across the village territory from one cabin to another. Stebler cited a fine example of seasonal mobility from the early years of this century:

> The "craziest" property belongs to my informant in Törbel, the peasant who has his principal residence during the winter in Mühlebach, 949 meters above sea level, down below on the valley road from Törbel to Kalpetran. Here he has a house and barn and he lives there up until the hay harvest. Then he goes with his whole family two hours higher up for haying at Bine, above the village at 1625 m. When that work is over, he and the entire household hike another hour away to make hay at Isch higher on the Voralp (1712 m.). After that he goes back into the valley to Mühlebach for the grain and second hay harvest; then once more to the Voralp and again to Bine. There follows some time in the hamlet Feld where he also has lands and back for the third time to Mühlebach for autumn pasturing of the stock and field preparation. As winter approaches, he with all his family and animals travel first to the Voralp to use that fodder. At New Years, he settles once more at Bine, and in February he spends the month in Feld. Then the yearly cycle begins again at Mühlebach. All together and all in the course of one year, he and his family change their residence twelve times—a nomadic life indeed. [Stebler 1922:102–3]

This case may well have been somewhat extreme, because the family concerned had its principal residence on the farthest down-slope edge of the village territory. But even a fortunate collection of meadows and barns accessible from the central settlement may require frequent movements of livestock and considerable travel time. A family in which the man spent the week on his job in a distant part of Switzerland and returned only on weekends maintained their three cows in the areas shown in Table 2.2. The longer trips made by the woman of the house in the course of foddering and milking her cows took place mostly after the depth of winter.

In the old days, when people moved out temporarily to houses in the farther meadows, Törbel village might be practically deserted during the midsummer hay harvests, with families reappearing only for Sunday

Table 2.2. *Movements of cows and schedule of barn use for a sample family*

Meadow area	Months used	Period (wk)	Travel time (min)	
			To	From
Siten	Late Oct.–Nov.	4	20	15
Rafgarten	Nov.	2	10	5
Schluocht	Nov.–Dec.	3	5	5
Agarte	Jan.	2	10	15
Hofmatten	Jan.–Feb.	6	5	5
Burgen	March	4	20	20
Hofmatten	April	3	5	5
Kumme	April–May	5	40	40
Burgen	Early June	1–2	20	20

mass (Stebler 1922:103). When mid-October brought an end to the major agricultural work for the year, the households could retreat to their most distant *Voralp* cabins for a few months of tending the animals in the stables. Only the children, who followed the steep paths to and from school every day, had to exert themselves. This season of comparative relaxation and plenty, living alone or in a small friendly cluster of long-acquainted families, is universally remembered as "the most beautiful days of my life." Not only was there easy personal warmth and a hospitable exchange of meals on the *Voralp*, but individuals also enjoyed privacy from prying eyes and busy tongues that typified daily life in the narrow confines of the village. When I asked one elderly man why he preferred his isolated hut to the comforts of his village apartment, he merely nodded toward some women nearby and waggled his fingers to imitate the rapid movements of a gossiping mouth.

The mountain environment mandates exploitation of several zones and maps a quilt of potential land use that the generations have transformed into a patchwork of holdings from which each household must assemble its dispersed, diverse collection. Amid the difficulties of terrain and the vagaries of climate, a farming strategy has been developed based on ensuring subsistence and minimizing risk. Fragmented farmsteads and seasonal minimigrations up and down the mountain gradient adapt agricultural work effort to these demands and make a virtue of variety and restless nomadism within a homogeneous and self-sufficient lifestyle.

For all its movement and its arduous succession of tasks, peasant farming in Törbel followed a calendrical cycle that probably altered little over the centuries. The agricultural year began in late April, with fertilizing, hoeing, and pruning the vineyards. At the same time, broad beans were sown. In May, potatoes were planted, the summer grain was broadcast, and cabbage and turnips were set out. Plowing of fallow grainfields (*Brache*) took place in June (*Brachmonat*), and gardens were weeded and grapes trimmed out. Around the end of June, the cows went up to the alp. After the first hay was cut in the lower meadows in July, the rye was ready for harvesting. Groups of reapers went out by 3 A.M. so that the grain still wet with dew would not drop ripe kernels as the sheaves were gathered. An additional task was irrigation of the meadows, done on an exact schedule such that a farmer might have to be out at any hour of the day or night to take his turn for water. People often mention how strenuous this midsummer period was and how weary they became from work and lack of sleep. August saw the second plowing of the fallow grainfields, which were later sown. Although the second hay harvest was lighter than the first, with none at all on the highest meadows, it remained a time-consuming labor. Cherries were picked and rye was threshed. The potato harvest came in September, and manure was carried from the barns out into meadows. From late September into October, the wine harvest (*Weinlese*) took place. With the cattle down from the alp about the eighth or tenth of September, they might be pastured for a week or two before being confined to the barns. Foddering the cows, cleaning the stables, milking, making cheese, and churning butter were the routine tasks of winter. The family allotment of firewood cut the preceding spring in the communal forest was snaked down the snowy paths with the help of neighbors and their mules. With early spring and the melting of the snow cover, the meadows were raked, and parties of men repaired tracks and walls on the communal alp. The new season of growth rolled round again.

The tools and the operations that extracted from the alpine fields and forests the food and warmth and shelter for the local population were relatively simple and straightforward. Most depended on human muscle-power or the energy of draft animals such as oxen or mules. What Wolf (1966a:19) has called a paleotechnic ecotype characterized the village until buses and trucks first made their way up the new road in 1937. Agriculture was not decisively altered until new alp stables with automatic milking machines were built after World War II and garden tractors with mowing attachments appeared in the meadows around 1955. In the past, each agricultural process employed a set of implements, certain skills, and various facilities, chiefly buildings. The tools were of

Bringing hay from the loft to fodder the livestock.

wood and fiber and metal, either locally made or maintained and repaired by village craftsmen. Because they were not expensive or complex, every household had its own, and every householder knew how to use them. Basic farm implements, like the various land types, were means of production that the average peasant family owned and controlled. Larger or more costly devices like the huge cheesemaking kettles and wine presses were owned by cooperative associations of users, or, in the case of the bread bakery, by the community as a whole. Water-driven flour mills, sawmills, and fulling mills were in the hands of private but still local entrepreneurs.

Because dairying played such a large role in the village economy, it is obvious that each household would have its own cattle plus a few goats to give milk when the cows were away on the alp. The fact that rights in meadowland were general suggests that the capacity to overwinter several grazing animals was a crucial factor in maintaining a viable household. Cows' milk was used directly as whey or as buttermilk for drinking; in the form of butter it provided the main cooking oil, and as cheese it was the most frequently consumed and most efficiently stored source of protein. Much of the dairy equipment was formerly of wood: milk pails, ladles, cream pans, churns, and milking stools. Every household had its own small copper replica of the alp kettles in which milk could be heated and stirred, then mixed with rennet, with the curds being scooped out by hand to mold into the cylindrical cheeses. Although some men were expert cheesemakers (*Sennen*) who presided over the alp huts of Törbel and were hired by other villages in this capacity, everyone knew enough of the process to make smaller cheeses at home when there was a surplus of milk. Both the man and the woman of the household milked, and either one along with the help of the children would bring down hay from the mow in a great apron to feed the cows, then sweep and shovel out the stalls, curry the animals, and lead them out to a trough for water.

The cattle were stabled in dim log barns (*Ställe*) with rough wooden mangers along the sides, and the ceilings were only about 1.7 meters (5.5 feet) high. It was said that this allowed the cows (but not some of the people) to stand upright and conserved the heat of their bodies. The haymow (*Scheune* or *Schiir*) up above the *Stall*, with steps leading down the outside from its lower doors and sometimes an upper door through which the newly cut hay was deposited, was often divided into sections so that each owner could keep his fodder separate. Like almost all structures in Törbel, the barns were built of squared logs, notched and fitted at the corners, with plank doors and wood rafters supporting overlapping slates. Manure of dung composted with straw or conifer needles and leaves was collected in neat piles outside the barn door. Owners might use the barn in turn, keeping cattle, sheep, and goats in it until their hay was exhausted, or if space allowed, several shareholders might keep stock in the barn at the same time. The average proprietor had rights in five different barns, but the average share was only about two-fifths of a structure. Few peasants owned entire barns, and their scattered fractional holdings necessarily were on or near the meadows from which their hay came. Although formerly there were no permanent barns on the alp for the cattle, there were a few communal cabins (*Alphütten*) for making cheese and accommodating the herdsmen, milkers, and cheesemakers. Because the cheese was later carefully divided among the owners of cows in proportion to the milk given by each animal, every household also required a cellar for storage of cheese. Cellars were windowless rooms with stone walls, often in the foundations of the log dwelling houses. The cheeses were kept first on shelves around a central post and later stored on edge on a suspended cheese ladder. In this way cheese could be kept for years without spoilage, and older cheeses were esteemed both for their taste and as a sign of the security and prosperity of the household.

Cows were both the principal source of milk for Törbel and, through their increase, a major means to a cash income, which was not easy to come by in a subsistence economy. A few breeding bulls are maintained by the community, and at least in this century, they have been pedigreed Simmental animals imported from Berner Oberland to improve the local stock (Stebler 1922:51). These reddish-brown spotted cattle are blocky and short-legged, more closely resembling an American beef animal than the taller Holstein. Because they have to negotiate steep pastures, they are somewhat lighter than the prize examples of this breed, averaging 440 kilograms instead of 700 to 800 kilograms (Imboden 1956:43). The Törbel herd also includes some animals of the Eringer breed from Lower Valais, a heavy animal of solid dark brown color known for its fighting ability on the first alp day, when the village cows establish their summer dominance hierarchy. Calves are born in the winter, and today the male animals are often muzzled so that they are not able to eat hay and can be sold at the age of 3 or 4 months as milk-fed veal. The calves are sufficiently developed to graze by spring; in the past, many of the young males were sold in the fall for butchering in eastern Switzerland. Older cows whose milk production and calf production have declined are either sold or slaughtered locally, and their meat is air-dried or made into sausage (*Hauswurst*). Törbel is well known for the quality of its cattle, and there has been a considerable trade in heifers and mature milk cows with neighboring communities, lower Valais, and the area around Frutigen on the northern slope of the Bernese Alps. Individual cattle dealers from Törbel and elsewhere carry on some of this commerce, but

Table 2.3. *Domestic animals owned in Törbel (1844–1969)*

Date	Cattle owners	Cows	Cows per owner	All cattle	Goats	Sheep	Pigs	Mules	Horses	Chickens
1844[a]	105	263	2.50							
1866[b]				351	76	412	55	19	8	
1876[b]				357	117	368	71	13	4	
1886[b]				530	120	381	77	21	6	
1896[b]				430	171	421	95	16	0	
1901[c]	106	242	2.28	521	114	391	109	10	2	
1911[d]		219		526	176	127	130	24	0	
1916[c]	111	280	2.52	634	191	137	82	31	0	
1936[c]	100	209	2.09	437	122	152	73	20	0	224
1946[c]	103	205	2.00	376	173	225	83	23	0	276
1951[c]	101	219	2.16	440	123	97	99	23	0	280
1956[c]	113	228	2.02	444	55	13	103	23	0	270
1961[c]	103	212	2.06	389	24	35	126	27	0	253
1966[c]	93	213	2.29	392	25	51	66	26	0	211
1969[c]	90	190	2.11	351	9	83	123	25	0	

[a]Data from community list of cow owners for special tax assessment to purchase church-tower clock.
[b]Data from Eidgenössisches Statistisches Amt, Bern.
[c]Data from Imboden (1967:20).
[d]Data from Stebler (1922:50).

many animals are sold in private transactions. In 1961, 83 individuals from the community sold at least one head of cattle each. Cattle changed hands mainly in the fall, after they had returned from the alp and before the long winter period of stall feeding began, but there were also many sales in the spring. In recent years, 80 to 90 percent of the animals sold were breeding stock, and about 56 percent of these were fully grown cows of 3 years or more.

Over the years for which we have statistics (Table 2.3), the total number of cattle in the village has varied, due perhaps to fluctuations in the hay crop and market conditions that influenced how many young stock were wintered and how many were sold. When we count only milk cows, however, the numbers are more nearly constant, varying from a low of 190 in 1969 to a high of 280 in 1916. A comparison with a household census made in 1970–1 shows that the numbers of cows and of cattle owners have both gone down, but the average number of milk cows per owner has not changed appreciably in the last 125 years. The number of cattle owners has also been quite stable, ranging from 90 to 107 and giving an average complement of milk cows of 2.00 to 2.52. A list of cow owners (Table 2.4) compiled by the community in 1844–5 to collect a special tax for installing a new clock in the church tower showed 105

Table 2.4. *Cows per owner in Törbel (1844–5 and 1970–1)*

	1844–5	1970–1
Total number of households	98	125
Number of owners	105	82
Number of cows	263	199
Average number of cows per owner	2.50	2.43
Owners with		
1 cow	21 (20%)	12 (15%)
2 cows	40 (38%)	31 (38%)
3 cows	21 (20%)	28 (34%)
4 cows	14 (14%)	9 (11%)
5 cows	6 (6%)	1 (2%)
6 cows	1 (1%)	0
7 cows	1 (1%)	0

individuals with 263 (presumably adult) cows. Cow ownership still clusters in the range of 1 to 3 animals, although the distribution of 1844–5 showed a higher percentage of owners at the 1-cow end of the spectrum and in the 4-, 5-, 6-, and 7-cow ranks. Although the keeping of cows is no longer a necessity, as indicated by the 34 percent of all households with no cattle whatsoever, the more affluent part-time herders of today can more often afford to maintain 3 milking animals. It is easy to see why older people today refer to the average or middle-class peasant households of their youth as "two-cow families." It is also interesting that the numbers of proprietors with larger herds were very small, and virtually no one had more than 5 mature animals. Given the small numbers of adult cows owned by each family and the crucial contribution they formerly made to subsistence, accident or disease leading to an animal's death was a severe economic hardship. Older people speak feelingly of how difficult it was to scrape together capital for the purchase of a cow as replacement for an unexpected loss. The narrow range of herd size, the large proportion of village households that had cows, and the almost stationary numbers of cow owners and cows per owner over the last century all suggest the operation of a kind of equilibrium in which animal numbers were limited by available meadow and pasture and access to these resources remained widespread and general within the community. Later on we shall consider the social conventions and legal rules that prevented the appearance of rich farmers with large herds and of peasants so poor that they did not own a single cow.

In the early part of this century, when young cattle were kept for some years to obtain a better sale price, the proportion of young animals (calves, steers, and heifers) in the village herd ranged from 52 to 58 percent. Since World War II, with more emphasis on milk for household consumption and less concern for other agricultural income, the percentage of younger animals has fallen somewhat to 45 or 50 percent. Other domestic animals have gone through wider vicissitudes as their economic roles in the community have changed (Table 2.3). Goats, once kept by almost every family to supply milk in summer when the cows were away on the alp, practically disappeared in the late 1960s. There were several reasons for this: Cows' milk was piped down from the alp, there was no village herder by the early 1950s to take the goats up to their high pastures every day in summer, and people were no longer concerned about utilizing every speck of forage on the crags and wastelands. Only an occasional elderly man or spinster kept a few goats in a stable.

Before 1900 there had been around 400 sheep in Törbel. They came from the black-faced black-stockinged old Valais breed (*Walliserrasse*) and produced both meat and the wool that went into local textiles and clothing. The sheep could graze freely above the timberline all summer with only occasional Sunday visits from their owners. Before the sale of the Oberaaralp in 1950, the Törbel sheep herd spent the summer there. Village women possessed the full range of wool-processing equipment, and once the animals were sheared, the women carded the fibers, spun them into thread on spinning wheels, twisted the yarn, and wove it on their looms or knitted it into socks.[2] A water-powered fulling mill would pound and soften the fabrics, and weavers from surrounding villages came to Törbel for this service. Wool may well have been a marketable commodity in the past, when there was some weaving as a cottage industry in Stalden and the Saas valley (Dubois 1965:18). But shortly after 1900, competition from foreign wool reduced the market for the Swiss product, and peasants found better economic opportunities in cattle raising. Since the 1950s the number of sheep kept in Törbel has begun to increase. Although the wool still has little market value, farmers who now keep fewer cows have some surplus hay. It requires little effort to fodder the sheep, and their meat is a welcome addition to the larder in a land where meat prices are always high. Inexpensive portable wire fencing also allows pasturing the sheep temporarily in various spots.

The keeping of a single pig that is bought as a weaned piglet from a traveling dealer and raised in a *Stall* for a year or two is customary in Törbel households. These pigs are fed on turnip greens and roots, potato peelings, and the whey from cheesemaking. Weeds from the garden and nettles that grow along the paths are also given to pigs. A task done every 2 or 3 days is the cooking of these plants, undersized potatoes, and whey in a large kettle for pig food. After the heavy frosts in November, the pigs

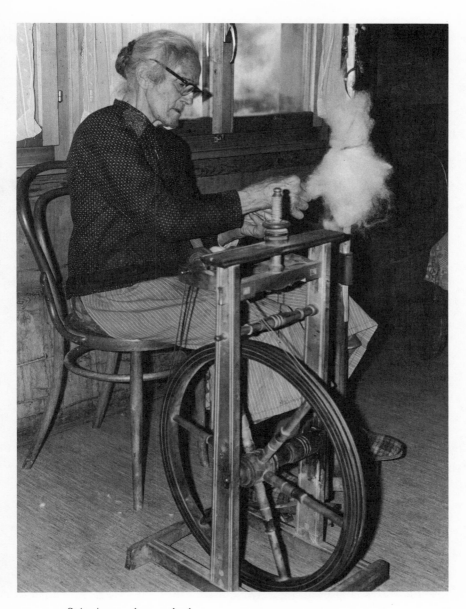

Spinning wool on a wheel.

are slaughtered. The hams, lightly salted, are dried in the *Speicher* storage buildings and eaten raw, a great delicacy called in the dialect *Hamme* rather than the standard German *Schinken*. Bacon is also preserved by drying, as was the loin until freezing facilities became available in the village.

Draft animals were always present but never prevalent in Törbel. Oxen were used to draw the plow and were fitted with packsaddles to carry loads up and down the mountain. In 1901 there were 23 oxen in the village, and 1 or 2 oxen remained as late as 1970. Horses may have been kept earlier, but not in large numbers. Mules, on the other hand, were very important beasts of burden. They were excellent pack animals, bearing 200-kilogram loads of manure, firewood, or household supplies along the rocky paths. On the few more level roads, they could pull a wooden sledge, and they were in general use for plowing. In the latter part of the nineteenth century, Törbel muleskinners guided daily pack trains to the summer resorts of Zermatt and Saas-Fee with mail, tourists, and supplies. Even after the coming of railroads and bus transportation, the small hotels and huts used by mountain climbers continued to be served by pack mules. To save fodder, mules and sheep were sometimes driven down to the Rhone valley during the winter and pastured on the sour marsh grasses (Stebler 1922:57). Several peasants might occasionally share the ownership of one mule, using and feeding the animal in turn. There were usually between 20 and 30 mules in the village, and although they may be underutilized for agriculture today, they still bring in some cash when they are rented to the Swiss army for maneuvers in the mountains. Because mules are still fed throughout the year and must be shoed regularly by a visiting blacksmith every 3 to 4 months, their upkeep is a significant expense. When a mule dies, it is butchered, and the meat is prepared for household use.

The economic role of draft animals in general and the numbers of oxen kept by village farmers have diminished in part because of the almost complete disappearance of grain cultivation. Cereal production is the only part of Törbel's traditional agricultural system to decline so rapidly. From 1919 to 1939 the amount of land used for grain went from 24.15 to 19.60 hectares, and even a government subsidy for Swiss cereals during the war years did not prevent further shrinkage to 15.11 hectares by 1944 (Imboden 1967:19). A further decrease by almost 50 percent to 8.42 hectares was evident in 1950, and by 1970 hardly a single hectare was still in use. Grain grown and milled in the community went from 19,982 kilograms in 1939 to 2,184 kilograms in 1965 (Imboden 1967:11), and most of the latter was used not for bread but for animal feed. Winter rye was the most important grain grown in this mountain environment; at

Loading a mule with pack saddle.

least 90 percent of the arable fields were devoted to it. Rye was synonymous with grain, and local people called it *Korn*. Small amounts of summer rye were occasionally planted, and a total area of about 1 hectare was sown in winter wheat. Even smaller amounts of barley, oats, and mixed grains were reported for earlier decades of this century (Imboden 1967:19).

In a patchwork of plots on the sunnier terraces and in swaths below the main village and below each hamlet, the rye fields (*Roggenäcker*) were planted and left fallow in alternate years (*Brachwirtschaft*). The choicest fields, called *Halmeren,* could sustain annual crops. Until the 1920s the major implement was a wooden, wheeled plow (*Holzpflug*) whose plowshare and moldboard were reinforced with iron. The depth of the furrow was only about 10 centimeters, but it could be adjusted. There was no knifelike coulter to cut the soil before it was broken and pushed into equal ridges on both sides of the spear-shaped point. The plow scratched the soil like a Mediterranean ard, rather than turning it. The plowman held in one hand the plow handle, made from a naturally forked branch, and guided with the reins a single mule or an ox. The fallow was plowed twice, in June and in August, and it was not harrowed. Smaller plots were prepared with a broad hoe (*Briethaue*). Seed carried to the field in a sack slung over the shoulder were sown broadcast in September. Even after the introduction of light all-metal plows, the final shallow plowing to cover the seed was often done with the old-fashioned wooden plow.[3] Plowing followed the contour of the slope, and sometimes it was done in one direction only so as to direct the earth upward. The hardy native rye of Valais (*Walliser Landroggen*) was especially resistant to drought and gave some return even on stony and steep fields (Imboden 1967:10). In the past, some grainfields went 10 to 20 years without fertilizer, and it was known that stable manure increased the quantity but adversely affected the quality of the rye (Stebler 1922:59).

The rye harvest might begin in the lowest fields by mid-June, but it was not completed in the late-ripening fields (up to 1,800 meters) until August (Stebler 1922:61). The grain was cut in the very early morning with the sickle (*Sichel*) or the scythe (*Sense*), gathered into sheaves (*Garben*), and bound with its own stalks. The sheaves were laid in chevron fashion, forming windrows in the field to dry. In order not to lose the precious grain, the sheaves were bound up in a large cloth and carried on the backs of mules or the harvesters themselves to the granary. These distinctive log buildings (*Stadel*), perched on timber pillars and the large mushroomlike stone disks that prevented mice from invading them, stood in or near the fields. Each had a broad open doorway and a central

Sowing rye.

passage separated from the individually owned granary sections by sturdy waist-high plank partitions. While the sheaves were being stored, they were knocked against this board wall, and the first of the grain was gathered up. In early winter, the rye was thoroughly threshed in the same corridor. The flail was a 2-meter pole with a heavy billet loosely attached to the end. Winnowing was formerly done in ingenious wooden machines (*Wannen*) with rotating paddles, and some of these devices were in use by the middle eighteenth century (Stebler 1922:63). The straw was carefully cut into lengths of 12 to 15 centimeters on a bench-mounted scythe blade (*Schrotbank*) to make better bedding material. Individual owners not only had a series of rye fields but also had fractional shares in a number of granaries and communal rights to a winnowing machine.

The threshed grain was kept in storehouses, again on stone plates, set in among the village houses. These *Speicher* were often divided into sections on one or two floors, and each compartment was entered through a door locked by an impressive iron key. This storeroom also protected bread during the 2 or 3 months that elapsed between bakings. Dried meat was hung there in the cooler months, and farm equipment, utensils, pieces of furniture, and clothing could be kept there as well. An observer has noted that the alpine subsistence economy was a "storage culture," and the wealth of special-purpose hay barns, granaries, *Speicher* chambers, and cellars bears out this conclusion (Wiegandt 1977). A peasant family obviously needed each type of structure in addition to land and dwelling houses. In the form of stipulated fractional shares (e.g., 1/4 of a barn, 1/28 of a granary), such holdings were widespread, jealously guarded, and precisely inherited. Of the total valuation of all individually owned real property in Törbel around 1920, almost exactly two-thirds was in land, and the remaining one-third was in buildings. Residential structures accounted for 60 percent of this valuation, whereas the rest pertains to shelters for animals and the specialized storage facilities for hay, grain, and processed foods. Without the techniques of preserving the products of summer for winter consumption and building up a stock of subsistence insurance against bad years and temporary climatic fluctuations, continued peasant life in the Alps would have been impossible.

All the major items of the Törbel diet could be stored for later use, and the means for transforming fresh foods into cured or preserved forms were known to everyone. The dry cool air of the Rhone valley allowed meat to be made into *Trockenfleish* (dried meat) without smoking and with only a minimum of salt. In the same way, chopped-up beef or pork could be mixed with potatoes, beets, and spices, stuffed into sausage casings, and dried for later use as raw *Hauswurst*. During the summer, meat was kept in the cool cellars along with the cheeses, which were still

*Village barns and storehouses (Speicher) set on posts with stone caps.
The roofs are of native slate slabs. In the foreground is a footpath
through meadows. The forest in the background and the meadow
clearings are all in Törbel territory as is the 2665-meter Schwarzhorn peak. Törbeltälli, from which flows the village stream, is at the
upper right.*

considered edible and suitable for grating when they were 20 years old.
Surplus milk could also be converted into butter and kept in a crock for
up to 1 year. Well-made wine improves in the cask, and the provident
vineyard owner could survive a year or two of poor grape harvests. A
board-covered hole in the cellar floor kept potatoes, and cabbage could be
shredded and saved in the sauerkraut barrel. Rye stored well in the dry,
rodent-proof *Speicher*, and even bread could be kept for months. Grain
ground locally in one of the mills with turbine-type waterwheels turning
the millstones was kneaded into a sour dough by the men of one or several
households working together. It was baked in the community oven in
batches of about 60 loaves weighing 2 kilograms each, with each baker
supplying his own firewood. Families customarily baked four times a
year: at Christmas, before the vineyard work in March, after the first hay
harvest in August, and at the end of October. The round rye loaves dried
and toughened in the *Speicher* until they required a vigorous cutting
action, or even a hinged knife mounted on a board for slicing. Winter-

baked and frozen rye bread will keep, it is said, for a year. Nevertheless, elderly people took pride in the fact that they could still chew the months-old bread. The crisp white wheat loaves that now come up daily on the bus from bakeries in the valley were in the recent past only for Sunday use. Before the turn of the century, white bread brought from Sion was so rare that it was kept in the *Speicher* as food for the very ill or for mothers who had just given birth. When local supplies of rye were inadequate, rye was brought in Visperterminin or Visp, and since 1900 it has been possible to buy polenta (maize meal) from Italy as a cheap supplemental cereal. Once the growing of grain became unprofitable in Törbel, the smaller fields that remained in use attracted all the birds in the area, and yields declined rapidly.

Small-scale gardening and the growing of potatoes continue to make an appreciable contribution to the part-time agriculture of Törbel. Vegetable plots averaging just under 80 square meters (Table 2.1) are manured in the spring, and the earth is thoroughly turned over and broken with large bent-tine forks (*Karste*). At the same time, soil that has washed to the bottom of the garden slope is loaded into pack baskets and carried to the upper margin of the plot. The soil is raked very fine and shaped into beds about 1.5 meters wide. The raised beds are separated by narrow walkways that allow the gardener to move about for planting, weeding, and watering. Although various green vegetables such as cabbage, lettuce, leeks, onions, and peas are grown today, it appears that gardening in the past provided more in the way of animal fodder than table food. Of 41,700 square meters listed in 1919 as devoted to vegetables, 38,800 square meters were designated for beans, probably the broad beans (*Grossbohnen*) fed dried to the livestock (Imboden 1967:19). People ate beans only briefly in the late summer, when they were still green, and they might use the dried beans in soup. Turnips and other roots (swedes, mangelwurzels) were also given to the cattle. A descendant of an affluent family recalls putting out about 300 turnip sets and the same number of cabbage. The gardens had no definite rights to irrigation water, but during dry spells water might be carried to the plants in buckets, or the overflow of a village fountain might be conveyed in movable hollowed-out wooden channels. Since the appearance of rubber hose and rotating sprinklers in recent years, gardens have been watered more frequently, either by means of siphons from a trough or directly from an irrigation channel.

The technology of potato cultivation was equally simple. Hand operations were used in preparing the field with a hoe or fork, except where the potatoes were rotated with grain in the same twice-plowed field. Rye could be sown for 1 or 2 years, followed by a manured crop of potatoes

(*Wechselwirtschaft*), and the field required no fallow. On smaller, steep potato gardens, the cultivator broke the ground in a chevron pattern of furrows angling up from the center of the plot toward each side. A narrow pointed hoe was used to unearth the potatoes in September. The green plant remains were formerly fed to the animals or plowed under as fertilizer for the grain crop. Small or damaged tubers were put aside for the pigs. In recent years, potato gardens have sometimes been cultivated by means of a plow pulled from the bottom to the top of the field by a motor-driven cable winch (*Seilwinde*), and this allows the plants to grow in straight lines instead of the less regular patterns of the past. Törbel people have also been able to purchase potatoes at government-subsidized sales, and their own local production has gone down. As late as 1965, however, some 6 hectares were still in potatoes, as compared with 12.39 hectares in 1919 (Imboden 1967:19).

Sketching in the climate and terrain of Törbel and briefly outlining the agricultural methods and land-use characteristics of its territory may demonstrate the possibility of a peasant economy, without proving that it existed in that form. Was agricultural self-sufficiency merely an ideal, or did people actually produce most of what they ate? My consultants in the village agreed on both the simplicity of the diet in the past and the high degree of self-reliance in the average peasant household. Breakfast was often bread with perhaps some cheese or the warmed-over soup of the night before. Sliced potatoes fried in butter (*Rösti*) were sometimes served. There might be milk to drink, but it (*Magermilch*) often featured the bluish whey left from butter and homemade cheese mixed three parts whey to one part whole milk.[4] Adults remember when coffee was only for Sundays or feast days, and the elderly recall a time when coffee was a special treat reserved for Christmas Eve. The midday meal was the big meal of the day, frequently based on potatoes, either peeled or boiled in their skins, and cheese. As in Ireland, a favorite repast was salted potatoes and buttermilk. Another preferred dish was boiled cabbage and potatoes with pigs' feet. Some dried meat might be cooked, but often meat was consumed just on Sunday. As imported carbohydrates like polenta and pasta became available, they were often cooked and served with butter or cheese in the same meal with potatoes. Some of the choicest foods, such as dried ham and sausage, along with bread and cheese and generous amounts of wine, were taken to the meadows for summer picnics during the hard work of haying. The same cold menu appeared for the late afternoon *z'Vieri* (at 4 P.M.), which might be anything from a snack to a kind of high tea. The evening meal, often after sundown, was usually a thin soup with meat broth and perhaps some vegetables and potatoes, but made heartier by grated or sliced cheese partially melted in the steaming liquid. Young nettle leaves might be gathered for the soup. Another soup was of potatoes and bacon, with milk mixed in just before serving. On the *Voralp* the family would gather around the kettle brought from the fireplace to the table and use their spoons to help themselves from the common pot. People say that potatoes formed a larger part of the diet than bread and that polenta was resorted to as a staple by poorer families or those with many children. More milk was consumed in winter than in summer, but even then there were periods when the cows might be dry or when a calf was taking half the cow's milk.

Although unexpected emergencies might require the sale of livestock to buy grain or polenta or an exceptionally dry year might drastically decrease the potato harvest, families strove for self-sufficiency in food. There was no regular store in Törbel until the 1920s, and the impact of the Great Depression followed by war slowed the growth of a local market economy. Young adults in 1970 could remember vividly the first time they were given an exotic fruit such as an orange or a banana.[5] Although no one talked of serious hunger of long duration, there was universal agreement that the diet until recently had been simple, nutritious, unvaried, and based on homegrown staples. Families might go for weeks without spending a single rappen (0.01 franc or a fraction of a penny), and the unvarying tribute to a respected peasant householder, whether rich or poor, was *Er hat einfach und sparsam gelebt* (he lived simply and frugally). Any surplus was stored or converted into cash that could then be invested in land or livestock or a house. The mode of production and food preservation meant that household consumption was carefully rationed and thrift was the watchword. Children thought of holiday white bread or a special loaf on baking day as a real treat. It is instructive that village feasting often required cooperation beyond the household. Not only was communally produced bread and wine distributed to citizens in public winter and spring celebrations, but rites of passage such as marriage and funerals often necessitated individual purchase of wine from the community cellars. Families would also tap their hoarded stock of old cheeses to entertain guests at a wedding or funeral.

Although we can enumerate the kinds of property necessary for a viable peasant household and demonstrate a pervasive ideal of self-sufficiency, it is much more difficult to decide just what amount of agricultural produce was actually consumed. We are unsure of mean yields of grain and dairy products in the past before improved varieties, chemical fertilizers, insecticides, better breeding, and feed supplements for cattle become available. There is also no way of estimating annual fluctuations in total food supply caused by climatic factors or the extent of variation related to the differing microenvironments of meadows and fields. Without attempting any reliable approach to carrying capacity, a few rough approximations may be useful. The local measure of hay is the klafter, a well-packed 1.95 cubic meters weighing 400 kilograms. It is reckoned that an adult cow needs 7 klafters of hay (approximately 1 per month) for the winter. Calves need 1 klafter, 2-year-olds 3, and heifers in their third year 5. It takes 10 sheep or 10 goats to match the consumption of a cow, so that 0.7 klafter would be the hay required for one of these animals. Using the 1901 count of animals from Table 2.3 averaged among 106 owners, mean hay needs would be approximately 27 klafters per owner.

Three full-time family farmers who estimated the production of their meadows for me in 1971 gave total klafters of 29.5, 26, and 24, an average of 26.5 klafters. Hay production varies widely according to the altitude, inclination, soil quality, and irrigation of individual meadows, as seen by land tax valuations varying from 0.05 to 0.53 franc per square meter and averaging 0.22 franc. There are suggestions, however, that it required 500 to 600 square meters of meadow on the average to produce 1 klafter of hay. Thus a peasant with a mean meadow area of 15,326 square meters might produce from 25.5 to 30.7 klafters.[6] There seems to be, then, a general relationship between meadowland in use, hay production, and livestock holdings, suggesting a fairly close adjustment to the potential of the local environment.

In a similar manner we may estimate rye production at 12 to 15 kilograms per 100 square meters (Imboden 1956:38) and average field area (omitting fallow) per cattle owner in 1919 at 2,278 square meters. This would produce 274 to 340 kilograms. One consultant guessed that the annual production of his household had been 250 to 300 kilograms, and larger families with unusually extensive *Aecker* judged they had 500 to 600 kilograms of rye annually. Because seeding required setting aside about one-eighth of the grain harvest, average consumption of grain may have been 300 kilograms or less. At the rate of 1.16 kilograms of flour per loaf, fewer than 260 loaves per year could be made from this amount, and it is not surprising that most families evidently purchased grain outside the community. A final rough tabulation of potatoes grown in Törbel used yields of 150 to 180 kilograms per 100 square meters (Imboden 1956) on the 1919 area of 123,900 square meters. Under these conditions, the average peasant family would have 1,753 to 2,104 kilograms. Estimates of annual potato production in the recent past made for me by representatives of six rather prosperous families ranged from 750 to 3,500 kilograms and averaged 1,988 kilograms. With perhaps one-fourth to one-fifth of this yield reserved for seed, a family would still have at its disposal around 1,500 kilograms, or well over 1.5 tons of potatoes. Although the preceding figures make no claim to precision, they do indicate rough agreement among land areas devoted to different agricultural uses, average yields, livestock supported, and consultants' estimates of household production.

The traditional material culture of production, processing, and storage in peasant Törbel was diverse without being complicated, functional without being mechanical, and ingenious but not innovative. The domestic animals and crops basic to the local economy made up an agricultural complex closely integrated with the alpine environment and capable of sustaining a human population over centuries without exhausting the resources of that environment. The necessary goods and tools were widely distributed in the village, most techniques were matters of common knowledge, and similar complements of land, buildings, livestock, and implements were available to all households. But we should not be deceived by surface uniformities into regarding Törbel as a homogeneous folk community, a boring collection of peasant stereotypes as undifferentiated as Marx's potatoes in a sack. Rather than plodding along an unchanging cultural furrow or responding dully to the dictates of a harsh physical environment, the Törbel householder was confronted continually by critical choices. Although the tasks and the tools of survival were common, the decisions on how to allocate time and effort, whether or not to sell a cow or buy a meadow, and what risks to take in the continual guessing game with the weather were ones that directly affected the family's livelihood. Everyone needed the same counters to play this game, but individual skill, knowledge, and luck influenced the outcome. And although we have been emphasizing the way in which a largely self-sufficient farmer encountered and won support from his particular portion of the landscape, the social world that nurtured him and that he in turn manipulated was part and parcel of his ecological arena. Although extremes of wealth and poverty were absent, one could rise or fall in the local scale of respect, as well as in terms of possessions. Choices involving whether or not to marry, when to marry, how to parlay a small inheritance into a comfortable estate, whether to migrate or stay put, what political stance to take on each issue of village policy – these gave scope to individuality and achievement, in addition to raising the possibility of failure and incurring the scorn of neighbors. Indeed, the extraordinary continuity of the community and the endurance of its culture were founded on the ever-renewed struggles of unique individuals defining themselves and their society in toil and anxiety and change. The ordered system in equilibrium so prized by the "scientific observer" is merely the distant and denatured view of a life lacking striving and stress, without color and conflict, one that negates growth as well as change. Perhaps the pale creature of custom, powerless against geographical determinism and pushed about by the invisible hand of economy, will take on flesh again as we examine the strategies people use to make their way against nature and compete cooperatively with their fellows in creating the history of a single little community.

3

Strategies of alpine land use

No man is an island, as the poet has reminded us, and no society is truly isolated and self-sufficient. But anyone attempting to understand human culture must make certain simplifying assumptions, reduce the variables being considered, and proceed as if a system of relationships existed in a kind of equilibrium. Anthropologists have attempted to model small preindustrial societies, often choosing real islands, in order to be able to deal with a bounded and relatively uncomplex unit that can be grasped and untangled by the single observer (Bayliss-Smith 1977). At the risk of seriously distorting a complex reality, we have taken a similar stance, viewing Törbel as an "island in the sky" where a local physical environment interacted with a set of cultural coping devices, including practical knowledge and technology to create food and other physical necessities of life. The outlines of an alpine subsistence system have appeared, but we have provided only an armature or a skeleton, without considering the processes that give rise to and maintain the system in working order. We must continue to simplify and abstract, but we can now begin to ask what strategic choices are made by individuals and by the group. In contrast to the situation involving the rather definite constraints of winter temperatures, plant requirements, how much hay a cow eats, and how far a man can walk to work, this approach involves options, alternative acts, and potentially conflicting decisions.

Given limited resources and equally fixed means for utilizing them, individual players of the peasant subsistence game may take several courses of action. We may term these strategies *intensification, expansion,* and *regulation* (Netting 1972). Intensification refers to getting greater returns from the same raw materials, usually by means of greater inputs of labor, mechanical energy, or capital. If more loads of hay are produced from a meadow by fertilizing it, or if steep wasteland is terraced into gardens, the use of that land has been intensified. An individual farmer may increase his yields by his own efforts, or he may serve the same ends in cooperation with his fellows on projects too large to be carried out with one pair of hands or paid for from a single purse. An alternative strategy is to gain new resources by expansion: claiming territory from another village, or buying property from an elderly bachelor. Expansion may involve perpetuating the peasant farming of the home area in newly opened land or securing a livelihood in quite different ways, as, for instance, a mercenary soldier or muleteer working for wages completely outside the community. Both intensification and expansion have finite limits. Technological breakthroughs have been rare in the Alps, and nothing like a frontier has existed in the area for 1,000 years. Perhaps the most pressing problem and the one that demanded specifically social solutions was that of regulation. How was access to the available resources to be allocated? What socioeconomic differences were right and proper, and which were illegitimate and intolerable? How were quarrels over property or tithes or the financing of public works resolved? Agreed-upon means of regulation may be embodied in law and religion. Disputes over policy also deal with regulation, but we call them politics. Intensification, expansion, and regulation are each both private strategies and public activities.

INTENSIFICATION

The present-day mixed-farming adaptation of Törbel and all the evidence we have of local agriculture back to the Middle Ages demonstrate the presence of a highly intensive system. The methods for increasing production from existing alpine resources were, for the most part, known in antiquity and used wherever the pressure of population on the environment made them necessary. There may well have been a considerable period corresponding to the late Neolithic expansion into Europe when nomadic herders made seasonal use of natural meadows in the Vispertal and even burned portions of forest to increase the grazing potential, as mentioned in Chapter 1. The shifting cultivation of grain may have been combined with cattle keeping, the gathering of forest products, and hunting to support temporary settlements. However, by the time Törbel entered recorded history, it was already a permanent, year-round settlement, probably situated in its current location, flanked by neighboring communities, and claiming a defined territory quite similar to that of today.

We have no means of determining thirteenth-century population or land use, but there are suggestions that the inhabitants had already felt the pinch of land scarcity. Established residence in the high alpine valleys entailed large-scale preparation and storage of hay. We have already noted that the favorable sun exposure of the Törbel slopes was balanced by their extreme dryness, and without artificial watering the meadows could not support grazing and a large hay harvest. With adequate irrigation, however, two cuttings of hay were possible. Such multiple cropping involved greatly increased application of labor to build and maintain a network of ditches, to guide the water to all parts of the meadows, and to systematically share the limited amount of water without wasting it. Without watering, there would be one-half to two-thirds less growth of usable grass. The time spent in cutting and carrying the second hay harvest (*Emd*) may be only half that for the first, but the amount of hay actually put in the barn averages less than half of the first cut. Maximum return on this effort could be attained only if soil fertility was enhanced and regularly restored by manuring. There is every reason to think that both these key techniques of intensification were already being practiced by 1200. Indeed, the two lower irrigation systems, both tapping the Törbelbach, were probably making maximum use of the available stream flow at that time. There is no other way to account for the purchase in 1270 by Törbel and Zeneggen of water rights in the Embdbach in Augsttal. This required not only a payment to an altar society of the church of Saint Niklaus[1] but also the engineering feat of channeling the water with a minimal gradient for 6 kilometers to Törbel and a further 4 kilometers to Zeneggen. The canal is named the Augstbordwasserleitung or Augstborder after its source, but it is familiarly referred to in the village as *die Niwa* (the new one). In operation, it brought water to the southwestern part of the territory (Bad, Riedfluh, Schaufel, etc.) and to all of the *Voralpen* above 1,800 meters. Although some of these areas may have been farmed earlier, their only natural water supplies were from small, spring-fed catch basins of meager and unpredictable flow. The allocation of the Augstbord water was also rationalized by assigning 6-hour periods (*Viertel*) to the members or sub-groupings in the association. This contrasted with the complex timing of water shares by a variety of sun and shadow marks (*Schattenzielen*) that characterized the smaller (and presumably older) irrigation systems (Netting 1974).

Irrigation demands both periodic communal labor and tightly scheduled individual work. Major canal systems are frequent in the circum-alpine culture area (Burns 1963), and the difficulties of bringing water along sheer cliff faces, over ravines, and across the paths of avalanches had already been met in eleventh- and twelfth-century Valais (Mariétan 1948). Coordinated group efforts were needed to build the channels and to clean and repair them every spring. There were dams to divert the flow of the feeder streams, settling pools to trap stones and gravel, wooden sluice gates, and log flumes to be maintained. Because a leak in the channel could rapidly soak lower slopes and lead to dangerous landslides, long canals had to be patrolled. A guard (*Wasserhüter*) was employed by the Augstbord association to walk the channel each day, checking for obstructions or gullying. A small waterwheel also powered a hammer whose rhythmic sounds signaled an unabated flow of water. All users of the water were subject to an annual labor contribution of 2 days, as well as emergency service and financial expenditures for major repairs in proportion to their stated irrigation shares. Leadership of the association (*Geteilschaft*) went in yearly succession to a representative (*Niventeiler*) from each quarter-day allotment, and he served as general supervisor.

Direct irrigation of a meadow is a simple but time-consuming procedure. The main stone-lined channel from the perennial stream may branch several times, with each subsidiary channel connected to a number of shallow feeder ditches (*Rus*) dug out of the soil and following the contour of the meadow. The farmer must often direct the water by means of several sluice gates (*Schieber*) or temporary earth and stone dams to his field and thence into one ditch at a time. Beginning at the tail of the ditch, the irrigator blocks the water flow at several points by slate plates (*Steinplatten*), thrown down with enough force to lodge in the earth sides of the trench. These dams partially interrupt the flow of water, causing it to spill over the edge of the ditch and cascade downhill. When the water reaches the base of the meadow, the stone plate is removed and placed 1 or 2 meters up the ditch to water the next strip of land. Because the progress of the water is difficult to detect in the thick grass, it is more efficient for a team to do the job. One person, often a child, can call from down-slope when the water arrives. Both men and women go out with the mattocklike tools (*Wasserbeile*) that can trim off bits of turf from the ditches and pack together or dislodge the temporary dams that guide the water. Only one meadow at a time can be irrigated because of the limited water source and the small capacity of each system. A user's turn during the 16-day cycle may come at any time of the day or night and may require not only 1 to 4 hours of actual watering but also considerable travel time to and from the meadow and perhaps partway up the branching system where the flow is diverted. My consultants estimated that these trips hither and yon across the village territory took 10 to 20 percent of all the hours put into a crop of hay. Another computation put hours of irrigating at double the time spent mowing, raking, and transporting the hay (Stebler 1922:81). Although the task is onerous and inconvenient, especially amid the other activities of midsummer, it is safe to say that it was never neglected in the past, and every effort was made to utilize the precious drops of *das heilige Wasser* (the holy water).

To achieve both the double crops of hay and heavy, dependable production from gardens, potato fields, and vineyards, it was necessary to conserve the soil and regularly restore the nutrients lost to runoff and to crop growth. Erosion was obviously a danger whenever slopes were cultivated. Although the meadows were never tilled, and a thick network of grass roots anchored the hillside turf, a water-soaked area of topsoil might give way, causing a destructive landslide. The irrigation system had to be continuously monitored, because a break in the channel could quickly result in damage. Water was the responsibility of the farmer whose turn it was to use it, and allowing it to run wild and uncontrolled (*herrenlos*) through the ditches was a punishable offense. Plowed or hoed fields had a normal tendency for earth to creep toward the lower edge over a single growing season. Low stone terrace walls in the rye and potato fields slowed this tendency, and the resulting patches were not level but merely less steeply inclined. The grainfields also had lines of fruit trees planted or at least protected along the contour terraces to further stabilize them. The back-breaking chore of loading dirt from the bottom of the field into a pack basket or a mule pannier and transporting it to the top of the slope was part of the annual spring preparation of gardens. The most precipitous terraced gradients were the vineyards above the Vispa River. Favorable land at this elevation was limited, and some of the terraces held no more than a single row of grapevines. A wall left unrepaired could wash out years of plantings and threaten all lower terraces. On the highest and least accessible terraces that have gone out of use in this century, the ravages of erosion are clearly visible.

The fertility of Törbel soil was maintained by a combination of fallowing, crop rotation, and manuring. We have mentioned the alternate-year fallowing of the rye fields that not only rested the land but also demanded several plowings to turn under weed growth and to pulverize the soil, thereby making it retain moisture better. The rye–potato rotation increased the total production of the land and built up fertility when the potatoes were manured. Törbjers have a high opinion of barn manure (*Stallmist*), which they prepare with care and apply judiciously to meadows, gardens, and vineyards. Cattle and small stock dung is always composted with stall bedding and piled neatly in stone or wood enclosures near the barn door. In the past there was never enough grain straw for this purpose (it was also fed to animals and was used to stuff mattresses), so larch needles and fallen leaves had to be scraped from the forest floor and carried to the barns. Moss and humus along with the conifer needles were raked and dug from even the most difficult ravines, and one observer saw the practice as detrimental to normal forest growth (Stebler 1922:98). Families collected 8 to 16 cubic meters of this material, with women and children bringing in much of the *Waldstreue* in large pack baskets (*Chris-Tschifferen*). In effect, the organic material of the forest was being taken to replenish the supply of agricultural nutrients. The stall bedding retained the liquid portion of animal wastes and helped to prevent loss of its nitrogenous components. Some of the stall manure was laboriously dried on the meadows to reduce its weight, then piled up again and taken by sledge or mule back down to the vineyards. After the meadows were fertilized in the fall, the residue of compost left after the winter snow had melted was raked up again and returned to the barn for bedding. Such conscious recycling indicates the importance of fertilizer in the agricultural system and the need to conserve scarce resources even at the expense of additional labor-intensive processes. Applying composted manure to hay meadows on a regular basis is reported to keep down the growth of broad-leaf weeds and promote a species composition in which desirable grasses predominate.

Although communal grazing grounds had lower average production than the meadows, they too were pushed to maximum capacity. In the spring, crews of village women raked up fallen twigs to increase the growth of grass, and men drained swampy hollows and repaired the paths, stone fences, and troughs. Once the cows had left the alp in the fall, other work parties went through the pastures above the timberline, swinging forks to break up and scatter the clumps of dung. It is said that this practice spreads the fertilizing effect and prevents the concentrations of manure that give grass a taste the cows don't like.

Irrigation, soil-conserving practices, and fertilization are all traditional methods for increasing the production of food from available resources and maintaining dependable yields. In the absence of major technological changes or new sources of energy, one must rely on greater application of human effort. As total production from a fixed land area goes up, average productivity in the sense of return per unit of labor declines (Boserup 1965). Skills may be refined, and more rational use may be made of various types of land or animals, but the chief contribution of the intensive farmer is time and work. A good example is the tending of the vineyard, always a secondary activity and today a kind of hobby of many men in Törbel. The average farmer now has several parcels totaling 300 to 500 square meters of vineyard, with 400 to 660 vines. From 30 to 50 man-days may go into the tasks of manuring, hoeing, pruning, breaking out unwanted growth, staking and tying up the vines, spraying, harvesting, and making wine, and in the past this included substantial travel time. An elaborate system of digging up low-yield elderly vines and fostering new shoots from their remaining deep roots shaped the surfaces of the terraces into lateral waves and helped to make the grapes drought-resistant. All this labor was expended for perhaps 200 to 400 liters of wine. The family work requirement for haying was a great deal higher. The support activities of preliminary raking of the meadow, irrigating, and manuring may absorb from 40 to 70 percent of the total time, which averaged 170 work days in three estimates by contemporary full-time farmers. If mowing were done by hand, this figure would be increased by at least 15 percent, bringing total labor for some 27 klafters of hay to 195 person-days. Because much of the work of haying was concentrated in 2 months, it is obvious that the labor resources of a household, even with the contributions of several children, often were severely taxed. Modern families in which the husband has a factory job or in which a widow is aided by young children manage only some 65 person-days per year on the hay crop.

Even routine winter activities of cattle feeding and milking require time. If the animals are in a barn 30 minutes' walking time from the village, 2 to 2.5 hours are spent twice a day. Packed hay must be cut with a spadelike tool so that the first cut and the greener second cut are mixed. Some people prefer to feed the animals once, then milk, water, and fodder a second time. A cow should be brushed and curried once a day, and the stall should be cleaned. Moving stock from one barn to another takes several people at least part of a day.

The years since World War II have seen a different type of intensification in which both labor and land resources have been replaced by power equipment and purchased raw materials. The numbers of mowing machines with gasoline engines grew quickly after they first appeared in the late 1950s. Equipped with metal lugs for clinging to the meadow slopes, they can cut all but the least accessible meadows. In comparison with the scythe, they can mow the same amount in one-quarter to one-fifth the time. Everyone agrees that only by substituting mowing machines for absent male labor have the meadows been kept in use. Small wagon attachments to the power unit increasingly serve to transport hay from fields near the road and carry the workers. Although the number of cows in the community has declined, their milk production has appreciably increased. The breed has been improved by importing superior sires; in addition, more hay per animal is provided, and grain supplements are offered routinely. The average milk yield of 13 to 16 liters per day is said to be double what cows formerly gave.[2] It is said that 4,000 liters per year is now a somewhat low average for village cows. Almost none of the grain fed to livestock is locally grown, and even baled straw for stall bedding is now imported in great truckloads. On the alp, portable automatic milking machines allow a few employees to milk the entire village herd and send the milk down a pipeline for cheesemaking in a single modern facility. Pumps at the alp barns send the manure through high-pressure hoses to fertilize the surrounding pastures. Some artificial fertilizer is also purchased, and considerable use is made of insecticides for spraying the vineyards and the potato patches. Vegetable and potato gardens are watered by hose and whirling mechanical sprayers. The intensive and autonomous land use involving compost from the forest, gathering wild grass in March to eke out the cattle rations, and scouring the woods for bits of fuel are activities of the past.

Self-sufficient full-spectrum peasant cultivation has given way to a specialized part-time farming system by which the families of factory workers and other wage earners fill their needs for most dairy products, meat, and vegetables by home production, purchasing other food, clothing, and consumer goods in the market. Individuals may sell some cheese and butter and livestock. Labor-intensive practices of meadow irrigation, manuring, viticulture, and animal care have been maintained with little change, but total farm work has dramatically decreased because of the use of motor power for mowing, plowing, and transport (Minge-Kalman 1977). Grain growing has lost its economic justification and all but disappeared. Yields have increased because of considerable recent investments in improved breeds of cows, supplementary animal feeds, veterinary services, and stall bedding. The Törbel farmer is now cushioned against agricultural fluctuations both by the cash from outside employment and by the multitude of government programs that insure his cattle, subsidize dairying, and periodically offer potatoes and fruits in bulk at below market prices. Although labor-saving equipment may continue to be adopted, and the number of full-time farmers, currently about six, may decline, it is economically unlikely that the modern trend away from the traditional intensive, diversified peasant household enterprise will be reversed.

EXPANSION

In farming societies in which land and other resources are not in short supply, intensification, with its attendant complex manipulation of the environment and high labor requirements, is seldom evident. Rather, the strategy of choice is expansion: moving onto unused land, or forcibly appropriating the flocks and herds of weaker neighbors. Perhaps the Keltic settlers of the Alps filled a niche that had supported only a few nomadic hunter-gatherers. Whether the Allemanic invaders of Valais in the ninth century were part of another *Völkerwanderung*, propelled by expanding population or the lure of greener pastures, cannot be known at present. By the time Törbel entered recorded history, expansion in terms of physical movements of peoples and the displacement of resident tribes or communities seems to have been over. Dorbia (the earliest name for Törbel) was bordered by the valley settlement of Stalden, known in 1245 as Morgia, a Gallic word meaning boundary or stone wall (Zimmermann 1968:21). A locality of Zeneggen, Sisetsch, mentioned in 1282, is derived from the Latin patois for fence (Zimmermann 1968:24). Embd boasts the foundations of a tower built in 1211 as a stronghold of the noble von Roten family, later resident in Raron (Stebler 1922:22). The name is derived from the Old High German *amat,* referring to the second cutting of hay. Bürchen, named in German for the birch trees on its lower slopes, is marked off from Törbel by a long stone boundary wall said to be 750 years old (Stebler 1922:42). If, as the poet tells us, good fences make good neighbors, medieval Törbel and the adjoining settlements must have existed in a state of considerable amity. There is, of course, no proof that the territories of these adjacent communities were absolutely fixed. But it is clear that named villages have existed in approximately their present locations for centuries and that Törbel could neither expand at the expense of its neighbors nor allow any trespassing. In 1551 an agreement with Bürchen provided for maintenance of a wooden fence dividing the respective alps (TGA C6). There may have been jostling between Embd and Törbel for alpine land and wasteland, as evidenced by an agreement providing a limited common-use area in 1672 (TGA C8), and the present boundary at Schreiende Bach was the subject of litigation in 1693 (TGA C9). Special-purpose land, such as that suitable for vineyards near the Vispa River, was never incorporated by Törbel but rather was purchased by individuals from Stalden or Zeneggen (documents from the period 1663–1742, TGA D52–7).

In conforming to the twin constraints of its alpine topography and the inflexible territoriality of the surrounding settlements, Törbel had little opportunity for expansion. At one time there must have been an internal frontier of woodland that could be put to more productive use as pasture. The opening up of high or outlying areas is commemorated by Germanic place-names, such as *Riedfluh* (rocky clearing), from the fifteenth century (Zimmermann 1968:47), and *Schwendi,* from the word for ring-barking and thus killing trees (Zimmermann 1968:49). The previously mentioned extension of irrigation to such high-altitude pastures allowed them to serve as hay meadows. A more decisive attempt to increase its natural resources is seen in Törbel's purchase of the Oberaaralp on October 16, 1514. A well-preserved parchment details the sale of this alp by Guttannen for 850 Bernese pounds; it was three days' march away from Törbel on the Grimsel pass, in the canton of Bern. The alp comprised some 350 hectares, of which half were unproductive. Törbel, at the same time, acquired rights of toll-free use of the pass, high and low hunting (with the exception of wolves and bears), and firewood collecting (Stebler 1922:48). By further payments in 1567 Törbel gained a right-of-way from the three Goms communities of Obergesteln, Oberwald, and Unterwasser, through which the Törbel route to the Oberaaralp passed (TGA C7). It appears that Törbel expected to pasture one-third of its livestock on the Oberaar (TGA C4), but it was used in recent times principally for sheep and heifers as well as horses and mules. In 1891 the 65-day summer grazing supported 400 sheep, 10 heifers, 19 young bulls, and 2 milk cows for the herdsmen (Stebler 1922:48). The initial expansion of Törbel into a relatively distant summer grazing ground can only reflect considerable pressure on local resources. The purchase price, equivalent to some 19,000 francs, must have required great efforts to raise. A presumably accurate listing of community members who lacked sufficient pasturage on the Törbel alp gives 74 names. The entries, often giving the names of wives, siblings, widowed mothers, or dead fathers of the individuals, seem to represent households. Each name is accompanied by a notation of cattle (*vaccis*) numbers ranging from 19 to 1, and totaling at least 332. If these indeed refer to total cattle holdings, as opposed to sheep and goats, the average per household would be 4.49, a close approximation of the average 2.5 cows, 1 heifer, and 1 calf found in the home herds of more recent Törbel peasants, as described in Chapter 2. Buying the Oberaaralp was obviously a carefully considered undertaking by the entire community, whose individually named members were entitled as cattle owners to the benefits of the new property.

If land and other natural resources were already scarce objects of competition early in Törbel's history, we would expect that community efforts to expand the new territory and intensify agricultural use through forest clearing and extended irrigation would be paralleled at the private level. Indeed, the individuals who enter the early records are almost entirely buyers and sellers of real estate. Moreover, the number of people involved, the varied and often fragmentary properties conveyed, and the significant sums involved suggest an active land market by the thirteenth century. In a series of useful historical notes published in the Törbel parish newsletter in 1976 and 1977 Brother Stanislaus Noti summarized the contents of 11 separate transactions from 1230 to 1251. Willermus de Fonte, perhaps a minor noble taking his name from the Törbel hamlet of Brunnen, acquired houses, vineyards, meadows with associated water rights, grainfields, granaries, a winepress, courtyards, and a *Speicher* storehouse from nine different individuals (Noti 1976). It is interesting that this mixture of land types and structures reflects almost exactly the mixture we have claimed was vital to the alpine peasant economy. Although some of those who either sold property outright or received cash and continued to use the land as a fief (*Lehen*) were also minor local lords, such as the knight Jakob von Visp and Canon Rimensteir, it appears that others were equivalent to yeoman farmers. They were certainly not dealing in extensive holdings in any way comparable to a manor. One sale for 9 pounds from Jakob de Campo (of Feld?) included ⅛ vineyard, ⅓ house, and another ½ vineyard. A larger deal consisted of a meadow in Heguerda (Agarte?), a vineyard in Sisetsch, ½ house, granary, and courtyard, and two parts of the tithe of Unter-Burgen (possibly a part of the Burgen hamlet). For these holdings Willermus was to pay the annual sum of 39 pounds. Although we might well consider this man who had land in Törbel, Embd, Grächen, and Stalden, and perhaps also some legal and administrative jurisdiction, to be a member of the feudal rural gentry, his forays into the market resemble those of a capitalistic farmer snapping up odd bits of his neighbors' land by sale, mortgage, and leasing. In these conveyances, he deals as an equal with individual men and with two women who sell property in their own names. He operates within a network of kinship, but these rights and duties allow economic individualism, alienation of land, and entrepreneurship. As Macfarlane (1978) has pointed out for medieval England, there is little indication of patriarchal peasant households bound to family land and refusing to treat such property as a commodity with market value. Willermus acquired some grainfields with his two nephews, but their distinct shares were specified. His own brother Walter in 1238 sold him a stone house and two outbuildings, but the transfer document included the consent of Walter's wife Beatrix, his three sons, and their wives.

Some form of individual ownership and private rights to acquire possession or use of defined properties are continuously evident in the Törbel records. The corporate community could also act as a legal entity in dealing with its members. In 1293 a certain Johannes an der Flüe sold the community parcels of land in several named areas (TGA D2). He was, in turn, granted feudal tenure of these scattered meadows for an annual payment of 10 percent of the purchase price. The village as a whole here takes the role of an overlord. No mention is made of labor or other services, and it is probable that communal ownership was only temporary. The transaction appears, in fact, to be a mortgage with a village citizen pledging his land as security for a loan from the community. The documents do not allow us to determine the distribution of land in medieval Törbel, nor whether the majority of local residents were villeins, customary tenants, or freeholders.[3] But the obvious economic power of the community and the number of named individuals, apparently local residents, engaged in property transfers suggest a fairly wide diffusion of ownership. During the fourteenth century, five noble families are mentioned as having land rights in Törbel, but also listed are nine peasants whose properties equal three-fifths of those belonging to the nobles (von Roten 1940).

Notarized and carefully preserved parchments in the community archives and privately held bills of sale from as early as 1642 indicate that land could always be purchased but that such transactions were formal, legally binding, and very expensive. A scribe from one of the valley towns, with authorization from the Bishop of Sion, set down the names and fathers' names for both parties, the type and location of the land, the names of other owners of bordering parcels, details of right-of-way and irrigation rights, and several witnesses. A *Kaufakt* of this kind in 1392 (TGA H1) transferred several grainfields to two buyers for 11 and 15 Mauriner solidi, and almost identical documents can be cited for this century. The acquisition of land evidently became so costly by 1672 that a special enactment forbade sales at a price higher than that determined by civic appraisers. Violators could lose their village citizenship (TGA B7). High local demand on a limited land base could drive prices far above what seemed reasonable in terms of alpine production. Stebler made the following observations on Törbel prices before 1920:

> For a good irrigatable meadow, one pays all together Fr. 40 per klafter [36 square feet or 11.1 meters square] and for a favorably situated meadow up to Fr. 50. No other region of Switzerland is known to me where the price of cultivated land is anywhere near as high. And yet the land hunger in Törbel is so great that continual inquiries [about land availability] are always being made. Of course the parcels are generally small. Even [in the 1850s] S. Furrer said that there were prosperous peasants in Upper Valais that saved all their extra money until the opportunity presented itself that they could buy a properly situated piece of land. A peasant in Törbel bought last year a mediocre meadow of 100 klafter at a price of Fr. 3700. . . . It is obvious that the land cannot give rise to so high a return as required for adequate interest on the capital, a proof that Mother Earth has a higher power of attraction for the mountaineer than the mere monetary. A result of these excessive land prices is that occasionally a farmer sells out and settles elsewhere where there is cheaper land.   [Stebler 1922:111]

The fall in land values that followed World War I sent prices down so rapidly that many owners could neither sell nor keep up with the interest payments on large loans they had taken to buy land. Törbjers have vivid memories of crushing debts and frequent bankruptcies during the Depression.

The high costs of agricultural assets that produced mainly subsistence goods rather than cash suggest that money was entering the system from outside. The expansion of individual landholdings often depended on wage labor. Although the outer world of cities and merchants, armies and kings, seldom penetrated the mountain fastness directly, the people of Törbel have long sought employment outside of the community and even abroad. Such work was often seasonal or limited to a few years. To the extent that the migrants returned to their native village and invested their savings in the farm enterprise, they remained peasants with traditional aspirations and life-styles. The premiere occupation of the alpine Swiss in the past was mercenary soldiering (*Söldnerdienst*). The Swiss Guard of the Vatican in Rome (most of whose members come from the Valais) remind us of this custom. It is estimated that Switzerland supplied 50,000 to 100,000 troops to neighboring states and principalities in the fifteenth century, and these numbers reached 275,000 in 1500–1700, peaking at 350,000 in 1700–1800 (Bickel 1947:48). As many as 35 to 40 percent of all excess births were later absorbed into the military (Bickel 1947:55).[4] From Törbel alone, 14 men died in France between 1689 and 1700. Swiss formed the royal bodyguard for French kings from 1497 to the Revolution. This service is commemorated by the grenadier uniforms and the Papal Guard uniforms worn by Törbel men in the village parade on Corpus Christi Day (*Fronleichman*). As late as the decade following 1846, Törbel soldiers were still going to Naples and elsewhere in Italy.[5] Many, of course, never returned, but the heroes of Törbel folk history were often officers like Hauptmann Peter Wyss, who fought in France and Belgium. He used his fortune to build and decorate the chapel at Burgen, whose wooden altar carvings show the captain and his relatives beneath the sheltering mantel of a baroque Virgin (von Roten 1945).[6]

A more mundane, but perhaps more frequent, source of cash was work as a farmhand, herder, or domestic servant in the Rhone valley or in Italian towns like Domodossola just across the Alps. The Swiss census of 1829 lists 14 men and 5 women as servants outside Törbel; in 1837 there were 8 of each sex, and in 1846 there were 10 men and 14 women. A few craftsmen may also have sought work elsewhere, but many of these individuals later returned to their natal community (Netting 1979a:51). Such servants tended to be young adults who were still single, and the periods they spent away from home may have allowed them to earn money for their eventual marriages and relaxed some of the pressure on their crowded natal households. Until recently, the custom was that wages earned by work away from the village were turned over to the worker's father. Only enough was retained for daily living expenses. The cash or the property purchased with it would be added to the paternal estate, which would be divided among all the children when the time came.

As mercenary service waned in the middle nineteenth century, near-at-hand seasonal jobs opened up in the nascent tourist industry. European, and especially English, interest in the Alps grew rapidly after Whymper climbed the Matterhorn in 1865. From Stalden, visitors, mail, and supplies for the hotels were taken to Zermatt and Saas-Fee by mule trains. The muleteers often came from Törbel. Even after the completion of the cog railway to Zermatt in 1891, the summer traffic to Saas-Fee continued to be by mule until the early 1930s (Schmid 1935). Törbel mule drivers also contracted to serve the huts frequented by climbers and hikers in various mountain ranges. A number of men continue to work as horse-taxi drivers, cooks, and porters in the resort centers that now have long winter seasons for skiing holidays. Two-thirds of the adult women in Törbel have been waitresses, chambermaids, or cooks before marriage. Because Törbel itself has only two small hotels, most tourist-related employment has continued to be outside of the community, and many wage earners have settled permanently in the resorts. As the natives of Zermatt, Täsch, and other Vispertal villages became increasingly employed as hotel workers, mountaineering guides, and skiing instructors, Törbel men often took on the herding and cheesemaking duties on other mountains. All such seasonal occupations took people away from haying and major farm work, leaving women and other members of the household to cope with the agriculture.

Longer-lasting and somewhat more lucrative jobs became available during the 1920s, when the peasant economy was being threatened by the Depression. Törbel men, along with others from Staldenried, Eisten, and elsewhere, found work as miners and laborers in the tunnel building associated with road, water-power, and defense projects. Upwards of 50 men were employed in this way at any one time, and 31 household heads in 1970 had mining experience. The work was dangerous, leaving many of the early tunnel workers (*Stollenarbeiter*) incapacitated with silicosis. Since World War II, such work has been entirely supplanted by industrial and craft positions. A large chemical complex at Visp provides both unskilled shift-labor jobs and apprenticeships taken by younger men to become plumbers, sheet-metal workers, electricians, and laboratory technicians. In 1970, 35 household heads commuted daily to the factory, and a number of others worked in power plants, sawmills, and small manufacturing concerns. Several truck drivers and bus drivers also continued to live in the village. A few construction workers and foremen come back to their families in the village only on weekends from distant jobs.

It is no longer accurate to think of wage earners as supplementing and attempting to expand their incomes from agriculture. Until the 1920s, cash earnings were the exception rather than the rule, and the goal for those who sought seasonal employment was to establish a household in the village and expand their landholdings. Stories are told of a man who worked for low wages on the Zermatt railway construction crews but was able to buy land and build a fine house in Brunnen. Five unmarried brothers carefully accumulated capital running the mule trains up and down the trail to Saas. They pooled their earnings and put up an imposing five-story house, and when it was completed they all married on the same day in 1921 and moved in (Netting 1972:137). A few occupations were available within the villages. Carpenters, tailors, and shoemakers worked part-time at their crafts, but there is no indication that they made much money, and indeed they may have come from among the poorer families of the village. Schoolteachers, on the other hand, commanded a dependable, but not large, salary. Until recent years, they came from Törbel itself, and they often acquired relatively extensive landholdings. There seem to have been few stores in Törbel until this century, but a thrifty group of celibate siblings did run a prosperous hardware store along with their farming activities. The village miller also had an above-average income. A natural outgrowth of the local dairy and livestock production is cattle trading, and one family has been active in this branch of commerce since the turn of the century. Today there is little evidence of outside earnings being invested in agricultural expansion. Milk and cheese production along with meat production for home use are maintained, but farming is part-time (*Nebenberuf*) or the occupation of the retired. Of 92 male household heads covered by my 1970 census, only 10 had never worked outside Törbel. The worker-farmer and his family can still derive extra food and some income from their holdings, and their inherited houses and building plots allow them to live somewhat less expensively than in the towns. But they are quite aware that Törbel now survives as an appendage of the factory and the national economy. Farmland has lost much of its value, intensification no longer pays (*Es rentiert nicht* is the inevitable comment), self-sufficiency is impossible, and the future of alpine agriculture is in doubt.

REGULATION

It is difficult to avoid a mechanical, almost deterministic, approach as we consider the strategies of intensification and expansion in an alpine peasant community. The goals are simple and physically direct: how people get enough to eat, clothing and shelter to protect them from the elements, warmth in winter, and sufficient stored goods to see them through a bad year or two. Their efforts take place within fundamental geographic constraints of altitude, slope, sunlight, and water. Their technology is largely homemade, manual, and so standard that any European folk museum could duplicate most of the implements. Long settlement has given them fixed boundaries and a limited territory with a fully known and exploited potential. It would seem that nature, a hoary system of alpine land use, a diet of bread and cheese, and a mountainous isolation from trade and conquest create a system in rigid equilibrium, with predictable energy exchanges and constricted marionettes rather than human actors.

Such a stereotype in which people respond to the push of climate or the pull of economic forces conveys a pleasurable sense of scientific clarity and mathematical inevitability, but it violates both real ethnographic uniqueness and the contrasts that other mountain societies place before us. There are indeed similar problems with which all high-altitude dwellers must cope, and the comparable solutions in the Andes, the Alps, and the Himalayas (Rhoades and Thompson 1975) are ecologically sound and provocative. But nothing in these accounts supports the stereotype of mountaineers as being incurious, superstitious, and conservative at the same time as they are vigorous, honorable, healthy, patriarchal, frugal, industrious, and provident. As Febvre so aptly noted:

> The truth is that there is no sort of mountain unity which would always be found wherever on the earth mountainous elevations exist; any more than there is one unity of plateau, or one unity of a plain; but simply that analogous possibilities are met with in different places, and that these have been turned to account in the same way, and the civilizations are in consequence comparable— if we omit their individual and truly characteristic features. [Febvre 1932:200]

It is just these "individual and truly characteristic features" that distinguish the southern Swiss mountain communities from their contemporaries in the Dauphiné, the Pyrenees, and the Tyrol, as well as definitively setting them off from the descriptions of English, French, and German rural villages that so strongly color our view of a north European peasantry. What we are talking about here is culture, and more particularly the social template of local political organization, rights to resources, and group means of securing cooperation and limiting conflict. The environment and the technology give no absolute answers to the questions of who has power to determine policy, who inherits property and when, and what happens when there is scarcity or surplus. Most societies most of the time do not ask these questions or do not propose revolutionary changes in the customary answers. What has happened in history, the weight of custom and law, that amalgam of accident and diffused ideas and learning and forgetting that all enculturated peoples carry about with them, gives an unmistakable shape and recognizable movement to a local ecosystem. But we are not talking about some ephemeral ethnic cachet, a distinction without a difference, that sets Törbel and similar Swiss alpine communities apart. The social rules of admittance to the village, use and conservation of common resources, intergenerational transfer of property, and democratic decision making are the crucial regulators that maintain the system in working order, provide personal security, and restore the precarious balance threatened by conflicting interests, death, and environmental perturbations.

We shall glance at some of those social processes that might be called servomechanisms or cybernetic factors, because, like the governor on a steam engine or a thermostat, they respond to changes in the atmosphere or the mechanism and restore the system to that range within which it works most effectively (Rappaport 1971a). In the accepted jargon, these are deviation-counteracting mechanisms. But because we must deal with them largely in a descriptive rather than quantitative manner, and because the system itself is a functional abstraction lacking even the kilocalories of measured energy flows, we shall be content to see our regulators as merely mechanical metaphors to be discarded or even sabotaged if they get in the way of understanding.

Perhaps the most pressing problem of a successful alpine community has always been the accommodation of physical growth within a framework of restricted but renewable natural resources. It is not possible to cut a pie of fixed size into more pieces without decreasing the shares of at least some participants. When the pie is a pasture or a forest, consuming it all may also mean that it will not reproduce itself next year, and the total size of succeeding pies will be radically reduced. Environmental degradation and poverty go together, and the individual in pursuit of his real economic interests may be squeezed by an invisible hand or find himself an unwilling actor in the "tragedy of the commons." If we are right in thinking that the alps attracted permanent late Bronze Age settlement and that medieval communities were already confronting scarcity by intensifying agriculture, asserting private ownership, and buying land, the problem of limiting access to these vital resources must already have been apparent. One reaction to such constraints may involve an emphasis on military defense of a territory against outsiders and attempts to take the land and chattels of others by force. The pre-Christian hill forts and the names of Allemanic strongholds like Burgen and Kastel may reflect such essentially tribal warfare, but early historic

Törbel seems already beyond such feuding. A corporate community of citizens with real, though circumscribed, power was negotiating with regional government, holding and transferring property, legally closing its membership to outsiders, and subscribing to written statutes providing for internal order.

Possibly the oldest document of upper Valais preserved in the archives of Visp (Noti 1977) gives evidence of the people of Törbel operating as a legal entity. In 1224 the priest of Visp agreed to give over two-thirds of the tithe[7] to the people of Törbel while retaining one-third for himself (TGA D1). In return, Törbel, through Wilhelm Albi (acting as a representative of the community?), promised to provide a body of fighting men when required and "4½ Mut of grain of the Visp measure along with 12 Dinars interest yearly on St. Michael's Day." In effect, the community was buying partial rights to a variable churchly tithe in exchange for a fixed annual rent. Property and perhaps tithing rights in Törbel after about 1050 were held by the cathedral chapter of Sion (von Roten 1940:85). The shrinking feudal dues of the thirteenth and fourteenth centuries, however, do not appear to cover the entire territory, and a list of holdings indicates a number of small, scattered, individually rented parcels of land (von Roten 1940:89). In 1297 the mother church in Visp released Törbel from its dues of one-half sester of oil annually. Fourteenth-century documents, giving the worth of several estates of petty nobles in Törbel, also list nine free peasants subject to no feudal obligation whatever and the community itself possessing goods worth 16 pounds (von Roten 1940:91).

The most commonly recorded transaction in medieval Törbel was one in which the corporate community bought specified lands for cash and the seller then received these same lands as a fief on condition of annual rent payments. The village and its unnamed leaders (*Herren*) were acting as a lord, granting feudal tenure to particular resident members. In 1293 Johannes an der Flüe of Törbel publicly acknowledged his duty to pay 10 shillings yearly to the community for property in Rafgarten, Hogiland, Blattmatten, and Millachern that he had sold for 5 pounds (TGA D2). He received these meadows and grainfields back in feudal tenure. In similar fashion, Johannes in der Bünden agreed in 1300 to pay one measure of grain for land in Stechen, Stapfen, Wüsti, and Ebnet (TGA D3). All of these place-names are still in use within the villages, and it is obvious that each deal covered only a small proportion of the total cultivable land in the community territory. Equivalent transfers of land rights were noted in 1306, 1307, 1312, 1331, 1333, 1334, 1339, 1350, 1354, 1370, and 1400 (TGA D). In effect, individual citizens were mortgaging their farms to the community, but both parties were operating as freeholders, with no indication that the transaction implied labor services, seasonal dues in produce, military duties, or the other complex requirements that characterized vassalage and servile status in other parts of feudal Europe. Where annual community dues to outside agencies are mentioned (e.g., 15 shillings to the bishop; 12 shillings to the cathedral chapter; 12 shillings, 4.5 measures of grain, and 0.5 measure of oil to the church in Visp; 35 pennies to private persons; TGA D16), they appear relatively modest and by no means confiscatory. When the tithe owed by the village came into the hands of such outsiders as two brothers of Embd, it could be purchased back, as it was in 1403 by 10 men in the name of the community (Furrer 1850:89).

By 1473 the community was regulating its affairs by written statute. To better administer the charitable contribution on the feast of Saint Theodul (Törbel's patron saint), the community pledged to give one loaf of bread from its grain revenues to each household. The poor were to be given their share before the propertied received anything (TGA B1). Törbel referred to itself as a *Bauernzunft* (peasant corporation) when in 1483 it laid down rules for the use and enjoyment of the alps, common lands, and forests in its territories (TGA B2).[8] A noncitizen (*Nichtbergmann*) who bought or otherwise occupied land in Törbel was not automatically entitled to rights (*Genossenschaftliches Nutzungsrecht*) in the communal alp, pasturelands, and woods. The community reserved to itself the power to grant such rights to a foreigner (*Fremder*). A citizen who sold his property in Törbel thereby relinquished his claims in the commons. The 22 named Törbel residents who witnessed this legislation were probably giving legal form to long-standing canons of group membership. Their action reflects an effort to control and limit community membership, not by preventing the free sale of property but by regulating access to communally held resources. The summer grazing on the alp was a necessity for sustaining the livestock and for freeing labor to cope with the haying. Fuel from the woodlands was an equally crucial resource. Although outsiders could be admitted at the pleasure of the community, competition for obviously scarce resources was decisively restricted.[9] The definition of citizenship was equivalent to erecting a barrier around the community, and it is typical of the autonomy displayed by Swiss village societies from an early date. The evidence points to the creation of a closed corporate community by a decision of its members rather than by a decree of a manorial lord or other outside authority.[10] Nor was closure a defensive reaction against colonial exploitation by a conquest state, as in the classic cases of Mesoamerica and Java (Wolf 1957). We may well see in the Törbel *Gemeinde* an association of free peasant landholders with a tradition of village-level self-determina-

tion rooted in the political forms of early tribal society.[11] Such independent behavior in response to what appears to be population pressure on
the local environment may also be fostered by alpine isolation, limited
opportunities for surplus production, and Swiss success in resisting
encroachment by the expanding nation-states. Political institutions and
their associated values are precipitates of historic origins and continual
functional adjustments. The Swiss version of the closed corporate
community, with its heritage of local independence, communal regulation
of key resources, household economic self-sufficiency, and individualistic
property holding, resists single-cause explanations across the entire
spectrum from vulgar materialism to refined idealism.

Evidently it was not enough for late medieval Törbel to wall itself off
from outside settlers. The relationships among citizens and their respective shares in the communal pool of land and raw materials were also put
under legal restraints. Because individuals were evidently encroaching on
bridle paths, footways, and forest tracks belonging to the community, an
ordinance of 1519 defined the width and use of these public roads. On the
sworn testimony of eight honest men, the extent of the common lands and
the communal forest was specified (TGA B3). An important regulation
of alp rights in 1517 (TGA C3) laid down the principle that "no one is
permitted to send more cows to the alps than he can winter." This made
the number of animals sent to the communal summer pasture directly
dependent on the amount of hay and thus the meadow area possessed by
each cattle owner. One could not merely put livestock on the alp and then
sell them at the end of the season. Although individuals might have
different numbers of cows, they could enlarge their herds and their shares
of the communal grazing resources only by acquiring land to ensure
sufficient winter fodder. The alp could not, in theory, be overgrazed,
because stocking was limited to the fixed number of animals that could be
provendered from a bounded village territory. At one stroke this simple
rule overturns the economic logic of the "tragedy of the commons" in
which the rational herdsman gains by using more of a communal good, to
the eventual detriment of the group and the environment (Hardin
1968).[12] The Törbel rule was given teeth by provision for one official (the
Gewalthaber or power-holder) to be chosen yearly to administer each of
the two alps. This individual had authority to fine anyone who exceeded
his quota at the high rate of 2 pounds per horse, 1 pound per cow or
heifer, and 5 shillings per sheep (TGA C3). Half the fine was kept by the
official "for his work." In 1971 similar penalties were exacted from
Törbjers who brought in animals for temporary alp pasturage or sold
cows within a stipulated period after the end of the alp season.

The most detailed rules for internal order were those in 24 statutes written on parchment and dated April 17, 1531 (TGA B4). They were set down with considerable formality by the Citizenry or Peasant Corporation of the Communities of Törbel and Burgen (*Burgerrecht oder Bauernzunft der Gemeinden Törbel und Burgen*). In addition to restricting immigration to and emigration from the community, as mentioned earlier, this code prescribed fines for hunting marmots on the alp without permission, for allowing small stock to trespass on others' property, for sending diseased infectious cows to the communal alp, for refusing to observe the rules regarding the proper time for entering and departing from the alp, for herding animals of a noncitizen on the commons, and for private haymaking on communal property. A preliminary mechanism for settling internal disputes before the *Gewalthaber* and two "honorable" men was provided, and if they failed, the matter went before the local judge (*Richter*). Individuals also had the duty of attending town meetings for governmental purposes, and unexcused absences and early departures were subject to fines. Village inhabitants could be forced to maintain their buildings and to give a day's labor to anyone erecting a new structure. Rules on protecting and sharing out forest products were to remain "according to ancient custom and usage." A *Gewalthaber* insubordinate or disobedient in his community duties could be punished by a fine paid into the village treasury. Sixty named males representing their own and nine additional families subscribed to this charter.

Although Törbel was certainly a face-to-face peasant community when these regulations were promulgated, they give convincing evidence of a highly autonomous corporate community protecting its territory, allocating its resources, ensuring cooperation, establishing official authority, and handling conflict. Nothing about the statutes suggests radical changes in the practices of local government or the relationships of village members. The strongest impression is that of custom codified and existing economic rights and duties defined. The same competition for agricultural resources that led to intensification and the purchase of the Oberaaralp had quite possibly increased local conflicts of interest and disputes over policy. The resort to written laws with procedures for enforcement and penalties for violation indicates that informal means of resolving differences were no longer effective. The people of Törbel had both the will and the power to institute their own binding regulations, rather than relying on external authorities or a local aristocracy of wealth or title. The fact that their rules met practical needs and were tailored to the characteristics of the community's own environment and population accounts for the long-continued observance of many of the code's provisions.

The democratic initiative and significant degree of self-determination exercised by the Törbel commune were made possible by the important benefits controlled by the group. Without communal property having significance for every family, there would be no reason for restricting membership and strictly regulating shares. But what was to prevent the scarce and desirable resources of alp and forest from passing into private hands and being exploited for personal gain? The presumption that human communities pass from a kind of primitive communism through clan holdings to private property was a staple of nineteenth-century evolutionism (Morgan 1963:551). It can be argued, however, that all food-producing societies have a mixture of individual rights in certain tools, animals, trees, and land areas, along with communal tenure and defined usufruct in other resources (Netting 1969, 1974, 1976). The spectrum of rights includes gradations in the degree to which property can be alienated and inherited as well as the range of kin who may enjoy its products. Layers of partial control may be vested in the state, religious groups, overlords, financial institutions, and occupants from landlords to squatters. The Törbel case is interesting because even the earliest documents reflect a situation in which clearly differentiated individual property and communal property exist side by side. Although all the household worked on the land and consumed its produce, a specific person could buy or sell that land for cash, and it was inherited in whole or in part by other individuals. This emphasis on private, alienable property apparently runs counter to the outright communal tenure that Wolf (1957) identified as a salient characteristic of the closed corporate peasant community. Adult married siblings and their surviving parents might continue to hold houses and land in common as an *Erbgemein-schaft* or joint inheritance, but married couples typically possessed property quite separate from their relatives. No suprahousehold kin groups, such as lineages or clans, had property rights. There was no vacant land or even long-fallow land, nor do we hear of periodic land redistribution, as among Russian peasants (Wolf 1957). At the same time, the village acting as an organized and self-conscious corporate group claimed and defended portions of the village territory, carefully controlling access to the resources in these areas. No one in Törbel could unilaterally dispose of such public land nor exploit it for selfish gain. This is not to say that there were never changes in the local land tenure system or the proportions held individually and communally.[13] It appears that the historic persistence of both types of property in a single community must be explained in ecological terms rather than solely as a projection of certain cultural or ethnic origins or the artifact of some system of legal ideas.

The types of property rights in the peasant community of Törbel were directly related to the agricultural system, the competition for scarce resources, and the productivity of the various natural zones; more specifically, land use by and large determined land tenure. We have already observed that almost all intensively farmed land in meadows, grainfields, vineyards, and gardens was privately held, heritable, and marketable in the early historical period. References in the various statutes of the late fifteenth and early sixteenth centuries make the communal possession of the alp, the forests, and the rough grazing grounds or wastelands (*Allmenden*) abundantly clear. In each case, common holdings and corporate administration by the village promote three things: an efficiency of utilization that would be threatened by fragmented private ownership; the potential for maintaining yields by enforced conservation; the equitable sharing of necessary resources by all group members.

The Törbel alps neatly demonstrate the advantages of communal control. The summer grazing is limited by the short season at this high altitude. Tree-shaded or high rocky pastures above the reach of efficient irrigation cannot produce stands of grass sufficiently dense and fast-growing to be harvested as hay. The Moosalp and adjoining Alp Bifigen crowning the Törbel territory are about 760 hectares in area, of which some 240 hectares are forest grazing, 40 hectares are pastured clearings, and 150 hectares are unproductive because of steepness or shallow soils (Stebler 1922:41; Imboden 1967:27). Until 1947, when it was sold as the site for a power-company reservoir, the Oberaaralp added another 350 hectares for Törbel's 10 weeks of summer grazing. To ensure effective use of these extensive areas of somewhat sparse forage, cows and heifers had to be moved from one area to another. Moosalp, for example, had five sections (*Stafel*), each with its cheesemaking building (*Sennhütte*) and several large stonewalled enclosures (*Ferriche*) sheltered by trees where the animals spent the night. A regular schedule was followed, with either 1 or 2 weeks in each section and 4 weeks at the home base, Moos. The cows were grazed in one spot after the morning milking, then taken higher up in hot weather to escape insects, returned to pasture in the late afternoon, milked again around 5 P.M., given further good grazing in the early evening, and turned into their enclosure at nightfall (Stebler 1922:43). The herder (*Hirt*) with his assistants was charged with using the pasturage in the most rational and even manner. Owners today often make a Sunday outing to visit their cows on the alps, and the performance of the herder in keeping the stock in good condition and promoting maximum milk production is carefully monitored.

Climatic variations affect the location of the best pasturage. Water is not evenly distributed, and the enclosures protected by great larches from the dangerous late spring and early fall storms are all situated between 1,900 and 2,100 meters. Obtaining the maximum benefit from these facilities, while at the same time using the widely spread grasslands in an optimal manner, requires a large fenceless area of open range. Overgrazing, which would decrease the alp's carrying capacity, must be rigidly prohibited, because alternative pastures are not available. Deterioration of the pasture and the effects of longer-than-average treks to the grazing ground are topics of immediate discussion in the village. In a very dry year, the cows may be brought down from the alp as early as mid-August.

In recent times, supervision of the alp has been in the hands of a three-man *Alpkommission,* elected by an alp association (*Alpgeteilschaft*), including all cattle-owning citizens of Törbel. They decide on the dates of entering and leaving the alp and select the days on which the membership will rebuild walls and trails, rake twigs, spread manure, and otherwise maintain the alp. Labor contributions or fees in lieu of work are in proportion to the cattle sent by each owner to the alp. Other elected officials, the stewards or *Vögte,* hire the necessary personnel, assess the alp costs on the membership, measure the sample milk production for each animal, and divide the finished cheeses among the cattle owners according to the milk yields of their cows (Imboden 1967:27). When cheese was still produced by traditional methods in the three alp dairies, a normal year provided 2,700 kilograms of cheese from Moosalp and 1,750 kilograms from Alp Bifigen (Stebler 1922:45). There are regular meetings of the alp association to review the accounts, elect officers, approve fines, and determine policy.

Labor economics combined with flexible and extensive grazing and range management helped to strengthen the communal alp institution. Two herders and their assistants supervised the grazing of about 210 cows and some 60 heifers and calves. Each dairy handled some 70 cows and was staffed by a cheesemaker, a female milker, and a weigher (Stebler 1922:44). The full-time workers, including several herders on the Oberaaralp, might total only 15 individuals, but they relieved over 100 households of the daily chores of feeding and milking the livestock. If only one member of each family devoted part time to dairying over the summer, the labor available for the demanding tasks of haying, irrigating, and grain harvesting would be substantially reduced. Herders and cheesemakers often returned year after year to the alp, and their work was concentrated and arduous. Their expert knowledge of the tasks involved and their efficiency commanded the community's respect, which is still evident when the garlanded cows are ceremoniously driven down from the alp and the alp staff are publicly toasted and congratulated.

Alp privileges have always been closely tied to the duties of village citizenship. Not long after the separation of the Törbel parish from Stalden in 1649, the bishop of Sion decreed that Törbel pay its priest 200 pounds per year plus a load of wood from each household (TPA 22). The arrangement was handled by giving each family a wooden marker (*Tessle*) once their firewood had been delivered to the priest. Without the *Tessle* to turn in at the alp reckoning meeting in the community house, the family could not pasture their cows with the community herd (Stebler 1922:39). Another wooden marker, with a distinctive house sign or initials inscribed on one side and the number of cows on the other, was used by each family in an elaborate system for dividing the whey left after the making of cheese and soft cheese (*Zieger*). After the *Tessle* were divided into groups and lots were drawn for their order, each household had a day assigned for fetching from the alps the whey, which was then fed to pigs (Stebler 1922:46). The essence of the alp administration was careful control of access, fair division of costs and rewards, and accountability of the officials and employees to the membership.

A diffuse natural resource of relatively low yield, such as an alpine pasture, loses productive value if it is split into private parcels, and it also requires considerably increased labor input because of duplication of effort. The cost of fencing alone might seriously reduce the profits of summer grazing. Changes from year to year in both grass growth and family herd size might make individual ownership of pasture tracts overly rigid. There are private alps belonging to individuals or groups who can dispose of the property at will, but these are rare. In Valais, 95 percent of all alpine pasture has been under common ownership (Carrier 1932:205). Although a number of Swiss alps may have been, at one time, claimed by great ecclesiastical or secular lords and rented for payment in cheese, they seem to have been taken over during the Middle Ages by the peasants who used them. Some contemporary alp divisions among private owners (e.g., Ausserberg) actually reflect the permanent habitation and haying of some high meadows that existed in the twelfth century (Gutersohn 1961:42). A similar situation in Turtmanntal was altered in the sixteenth century when associations bought up and consolidated a large number of small private pastures (Gutersohn 1961:70). Where the alp is relatively close to the village, as in Lötschental, individual family members may move to summer huts and tend their own stock (Friedl 1973).

Over the years the Törbel communal alp holdings may have expanded somewhat and also contracted. The community bought or traded for private parcels on the alp or bordering the alp in 1400, 1632, 1701, 1726, 1769, 1772, and 1832 (TGA C,D). Some very high meadows, such as Breitmatten and Hannig, were private property until the eighteenth century, when the community bought them to accommodate a growing cattle herd (Stebler 1922:43). Such unirrigated *Voralp* lands probably furnished, at best, poor and irregular crops of hay. Other parcels were acquired as convenient rights-of-way between pastures. It is also possible that gradual climatic changes made some meadows less productive and better suited for communal uses. A field called Galtacker (barren acre) lies just below the timberline in an area now too high for planting rye. Efforts to convert parts of the alp back to private purposes (as a sanitarium site or hotel location) have been strongly resisted by the community. Tourists, it was said, would tread down the grass needed by the cows. Development plans since the turn of the century have been defeated by votes in the town meeting, and only recently have a small restaurant, a hunting lodge, and a ski lift been permitted on the communal land.

Although a few scattered parcels of forest were in private hands, the major source of both fuel and timber was the communal forest (*Gemeindewald*) covering the lower slopes of the alp. Firewood was formerly an absolute necessity for heating houses by means of the large stone stove (*Steinofen*) in the corner of each bedroom/sitting room (*Stube*). All cooking was done over a wood fire in the kitchen's large open fireplace. Heavy notched and squared logs were basic to the construction of houses, barns, granaries, and storage buildings. Until recently, the forest floor was scraped to supply needles for strewing the cattle stalls in winter (Stebler 1922:98–9). Growing timber also anchors mountain soil, preventing erosion and rapid runoff of water from melting snow. Woodlands above the cultivated area lessen the danger of destructive avalanches and provide shelter for livestock on the alp. Maintenance of fuel and lumber supplies, plus watershed protection, enjoins strictly limited and selective cutting through the entire forested area. Private ownership of woodland would interfere with obtaining controlled continuous yields and would present problems in filling the minimal needs of each household because of intergenerational demographic changes. Communal administration of the forest allowed the annual cutting to be determined by the elected village council. These officials further divided the marked trees into equal shares that were allocated by lot (*Los*) to teams of three households. These self-selected teams provided the necessary cooperation for felling and snaking the logs down the mountain on the winter snow. Children on half-holidays from school were sent with pack baskets into the woods to gather fallen branches and pinecones. The pressing need for fuel led people to scour the forests until not a twig was left lying about. Dead limbs were pulled down with hooks or long staves, suggesting the old English rule that villages could have whatever wood from the manorial forest they could procure "by hook or crook." Windfalls and dead standing timber were auctioned off by the forest steward (*Waldvogt*) on Sunday after the mass (Stebler 1922:98). Because little could be done to increase timber production, the emphasis was on restricting resource use to the renewal rate of forest growth, leaving undamaged the protective function of the woodland, and giving equal shares to all households. Communal forest ownership would appear to meet these requisites most efficiently. Although individuals might put aside part of their timber allotment for building repairs, it appears that major construction over at least the last century necessitated buying logs in other communities.

Wastelands or *Allmenden* tended to be bare, rocky, or otherwise minimally productive lands scattered through the village territory. Those areas thus designated in Törbel were cliffs, steep ravines, and mountain peaks where little or no grass grew. Such rugged slopes, too precipitous for cattle, could afford sparse browsing for goats, and it was to them that the village goat herd was taken in summer. Wild grass was pulled from the crags to supplement the hay supply at the end of winter. Villagers could freely take stone for foundations and roofing slate from these common lands. Moreover, such areas were protected from outsiders who might occupy them to the detriment of inhabitants. The high mountain catchment basin of Törbel's principal irrigation stream also was treated as common land, thus guarding the vital water rights of the village.

The need for communally owned and maintained paths and roads is obvious. With intense competition for every scrap of meadow and arable land, access routes could become a source of contention. In 1402, Johann Ester publicly threatened all trespassers on his land (TGA H2). To this day, lack of an agreed-upon right-of-way can render land useless to its owner. Thus the community must specify the width and type of traffic permitted on its traveled ways, resist infringement or rerouting, and keep the paths in repair.

Communal property was regularly distinguished from property under individual tenure by its lower average production, the variability of its yields, its larger extent, and the sizes of the exploiting groups (Table 3.1). On a continuum of land use, it was at the extensive end, but its products were critical to the self-sufficient peasant household. The centuries-long

Table 3.1. *Land use and tenure in Törbel*

Nature of land use	Land tenure type	
	Communal	Individual
Value of production per unit area	Low	High
Frequency and dependability of use or yield	Low	High
Possibility of improvement or intensification	Low	High
Area required for effective use	Large	Small
Labor and capital-investing groups	Large (voluntary association or community)	Small (individual or family)

survival and continued productivity of both alp and forest testify to the effectiveness of communal management, the wisdom of conservation measures, and the continued enforcement of rules against overgrazing and indiscriminate timber cutting. Perhaps the modicum of ecological fitness seen in the dual system of Törbel landholding has been preserved only because the combination of mountain isolation and well-defended Swiss neutrality has forestalled any thoroughgoing imposition of feudal, capitalistic, and communistic tenure systems. There have never been the political means or perhaps the economic incentives for outsiders to confiscate Törbel lands, collectivize its farming, or transform it by investment into a ski resort. The checks and balances of local decision making allowed property to reflect the logic of alpine land use.

4

Family-line continuity in a closed corporate community

It is easy to assert that European peasant villages often show striking continuity in terms of place and name and territorial extent from the early Middle Ages to the present. Documentary evidence and some sparse archeological evidence suggest widespread emergence of nucleated settlements by the tenth century, and the parishes founded between the seventh and ninth centuries in France had local political organizations and boundaries that correspond closely to those of present-day communes (Cheyette 1977). Törbel's existence was first recorded somewhat later, but it shows a similar persistence as a physical entity, enduring plagues, warfare, and years of dearth with amazing tenacity. Indeed, the best evidence of the adaptiveness of the peasant mode of production and social system is their survival. The community could fall back on its own resources and provide at least the minimal necessities of life for its people despite the cycles of growth and decay through which the surrounding urban and state societies passed (Greenwood 1974). In the preceding chapter we illustrated some of the ways in which farming households and cooperative institutions lessened the risks from climatic fluctuations, conserved both food and capital, and regulated the consumption of plant and animal products to match the natural rates of renewal.

Community stability is presumed in the classic models of peasantry, where social homogeneity is maintained by a network of kinship relationships, relative isolation, economic self-sufficiency, and group solidarity within a larger literate and politically dominant society. Change and innovation appear more rapid in the impersonal mercantile spheres, with their specialists, ethnic diversity, and class stratification that touch but do not fundamentally alter the ways of the rural folk (Redfield 1955, 1956). But the mere maintenance of village identity and a distinctively conservative life-style says nothing about the continuity of an actual population. Did peasants, in fact, cling piously to the lands of their forefathers and remain unquestioningly in their birthplaces under the sway of stern but benevolent patriarchal authority? Was Tönnies's *Gemeinschaft* (1961) of blood, place, and mind built on the continuity of kinship, neighborhood, and friendship a real community or a romantic abstraction contrasting with all that is transitory and superficial in modern industrial life? It is a testimony to the strength of this pastoral ideal that many of us assume that peasant families remain in the same localities for generations and that the ancestral names on the churchyard gravestones or in the family Bible reflect roots in the local soil that extend deep into the centuries. Actual behavior may never have been so predictable, and the recent investigations of historical demographers show, at least for rural England, restless movements of individuals from one parish to another and rapid scattering of descendants from almost every household (Laslett 1965, 1969). Similar degrees of mobility characterized France and the Scandinavian countries, but the case of Törbel shows a very different system at work. In the last 300 years, many Törbel family lines have exhibited unbroken continuity, and not one new patriline has become established and perpetuated itself. To account for such a stubbornly sessile population, we shall have to look not to peasant values and sentimental attachments but to the realities of alpine farming and herding, the workings of a system of partible inheritance, and the special properties of village citizenship. Scarce agricultural resources and the voluntary constraints of the closed corporate community restricted migration and increased the benefits of producing and reproducing in the home community.

The first indication that Törbel family lines were founded early and long continued was the parish genealogy book.[1] Families were listed under the following 15 surnames:

Andres	Kalbermatten	Seematter
Carlen	Lorenz	Summermatter
Hosenen	Petrig	Williner
Jungsten	Ruff	Wyss
Juon	Schaller	Zuber

Twelve of these groups were represented by adults of both sexes when I first entered the village in 1970, and three lines (Andres, Jungsten, and Williner) had died out or emigrated within living memory. Genealogical linkages set out in a comprehensive and generally reliable manner in the parish record linked living descendants and extinct families to specific ancestors resident in Törbel before 1700. Because the family trees had been written down only in the period 1840–60,[2] some surnames were absent there that had appeared in notations of birth, marriage, or death in earlier registers. The names Gattlen, Gerwer, Imwinkelried, Jungen, Sub Colle, and Werlen became extinct in the eighteenth century but appear sufficiently well attested to rate as Törbel citizens from an earlier period. In all, 12 of 21 surnames continued in the male line from before 1700 until 1970.

Many of the surviving village family lines may extend several centuries further into the past. The first mentions of individuals in the archive of community parchments designated by recognizable place-names those arranging mortgages or sales and subscribing to laws or charters. De Brunnen (or, in the Latin, ab Fonte) refers to a family living in the hamlet of Brunnen, and other labels connect people with the localities of Bad, Fellach, Steinhaus, and Rafgarten. It is not clear whether these lines were terminated by the Black Death that apparently took a heavy toll of the village population in 1532–3 or whether they took new surnames. An unsystematic review of extant documents gives a probable mention of the Wyss family as early as 1224, with Kalbermatten in 1424, Carlen and Jungsten in 1453, Juon, Ruff, and Hosennen in 1517, and Lorenz and Jungen in 1531. New families may well have entered the community after 1532 (Furrer 1850:87), and there are references to Seematter in 1533, Zuber in 1584, Andres in 1633, Williner in 1644, and several Summermatters who were admitted to citizenship in the later part of the seventeenth century. The family names are not unique to Törbel, with Carlen being frequent in the Goms area, Kalbermatten and Zuber widespread in upper Valais, and frequent occurrences of Andres, Schaller, Summermatter, and Williner in other villages of Vispertal. In the Törbel context, surnames have sometimes changed either in spelling (e.g., Carlen became Karlen in the 1850s, and Ruoff was later written Ruff) or when the Latin form alternates with the German cognate (as in Sub Colle and Hinterdembiel). There may be doubt whether or not contemporary Williners and Wildiners were relatives and whether or not they descended from an old stock called in der Wildi (in the wastelands). None of these linguistic quibbles, however, weaken the impression that a significant number of family lines maintained an uninterrupted presence in Törbel for at least a dozen generations and often for much longer periods.

Studies of surname persistence and the rate of extinction of elite family lines have provided some rough comparisons to the Törbel records and given indications whether lineal interruption is responsive to regular demographic processes or to unpredictable events such as wars, epidemics, or political transformations in the external environment. The turnover of surnames has been traced for the period 1280–1700 in the English Midlands village of Kibworth Harcourt (Howell 1976:124). Tithing lists, rent rolls, and court rolls show that of 39 surnames present in 1280, all continued until 1340. The number declined to 29 in the plague years of 1348–9 and then in fairly regular steps to four surviving lines in 1557. Thus 35 surnames disappeared in 277 years, or an average of one every 7.9 years, as compared with the average Törbel surname failure of one every 30 years. In the same 277-year period the English village gained 65 new surnames, of which approximately 16 were maintained in the population until 1557. The rapid extinction and turnover of surname groups in what appears to have been a relatively stable community of landholders contrasts with the slower rate of extinction and the marked resistance to immigration characteristic of the Swiss mountain village. Whereas 57 percent of Törbel surnames survived 270 years, only 10 percent of the English surnames persisted through a like number of years.[3] Similarly, the Leicestershire village of Bottesford, with a population generally in the 700 to 900 range, had only one family that "replaced itself and continued its surname from the 1580s to the middle of the nineteenth century" (Levine 1977:42). This contrasts with the 12 distinctively surnamed lines maintaining seemingly unbroken continuity over an equal time span in the smaller community of Törbel.

Although the surname groups provide a rough index of family-line persistence, a more precise and demographically significant measure is that of the patriline traced from a single male founder. Genealogical links of this kind are recorded in the parish genealogy book and substantiated by the other registers of vital statistics, the Swiss censuses existing in manuscript form from 1798 to 1880, and by local civil records kept since 1875. Some family lines were represented by only a single male ancestor living at or before 1700. Fourteen lines stem from single known progenitors: Hosennen, Juon, Kalbermatten, Petrig, Ruff, Schaller, Seematter, and Wyss survive, whereas Gattlen, Gerwer, Imwinkelried, Jungen, and Sub Colle have become extinct. Other lines were already represented by two or more contemporaneous families when they entered the records during the late 1600s. Family heads might have been brothers, cousins, or very distant relatives who had the same surnames, but for documenting continuity or extinction, we may treat each traceable line as distinct. By these criteria, the Summermatter family had two lines, Jungsten and Zuber had three lines each, and the surnames Andres, Karlen, Lorenz, and Williner were each carried by four lines. These differences are recognized in the genealogy book by assigning Roman numerals to each line, and we have labeled distinct patrilines by lower-case letters within each numbered surname group (Figure 4.1).

Of the 38 distinguishable patrilines present in 1700, 22 had no more living male or female members in 1970 (Figure 4.1). A patriline became extinct on the average of once every 12.5 years. It should be emphasized here that we define a patriline as the direct descendants of a paternal

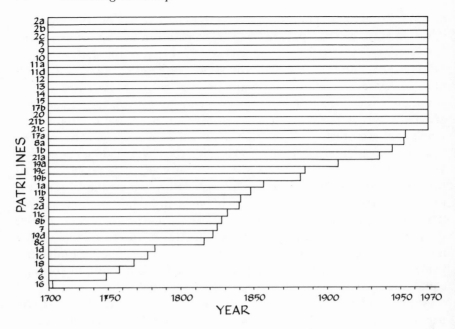

Figure 4.1. Persistence of patrilines in Törbel (1700–1970).

ancestor in the male line. It includes all demonstrably related males who bear the ancestor's surname and their female siblings who are genealogically members of the patriline but cannot pass on this membership to their offspring. Households in Törbel have characteristically been either nuclear and neolocal or extended with some co-resident relatives beyond the nuclear family. Multiple- or stem-family households were rare (Netting 1979a), and the holding of common property by kin groups larger than the nuclear family household was infrequent and transitory.[4] Kinship relations within and among patrilines seem to have been well known, though transmitted orally. There is little evidence, however, that patrilines functioned as corporate lineages, given the facts of residential dispersion of members, individual property as opposed to a corporate estate, and bilateral partible inheritance that conveyed resources equally to male and female descendants. No titles or other prerequisites were passed on by primogeniture, and there were no apparent persisting differences in socioeconomic status between senior and cadet lines of the same patriline. Patrilines per se may have had certain continuing allegiances in village politics and marriage alliances, but such competing groups appear as statistical regularities quite apart from cultural conceptions of lineage homogeneity or obligatory solidarity (see Chapter 9). No stigma seems to be attached to patriline extinction as far as contemporary

Törbjers are concerned, and there are no methods for legally adopting male children or altering the names of sons-in-law in order to continue a line in which there has been a failure of male heirs.[5]

The extinction rate of patrilines may be more accurately evaluated if we use component lines with demonstrated genealogical descent rather than surname groups. The 38 lines charted in Figure 4.1 appear to have a somewhat irregular pattern of extinction, with 6 dying out in the eighteenth century, 11 in the nineteenth century, and 5 in the first 70 years of this century. The greatest frequency was in the period 1800–49, when 8 lines disappeared. The annual extinction rate for 1700–99 was 0.060 and for 1850–1970 was 0.067, but for the 50 years at the beginning of the nineteenth century, an average of 0.16 line per year ended. Total Törbel population was increasing rapidly at that time, and neither epidemic diseases nor warfare appears to have made special inroads (Netting and Elias 1980). Major permanent emigration did not begin until the decades after 1850. It is possible that some of the local disturbances accompanying the Napoleonic occupation of Valais around 1800 adversely affected some smaller patrilines, but the evidence for military requisitioning of food supplies or conscripting a labor force for road contruction in the Simplon pass is only anecdotal.

The Törbel extinctions do not show the remarkably regular pattern of the English baronetcies examined for the period 1611 to 1769 (Wachter and Laslett 1978). The 203 patrilines in the English samples appear to have become extinct with a regularity that was little modified by historical events such as the Civil War. With 115 patrilines becoming extinct in 158 years, the proportion of patriline extinction per year is $(E/P)/N$, where E equals extinct lines, P equals total patrilines, and N equals number of years. With this formula, the Törbel extinction rate is 0.00214, as compared with a rate for the English baronet lines of 0.00358.[6] Whereas 60 percent of the English patrilines terminated in 150 years, only 37 percent of the Törbel lines became defunct in the same length of time, and only 58 percent in the entire 270-year period. The somewhat startling conclusion is that relatively poor Swiss peasant farmers in an isolated community had a decidedly better chance of perpetuating their family lines than did a portion of the English titled aristocracy with landed estates and elite status. Although maintaining kinship ties with baronets would seem to have had substantial material advantages for potential heirs to a title, it appears that in practice families kept track only of close cousins (Wachter and Laslett 1978). More distant relatives of the sort who would still bear the family surname in the narrow confines of the Swiss village might be more rapidly dispersed and lost to effective contact in the English setting, with its higher geographic and socioeconomic mobility. The claim that the British data measure "an ordinary or normal, sustained, presumably demographically-determined rate of extinctions" (Wachter and Laslett 1978) is open to question if indeed the authors wish to imply cross-cultural or diachronic significance for their findings.

THE ECONOMIC AND POLITICAL BACKGROUND OF PERDURING PATRILINES

If the Swiss mountain peasant patrilines we are considering here show remarkable continuity, what factors in their environment promoted this fixity in place and resistance to extinction? The ecological limitations of subsistence agriculture and herding in the alps and the persisting political means for regularizing access to local resources certainly put a premium on family members remaining within the village and restricted the settlement of newcomers. Given the fundamental requirement for varied types of land, buildings, and domestic animals to ensure household viability, each generation had limited options in production and repro-duction, as we have seen in Chapter 3. Until the latter half of the nineteenth century, there were few opportunities for employment outside the community, and neither mercenary soldiering nor farm labor and domestic service were adequate to support a family. In order to marry, a man and woman needed the full complement of fields, meadows, barns, and cellars, and these were almost always acquired through inheritance. The rule of strict partible inheritance with equal shares to siblings regardless of sex further necessitated combining shares received by each potential spouse. The creation of an adequate estate encouraged village endogamy (about 86 percent of 917 Törbel resident marriages have been with other community members) because the property of an in-migrant wife or husband might be too far away to be utilized effectively (Hagaman, Elias, and Netting 1978). Further inheritances from bachelor uncles and spinster aunts were important in Törbel, with its high incidence of celibacy, and only continued residence in the village allowed one to fully exploit such holdings. The ownership of land was practically synonymous with village membership, and although some householders might rent or sharecrop particular plots, there was no class of landless laborers, and paupers were rare. Acquiring land by means other than inheritance was possible, but the almost unreasonably high cost of a parcel restricted the frequency of sales (Stebler 1922:111), and mortgages were given sparingly to local citizens by their elected village council from capital belonging to the community or the church. The peasant farmstead was both the most familiar and the most secure livelihood known to the people of Törbel, and the best strategy for acquiring and enlarging the requisite property was to remain in the natal community where one could inherit, marry, manage family labor, get loans, and make deals.

In situations where land is passed on by primogeniture or held on the basis of short-term tenancies, a great deal more mobility can be expected. Seventeenth-century English villages showed rapid turnover of population, although their total sizes varied little. In Clayworth, Nottinghamshire, 61.8 percent of the people living there in 1688 had not been there in 1676, and Cogenhoe, Bedfordshire, had 50 percent new names in the 10 years before 1628 (Laslett 1965:146–7). If only 15 percent of the children born in a parish are there after 25 years, a steady annual loss of some 8 percent of the population can be assumed, a rate that Hollingsworth (1970) did not find high for the English evidence. A similar *grande fluidité* has been noted for French rural populations of the eighteenth century (Valmary 1965:73), and in a Swedish manor parish of the 1740s there were significantly more in-migrants and out-migrants than births and deaths (Gaunt 1977). Contributing to this mobility was the north European custom of employing unmarried young people of both sexes as servants who lived in the household. In some English cases they formed 12 to 13 percent of the entire population (Schofield 1970), and the leaving of the parental home to be a servant elsewhere characterized the life cycle of some 40 percent of all children (Laslett 1977:43). Conversely, few Törbel households contained servants from outside the community, and of the somewhat larger numbers who sought work elsewhere, most returned after a few years to found or rejoin their own families in the home village (Netting 1979a). The factors contributing to high mobility in preindustrial England, including severe underemployment and endemic poverty, tremendous variations in annual mortality, and the small sizes of individual communities (Levine 1977:35), were less effective in Törbel, where the land base could absorb a great deal of intensive labor, where relative independence from the market economy emphasized household self-sufficiency, and where isolation moderated the wide variations in mortality due to epidemic disease (Netting and Elias 1980). But perhaps most important was the strong economic attachment to real property that held owner-occupiers and provided them with a security not available in either cottage-industry work or wage work. As Gaunt (1977) noted in a comparison of Swedish parishes, "farmers were the most inclined to stay put, while servants and other landless had a greater propensity to move."

Whereas individual peasant strategies for maintaining a predictable subsistence and establishing a viable household may have contributed to Törbel patriline continuity, they were undoubtedly reinforced by corporate political decisions and communal institutions. The typical Swiss *Gemeinde* or commune is perhaps the primary governmental unit for its resident members, functioning historically with considerable autonomy to protect community interests and resolve local conflicts. Resembling a state in microcosm, the community has its own name and identity extending centuries into the past, its own territory clearly demarcated from that of its neighbors, its own citizenship, and its own political structure with elected representatives and highly democratic town meetings. Residence, even when it included ownership or lease of local lands, did not give political and economic rights of membership in the Swiss community. This strict interpretation of *Burgerrecht* or citizenship fundamentally differentiated the Swiss *Gemeinde* from the more open rural villages of England and France. The emphasis on acquiring land by inheritance from kin combined with the rule that citizenship was acquired by descent in the male line from a prior member of the community slowed out-migration and decisively limited the settling of "foreign" males in the village.

The statutory laws on immigration outlined in Chapter 5 were prominent in the fifteenth- and sixteenth-century codes or charters that the people of Törbel caused to be formally drawn up and to which they subscribed by name. It was clearly stated in 1483 that a landholder in Törbel who sold or otherwise conveyed real estate to any outsider with no right to a *Viertel* (a time period of irrigation water) or a *Schnitz* (permitted timber cutting) could not give any rights in the alps or the commons or the forests or the pasturage of the community.[7] The crucial nature of summer grazing privileges on the alp and a share in fuel for heating and cooking from the communal forest was obvious. This regulation did not mean that all outsiders were forever denied community membership. Women from other villages married Törbel men and thus acquired rights to use these resources both as wives and as widows. Their children by the Törbel husbands were, of course, citizens by birth. But no man lacking direct descent from a Törbel male was entitled to citizenship by virtue of land purchases in the territory or by taking a Törbel wife. Such resident in-marrying males are present today, but they are still singled out as noncitizens (*nichtburger*) and denied communal rights. Certainly such requirements were relaxed when epidemics had drastically lowered local population, and in 1483 the community explicitly reserved the right to admit new members. This required formal agreement (and probably a two-thirds majority of citizens) as well as payments into the community treasury and the sponsoring of a feast for the village. The most recent admissions to citizenship, in 1692, involved one man who paid 200 pounds cash, a double-measure pewter tankard, and a mule load of wine, whereas a second entrant reimbursed two village irrigation associations with 24 Spanish doubloons for a drinking party, to which he added a *Lagel* (50 liters) of wine "by his own free will."

To this day Swiss citizens have both the rights of the national state, giving them protection under the laws and voting privileges regardless of where in the nation they live, and local citizenship rights inherited in the male line and conferring membership in their ancestral communities. The economic rights to use communal resources and take part in corporate decisions concerning them are, of course, of little importance to migrant urban dwellers. Yet membership along with records of vital statistics and local citizenship documents (*Heimatscheine*) are still maintained in the natal community. Descendents of a foreign national who married a Törbel woman in the early nineteenth century and have never lived in the village are still listed as citizens. Conversely, even the most influential and wealthy immigrants may be long denied community membership, as was the case with the famous hotel-owning Seiler family in Zermatt (Kämpfen 1942). Men who married into Törbel in the past and actually took up residence there were usually artisans who worked as stonecutters or blacksmiths or in some other craft that made them less dependent on farming. Most left after a few years, and of those who remained, no male offspring themselves founded families in Törbel. Men who left Törbel usually did not continue to be peasant farmers, because other alpine communities had similar prohibitions. Only from such specialized cash cropping as growing fruit or making wine in lower Valais could a family live solely from the production of its own land without relying on goods from the commons. The local autonomy that allowed communities to legislate and enforce standards of village citizenship was recognized and historically supported by the cantonal and national authorities of the Swiss confederation. A large measure of territorial sovereignty, direct rather than representative democracy on issues of local importance (Barber 1974), and both the levying and the allocation of significant tax revenues by the community itself combined to make legal membership in the closed corporate community an important and jealously guarded status.

Although the patrilines of Törbel are not classic unilineal descent groups, they do act as kinship statuses conferring distinctive and exclusive rights within a closed corporate community. Citizenship, combining access to communally held subsistence resources and a voice in political decision making, has been traditionally a kinship perquisite rather than a result of voluntary association or residential choice. Legal and economic barriers have restricted in-migration, thereby lessening competition for scarce goods and increasing the stability of the peasant subsistence

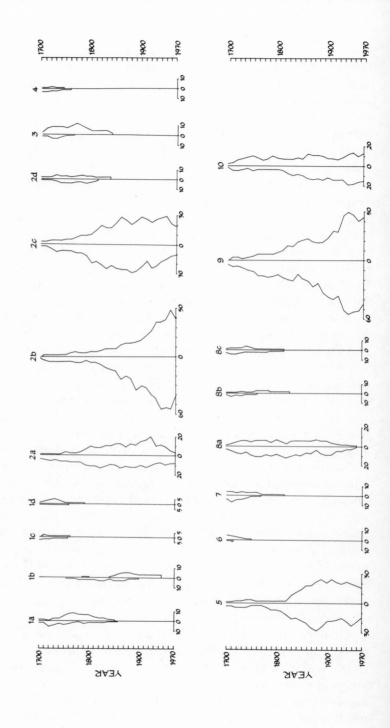

YEAR

YEAR

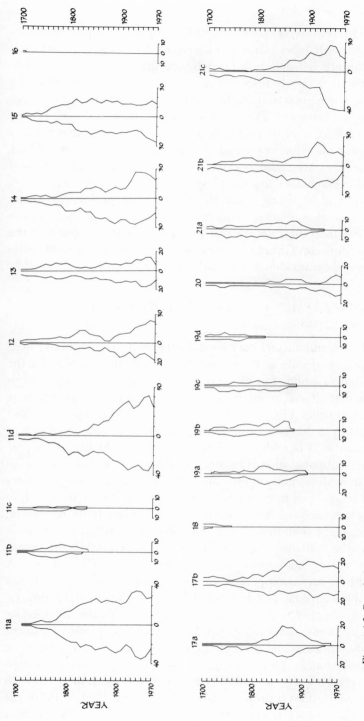

Figure 4.2. Population dynamics of Törbel patrilines (1700–1970). Numbers of males are shown in the left of the central axis and number of females to the right.

adaptation. The requirements of self-sufficiency in an alpine environment combined with inheritance rules, rigidly defined group membership, and a largely self-determining polity to limit individual mobility and perpetuate local family lines. Simply put, for rightful members the costs of leaving were great and the benefits of staying in the village were palpable and predictable. The established social boundaries of the community acted as semipermeable membrane, selectively absorbing a few outsiders and allowing its own surplus population to filter out. These regulatory mechanisms could operate best in a state of geographical isolation, buffered against wars and plagues, little affected by conquerors or the exactions of a strong centralized state, and peripheral to the explosive growth of a market economy. Such conditions may be the exception rather than the rule in rural Europe, but they suggest that the perduring patrilines of Törbel have a reasonable basis in the local Swiss circumstances of peasant choice and institutional structures.

DEMOGRAPHIC DYNAMICS OF INDIVIDUAL PATRILINES

Political and economic factors may have contributed to a singularly high rate of patriline continuity in the village, but they cannot account for the internal differences among families, the contemporaneous growth, stability, or decline that altered membership in the various descent groups over the same span of time. The demographic dynamics of each patriline can be represented by a diagram (Figure 4.2) based on computer-generated counts of the numbers of males and females present in the line at 10-year intervals. Each subpopulation is created by adding births and subtracting deaths as well as all permanent out-migrants.[8] For comparative purposes the lines can be grouped into four types: those that became extinct before 1950 and others defined on a somewhat arbitrary basis as stable, slow-growing, and expanding (Table 4.1). We use only the period after 1700 (when vital statistics began to be uniformly recorded) and before 1950 (when village self-sufficiency had practically disappeared). A number of lines that disappeared in the eighteenth century are not included in the comparative tabulation because of their small numbers, and two lines (8a and 17a) that died out after 1950 are included as surviving populations. Surname group 2 shows all four possible patterns of patriline dynamics, with 2d becoming extinct, 2a maintaining a quite regular vertical profile with the number of males varying only between 4 and 13, 2c growing to around 25 males before declining, and 2b broadening steadily into a pronounced pyramid from 1800 to 1950. All lines begin with five or fewer members of each sex in 1700, in part

Table 4.1. *Patrilines grouped by relative demographic stability*

Type	Characteristic	Tabulated lines	Untabulated lines
I	Extinct before 1950	1a, 1b, 2d, 3, 8b, 8c, 11b, 11c, 19a, 19b, 19c, 19d, 21a	1c, 1d, 4, 6, 7, 16, 18
II	Stable (never more than 15 males)	2a, 8a, 12, 17a, 17b, 20	
III	Slow-growing (never more than 16–25 males)	2c, 5, 10, 13, 14, 15, 21b	
IV	Expanding (reached 26 males or more)	2b, 9, 11a, 11d, 21c	

because of the methodological need to trace each line to individuals whose presence and kin relationships can be documented only after 1665.

Which demographic variables can account for the apparent differences among lines in their historical profiles? More specifically, are extinction, stability, and growth clearly related to differences in fertility, in migration, in mortality, or perhaps in all three? The answer seems to be that only the patrilines that died out are statistically distinct, and the characteristics that set them off from surviving lines are obvious (Table 4.2). Extinct lines had significantly fewer offspring per family and male births per family than did the other types, but the conclusion that a group with smaller average reproduction will not maintain itself is hardly surprising. Of more interest is the fact that stable, slow-growing, and expanding lines had children at a rate of 4.88 to 5.26 per family, and within this narrow range, the stable lines had the highest average numbers. Preadult mortality and the percentage of children per family who themselves married do not appear to distinguish the four types from one another.

A hypothesis that informed much of our attention to the dynamics of family lines was that stable lines would enjoy some economic advantages over rapidly growing groups because the family estate would be less fractionated in succeeding generations. Thus, any factors limiting the number of inheriting offspring (lower birth rate, higher preadult mortality, or higher proportion of celibate children) would result in population stability of the line and maintenance of the economic base. The data on fertility, marriage, and mortality do not demonstrate regular differences that would mark off stable lines from expanding lines or suggest that those groups showing little or gradual growth were either consciously or unconsciously limiting family size. Age-specific female fertility, birth

Table 4.2. *Comparative demographic attributes of patriline types*

	I (extinct)	II (stable)	III (slow-growing)	IV (expanding)
Number of births per family	3.74	5.26	4.88	5.13
Male/female ratio of offspring	93:100	106:100	103:100	109:100
Percentage of children dying under age 20	28	22	26	23
Percentage of children marrying	42	43	46	48
Percentage of children emigrating	10	17	19	23

interval, and mother's age at birth of last child also gave no indication of departures from unrestricted natural fertility at any period from 1700 to the present (see Chapter 6). In these admittedly small subpopulations it appears that essentially chance factors operated either to reduce fertility below the replacement rate or to influence the degree of growth in surviving lines.

It is plain that emigration could decisively alter the number of patriline members present in the community. Indeed, some fairly substantial lines such as 19a, 19b, and 19c lost at least 10 members in the South American exodus of the 1860s and 1870s, thus contributing to the extinction of these groups. Line 8a had 2 males going to America, 2 males settling elsewhere in Switzerland, and 1 male dying as a soldier in Naples. Usually, migration merely added to the apparently random effects of low reproduction or an unbalanced sex ratio, as in 21a, where 5 children left the village, 1 son was childless, and the remaining 4 offspring were females, who could not continue the line. Line 17a lost 1 male to out-migration, but a more important cause of its decline was that 6 sons in two separate families never married. However, when migration is considered by patriline type, such idiosyncratic differences disappear, and the proportion of children per family migrating is seen to correlate directly with relative growth of the line (Table 4.2). Thus lines that became extinct had, on the average, only 10.4 percent of their offspring leaving the village, whereas expanding lines lost 22.7 percent of their children. The frequency of emigration was one-third higher for expanding lines than for stable lines. It seems clear that when there were fewer potential heirs in a line and individuals were thus assured of more adequate agrarian resources, permanent migration was economically less necessary and less attractive. On the other hand, when the pool of prospective property holders widened to the point of increased competition and small shares, the alternative of seeking one's fortune elsewhere was increasingly

Table 4.3. *Comparative wealth by patriline type*

	I (extinct)	II (stable)	III (slow-growing)	IV (expanding)
Mean patriline wealth as proportion of total village wealth	1.09	3.11	5.73	7.38
Mean family wealth as proportion of mean family wealth in village as a whole (1.00 = mean family wealth)	0.82	1.28	0.98	1.01

chosen. However, even the drain of greater average migration did not reverse the cumulative growth of expanding family lines.

PATRILINES AND RELATIVE WEALTH

Given the fact that the peasant subsistence adaptation of Törbel was based largely on strictly circumscribed resources of land, animals, and agricultural equipment and that the local population had few alternative sources of livelihood until the present century, individual family wealth was acquired largely through inheritance, and additional property was difficult to obtain. It is plausible, then, that those family lines whose numbers were stable or declining would be in a better position to maintain or even augment their wealth. Expanding patrilines, on the other hand, would risk progressive impoverishment. Suggestive, but by no means definitive, evidence on this issue is available from property assessments for taxation purposes in the cantonal archives at Sion. For a sample of years from 1845 to 1915, these assessments were abstracted, tabulated individually as proportions of the total village assessed wealth for that year, and compared according to the patriline memberships of the various household heads.

The results of comparing total wealth of patriline and demographic type (in Table 4.3) show a correlation indicating that in the late nineteenth century the total property of a group was proportional to the number of members. Expanding patrilines with more male members and more family households had the largest shares of wealth, with slow-growing, stable, and dying lines at successively lower levels. We must remember that wealth was not at any time held corporately by a patriline, and it was possible to have individual families with substantially above-average wealth and below-average wealth in a single patriline at any point in time. Furthermore, there may well have been a developmental cycle in the course of which individual households began with a small

Traditional woman's holiday dress with embroidered jacket and cap.

estate, added to it as various relatives of both spouses died, and finally
dispersed it to heirs as the original couple retired. Yet, even with these
qualifications, it does not appear that the population growth of a line
operated decisively to reduce the average wealth of its members.

Table 4.3 indicates that average family wealth in expanding lines and slowgrowing lines was almost exactly that of all families in the village. Families in stable lines were somewhat richer than average, and families in lines destined to become extinct were somewhat poorer, but the differences are not great and are by no means statistically significant. Small stable lines did not monopolize property, as might be the case in a highly stratified village society. Indeed, demographic chance affecting the number of heirs and the number of relatives from whom they received legacies varied widely among families, and the luck of marriage to a rich or poor spouse further increased the range of individual outcomes. The rule of partible inheritance may have meant a rich windfall for an only child or for the man who had two well-endowed wives, but the celibate whose parental property was divided with a number of married siblings and who never combined it with the portion of a spouse may have been relatively poor.

The lack of congruence between family-line growth and average wealth is perhaps more understandable if we evaluate it in terms of individual strategies of accumulation and transmission between generations. The close connection between marriage and the availability of land and goods necessary to support an independent household will be considered in Chapter 8. The continued adherence to this principle meant that there were no landless people in Törbel nor any class of noncitizens lacking rights in the communal resources. Although a married couple might be well aware that a single child of theirs would get more property than if there were numerous brothers and sisters, their own immediate interests were in having many offspring. This protected them against unpredictable losses through high infant mortality and also contributed to a household labor force. Parents also could effectively retain their productive property until death or until their own voluntary retirement. Either single or married offspring remained with them and cared for them in their declining years, but in neither case did the presence of many children decrease the parental estate while its owners still had need of it. A further advantage of large families was that adult male children could support their father politically and wield more power in the democratic elections that decided most important village controversies.

Although the welfare of children was often subordinated to that of their parents, insofar as marriage in the younger generation might be delayed and single children kept long years in a dependent role, the wealth of children was not determined solely by what they could eventually inherit. Seasonal work outside the community might bring in some cash, artisans and schoolteachers were employed in the village, and a judicious marriage could add considerable amounts of property.

Because of such opportunities, a cooperating group of hard-working thrifty brothers could expand the parental estate and compensate for the fact that their final shares in it might not be large. It is therefore intelligible that joint patriline wealth went up with an increase in numbers and that conscious restrictions on growth did not figure importantly in the apparent demographic decisions of individual families.

CONCLUSIONS

The historically attested continuity of patrilines in Törbel reflects both the special social and political circumstances of a Swiss closed corporate peasant community and the persistence of similar economic strategies in the individual family. A limited territory allowing a large measure of agrarian self-sufficiency but restricting surplus production put a premium on communal regulation of man/land ratios. Geographical isolation and the tradition of Swiss local independence and self-determination made possible the establishment of patrilineally inherited village citizenship and the effective prevention of male in-migration. Socially enforced adherence to standards for forming new households only on the basis of viable peasant holdings made inheritance of property a necessity for marriage and avoided the development of a landless class. The system emphasized stability, buffered as it was against the disruptions of war, external exploitation, and the more active market participation that characterized much of rural Europe. The strong persistence of owner-occupied farmsteads resulted in a population more sessile than the tenants, laborers, and servants whose mobility was so striking in English, French, and Scandinavian preindustrial communities.

It is apparent, however, that maintenance of the line was not an end in itself among Törbel families. Adoption was not practiced. Primogeniture was never the rule, and partible inheritance distributed property equally among male and female heirs, creating new holdings through division and recombination in each generation. Patrilines did not operate in an economically corporate manner, and individual family households formed the significant units of production and consumption. The perpetuation of the line was in part a by-product of the general desire to increase the household labor force and guarantee the security of the parental couple in their old age. Although restricting the number of heirs might have contributed to the heirs' future economic standing, the more immediate advantage of the household heads encouraged the propagation of children. The chance factors of child survival, celibacy, and advantageous marriage increased the risks inherent in intentionally limiting family size without increasing its benefits. Lines that became extinct

under these circumstances did so because of lower-than-average reproduction, and no substantial differences in fertility, mortality, or nuptiality
regularly distinguished stable, slow-growing, and expanding family lines
from one another. Migration functioned partially to counteract deviation
in the size of the group, reducing numbers in proportion to growth.
Expanding lines did not suffer gross declines in wealth, and although
individual families may have been, on the average, somewhat poorer than
representatives of stable patrilines, considerable variations in wealth
among families within a line, in a single family over time, and in
patrilines of the same type partially obscured such differences. The initial
picture emerging from a comparison of Törbel patriline dynamics and
relative wealth is of a fairly egalitarian society, lacking extremes of
poverty and great wealth, and without any defined reproductive strategy
for the accumulation and consolidation of property.

Genealogical depth and lineal continuity are by no means invariant
attributes of the peasant community. Yet when political and economic
circumstances restrict in-migration and out-migration, provide an
adequate livelihood for village members, and confer necessary rights to
resources and governmental participation on the basis of a descent
rule, family lines may show an astonishing potential for survival.
Individual family economic interests run parallel to and support patriline
continuity in an ecosystem as finely calibrated and dependable as an old
Swiss watch.

5

The village population:
growth, decline, and stability

Much that we have said about the ongoing ecosystem that is Törbel has been based on certain premises about population. A major impetus for the original research project was the idea that in a situation of environmental limitations on the kinds and quantities of subsistence goods and of a relatively unchanging means of production, the mechanisms for regulating local population could be isolated and analyzed. The requirements and constraints of peasant land use and herding evidently contributed to a stable, self-perpetuating village society in which households could provide themselves with a reasonably secure agricultural livelihood. There were no indications of either sudden famine or gradual impoverishment to indicate that the population had grown to the point where its natural resources were inadequate. The grim Malthusian positive checks of starvation, disease, and warfare were not apparent, at least in their dramatic forms. Rather than being a society that periodically exceeded its carrying capacity, only to be ruthlessly cut back, Törbel seems to have approached a homeostatic condition in which density-dependent mechanisms such as a high age at marriage, celibacy, and migration kept population growth within supportable limits. The findings that Törbel kept soil erosion in check, did not overcut its timber, and did not experience declining yields of hay and grain suggested the achievement of an equilibrium, presumably at some point comfortably within "carrying capacity." Permanent boundaries, inflexible altitude zones for different crops, the constancy of total and average individual cattle herd sizes, and the continuity of family lines all contributed to this impression of stability, of a delicate but enduring balance struck between the environment and its human inhabitants. Although the system generally maintained itself constant, its equilibrium could be disturbed without being destroyed.

We have suggested that prehistoric adjustments were necessary as sedentary villages replaced migratory herding and as a growing peasant population pressed on its land base, causing the intensification seen in irrigation, manuring, and individual land tenure.[1] On the other hand, Törbel was not immune to bubonic plague, influenza, typhus, or occasional crop failure. However, it is not enough to describe the functional operation of this ecosystem or the means by which it countered deviations due to unpredictable "environmental perturbations." We need to chart these processes quantitatively in a real population as it evolved through time. Growth is not the result of a single factor, nor does one cause produce a steady state. The history of social behavior and physiological responses crystallized in the demographic records of a peasant village may be inadequate to answer many questions, but the documents have seldom been fully utilized to understand those profound dynamic processes that await the patient investigator.

POPULATION RECONSTRUCTION AND FAMILY RECONSTITUTION

The most direct means of entering a small demographic universe is to abstract from a continuous registry the raw numbers of births, marriages, and deaths for every year that they are present. Such "aggregative statistics" give clues to trends, such as an increasing annual number of births, or to dislocations, such as the passage of an epidemic marked by a year of disproportionate deaths. Relating the various indices can also give information on natural increase or on the average fertility of a marriage (births/marriages). Although such data may allow crude comparisons between time periods or comparisons with other contemporaneous examples, they do not allow the application of more precise demographic measures. In order to make use of even the simplest birth and death rates (Wrigley 1966a:100), we need to know the size of the population. Without the ages of those dying, we cannot derive age-specific mortality or estimate life expectancy. Until births can be credited to particular women at known points in their life cycles, we cannot discuss birth intervals, variations in fertility, or the possibility of contraception.

To meet these needs for studying local demography before the advent of modern census techniques, the method of family reconstitution was developed (Fleury and Henry 1965). Isolated notations of vital events can be brought together in a context of specific families, where, for instance, birth dates for both parents indicate their ages at the recorded time of their marriage, and successive baptisms make apparent the number, sex, and spacing of their children. Burials then specify the life spans of these individuals. It is not necessary to have full data on each family or person for partial reconstitution (Wrigley 1966a:96). A fertility history of a woman is possible if we have marriage and death dates, with intervening births, even if we lack her own birth record. Children may be present in a community until they marry and go away, but we may keep track of them (or, as the demographers say, keep them in observation) from birth to migration and compare them with other children who pass through or die in the same age brackets. Lacking a total population, we can base rates on various subsamples, such as families for whom marriage and childbearing histories are complete, or women married and therefore at risk of pregnancy between the ages of 25 and 29 years. Samples may indeed be skewed, as when many people marry outside of their natal villages and therefore lack birth records (it is, unfortunately, seldom possible to find reliable registries in a series of adjacent parishes or towns for the same time period, and therefore documentation on many individuals is only partial). The more migration and the more rapid the turnover of local populations, the fewer families can be reconstituted (Wrigley 1966b:147; Thestrup 1972; Smith 1977). It has been estimated that most village studies consist of samples in which only about 15 percent of all families are reconstituted (Hollingsworth 1970:93). The French registers for the village of Crulai in Normandy allowed determinations of age at marriage for 45 percent of marriages in 1710–42, but in only 27 percent of the cases were ages present for both partners. In just 19 percent of the marriages were the dates of both birth and death for both parties known (Gautier and Henry 1958; cited by Wrigley 1966a). Questions may then arise as to the representativeness of families who remain for their entire lifetimes in one locality, unlike their more mobile neighbors. Despite these caveats, family reconstitution is obviously an indispensable tool and the only one now available for population reconstruction of small communities before censuses.

English historical demographers have recognized the limitations of the family reconstitution method, even as they have applied it most effectively and extensively. To the degree that Törbel, unlike the typical English or French rural village, was indeed a closed corporate community, it is even better suited to this type of analysis. Well over 90 percent of resident families can be fully or partially reconstituted because of the economic and political forces mentioned in the last chapter that kept them at home and restrained in-migration. The continuity and generally high quality of the parish registers increase the accuracy of individual identification. Baptisms are listed beginning in 1665, deaths in 1687, and marriages in 1703. Baptismal records uniformly give the maiden name of the mother, and the marriage book notes the names of the couple's parents as well as the bride's birthplace, if it was not Törbel. In accordance with the Roman Catholic emphasis on prompt baptism to allow the new Christian soul to enter heaven, baptism occurred immediately after birth or at the most a day or two later. The distinction between birth and baptism dates is therefore unimportant, and the fact that all villagers were practicing members of the same parish congregation also contributes to the completeness of the birth registration (Knodel 1970).[2] Cross-checking between the parish entries and Swiss manuscript census returns is possible for the whole of the nineteenth century, and parallel civil registries exist for vital statistics from 1875. Tax listings with the names of all Törbel property holders at annual intervals commence in 1851. The tremendously time-consuming process of manual reconstitution of families[3] was not even necessary in the Törbel case because of the genealogy book, which required only the addition of exact dates, the occasional missing births of children who died young, and extinct family lines to provide coverage of roughly 1,000 families and some 5,500 individuals.[4] The high degree of endogamy in Törbel, where until this century some 85 percent of all marriages were of native villagers with each other, also meant that people remained available for long periods of time to demographic observation (Hagaman, Elias, and Netting 1978). By contrast, the English agricultural village of Bottesford had less than 10 percent of all parish marriages from 1610 to 1851 in which both bride and groom were born in the community (Levine 1977:39). The custom of maintaining a resident parish priest and the long terms of most of these *Pfarrer* in the community probably promoted the accurate keeping of unbroken series of annual records in Törbel. Once filled, a book of baptisms or deaths was stored with other parish records in the priest's home.

Although the Törbel parish registers make possible a high proportion of family reconstitution and allow the continued observation of a relatively large number of individuals, they are not without problems. Because we have almost no reliable dates before 1665, and because routine recording of all vital events including death and marriage was not in operation until shortly after 1700, there can be no useful comparisons with the English cases that begin around 1550 and the earlier French family reconstitutions from the seventeenth century (Wrigley 1966*b*). The earliest Törbel death records often lack the names of parents and spouses. Because there were few surnames and only a small assortment of given names regularly used in the village (boys were baptized Johann, Joseph, Peter, Christian, and Anton, and girls received the names Maria, Katherina, Anna, and Christina, either singly or in combination), there might be several contemporaries with the name Maria Carlen or Johan Kalbermatten.[5] Comparison of the file cards containing all possible

Table 5.1. *Data reliability for Törbel natives (migrants excluded) (1650–1974)*

Birth cohort	Birth date					Death date					
	Present	After	Before	?	Total	Present	After	Before	?	L	Total
1650–99	265	2	33	5	305	204	11	18	72	0	305
1700–49	507	4	26	4	541	408	29	6	98	0	541
1750–99	485	1	0	3	489	382	25	32	50	0	489
1800–49	649	1	9	4	675	649	12	5	9	0	675
1850–99	770	3	0	1	771	712	18	1	4	36	771
1900–49	578	0	0	4	582	302	0	0	0	280	582
1950–74	289	0	0	0	289	25	0	0	0	264	289
No birth date						394	10	2	71	1	478

Present = recorded date securely documented and attached to individual case.
After = date (usually year) after which village resident is known to have been born or died.
Before = date (usually year) before which village resident is known to have been born or died.
? = questionable attribution in which individual birth or death could potentially have been attached to another contemporary individual with the same name.
L = living individual in 1971.

candidates for a particular death date sometimes resulted in a questionable attribution (Table 5.1), but such decisions were noted and flagged for computer tabulations. Death dates in the late seventeenth and early eighteenth centuries were clearly useless in determining age when the individual concerned had been born before the baptismal listing began. Women born in other communities and marrying in Törbel also often lacked birth dates. A more serious difficulty was the appearance of people for whom only a birth date was recorded, with no reference to subsequent events, presumably because of infant or childhood death or emigration before marriage. We have referred to these cases as uncomputables, and we shall discuss the way in which they have been handled in the following sections on migration and mortality.

Despite such occasional lacunae in the otherwise dependable sources, it was possible to reconstruct the total population of Törbel by combining all individual computer records and tabulating annual totals. In each year, births were added to the previous year's total and deaths were subtracted. New residents, usually in-marrying spouses, were added at the date of the wedding. Those who left the village permanently and settled elsewhere were dropped from the total on the date of migration, if known, on the date of marriage with an outsider, or, rather arbitrarily, at age 20 years. This does not take account of seasonal migrants or those, like soldiers, who might stay for years away from Törbel but who eventually returned to found families and die there. When only a birth date was listed and no indication of life span was available, the uncomputable individual was neither added to nor subtracted from the local population. When an exact death date was unknown but the person concerned had been in the village up to at least a certain period (e.g., a parent up to the birth of the last offspring, or a bachelor listed on a Swiss census form), a year was given with the notation *A*, meaning "dead after" the given date. Similarly, when a child was given the same name as a prior sibling, we knew, according to local custom, that the earlier sibling had predeceased the newborn infant. If a death date was lacking for the earlier sibling, the year of birth for the same-named infant could be listed with a *B*, standing for "before" the given date (Table 5.1). The goal of this reconstruction was to approximate the number of living people at any given time who considered Törbel to be their permanent home. Unlike the family reconstitution studies, this procedure provided an estimated *total* village population for the calculation of various demographic rates. It also, and most significantly, charted population fluctuations and trends over 270 years and suggested more specific investigations of the causes influencing such dynamics.

The Törbel reconstructed population as represented in Figure 5.1 gives us some basis for discussing village demography in the century before the first official census in 1798 and illuminates short-term changes between the periodic censuses.[6] Because the Törbel count lacked a base population with which to begin and was aggregated only with births after 1665, it is not until 1700 that the count may approach a reliable estimate. When adjustments are made for deaths of individuals who were not included in the tabulated population because they lacked birth dates, the totals for the period 1700–40 should probably be adjusted upward by about 5 percent. After 1740 the estimated population (as indicated by points at 20-year intervals on the dotted line) is very close to the tabulated total. After 1798, the reconstructed population parallels the official census population in both aggregate totals and trends, indicating that both are measuring independently the same local universe. Discrepancies in 1837 and 1846 are due to the inclusion by the Swiss enumerators of Törbel citizens who had migrated to other villages or left the country. Our estimate of de facto population is less than the official de jure count, but as soon as official usage changed in 1850 to the modern method of listing only those physically present in the community on the day of the census, the two totals become almost identical. From 1880 on, and increasingly after 1910, the reconstructed population exceeds the official figure. This can be traced directly to the growth of more distant wage work requiring village residents to remain away from the village for

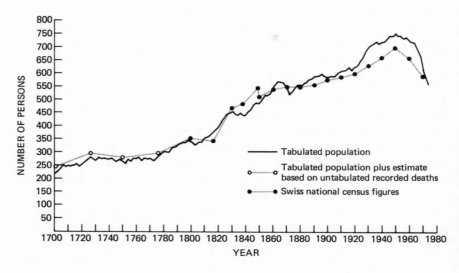

Figure 5.1. Aggregate population estimates for Törbel (1700–1970).

weeks or months at a time. If such individuals maintained a permanent residence in Törbel or eventually returned to homes there, they are retained in our annual estimates. It requires a fair amount of temerity to claim that the population of a Swiss peasant village can be meaningfully estimated on an annual basis for 270 years, and the drawers of file cards and stacks of computer printout that led to these conclusions cannot by weight alone vouch for the reliability of our numbers. However, tabulations are grounded on a great many bits of factual and internally consistent data from the uniquely controlled context of carefully kept parish records in a closed corporate community. Although we may have underestimated totals in the early years because of missing birth dates and the presence of children who grew up in the village and then migrated, we are confident that our counts, supported by Swiss census results, adequately reflect the general levels and historical changes in local population.

If the apparent trends in the chart of Törbel demography are largely accurate, the initial hypothesis of a stable population within fixed and inflexible economic constraints must obviously be revised. There are indeed periods such as the first three-quarters of the eighteenth century and the span from 1875 to 1910 when population remained either static or expanded gradually. This configuration would be just what one might expect if the local community had arrived at a kind of equilibrium with its environment and limited productive resources. But the impression of stability is contradicted by three consecutive spurts of growth, separated by short plateaus, that carried Törbel from 280 to 572 inhabitants between 1774 and 1867. These 93 years of sustained increase more than doubled a village population that was still agriculturally self-supporting and had probably not yet felt the benefits of modern medicine or public health. Another period of rapid growth did not begin until about the time of World War I, and it continued until 1950, when population began to fall sharply.

The general shape of population growth in many parts of Europe is not unlike that of Törbel. After a period of demographic stagnation in the seventeenth century (Hobsbawm 1967), there was mild growth from 1700 to 1750 and a strong increase from 1750 to 1850. This was noted in a large sample of English parishes by Laslett (1977:125) and in several German communities by Lee (1975).[7] French population began to expand well before the agricultural revolution, growing 30 to 35 percent between 1720 and 1790 (Goubert 1971), and Denmark doubled in numbers between 1787 and 1865 (Utterström 1965:529). Switzerland went from 1,680,000 inhabitants in 1798 to 2,393,000 in 1850 (Brugger 1956:11). In the Visp district, including Törbel and other alpine villages but also the commercial center of Visp and the new tourist industry in Zermatt, population practically doubled from 1816 to 1900 (Figure 5.2).[8] We should not expect to find in a single mountain peasant community the same causal factors that powered "the modern rise of population" in a whole continent, but the microcosm does provide a test case for the interplay of fertility, mortality, and migration in a situation of significant demographic growth far removed from the burgeoning urbanism, the expanding trade, the factories, and the hospitals that figure so largely in many explanations of European growth.

MIGRATION

Rather than attempting at the outset to plumb the mysteries of birth and death in Törbel, it may be useful to briefly survey the influence of migration on the population.[9] We have already noted (Chapter 4) that political and economic restrictions effectively denied men from other communities the opportunity to gain citizenship and rights to village common resources. Only three men appear to have settled in Törbel, married, and had children there since 1700. One later left with his family; one had living descendants, but his married son has not founded a family; the third is currently living. Because the surnames of in-marrying individuals or notations on their marriage records indicate that they were not Törbel natives, it is possible to distinguish 129 people over the last 300 years who entered Törbel. Only 14 percent of the 917 marriages of Törbel residents involved in-migrants, and nearly all of these were women (Hagaman, Elias, and Netting 1978). Marriages with outsiders

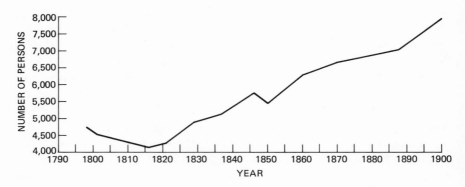

Figure 5.2. Population of the Visp district (1798–1900) based on census totals reported in Meyer (1907).

were most frequent between 1700 and 1729, when an average of 1.23 per year took place. From 1730 to 1799 this declined to 0.44, and in the 30 years from 1780 to 1809 there were only 2 such marriages. An average of 0.53 marriage per year with nonnatives took place between 1810 and 1879, and from 1880 to 1969, there was only 0.14 marriage per year. It is no wonder that the few spouses from outside the village admit to feeling lonely there and often comment adversely on the close-knit clannish society that has never fully accepted them.

Available mates for men in a peasant community are obviously those from a similar farming background and of similar social standing who live near at hand. When Törbel males married outside the village, they most frequently chose women from the adjacent settlements. Törbel and its neighbor Embd were often in conflict over irrigation water, but they had a long common border with good meadowlands on both sides (Figure 1.1). It was therefore possible for a Törbjer to effectively use any land within walking distance that his wife from Embd might inherit, and 23 marriages with Embd women actually took place (Figure 5.3). Much of Törbel's contact with the outside world took place through the valley village of Stalden, and this was the source for 14 spouses. Zeneggen and Bürchen were somewhat farther from Törbel, and they lacked adjacent farmlands; so fewer marriages were contracted there. In all, 51 percent of the in-migrant women came from the four nearest communities. Transport, trade, and summer alp employment often took Törbel males up the Mattervispa valley toward Zermatt, and 16 marriages were with women from Randa, Zermatt, Saint Niklaus, and adjacent villages, 7 marriages were with women from the Saastal, and 6 marriages were with women from Visp and Visperterminen. Thus 79 percent of the marriages in which the wife's origin was noted and in which the couple settled in **Törbel were** within the Visp valley system. A total of 10 more wives came

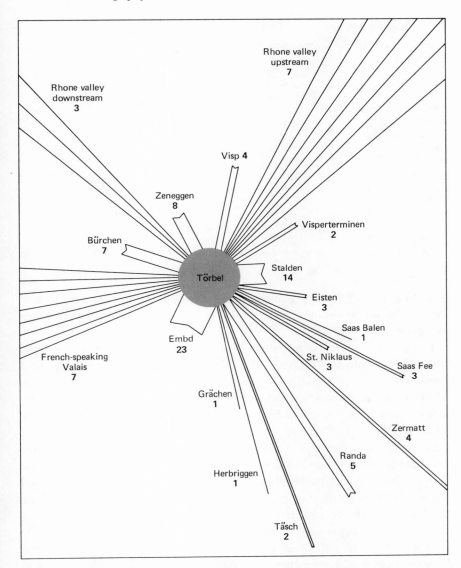

Figure 5.3. Numbers and places of origin of wives immigrating to Törbel. The thickness of arrow indicates number of women; the length of arrow indicates distance of place of origin from Törbel.

from German-speaking upper Valais and 7 from the French-speaking part of the canton. Only 2 women came from other cantons in Switzerland and 2 from Germany. It appears that in-marrying women tended to be neighbors or at least natives of the geographically and politically connected Visp district. Most came from alpine villages similar to Törbel,

Table 5.2. *Törbel net migration (1688–1962)*

Period	Tabulated in-migrants	Tabulated out-migrants	Net migration	Average annual migration	Rate per 1,000[a]
1688–1712	37	17	20	0.8	3.65
1713–37	22	11	11	0.44	1.57
1738–62	10	10	0	0	0
1763–87	8	8	0	0	0
1788–1812	6	13	−7	−0.28	−0.82
1813–37	14	26	−12	−0.48	−1.11
1838–62	13	46	−33	−1.32	−2.74
1863–87	7	108	−101	−4.04	−7.58
1888–1912	6	61	−55	−2.20	−3.79
1913–37	3	74	−71	−2.84	−4.41
1938–62	3	207	−204	−8.16	−10.94

[a]Based on tabulated midyear total population: e.g., 1700, 1725, 1750, 1775, etc.

including a few from the French section of the canton. The numbers of spouses from elsewhere in Switzerland or beyond who took up residence in Törbel were negligible.

In the past, most of the other Törbel residents not born there were temporary sojourners. There was always a priest who hailed from elsewhere, and occasionally a priest brought his housekeeper with him. There might be a local woman widowed in another village and spending a few years in her original home with her children (who could not be Törbel citizens and seldom remained as adults). The others were all servants or hired hands, some of whom might marry in Törbel, but most of whom left when their employment was over. In 1846, for instance, the census listed 4 maidservants and 2 farm workers (*Knecht*). Total permanent immigration into Törbel was light, coming chiefly as a trickle of in-marrying spouses who seldom accounted for more than one marriage every other year.[10] The new Törbel residents contributed little to population growth, and from the end of the eighteenth century, in-migration was increasingly overbalanced by a strong flow of those leaving the village.

Table 5.2 is based only on migrants from whom information on birth date and date of departure from or entry into the village can be tabulated. There may well be undercounting of emigrants during the early 1700s, when a significant number of individuals born into the village merely disappear from our records. The general impression of migration over 25-year periods is that numbers were initially quite small, with a positive net in-migration from 1688 to 1737, due mostly to women entering the community at marriage. There followed a period of equilibrium until after 1788, when the weight shifted to gradually increasing net out-migration. This peaked in the quarter century around 1875, declined somewhat from 1888 to 1937, and then rose rapidly in the 1940s, 1950s, and 1960s. The same picture emerges from a 9-year moving average of tabulated out-migrants (Figure 5.4).

The small but fairly steady emigration from Törbel in the late seventeenth century and the eighteenth century is documented chiefly in the deaths of mercenary soldiers abroad. The village seems to have provided troops and occasionally officers for the armies of France, Spain, the Vatican, and other Italian states. Such men enlisted in units recruited in the canton and contracted to serve for a period of years. They appear to have been young unmarried men who expected to earn cash and qualify for pensions that would allow them to return home and set up households in Törbel. Those who survived combat and the even greater danger of disease in a foreign army could return as prosperous and honored citizens who often held posts such as *Kastlan* in the village and district governments or became officers in the cantonal militia. Many never came back, however, and there were 15 deaths in France recorded from 1689 to 1699, with 9 deaths in the year 1690 alone. At this time there were 2,400 men from Valais in French armies (Bridel 1820:251). In the first decade of the eighteenth century, 7 more soldiers perished in France. Single deaths are listed for France in 1744, 1749, 1761, and 1810, for Spain in 1712 and 1824, for Milan in 1761 and 1763, for Naples in 1846, 1850 (2), 1851, and 1857, for Italy in 1713, for Rome in 1851, and in unknown foreign countries in 1713, 1847, and 1851. In all, there were 41 deaths of mercenaries abroad from 1689 until 1857, when this type of service practically ended. The 1837 census listed 4 men as soldiers in Rome and 1 man in Naples; in 1846 there were 2 in Rome and 3 in Naples. Although the loss of men in the military may have been appreciable in the small village population of the late 1600s and early 1700s, foreign soldiering was probably not a significant drain of local manpower at later periods. Using men who would quite possibly have spent the same years as bachelors waiting to marry, the community received cash remittances while at the same time temporarily or permanently reducing what may have been a surplus of agricultural labor.

A more concentrated and obvious effect on the Törbel population was produced by a migration to the New World, especially the Santa Fe area of Argentina, from 1866 to 1886. The pronounced decrease in village population that occurred between 1868 and 1878 (Figure 5.1) was due to the permanent resettling of 63 individuals, including seven complete families, in South America. About 11 percent of the 1868 population was

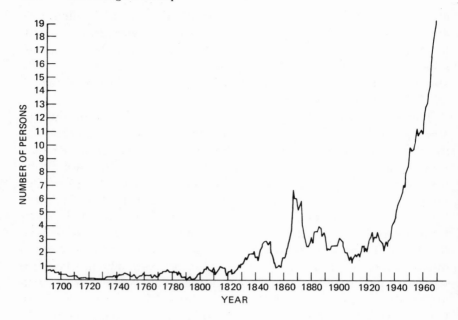

Figure 5.4. Permanent migration from Törbel (1690–1970). The lines represent nine-year moving averages.

eventually involved. The emigration was organized by a firm of Swiss agents from Basel who received land in Argentina and obtained exclusive permission from the Swiss Department of Interior to recruit in Valais. They arranged the sea voyage and land grants in colonial settlements such as Esperanza and San Geronimo (Joris 1979:126). Although Valais had less intensive out-migration than the cantons of Ticino, Schaffhausen, and Glarus, an 1878 newspaper claimed that 5,998 persons had already contracted the emigration fever (*Auswanderungsfieber*) and departed (Joris 1979:120). In 1 year, 0.46 percent of the Valaisan population left, and most of those migrating were from mountain communities (Wiegandt 1977*a*).

Individuals in Törbel remember the names of granduncles and cousins who went to Argentina, and cantonal lists show that there were a few people from almost every one of the village surname groups. Some married other settlers from upper Valais and continued to live in German-speaking farming or ranching communities. Some found America not to their liking and returned to Törbel. There remain stories of success such as that of one man visiting his boyhood home who remarked that the village was proud of its 400 cattle on the alp but that he himself **owned** more animals than their entire herd. There are also grimmer tales of a well-to-do Törbel peasant who was blackmailed by covetous fellow villagers into selling his property cheaply and leaving for "the streets paved with gold." The sons of this man walked unwillingly out of the village threatening to come back and have vengeance on those who had cheated their father. Beside their names in the parish records is written simply *Verschwunden* (disappeared).

Törbjers agree that it was not the poorest people who migrated. Indeed, without sufficient property to cover the costs of the trip and a character judged responsible by the agents, no one could make the long overseas journey. Bell (1979:342) noted that among nineteenth-century Italian peasants it was the threat of lowered living standards rather than absolute poverty that induced emigration. The priest of Visperterminen across the valley from Törbel noted in 1888 that 174 people had already left his parish and that although many were poor, they had taken with them all of 80,000 francs in 1 year (Studer, cited by Heinzmann n.d.:16). Those who remained in the village went into debt to buy the suddenly available land. The exodus from Törbel came toward the end of almost 100 years of population growth, and it is apparent that competition for land and attempts to secure a larger cash income were increasing. The safety valve of mercenary service had also been recently closed. Although some contemporary observers accused the migrants of lack of patriotism or lack of religious convictions or dismissed them simply as lazy people (Joris 1979:120), others recognized that their discontent arose from limited future prospects and the chance of gaining fruitful farmlands and a prosperity not to be hoped for in the homeland (Franscini 1848:549).

There are indications that the growing pressure of population on a limited land base was generating conflict within the community. There were few alternate sources of income, and the Industrial Revolution had not yet been felt in Valais. In 1866 there were only nine factories employing 179 people in the entire canton (Wiegandt 1977a:128). Although emigration took the young and strong from the labor force, the parish priest of Visperterminen saw advantages for public tranquility in the emigration: "For about the last twenty years there has been a lot of quarreling and fighting in our community, especially among the young people. Thank God, however, that this has all ceased in our days, because this scrapping rabble has all left our village and gone to America where their lust for fighting has surely vanished" (Studer, cited by Heinzmann n.d.:16). One suspects that those who were worsted in the endemic Törbel political rivalries sometimes emigrated. A young man who made the mistake of getting his deaf-and-dumb cousin with child was also forced to depart for Argentina.

The American migration was only one short incident in the growing movement out of Törbel. Both before 1850 and after 1880 there were numbers of young people who took jobs as servants or laborers in surrounding towns, and some of them never returned. In 1837, eight young women were maids in Visp, Stalden, Zeneggen, and Bürchen, and six men and boys worked as hired hands in the same region. A clerk lived in Sion and a smith in Visperterminen. Seven men were servants in Domodossola and elsewhere in Italy. A total of 47 men, women, and children were listed in the 1846 census as resident outside of Törbel. Those who acquired education or learned a craft seldom came back to the village, and women were quite likely to marry in the communities where they worked. If a young man was bright and his parents could support his studies in the *Collegium* at Brig, he might become a priest and serve in parishes or schools in the canton. By 1920 there were 28 Törbel natives who had been priests (Stebler 1922:28). With the opening of Zermatt, Saas Fee, and other Vispertal communities to tourism in the latter part of the nineteenth century, some Törbjers found work as mule drivers, hotel porters, carpenters, cooks, and chambermaids. These positions sometimes led to permanent relocation, but more often they were seasonal, with the employee continuing to live in the home village. A civil register giving deaths of Törbel citizens away from the village shows a steady climb from an average 1.75 per year in 1876–9 to 4.6 per year in 1900–4. Thereafter, until 1925, the average fluctuated between 3.4 and 4.2. All but a few died in Valais, indicating the short-range nature of migration.

Although the total population of Törbel rose steadily from the time of World War I, there was no corresponding increase in out-migration. Indeed, there is reason to think that the economic recession followed by depression that characterized the 1920s and 1930s had the effect of keeping the alpine villagers at home. There were no permanent jobs for them elsewhere in Switzerland, and the peasant homestead at least guaranteed subsistence.[11] As one man said, who had graduated from teacher training school and could not find employment, "For two years I foddered the cows with my diploma." High wartime prices for farm products had fallen sharply during the Depression, and Törbjers who had bought local land before the economic crash were saddled with heavy mortgages and the threat of bankruptcy. Only by staying on the farm, eating what they produced, and saving every penny was it possible to survive the *Krisenjahre* (crisis years). Even the men who found work as miners and tunnel builders kept their families in the village and maintained agriculture as a necessary hedge.

Migration became the dominant factor governing local population only in the 1950s and 1960s, when it soared (Figure 5.4) and began to markedly reduce the number of residents (Figure 5.1).[12] Although alpine

Table 5.3. *Occupations of Törbel migrants in 1970*

Occupation	Male	Female	Total	Spouses
Hotel and restaurant (cook, waitress, chamber-maid, porter, coachman, ski teacher, mountain guide)	24	25	49	3
Artisan (carpenter, mason, roofer, butcher, baker, mechanic, plumber, printer, seamstress, hairdresser)	25	3	28	33
Clerical and administrative (police, post office, bank, telephone, teacher, nurse, forester)	18	9	27	11
Factory labor (shift work, foreman)	17	8	25	12
Transport (truck driver, railroad worker, bus driver)	20	1	21	11
Labor (road maintenance, construction, aerial tramway, charwoman)	13	3	16	2
Managerial (restaurant, hotel, garage, dry cleaner, butcher shop)	7	7	14	—
Sales (salesman, shop assistant, kiosk attendant)	7	4	11	4
Religious (priest, nun)	5	3	8	—
Technical (engineer, architect)	4	—	4	5
Farming	3	—	3	6
None listed	22	58	80	—

farming had not necessarily declined in profitability, it could not compete with the opportunities for permanent wage labor in the rapidly expanding Swiss economy. At the same time, secondary education and vocational education were becoming generally available to the young. A high school in Stalden allowed all Törbel youngsters to go beyond the sixth grade, which was the highest grade provided in the village, and boys found it easy to become apprentice cooks, electricians, mechanics, and laboratory technicians. Factories in Visp, Saint Niklaus, and Stalden hired workers, the resorts expanded to handle winter skiers as well as summer visitors, and national railroad, bus, and postal services grew. Once the acquisition and consolidation of agricultural land ceased to be an overriding concern, the young men and women of Törbel began to marry outsiders with much greater frequency. Neither husbands nor wives who had not grown up in the community showed any desire for life in the old houses lacking modern conveniences, and they had no incentive to take up the tasks of peasant farming. Few new couples settled in Törbel after marriage.

The occupations of Törbel migrants and their spouses show a concentration on skilled labor and crafts, with few requiring higher education or professional training. Local consultants gave me lists of the jobs and

Table 5.4. *Törbel migrant destinations*

Permanent residence	Male	Female	Both
Zermatt	27	14	41
Stalden	12	13	25
Grächen	6	5	11
Saas	6	3	9
Embd	0	6	6
Saint Niklaus	0	4	4
Zeneggen	2	0	2
Vispertal total	53	45	98
Brig	22	21	43
Visp	19	15	34
Other Oberwallis villages	7	26	33
Upper Rhone valley total	101	107	208
Zürich	7	16	23
Basel	8	10	18
Bern	4	2	6
Towns and cities in German- speaking Switzerland	22	21	43
German-speaking Swiss total	142	156	298
Lower Valais	13	18	31
French-speaking Switzerland	10	11	21
Italian-speaking Switzerland	1	1	2
Swiss national total	166	186	352
Other European countries	1	0	1
Outside Europe	2	0	2
Away (residence unknown)	6	4	10
Total migrants	175	190	365

current places of residence for 286 of their absent children and/or siblings (Table 5.3). Occupations were also mentioned for 87 spouses, usually the husbands of local women. Women migrants for whom no occupation was listed were usually housewives, and the men they married tended to be artisans, factory workers, transport personnel, or clerical employees. These same job categories were strongly represented among Törbel migrant men.[13] Whereas the generation of Törbel men over age 45 who stayed on in the village tended to be unskilled worker-peasants or retirees from tunnel building, construction, and hotel-related jobs, their sons, with few exceptions, have learned trades and gone through formal apprenticeship programs. Only a handful of carpenters, electricians, and masons can work within the village, and a few more can find jobs in factories near enough for daily commuting. The rest have moved away and generally married out of the community.

Despite the current large numbers of adult out-migrants, sizable numbers have remained in Oberwallis (German-speaking upper Valais), within a few hours' travel of Törbel. Table 5.4 shows that 27 percent are resident in Vispertal and 57 percent in the upper Rhone valley system. The largest numbers have gone to tourist areas such as Zermatt, Saas, and Grächen or to commercial and industrial centers like Brig and Visp. Few have moved to Törbel's nearest neighbors Embd and Zeneggen. Elsewhere in Switzerland there is no real concentration of Törbjers, although all the major cities have some representation.[14] The preference for German-language regions (82 percent) over French regions (14 percent) is clear. A great many foreign workers have come to Switzerland from Spain, Italy, and elsewhere to work as laborers and unskilled employees. Törbel people who earlier took such positions now have steadier positions as skilled blue-collar and semiprofessional workers, and opportunities have been so good that very few have left their country. Specialized training is readily available, but university and professional education is limited, with only a few local young people going into occupations such as architecture, law, and the church. Many migrants remain in close contact with their homes, visiting relatives and frequently telephoning. Several have built or refurbished houses as vacation chalets, and some may eventually retire to Törbel. Given the occupational specializations of the younger generation, the continued economic prosperity of Switzerland, and the mobility characteristic of modern urban life, it is doubtful that out-migration will diminish or that village population will increase substantially in the near future.

Modern migration does not appear to forecast either collapse of the community, as in depopulated alpine lands of the French Dauphiné (Burns 1961), or the rural exodus noted among relatively prosperous Basque farmers (Greenwood 1976). Neither does it appear that the village will expand rapidly like Saas-Fee or Grächen with business activity and new residents attracted by tourism. Although apartments in the old log houses of Törbel continue to be deserted, new chalets are going up on the village outskirts, and these have electrical appliances, plumbing, and comforts similar to those found in Swiss cities. Full-time peasant agriculture has indeed shrunk drastically in postwar Törbel, but it has been replaced by the economically attractive combination of wage-work commuting and part-time farming, with women and children contributing to the enterprise. Access to building sites on inherited land makes it possible for younger people to acquire housing perhaps more readily in the village than in valley towns. Good bus service, telephones, a tower for improving local TV reception, a new school, and increasing car ownership all have reduced the isolation that formerly characterized the community and have opened it to communications from the wider world. The Törbel couples who have decided to remain at home over the last 15 years take pride in their cows and sheep as well as the amenities of their homes, and they participate in the musical groups and thriving voluntary associations in the community. Some are planting vineyards, and others turn out to repair the village chapels. The *Fronleichnam* procession and the *Alplerfest* are attended by crowds of migrant kin as well as by the local population. The people who leave Törbel do not appear to do so because of any high value they place on modern urban life nor because they perceive farming as a demeaning occupation inconsistent with personal dignity (Greenwood 1976:154). On the contrary, they seem to respect the way of life of their fathers, and many willingly devote their vacations to work on the meadows. Change has come so rapidly and opportunities for earning cash have been so readily available that intergenerational conflict has not been severe, and children have been able to go directly from the alpine homestead to a secure urban or suburban niche with the distinct possibility of returning some day to Törbel if they wish. Both the Swiss attachment to a romantic ideal of mountain peasantry and a Germanic sense of the inherent value of working the soil in an environment of rural *Gemeinschaft* (Cole and Wolf 1974) may be effective in maintaining the attachment of these migrants to their home villages. Although the economic independence of the village has been eroded, its social viability gives fair promise to endure.

6

The balance of births and deaths

The fundamental facts of demographic history are births and deaths, and it is an understanding of these variables in their economic and social contexts that should provide the key to the population dynamics of Törbel. Net migration has played a role, adding to the population slightly in the early eighteenth century and draining off what may have been an excess of local residents in the nineteenth century (Table 5.2). But only in the periods of pronounced emigration, 1863–87 and 1938–62, was there an average annual change of more than three people per year in either direction. Migration appears to have been a response to underlying trends in the tabulated population rather than a cause. For instance, when village numbers were stable or slightly declining in the first half of the 1700s, the inflow of women did not lead to an increase in the total. The long rise in population after 1774 was not fueled by immigration. Indeed, the tide of out-migrants ran counter to this growth and temporarily reversed it after 1868. Migration operated as a brake on the expansion of village population, but it seems not to have become a dominant factor until after World War II.

The changing relationship between births and deaths accords closely with the cycles of growth and stability that appear in our reconstructed population (Figure 5.1). The records of those entering and leaving the local population at birth and death have been handled in two ways. Table 6.1 gives aggregate totals of births and deaths from the parish records for 10-year periods along with the apparent positive or negative effects on the population and the ratio of births to deaths. Figures 6.1, 6.2, and 6.3, based on tabulated births and deaths (those for individuals whose other vital statistics allow them to be kept in observation for a computable time period), show 9-year moving averages of the annual numbers. Both procedures yield similar pictures. After death records begin in 1687, there are four periods in which deaths exceed births (Table 6.1), and until 1764, even in periods of net natural growth, the ratio of births to deaths is only a few tenths of a point above unity. The moving averages (Figure

Table 6.1. *Population increase (births − deaths) (recorded figures from parish register)*

Period	Births	Deaths	Population increase (N)	Ratio B/D
1687–94	65	109	−44	0.60[a]
1695–1704	87	73	+14	1.19
1705–14	105	109	− 4	0.96
1715–24	100	82	+18	1.22
1725–34	95	100	− 5	0.95
1735–44	98	90	+ 8	1.09
1745–54	107	84	+23	1.27
1755–64	90	76	+14	1.18
1765–74	72	52	+20	1.38
1775–84	109	53	+56	2.06
1785–94	110	42	+68	2.62
1795–1804	87	92	− 5	0.94[b]
1805–14	139	78	+61	1.78
1815–24	148	85	+63	1.74
1825–34	131	121	+10	1.08
1835–44	144	97	+47	1.48
1845–54	182	115	+67	1.58
1855–64	180	131	+49	1.37
1865–74	159	113	+46	1.41
1875–84	221	103	+118	2.15
1885–94	194	138	+56	1.41
1895–1904	156	121	+35	1.29
1905–14	172	123	+49	1.40
1915–24	194	140	+54	1.39
1925–34	210	118	+92	1.78
1935–44	161	88	+73	1.83
1945–54	191	91	+100	2.10
1955–64	163	89	+74	1.83
1965–73	76	69	+ 7	1.10

[a]Deaths exceed births in 6 of 8 years.
[b]Deaths exceed births in 4 of 10 years.

6.1) show births and deaths following parallel and often almost identical courses until 1765. Under consistent conditions in which almost as many people die as are born, it is self-evident that population growth must be absent or very small. If, in fact, some deaths were not recorded, there could have been minor declines in the total of villagers during this time, especially in the late seventeenth century, before our reconstructed population begins.

The era of fluctuating and generally stagnant village population ended abruptly in the two decades after 1775, when the numbers of births were 2 to 2.5 times the numbers of deaths (Table 6.1). Births increased

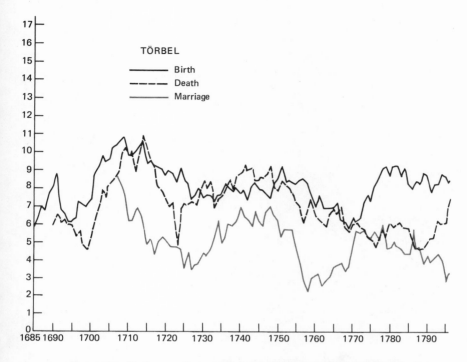

Figure 6.1. Births, marriages, and deaths in Törbel (1685–1800). The lines represent nine-year moving averages.

somewhat over those for the preceding periods, and deaths declined precipitously. The widening gap between birth and death indicators (Figure 6.1) may have been exaggerated by underreporting of infant deaths, as will be discussed later, but the surplus probably set in motion the population growth that continued with minor interruptions until the 1860s.[1] A slower but still appreciable natural increase continued into the nineteenth century, with an average birth/death ratio of almost 1.5. Only the decades of 1795–1804 and 1825–34 showed a small net loss or a minimal gain (Table 6.1). There was another brief peak in births from 1875 to 1884, and a strong net natural growth in the modern 1905–64 period produced an average birth/death ratio of 1.68.

Although we have emphasized the contrast of stability and expansion in the Törbel population, even the most vigorous local growth was well below the rates noted in developing countries today. Using estimates and interpolations where official census figures are not available, Table 6.2 shows growth exceeding 1 percent per year only in the 1800–25 period and a decline of more than 1 percent only in the recent 1950–74 period. Table 6.3 indicates that long-term periods of growth showed annual rates of 0.8 to 0.9 percent interspersed with relatively stable stretches of 0.06

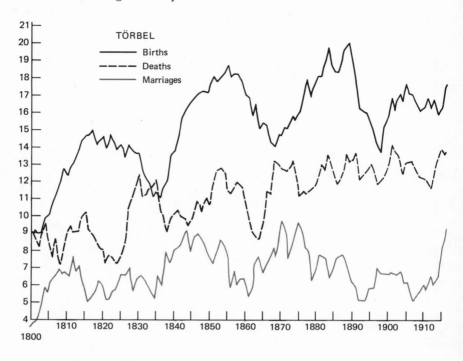

Figure 6.2. Births, marriages, and deaths in Törbel (1800–1920). The lines represent nine-year moving averages.

percent to −0.03 percent. The narrow range of fluctuations in growth and the long periods of remarkable stability suggest the operation of finely tuned homeostatic mechanisms in the local ecosystem.

MORTALITY

Attempts to explain both the rapid growth that has recently characterized Third-World countries or developing countries and the historically declining rates of increase in Western countries have used the theory of the demographic transition.[2] The theory predicts that a decline from traditionally high levels of mortality precedes the corresponding fall in fertility, and it is the excess of births over deaths during the transitional period that rapidly inflates population. Mortality responds rapidly to improved medical and public health practices, whereas births continue at the high rate formerly necessary to make up for large numbers of infant and child deaths. Only when modern birth control is adopted does the spiral of growth moderate. At first glance, the dynamics of population in Törbel appear to reflect substantial though somewhat slow growth in the number of villagers, accompanied by a gradual decrease in mortality and

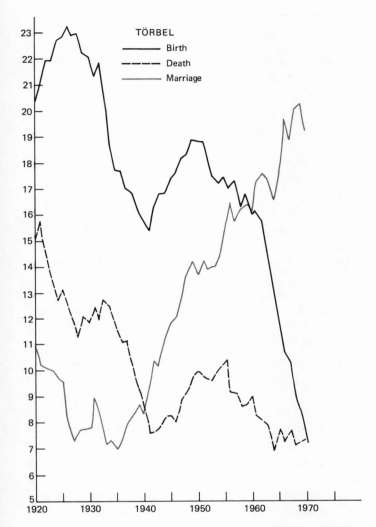

Figure 6.3. Births, marriages, and deaths in Törbel (1920–70). The lines represent nine-year moving averages.

an increase in fertility from rather low levels to medium levels. A closer examination of mortality may suggest the relative effect of this variable and some reasons why it does not seem to function as the single prime mover in demographic change.

Mortality in preindustrial Europe was usually linked to periodic crises (either epidemics of contagious diseases or years of poor crops and resulting famine) that caused massive loss of life (Meuvret 1965). Such dangers, often exacerbated by warfare, could virtually wipe out the inhabitants of small regions or ravage large parts of the Continent, as in

Table 6.2. *Annual growth rates of Törbel population*

Period	Initial population[a]	Final population	Annual rate of growth (%)[b]
1700–25	241	294	0.80
1725–50	294	279	−0.21
1750–75	279	292	0.18
1775–1800	292	350	0.73
1800–25	350	450	1.01
1825–50	450	508	0.49
1850–75	508	546	0.30
1875–1900	546	571	0.18
1900–25	571	610	0.26
1925–50	610	693	0.51
1950–74	754	583	−1.07

[a]Population totals were estimated from tabulated totals (1700, 1725, 1750, 1775), taken from official censuses (1800, 1850, 1900), or interpolated using nearest preceding and following censuses (1825, 1875, 1925, 1974).
[b]Annual rate of growth was calculated using the formula of Barclay (1958:207).

$$G = P_2/P_1 \quad \log G = n \log (1 + r)$$

where P_1 is population at year 1, P_2 is population at year 2, n is number of years between censuses, and r is annual rate of growth.

the outbreak of the Black Death in the fourteenth century. Törbel was not immune to such visitations, and one disastrous bout of plague (*die grosse Pest und Sterben*) is remembered in a grim local folktale. The disease probably struck in 1533, some few years after the populous village had drawn up its statutes regarding rights to use of the common lands and purchased the Oberaaralp. The plague was so severe that the cantonal congress (*Landrat*) suspended meetings until it abated. The Törbel legend has it that only eight people, enough to sit at a single round table, survived in the village. A mysterious foreigner named Caspar Dilger, perhaps a German deserter from the English army, was responsible for transporting the corpses from Törbel to Stalden for burial (Stebler 1922:33). He appropriated a great stack of linen shrouds, and the experience of hauling away all of the bodies so brutalized the man that he took up a life of murder and robbery in a solitary house on the path to Zeneggen. His victims were merely added to the daily mule load of corpses. A maid he had taken from a family whose other members he killed finally exposed Dilger. Having promised under duress to tell no man of his evil deeds, she went to church and on the way home told all to a heating stove (*Ofen*) in the house of friends. She also mentioned that Dilger was in the habit of resting his head on her lap for delousing[3] after the midday meal and then going to sleep in the sun. The legend has it that he could be seized and his great strength nullified as long as he was kept

Table 6.3. *Periods of growth and stability in Törbel population*

	Initial population[a]	Final population	Annual rate of growth (%)
Periods of growth			
1775–1867	281	590	0.81
1919–40	613	734	0.86
Periods of stability			
1730–70	275	282	0.06
1867–1919	590	613	0.07
1940–60	734	729	−0.03

[a]Population totals from computer tabulation shown by solid line in Figure 5.1.

from contact with the earth. The scheme to capture Dilger was successful, and he was condemned in court to be hanged. He was also denied his last wish to kiss his maid goodbye, a fortunate decision, because he had planned to bite off her nose (Stebler 1922:34). The folktale captures the horror of plague, its capacity to bring out all that is inhuman and antisocial in men, and the eventual triumph of humble morality, law, and godliness. There is also the trace of xenophobia in the labeling of the outsider as an unrepentant monster.[4]

Death, for all the fear it must have inspired in the Törbel of the past, was met with solemn religious ceremony and the customary display of community solidarity. The dead were laid out in the main room *(Stube)* of the family home, with candles and flowers at their heads. Unmarried women and children were clothed in white and covered with lace sheets. An infant who died was known as an angel child and was thought to go directly into heaven because the soul was without sin.[5] Rosaries, necklaces, fine knitted caps, and embroidered garments decked the body (Chappaz 1979:129). An infant's funeral in the church is attended by siblings, parents, the brothers and sisters of the parents, and the grandparents. During the two nights that a body lies in state, village members attend a wake at which the rosary is repeated in alternate chorus by men and women. A new group takes up the task about every 2 hours. For an older child or an adult, at least one member of every family is expected to take a turn in the praying. On the day of burial, a procession accompanies the coffin *(Sarg)* through the village streets to the cemetery. A black flag, crucifix, a group of older praying women *(die betende Schar)*, schoolchildren, and the flags and members of any organizations to which the deceased belonged precede the priest with altar boys and a bearer of holy water. The pallbearers are cousins, and they are followed by boys with wreaths, the mourning family and near relatives, and other villagers. The procession for the funeral of an adult man that I witnessed had 270 to 290 participants. While the coffin rests in the village square, individuals come forward to sprinkle it with holy water. The grave, dug always by unrelated next-door neighbors, is filled in after a short service. Traditionally the kin of the dead were invited to a repast (*Vergrebt*) of wine, bread, and cheese in the *Gemeindehaus* after the interment. Even distant relatives must be specifically invited.[6] The wake, the procession and burial, and the *Vergrebt* bring together a wide range of kin and involve every household in the village. The sacred ceremonies of mourning effectively cancel out the personal rivalries and political schisms that color so much of village social interaction, and they emphasize the abiding unity of communal life, the shared suffering, and the virtues of cooperation.

We have no reliable way of knowing the complex of beliefs that surrounded death in the local peasant society of earlier centuries and no way of knowing the ritual observances that accompanied burial. It can be presumed that since the establishment of an independent parish with a church and resident priest in Törbel about 1650, the formal ceremonies of the Roman Catholic church have undergone few major alterations, and there is no reason to think the village or kin-group participation in funerals was markedly different. We can, however, make some effort to quantify the occurrence of death as contained in the written records and to analyze changes in mortality rates and perhaps even causes of death through time.

The simplest approach to mortality in the context of a single peasant agricultural community is to account for any abnormally high number of deaths in any given year by matching the time with known environmental fluctuations such as harvest failures or epidemics. Crisis mortality, defined as a death toll of more than double the annual average (Lee 1977), affected Törbel in 1690, 1693, 1704, 1718, 1728, 1763, 1803, 1831, 1881, and 1918. For several of the years in the late seventeenth and early eighteenth centuries Törbel recorded the deaths of 24 to 26 individuals, totals not surpassed until 1831 and 1918, each with 28 burials. No single year comes close to the seventeenth-century mortality in some French communities, which was more than seven times normal (Meuvret 1965:513), or the carefully documented onslaught of disease in Colyton, Devonshire, in 1648, when 20 percent of the local population was carried off (Wrigley 1966a). After its devastating encounter with plague in the sixteenth century, Törbel seems not to have been revisited, and there are no signs of the 1720 outbreak that killed one-fourth to one-third of the people in some European urban centers

(Langer 1972).[7] The heavy mortality of the 1690s (perhaps 2.5 times normal in the worst years) may well have been connected with bad harvests: "Cold seasons were particularly severe on the cereals of the high Alpine valleys, where even in a normal year they had difficulty in surviving the rigors of the mountain climate. The Alps had cold, and often wet and dull, spring summers in 1687, 88, 89, 90, and 92" (Le Roy Ladurie 1971:68). In 1693–4 many parts of France had death rates 2.7 to 4.3 times higher than the preceding year, and the similarly inflated grain prices make clear that it was a time of severe dearth (Meuvret 1965:517). It is also possible that Törbel's mercenaries, nine of whom died in 1690, may have brought diseases home with them from foreign battlefields. The 1690s were unhealthy years in England as well (Clarkson 1975:13).

The climate continued to be unfavorable for agriculture through the first half of the eighteenth century, with deaths exceeding births in Törbel in 18 of 50 years. The 1720s and 1730s showed the same phenomenon in England (Clarkson 1975:14), with the winters of 1708–9 and 1740 being particularly long and harsh. The so-called Maunder minimum of severely depressed solar (sunspot) activity of the sixteenth through early nineteenth centuries correlated with a period of unusual cold in Europe, making for winters that were most severe around 1675. The climate had not fully returned to normal until after 1750 (Eddy 1977). There were glacial advances in the Alps, Norway, and Iceland in the periods 1698–1707, 1715–22, 1742–52, and 1770–9 (Manley 1966). Such forward movements of the great alpine ice sheets in the Vispertal and surrounding alpine valleys follow cold springs and cool summers, reflecting the accumulated summer temperature with about a 9-year lag (Manley 1966:36). The Bies glacier above Randa near Zermatt advanced in 1726, 1736, and 1786, and the repeated flooding of the Mattmarksee in the Saas valley marked the period 1740–50 as a time of glacial advance (Le Roy Ladurie 1971:166, 198). After 1728 in Törbel, years of high mortality became less frequent, in part, perhaps, because of improvements in climate and more secure food supplies that were both locally produced and imported. It appears, however, that not even abnormal weather conditions in an already somewhat marginal environment could disrupt the local ecosystem sufficiently to bring a famine of real crisis proportions.[8]

The major late-eighteenth-century crop failures of 1770–1 caused deaths to peak in alpine villages near Lucerne (Pfister 1975:185) during a period of cool wet summers that affected much of northwestern Europe (Le Roy Ladurie 1971:60). High agricultural prices resulting from bad harvests between 1766 and 1771 have been correlated with volcanic eruptions and the global veils of dust that interfered with solar radiation

(Post 1974). Törbel had a slight surplus of deaths over births in 1761, 1768, and 1769, but there was no sign of unusual mortality.[9] Similarly, between 1815 and 1817, when west-central Europe had temperatures considerably below the mean, and in Switzerland there was enormous loss of livestock along with a 235 percent increase in wholesale grain prices (Post 1974), Törbel had no increases in deaths.

The above-average mortality of 1800, 1801, and especially 1803 may be traced to dislocations arising from the French conquest of Valais rather than to poor weather conditions. Troops led by one of Napoleon's generals defeated the militia of upper Valais in a decisive battle at the Pfynwald in May of 1799. There was further fighting near Visp, in which Austrian forces supported the Swiss, but again the French were victorious (Borter 1965/66). Visperterminen was plundered, with livestock killed, wine barrels smashed, and the chapels robbed of their chalices. Some people were killed in the battles and during looting, and heavy indemnities in cash and farm produce were exacted over the next year (Heinzmann n.d.:117). There was some minor resistance to the French below Zeneggen, and in an engagement at Stalden the inhabitants were driven out and 27 local men lost (Kämpfen 1867:140). Törbel was spared when the priest there recognized the enemy officer as an old school companion and begged him to have mercy on the "poor devils" of the village. However, it is probable that Törbel men died in the battles of the Rhone valley (Carlen 1974) and that food supplies were requisitioned from the community as a whole. The priest of Embd was taken as a rebel by the French and died during imprisonment at Chillon (Heinzmann n.d.). Although there is no direct evidence of conscription, Napoleon certainly required many Swiss laborers in constructing his new pass road over the Simplon (1800–6), and Swiss soldiers are known to have been used in the Russian campaign. In any event, the early years of the century are remembered as a period of cruel and repressive military occupation in upper Valais (Jossen 1973), and increased mortality evidently reversed the growth of the local population at that time.

Political conditions no longer threatened the Vispertal after the departure of Napoleon's troops in 1802 and the disappearance of French influence after 1813. Although there are frequent mentions of bad crops or other natural calamities in the nineteenth century, they are not directly reflected in higher death tolls. The years 1816 and 1817 were so-called *Hungerjahre* (Heinzmann n.d.), and there was a general Swiss famine in 1817 (Brugger 1956), but Törbel had no marked increase in mortality. The same is true of crop failures in 1852, 1867, 1872, and 1895 (Zurbriggen 1960). Although cold damp summers were always a danger, dry springs could cut back the rye harvest, and lack of summer precipitation could lead to a fodder shortage. Törbel and its neighbors Stalden, Staldenried, and Zeneggen were especially subject to drought. Rain was so rare in 1870 and 1885 that several of these communities made a pilgrimage to Saas-Fee to seek divine intercession, and 1893 was similarly dry (Zurbriggen 1960). Contagious cattle disease was present in 1852, 1879, and 1885 (Zurbriggen 1960). An earthquake in 1855 damaged the Törbel church and cut the Augstbord irrigation canal, forcing a decrease in the number of cattle in Zeneggen from 200 to 50 (Gutersohn 1916:58). Although Törbel's population had risen considerably by the middle of the nineteenth century, none of these environmental fluctuations resulted in unusual numbers of deaths.

Disease probably had greater potential for raising mortality in Törbel than temporary bad agricultural years. The last time there was a significant increase in deaths was during the familiar 1918 influenza pandemic. In 1803 there were 19 infant deaths between January and August, 13 of them in May and June alone. There were similar clusterings of children's deaths in April through June in the years 1728, 1830, and 1842. These may have resulted from gastrointestinal disease and dysentery spread by contaminated milk. Similar phenomena occurred during a period of possible food scarcity before the June–July grain harvest. In 1831, 11 infants, children, and adolescents died before the end of July. Spring also saw the deaths of 11 children from 1 to 7 years of age in 1856. One wonders if this reflects the epidemic smallpox known to have struck Visperterminen children in 1820 and 1857 (Heinzmann n.d.:120). People in that village did not submit willingly to inoculation until after the 1857 outbreak, suggesting that even such relatively early improvements in disease control did not become effective in the alpine villages until much of their population growth had already taken place.[10] There are no records to indicate whether or not Törbel suffered from the typhus epidemics that hit Visperterminen in 1850 and 1860 (Heinzmann n.d.:120) and Saas-Fee in 1864 (Zurbriggen 1960), with very high infection rates and substantial numbers of adult deaths. Of the 22 Törbel deaths in 1881, 12 were children, and there is a possibility that they were victims of scarlet fever, which spread through the Saas valley in 1877–8 (Zurbriggen 1960).

It is possible only to infer the kinds of epidemics that may have come to Törbel, and we are also unsure about normal causes of death and morbidity. The civil registry lists causes for 1893–5 and 1913 through part of 1918. The diagnoses were frequently quite general and may often have been determined without any direct medical assistance. There was never a resident physician in Törbel. Prior to completion of the motor road in 1937, a doctor had to be brought by mule from Visp or Stalden.

Of 98 deaths with causes attributed, 17 were due to *Altersschwäche* or *Lebensschwäche* (the weakness of age and life weakness, respectively). It is understandable that respiratory diseases should be prevalent with the temperature extremes and often crowded living quarters of an alpine village. Thirty-four percent of deaths were credited to pneumonia (*Lungenentzündung*), influenza (*Grippe*), and tuberculosis (*Auszehrung*). Pneumonia alone accounted for 18 percent of all deaths, and this agrees with the recollections of contemporary doctors. Although 3 people died of heart disease, 10 perished from edema or dropsy (*Wassersucht*) that may have been associated with coronary problems. Nervous disease, brain fever, and strokes were believed to have been the causes of 7 deaths. Cancer claimed 3 people, and 3 women died in childbirth. Various less specific ailments, such as fever, blood poisoning, throat sickness, and stomach pains, were named in 7 cases.

Public health measures that could appreciably affect Törbel's mortality were probably not effective until this century. The draining of swampy areas in the Rhone valley and the river canalization to reduce flooding were carried out in the 1870s (Zurbriggen 1960). The malaria that had previously threatened lowland populations had presumably never been a danger in the alpine villages. Sanitariums for tuberculosis patients were being built in Valais after the turn of the century, but there is no reason to think that the incidence of the disease declined until the introduction of new antibiotic drugs after 1940. A few Törbel families installed private water systems and septic tanks in the 1950s, but village-wide piped water and sewers were not available until 1974. People had traditionally relied on a number of fountains and troughs scattered through the community that provided water for drinking and for washing clothes, as well as for the animals. Outhouses were periodically emptied and the night soil used in manuring the meadows. There had always been midwives who assisted in childbirth, but the first trained resident midwife took up her duties in 1916 and delivered 8 to 12 babies annually for many years. Only since World War II has it become customary to go to a hospital for childbirth.

There seem to have been few endemic health problems peculiar to alpine regions. Some doctors have speculated that goiter and its related mental retardation and deaf-mutism may have increased the mortality. After iodized salt was made compulsory, in some mountain cantons by 1922, deferments from Swiss military service for reason of goiter fell rapidly (Schaub 1949:34).[11] Goiter of the newborn decreased almost immediately, and cretinism was expected to become less frequent 20 years after the treatment of salt began. Any resulting changes in mortality came too recently to be associated with the earlier rise in Törbel population.

Table 6.4. *Crude death rate estimates*

Year	Tabulated population[a]	Tabulated deaths in 25 years[b]	CDR I[c]	Census (or estimated) population[d]	Recorded deaths in 25 years[e]	CDR II[f]	Recorded deaths plus uncomputable births[g]	CDR III[h]
1700	219	179	33	(241)	255	42	305	51
1725	281	192	27	(294)	215	29	255	35
1750	266	200	30	(279)	194	28	255	37
1775	279	150	22	(292)	138	19	190	26
1800	340	188	22	350	185	21	219	25
1825	433	240	22	(450)	249	22	282	25
1850	481	277	23	508	304	24	338	27
1875	540	296	22	(546)	291	21	323	24
1900	580	322	22	571	312	22	327	23
1925	644	327	20	(610)	319	21	322	21
1950	746	218	12	693	219	13	221	13

[a]The tabulated population is created by incrementing annually the number of births and in-migrants to the population and subtracting the number of deaths and out-migrants. It does not include uncomputable cases for which there is a recorded death date but no birth date.
[b]Deaths are tabulated for the listed year, for the 12 preceding years, and for 12 following years, and then summed to give a 25-year total. Thus the 179 deaths given in the 1700 row refer to all deaths tabulated in the period 1688–1712 inclusive.
[c]Crude death rate I (CDR I) is obtained by dividing average number of tabulated deaths per year by the tabulated population and multiplying by 1,000. The crude death rate per 1,000 is rounded off to the nearest whole number.
[d]Total population is estimated in the eighteenth century by increasing tabulated population to take account of untabulated deaths (deaths of individuals lacking birth or marriage dates) during each 25-year period. In the nineteenth century, estimates are interpolated between known census figures.
[e]Recorded deaths are all those mentioned in the parish burial register or civil register. This does not include certain deaths away from the village, for which approximate dates of death have been tabulated.
[f]CDR II is based on the recorded deaths and the census or estimated population. It differs substantially from CDR I only in 1700, when the number of recorded but untabulated deaths was highest.
[g]Uncomputable births are those for which no further vital statistics occur in the records. Treating all these as early deaths gives a maximum mortality estimate.
[h]CDR III is based on recorded deaths plus uncomputable births regarded as deaths and on the census or estimated population.

The nature of the evidence for deaths in Törbel means that we cannot be sure of causes, and we can only suggest through the dating of unusually high numbers of burials that harvest failures were still a threat to health in the late seventeenth and early eighteenth centuries and that epidemic disease was a greater killer in later periods. This appears plausible in the light of general European trends. Törbel's peasant self-sufficiency and geographical isolation may also have protected it

Table 6.5. *Comparative crude death rates*

	1700	1750	1800	1850
Törbel I	33	30	22	23
(Average of I, II, III)	42	32	23	25
Speicher (Appenzell)[a]	30	38	36	27
Gais (Appenzell)	—	38	34	23
Muotathal (Schwyz)	—	21	31	29
Engelberg (Unterwalden)	22	29	26	23
Entlebuch (Luzern)	—	23	25	—
Lumbrein (Graubünden)	29	31	29	26
Conthey (Valais)	—	—	28	19
Luzern (city)	30	31	42	27

[a]All comparative rates from Ruesch (1979:168).

from the more severe crises that afflicted other rural groups in parts of France and England.

In order to gain a more detailed understanding of historical changes in local mortality, we must construct rates for the village population as a whole and for age and sex groups within it. A first approximation is the estimate of crude death rates. Twenty-five-year calculations have been made using computer-tabulated base populations and deaths (crude death rate I or CDR I), the combination of estimated populations and recorded deaths (CDR II), and the pessimistic assumption (CDR III) that all uncomputable births were of infants who died (Table 6.4). They differ markedly only in 1700, when many of the deaths in the parish registry were those of individuals lacking birth dates and therefore not included in our tabulated totals. Yet regardless of whether CDR I, II, or III is more accurate (and they never differ by more than 4/1,000 after 1775), they all indicate a similar pattern.

There appears to be a contrast between the high rates for periods through 1750 and the lower but relatively stable rates from 1775 through 1850. Using a 25-year average of recorded deaths and the midyear (1700) total population, the period from 1688 to 1712 appears to have had an incidence of death above 40 per 1,000, whereas that for 1700 to 1750 averaged 33.5 per 1,000 (Table 6.4, CDR II) or, if all uncomputable births are assumed to be early deaths, 40.6 per 1,000 (Table 6.4, CDR III). The following long period from 1775 to 1925 had either quite stable rates averaging 21.9 (CDR II) or gradually declining rates from 26 to 21 (CDR III). Only in the most recent quarter century has mortality decisively dropped to 13 per 1,000 (Table 6.4). The general profile of the Törbel death rate is that of stairsteps, descending from fairly high levels with frequent bad years in the early eighteenth century to moderate levels

Table 6.6. *Male age-specific mortality rates for 50-year periods (1650–1949)*[a]

Age	1650–99	1700–49	1750–99	1800–49	1850–99	1900–49
0	58	99	54	108	163	186
	(178)[b]	(193)	(162)	(174)		
1–4	92	91	69	67	70	53
5–9	57	57	55	48	59	51
10–14	36	38	32	30	31	11
15–19	50	27	34	5	14	11
20–24	26	33	21	37	47	39
25–29	27	58	28	71	10	23
30–34	14	62	36	58	35	47
35–39	42	57	68	37	21	25
40–44	103	90	65	45	42	44
45–49	66	99	87	61	44	46
50–54	88	171	133	72	74	c
55–59	135	132	154	116	74	
60–64	267	153	156	70	107	
65–69	242	300	246	179	179	
70–74	480	143	408	287	255	
75–79	538	400	517	468	341	
80–84	500	611	500	455	426	
85+	1,000	1,000	1,000	1,000	1,000	

[a]For tables on which these rates per 1,000 are based, see the Appendix, Tables A.2–A.7.
[b]Estimated infant mortality is given in parentheses. The derivation of this rate and a methodological discussion are given in the Appendix.
[c]The rates for 1900–49 are left incomplete because many of the people born in this period are still alive, and their mortality cannot be predicted.

for the following 175 years and then to a markedly lower rate, probably reflecting the advent of modern medicine, from the late 1930s.[12]

Comparison with crude mortality data for other Swiss mountain villages (Table 6.5) shows Törbel somewhat above average in 1700, midway in the 1750 distribution, and slightly below average in 1800 and 1850. Törbel's death rate is somewhat below that for the French-speaking Valais town of Conthey and considerably under that for the city of Luzern. Estimates for English death rates by 1800 are in the high 20s per 1,000 (Clarkson 1975:172); then they settle at an average 22 after 1838, until beginning to fall once more in the 1870s (Flinn 1970:40). Although the decline in mortality in Törbel seems to respond to peculiarly local circumstances, it falls within the general range for other European cases and follows a broadly similar course.

Crude death rates tell us little about the changing risks for different age groups in the population or the possible contrasts for males and females. In fact, the overall trends obscure the real and inevitably complex processes of mortality through time in a single village ecosystem. Even when there has been reasonably consistent recording of deaths and when family reconstitution allows the calculation of age at death, a small population like Törbel's may well show somewhat random fluctuations in, for instance, the proportions of men 25 through 29 years of age who die during successive 50-year periods. The finer detail of age-specific mortality tables by sex (Table 6.6) shows some general improvement in health but a great many minor oscillations. There is a decline from 1700–49 to 1750–99 in deaths during the first year of life, but these rates bounce back and even increase up to this century. This may be due in part to possible underreporting of infant deaths before 1800, and it is possible to suggest plausible revisions for some of the earlier figures (see Appendix). Childhood mortality for males went down over time for those 1 to 4 years of age but underwent little change for those 5 to 9 and 10 to 14 years of age. Adult men 40 to 54 years of age had a steady improvement in life chances after 1700. The mortality experience during 1800–49 was better for men 35 to 84 years of age but poorer in the groups 20 to 34 years of age than it had been in the preceding half century. Further declines in death rates occurred among males for most of the age groups between 25 and 59 years in the 1850–99 period. Men born during 1850–99 were, in their adult years of 25 to 59, much healthier than their ancestors had been 150 years earlier. However, there is no indication of continuing improvement in the young adult years for the 1900–49 cohort. Females show, if anything, a somewhat less erratic pattern (Table 6.7), with steadily declining mortality for the age groups 35 to 39, 40 to 44, 45 to 49, and 55 to 59 years. The death rate was lower at every age after 35 in 1700–49 than it had been in 1650–99. In 1750–99, women had a lesser risk of death in seven age categories and a greater risk in five categories when compared with the previous half century. The years 1800–49 showed significant improvement for adults across the board from 15 to 64 years, and further improvement was evident by 1850–99 for females aged 40 to 84 years. The long-term trend as established by 1800–49 was of lower mortality at most stages of the life cycle but a radical improvement over 1650–99 in the childbearing and later adult years.

Although female mortality was clearly greater than that for males in the corresponding age ranges during the seventeenth and eighteenth centuries, the differences after 1800 were not consistent. If we compare only the death rates for married adults, however, women show consistently higher rates between the ages of 20 and 45 years (Figure 6.4). A reasonable inference is that childbirth remained a significantly life-threatening event whose danger went down sharply only in this century. The higher mortality for young adult women as compared with men, plus the possibility that out-migrant women were not equaled by in-marrying

Table 6.7. *Female age-specific mortality rates for 50-year periods (1650–1949)* [a]

Age	1650–99	1700–49	1750–99	1800–49	1850–99	1900–49
0	67	98	47	95	104	106
	(106)[b]	(125)	(114)	(116)		
1–4	83	80	92	73	60	40
5–9	52	100	68	39	47	26
10–14	41	60	14	20	13	32
15–19	43	45	37	31	27	22
20–24	76	57	38	22	23	34
25–29	161	40	56	49	43	6
30–34	58	74	50	40	50	29
35–39	102	91	88	54	57	6
40–44	182	113	87	83	77	24
45–49	111	70	77	69	54	19
50–54	281	106	140	82	70	[c]
55–59	174	169	122	114	54	
60–64	316	163	215	183	101	
65–69	462	220	216	281	112	
70–74	571	219	400	469	234	
75–79	1,000	400	583	412	382	
80–84		667	600	650	361	
85+		1,000	1,000	1,000	1,000	

[a]For tables on which these rates per 1,000 are based, see the Appendix, Tables A.2–A.7.
[b]Estimated infant mortality is given in parentheses. The derivation of this rate and a methodological discussion are given in the Appendix.
[c]The rates for 1900–49 are left incomplete because many of the people born in this period are still alive, and their mortality cannot be predicted.

counterparts, produced a difference in village sex ratios. In our reconstructed population, the number of resident women never equaled that of men until about 1925. In the eighteenth and nineteenth centuries, females composed 43 to 49 percent of village inhabitants, and only since about 1925 have they been numerically dominant. The change in sex ratios coincides neatly with improved access to modern medical assistance during pregnancy and childbirth. During the corresponding period in this century, male mortality may have increased to some degree. With the greater availability of wage work out of the community, men have been exposed to accidents and occupational diseases not encountered in peasant farming. Mining and tunnel building in the 1920s and 1930s before the dust problem was adequately controlled led to silicosis, which has been the cause of disability and premature death for a number of village men. There have also been accidents with heavy construction machinery and vehicles.

A more economical and intuitively acceptable way to look at changing

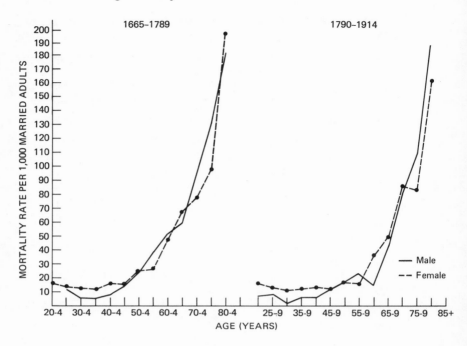

Figure 6.4. Age-specific mortality among married adults in Törbel (1685–1789 and 1790–1914). Tabulation by the Cambridge Group for the History of Population and Social Structure.

mortality is by means of average age at death. Rather than examining the mortality experience of successive birth cohorts, we can simply average the ages of those dying in a particular period. Table 6.8 shows a temporary increase of over 10 years in average age at death for both men and women during 1775–99, then a return to earlier levels of about 42 years for males, whereas females fell to 37 years. Male average age at death advanced slowly, passing 50 years only after 1925 and 60 years after 1950. For females, the average age at death remained in the 40s and low 50s from 1825 to 1949 and reached almost 69 years in the most recent period. A more usual and technically accurate method for dealing with changing mortality is to construct age-specific mortality rates for the village population during various periods, compare these with different model life tables (Coale and Demeny 1966), and arrive at estimates of life expectancy at birth and at various more advanced ages. This is the procedure used by Schofield and Wrigley (1979) for evaluating infant and child mortality in eight English communities. Life expectancy (Table 6.9) is a handy summary statistic for suggesting gross historical changes in Törbel and for comparing this Swiss alpine village with other peasant

Table 6.8. *Average age at death*

25-Year death cohort	Male Average age	Male Number	Female Average age	Female Number	Both sexes Average age	Both sexes Number
1725–49	41.0	81	29.7	71	35.8	152
1750–74	42.9	75	31.8	69	37.6	144
1775–99	51.4	75	42.2	58	48.6	133
1800–24	42.1	100	37.0	82	39.8	182
1825–49	42.3	125	45.3	101	43.7	226
1850–74	45.2	127	42.3	115	43.8	242
1875–99	49.0	148	49.2	147	49.1	295
1900–24	45.5	183	51.5	154	48.2	337
1925–49	55.6	149	45.9	118	51.3	267
1950–74	62.4	165	68.6	115	65.0	280

groups. But the small size of the population and various methodological problems[13] make fitting the local data to model life tables difficult and capable of providing only rough-and-ready approximations. The outlined changes in life expectancy are at least plausible. Males born from 1650 to 1699 had substantially longer lives, on average, than those born from 1700 to 1749. The following century, 1750–1849, saw life expectancy in the upper 40s for men, and it jumped to about 56 years for the 1850–1949 period. Female mortality was very high for the 1650–99 cohort, resulting in unusually low life expectancy. This rose in 1700–49, slipped back in 1750–99, and then rose steadily at a rate of 5 years or more per half century until 1949. The fact that women's life spans increased dramatically among those born after 1900 points again to the declining risks of childbirth, whereas the stable life expectancy for men may reflect the fact that better medical care was counterbalanced by increased occupational hazards.[14] Average life expectancy in Törbel did improve over time, but the rise was irregular and was not consistent for men and women. Viewed against other European populations, Törbel longevity appears to have been within the expected range of variation. Estimates for late-eighteenth-century France give a life expectancy at time of birth of 29 years, whereas for Crulai in Normandy in 1675–1775 it was about 30 years (Wrigley 1969:131). A sample of eight English parishes from 1550 to 1649 yielded life expectancies of 35 to 40 years, "an unusually high level by the general standards of early modern Europe" (Schofield and Wrigley 1979). The estimates for rural departments in late-nineteenth-century France ranged from 41 to 46 years for males and 43 to 50 years for females (Wrigley 1969:175).

Table 6.9. *Life-expectancy estimates*

Period	Model life tables[a]	Life expectancy at birth (range)	Life expectancy at birth (estimate)
Males			
1650–99	West 11–15	42.1–51.8	47.1
1700–49	North 7–12	32.0–44.3	36.9
1750–99	North 11–16	41.8–53.9	49.1
1800–49	North 11–15	41.8–51.5	46.7
1850–99	North 15–18	51.5–58.8	56.3
1900–49	West 15–18	51.8–58.8	56.5
Females			
1650–99	West 1–4[b]	20.0–27.5	22.5
1700–49	West 5–12	30.0–44.5	37.5
1750–99	North 5–10	30.0–42.5	35.0
1800–49	West 6–12	32.5–47.5	40.0
1850–99	West 10–15	42.5–55.0	47.5
1900–49	West 11–22	45.0–72.5	57.5

[a]Values for age-specific mortality rates cluster in the listed model life tables from Coale and Demeny (1966).
[b]High mortality in this period made for a poor fit with any of the available model life tables.

Decreasing mortality resulting in rising life expectancy contributed to Törbel's population growth, especially among men born from 1750 to 1799 and women from the 1800–49 cohort. These cohorts were pruned less rapidly by death during infancy and childhood, and there were also smaller losses in many of the adult age categories. Population crises caused by a bad harvest or disease or a combination of the two became less frequent in the course of the eighteenth century, and the documented years of poor climate and crop failure in the 1800s led to no immediate increases in village mortality. We cannot reconstruct causes of death in earlier centuries, but modern medical and public health practices seem to have had little impact until after 1900. Decreases in the crude death rate and in age-specific mortality after 1750 were presumably too early to reflect advances in the healing arts (McKeown 1976). Thereafter, only gradual declines in mortality are evident until around 1925, when the crude death rate begins falling to essentially modern levels, childbirth becomes obviously less dangerous as testified by the higher proportion and life expectancy of women in the population, and the average age at death turns sharply upward. The presence of a trained local midwife, a road allowing easier access to physicians and hospitals, state programs of vaccination and chest x-rays for schoolchildren, and subsidized national health programs since World War II have all contributed to recent health improvements. It does not seem reasonable, however, to credit Törbel's earlier major population growth commencing before 1800 to the introduction of scientific medical services or improved sanitation. There is also no indication of substantial changes in village isolation or agricultural technology during this period. The effects of declining mortality may have been strengthened by rising fertility, and it may well be that both processes were responding to the same ecological cause.

FERTILITY

Birth in Törbel involved little of the ritual recognition and community attention that regularly accompanied death. It is true that prompt baptism on the day of birth or shortly thereafter was important, but this may often have taken place at the house of the parents. Even today, when an infant is baptized in the church, the ceremony takes place after mass, when the worshipers have left. Only the parents, the godparents, who are often siblings or other close relatives of the parents, and a few other relatives attend. It is said that in the past a birth was announced by ringing the church bell with a single toll for a boy and two tolls for a girl. The priest registered the names of the child, parents, and godparents with a Latin formula in his baptismal book, but there was no further religious occasion in the life of the child until first communion. It is little wonder that with the mortality of 30 percent or more for children there should be a minimum of public involvement.

Törbjers treat the coming of children to a married couple as normal, desirable, even inexorable.[15] They speak of large families as a good thing and say with a trace of regret that few of today's young people will have 8 or 10 children, as was common in the 1920s and 1930s. A woman may speak of hard times when poverty was accompanied by "a child coming every year." But there is never the suggestion that families should be limited, and the solidly conservative Roman Catholics of the village believe contraception to be a sin. Men apologize for having only two children, noting the fact that they married late in life and that a wife in her late thirties could not bear many offspring. When I suggested that having few children and thus avoiding subdivision of the family lands would have been an effective way to preserve wealth in the household, people agreed, but they claimed that no one chose voluntarily to limit their procreation.[16] Just as it was the duty of married people to have children, it was a moral obligation of both men and women to remain chaste before marriage and continent if they were celibate. Illegitimacy was formerly rare in the village, and premarital conceptions, though they occurred with some frequency, were still considered both unfortunate and shameful. The common socially tolerated illegitimacy of parts of the

Austrian Alps (Gerschenkron 1971; Shorter 1978) seems not to have been present in Valais.[17] A favorite diatribe of the clergy was directed against premarital sex, and the virtues of a pure life were extolled at the funeral of an elderly virgin.

A pregnant woman was expected to continue her household chores and her work in the barn and the fields until shortly before she gave birth. The midwife and the mother or a sister of the woman came in to help during labor. The newborn child was cleaned and swaddled in a length of linen cloth so that its body was rigid and its bones would grow straight and strong (Anneler 1917:61).[18] The mother, at least in the earlier part of this century, spent about 10 days in bed to recover her strength and allow her internal organs to come back into place. Herb teas were administered, and a special soup of white bread cooked in butter with onions, water, a little milk, and cheese was prepared for the new mother. While she was confined her husband did the cooking, and the midwife as well as female relatives would come in every day. The infant was kept in a cradle (*Wiege*) and carried about in a basket for the first few months. Swaddling continued until the child was 2 or 3 months old, and it was not unwrapped to nurse. The practice was maintained in Törbel until the 1920s. When the family moved to the *Voralp* or to a hamlet, the mother carried her baby tied to her back with a cloth. Nursing and supplementary feeding practices will be discussed later.

The factors underlying changes in fertility may have been more subject to human control than those connected with mortality in the preindustrial world. It is clear that both the age at marriage and the prevalence of celibacy could affect fertility and that both were important variables in the distinctive north European marriage pattern (Hajnal 1965). Analysis of the Törbel birth records in terms of reconstituted families allows a systematic check on changing fertility and its regulation by essentially social factors. We can ask whether fertility rose to make up for periods of high mortality and fell in some deviation-counteracting fashion with the increasing pressure of local population. A simplified homeostatic model would predict that as the resident farming population went up, land would become scarcer, marriages would be delayed or postponed as young adults waited for an inheritance, families when finally formed would have fewer children, and a larger proportion of adults would stay single permanently.

When crude birth rates are calculated, it appears that fertility indeed rose to counterbalance high mortality and declined during periods of population growth (Table 6.10). Crude birth rate II (CBR II) hovers between 34 and 37 per 1,000 in the periods around 1700, 1725, and 1750, when death rates were high (Table 6.4) and the population was stable or

Table 6.10. *Crude birth rate estimates*

Year	Tabulated population[a]	25-Year average of tabulated births[b]	Crude birth rate I[c]	Census (or estimated) population	25-Year average of recorded births[d]	Crude birth rate II[e]
1700	219	8.24	38	(241)	8.88	37
1725	281	8.48	30	(294)	9.92	34
1750	266	8.08	30	(279)	10.12	36
1775	279	7.52	27	(292)	9.40	32
1800	340	9.69	29	350	10.52	30
1825	433	13.44	31	(450)	13.92	31
1850	481	17.00	35	508	17.52	34
1875	540	16.72	31	(546)	17.84	33
1900	580	16.36	28	571	16.56	29
1925	644	20.04	31	(610)	19.76	32
1950	746	17.12	23	693	17.32	25

[a]The tabulated population is created by incrementing annually the number of births and in-migrants to the population and subtracting the number of deaths and out-migrants. It does not include uncomputable cases for which there is a recorded birth date but no marriage or death date.
[b]The 25-year average of tabulated births is calculated in the same manner as the deaths in Table 6.4.
[c]Crude birth rate I is obtained by dividing the average number of tabulated births per year by the tabulated population and multiplying by 1,000. The crude birth rate per 1,000 is rounded off to the nearest whole number.
[d]Recorded births are all those mentioned in the parish baptismal register or the civil register.
[e]Crude birth rate II is based on the recorded births and the census or estimated population.

shrinking. As mortality went to lower levels in the successive periods from 1775 through 1825, the birth rate dropped to 30 to 32 per 1,000. Although the crude death rate (CDR II) remained in the low 20s for the next 100 years, the birth rate climbed slightly in 1850 and 1875 before coming down, and both birth and death rates touched their lowest levels around 1950. There is a general contrast between birth rates during a time of stagnant population, 1688–1762, which averaged 36, and those during the growth period, 1763–1862, which averaged 32. Even these fluctuations are relatively moderate when compared with those for seventeenth- and eighteenth-century Swiss cities and areas of cottage industry, where crude birth rates ranged between 41 and 48 per 1,000. Contemporary alpine herding communities, on the other hand, displayed similar rates in the middle and low 30s (Ruesch 1979:168). After a plague or period of crisis mortality, the premodern birth rate in Switzerland might climb to 40 or 50 per 1,000, but the average was perhaps below that for other European states, and Malthus commented on the low fertility of the Swiss (Bickel 1947:47).

Table 6.11. *Mean values for birth, survivorship, nuptiality, and celibacy of children per family (1700–1949)*

	1700–49	1750–99	1800–49	1850–99	1900–49
Number of families[a]	147	105	160	160	157
Births per family	3.84	4.69	4.88	5.07	5.66
Standard deviation	3.20	3.57	3.62	3.34	3.75
Uncomputable births[b]	0.76	0.83	0.43	0.27	0.12
Children reaching age 1[c]	2.44	3.49	3.62	3.71	4.75
Children reaching age 20	1.86	2.84	3.09	3.22	4.46
Children reaching age 20 as percentage of births per family	48	61	63	64	79
Gross replacement rate (children marrying per family)	1.45	2.26	2.20	2.16	3.13
Net replacement rate	0.73	1.13	1.10	1.08	1.57
Celibate children	0.41	0.58	0.89	1.07	1.33
Celibates as percentage of children reaching age 20	22	20	29	33	30
Emigrating children[d]	0.06	0.28	0.79	0.92	2.38

[a]Families formed by marriages taking place during the specified 50-year periods and remaining resident in the village so that family reconstitution and reproductive histories are possible.

[b]Births for which no further dates of marriage, death, or presence in the population exist. Such cases appear to have an unpatterned distribution according to family size, birth order, and the presence of documented siblings in the same families. They may represent unreported infant and child deaths in large proportion, but some cases may be children who migrated permanently from the village before marriage. As documentation improved in the nineteenth century, the number of uncomputables declined.

[c]Number of births minus those known to have died in the first year and uncomputables.

[d]Emigrants are those who settled permanently outside of the village. They include both married and celibate offspring. Labor migrants who sought temporary or seasonal work away from Törbel but maintained permanent residence there are not included.

If crude birth rates were going down during the time when Törbel population grew, does that mean that individual families were having fewer children? This is clearly not the case, as Table 6.11 demonstrates. Because few children were born out of wedlock, the increase in marital fertility (births per family) between 1700–49 and 1750–99 indicates that the average wife was bearing substantially more children than she had before. The increase continued at a gradual rate, reaching just over 5 births per family in 1850–99 and jumping again to 5.66 in this century. Parallels to this growth in marital fertility are provided by other Swiss communities (Table 6.12). This does not mean that a long-standing peasant pattern of having few children was undergoing revolutionary change. There may well have been other periods of generally high fertility in the sixteenth and seventeenth centuries, with the rise in the period we have surveyed being merely a return to normal (Flinn

Table 6.12. *Comparative births per marriage*

Community[a]	1650–99	1700–49	1750–99	1800–49
Büron (Luzern)	4.0	—	5.1	6.2
Triengen (Luzern)	—	4.5	5.4	6.3
Speicher (Aarau)	3.7	4.3	4.5	5.2[b]
Appenzell	4.6	4.5	5.6	6.0[b]
Entlebuch (Luzern)[c]	2.7	3.9	4.9	5.9
Törbel (Valais)	—	3.8	4.7	4.9

[a]Data on Swiss communities other than Törbel from Ruesch (1979:174).
[b]1800–29.
[c]The figures for Entlebuch are from the periods 1680–99, 1735–59, 1760–99, and 1800–29, respectively.

1970:30). Wrigley (1966a) showed a general increase in fertility for the Colyton women of 1770–1837 over those of 1720–69, and Hollingsworth's study (1964) of British peers cited a low ebb of fertility in those women born from 1700 to 1724, with fertility for each succeeding generation being higher. Although the Törbel crude birth rate was declining, marital fertility was going up. While fewer families were being formed during 1750–99 and the proportion of celibates was growing, those women who did marry were reproducing at a greater rate than before. This increase, along with falling mortality, contributed to the population growth that became stronger during the first half of the following century.

There are several ways in which childbearing can increase: (1) The age of marriage can go down, allowing women to be exposed to pregnancy during a longer period of their fertile years; (2) a larger proportion of eligible women may marry instead of staying single; (3) the average duration of the marriage spanning the reproductive years can increase because both partners tend to live longer; (4) family limitation methods operating within marriage may be relaxed; (5) births may come closer together, allowing more children to be born in a given length of time. Which of these explanations best fit the Törbel evidence?

Marriage age

The immediate cause cited for the increasing marital fertility among European preindustrial groups has been the younger age of women at marriage. This is grounded in the notion that essentially "natural" fertility was the norm among noncontracepting populations and that the earlier an ovulating woman began intercourse, the greater the probability that her total number of conceptions would increase. Where marriage

Table 6.13. *Average total births by mother's age at marriage*

Age	Births	N
15–19	6.58 ± 4.13	33
20–24	6.47 ± 3.72	171
25–29	5.62 ± 3.20	227
30–34	4.35 ± 2.47	122
35–39	2.48 ± 2.22	65
40–44	1.34 ± 2.64	35
45–49	0.91 ± 2.39	11

was conventionally quite late, as seems to have been the case in much of northwestern Europe[19] from the sixteenth century or earlier (Chaunu 1974), a decrease in the age at marriage would bring greater exposure to pregnancy during the woman's early 20s, when fertility should be at its highest. Using only Törbel data (Table 6.13), it is apparent that a woman's age at marriage was closely related to her average childbearing capacity. The later she entered marriage, the fewer children she was likely to have. Women who began their reproductive careers between 30 and 34 years of age had two fewer children than those who had married 10 years younger. Although teenage brides had the most childbirths, their fertility was not much greater than the fertility of those who married at ages 20–24, perhaps because the sample of very early marriages was small, but also suggested are the possible lingering effects of adolescent sterility. It is noteworthy that even the women with the longest reproductive histories did not approach the average of 10 births per marriage found in modern Hutterite and French Canadian populations (Henry 1961). At the other end of the spectrum, even the few Törbel women who married at age 45 or older seemed still to have had the potential to conceive. From Table 6.13 we can also observe that lowering the age of marriage by 1 year at any point would add 0.25 birth to the average family size, and a 5-year lowering of the marriage age would increase the number of births by 1.25.[20]

A decreasing marriage age has often been a signal that the chances for forming a household suddenly improved because of adult deaths due to epidemic disease (Herlihy 1977) or that there were new economic opportunities that encouraged family formation to fill labor needs. The growth of cottage industry allowed individuals to earn a livelihood with only a small investment in a loom or knitting frame. The scarcity of land and the dependence on inheritance that were the major bars to marriage in peasant society were abruptly removed. As Malthus pointed out, "In many manufactures, children are able to maintain themselves at an early age, and so entail little expense to their parents, to the obvious encourage-

Table 6.14. *Age at first marriage*

50-Year period	Females' average age	Males' average age
1700–49	28.33	30.85
1750–99	27.11	31.33
1800–49	28.48	30.05
1850–99	29.10	33.44
1900–49	28.85	32.55
1950–74	27.13	30.60
Total[a]	28.24	31.49

[a]Based on 734 families for males and 674 families for females.

ment of marriage" (Habakkuk 1971:40). Protoindustrialization involving a putting-out system of textile manufacture in the eighteenth-century Zürich hinterland had just this effect. Contemporary observers railed against the early marriages of poor people and noted the explosive growth of a landless laboring population that followed from these "beggar weddings" (Braun 1978:312–15). In the frame-knitting English village of Shepshed, the men and women at the second quarter of the nineteenth century "were both marrying about five and one-half years earlier than they had before 1700" (Levine 1977:175). This largely accounted for an increase in the average number of children born per family from 4.38 to 6.16 (Levine 1977:74), reflecting both the growing ease of founding an economically independent household as cottage industry became the dominant occupation and the positive financial incentive of acquiring a wife and child for direct assistance in the craft work (Levine 1977:80).

Törbel had neither a plague nor an occupational alternative to peasant farming in these times. There were, in fact, no major fluctuations in the extraordinarily high age at marriage (Table 6.14). It may have been that a small decrease in the female marriage age during 1750–99 followed from the somewhat higher mortality of that period, but alone it would have produced only an increase of 0.29 in the number of children per household instead of the 0.85 (Table 6.11) that actually appeared. Average age at marriage indeed rose 2 years for women in the 1750–1899 period, when population was dramatically increasing. The evidence is persuasive that both marriage age and average number of adult celibates (Table 6.11) went up along with the growth in population. These mechanisms, whose effect was to slow the surge in village numbers, were damping the growth rate rather than fueling it. The factor that imposed this preventive check on reproduction, presumably the need of both partners to inherit adequate agricultural resources to found a family, seemingly did not diminish during the entire period. The obligation to work for the family enterprise and to support aged parents who remained in control of the household persisted in the village value system. Long engagements and a premium on premarital chastity continued to be the rule (see Chapter 8). It was not incumbent on a household head to retire and divide his estate among offspring until he desired to do so, and children marrying before this formal division could not count on access to land (Netting 1976).

Marriage and celibacy

Marriage was the socially defined strait gate that regulated who could reproduce and when. As Goubert (1971) noted, "marriage is the main act of demographic significance that depends on the human will." Continuity of the family line, transmission of property, and the socioeconomic standing of succeeding generations depended on marriage, and decisions concerning alliance furnished a crucial element in the peasant household's strategy of survival (Bourdieu 1976). Not only was marriage in Törbel delayed well beyond physical maturity, but many adults never entered into matrimony at all. Table 6.11 indicates that although both the gross reproduction rate of children born per household and the number of children surviving to adulthood were increasing from 1700 to 1900, the number of those children who themselves married remained constant at about 2.2 from 1750 to 1900. Once the necessity of subsisting solely on local resources lessened and the pressure to find a mate from within the village relaxed, the average number of those marrying in this century jumped up.

Assuming that there is no sex-specific difference in marrying children, the net replacement rate is found by dividing the number of marrying children by 2 (Levine 1977:75). This suggests that the 1700–49 population was not replacing itself, and indeed there may have been a slight downturn in population during this time. Almost 80 percent of all surviving children in families formed during 1750–99 went on to marry, but this proportion slipped to 71 percent and then 67 percent in the following 50-year periods. A replacement rate near 1.1 was maintained, and the proportion of eligible individuals marrying went down in inverse relation to population growth. Normally, such a low replacement rate would have restrained the annual rate of population increase, but both the number of children born per family and the number of these offspring surviving were climbing. Clearly the average number of those remaining celibate was rising too (Table 6.11). Between 1700 and 1899 the actual number of surviving children per family who never married went up more than 2.5 times. In relative terms, the proportion of adult offspring who remained bachelors and spinsters went from approximately 1 in 5 to a high of 1 in 3.

Celibacy without continence would naturally have exerted much weaker demographic control. If an increasing age of marriage had been accompanied by a growing rate of illegitimacy, the crude birth rate might have risen even while marital fertility was falling. There is every indication that social mores and religious strictures in Törbel successfully prohibited premarital sex, except in some cases of engaged couples, who almost always married before their child was born. The pairing off of young couples was a public and institutionalized process. Acquaintance or *Bekanntschaft* was recognized when the young man and woman, usually already in their 20s, began to walk together after mass. He might visit her in her parents' house on Sunday afternoons, and he might give her small gifts. This period might continue for years, and it was equivalent to engagement. Although parents might express strong preferences for and objections to particular individuals, often in terms of their relative wealth or political affiliation (see Chapter 9), there is no suggestion that marriages were arranged or that the wishes of the young people could be routinely overruled. Perhaps more vital were the obstructions and delays that some parents might put up against a particular wedding date or against any match at all (see Chapter 8). Although mountain families appeared strongly authoritarian in the recent past, with children using the formal *Ihr* rather than the familiar *du* when speaking to their parents, there was a pervasive tendency to consult with children as equal partners in difficult decisions. This consideration, especially in matters of property, was noted by Rousseau during his 1744 trip through upper Valais (Bellwald 1960).

Sex outside of marriage could dishonor the family, harm social standing in the community, and interfere with the orderly transmission of property so crucial to the peasant economy. To the practical considerations of avoiding parental disgrace and community scandal were added the religious sanctions reiterated from the pulpit and enforced by the unassailable decisions of the parish priest. Sexual prudery was insisted upon to the point that the priest decreed long sleeves for women raking hay under the summer sun. Bare female arms might cause men to have "bad thoughts." It is no accident that the only representation of human nakedness visible in Valais is a medieval mural in the church of Raron showing the agonies of writhing sinners in hell. It is probable, though perhaps difficult for a more permissive age to grasp, that in traditional Europe large numbers of adults had no coital activity whatever. Society "feared eroticism as it feared the plague, and maintained ferociously the

Table 6.15. *Illegitimacy*

25-Year period	Illegitimate births	Total births	Rate/1,000	Illegitimacy ratio (%)
1800–24	5	330	15.2	1.5
1825–49	4	338	11.2	1.1
1850–74	6	438	13.7	1.4
1875–99	5	486	10.3	1.0
1900–24	7	451	15.5	1.6
1925–49	13	468	27.8	2.8
1950–74	11	338	32.5	3.3

link between marriage and intercourse" (Shorter 1977). The closed community of Törbel maintained a level of vigilance on its members that militated against any clandestine sexual activity. From the small windows of the black log houses there are always eyes on the street. There is no movement on the paths or across the meadows that cannot be identified both as to who it is and what they are doing. It is instantly known whether or not the observed person can possibly have business in that place at that time of day.[21] The canons of appropriate behavior are so inclusive and the scrutiny of neighbors so continuous that repression may become second nature. In this sense privacy is the enemy of the moral community, and the Törbel of times past trusted its members no farther than it could see them.

Abstinence was a valued goal, and there were punishments for violating the standard of premarital chastity. An infant born out of wedlock was baptized under a black veil, and the public judgment this symbolized clung to him more or less his whole life (Bellwald 1960:44). Congenitally handicapped or severely retarded individuals were less subject to social censure, but they were not permitted to marry, and anyone getting a child with such a person could be expelled from the community.[22] Illegitimate (*uneheliche*) births are clearly marked in the parish registry, and many of these children either died young or left the community before adulthood. Few are mentioned in the Törbel books before 1800, and in one seventeenth-century case the lack of a father was partially compensated for by special baptismal blessings of priests from Törbel and Visp and of four leading male citizens and two females as godparents. It is possible that some unmarried pregnant women left Törbel to have their babies, and some of the local illegitimates were born to women of other villages. In any event, from 1800 to 1924 the ratio of illegitimate births to legitimate births was fairly constant and very low (Table 6.15). Only with the increasing exposure of Törbel women to urban life and wage work outside the community in the last 50 years has the rate increased.[23] The low incidence of illegitimacy parallels observations in Lötschental around the turn of the century (Bellwald 1960:40) and in English parishes of 1640–1710 (Laslett 1977:125). More recent local records in England give ratios of 4.2 to 5.5 per 100 births, and since 1900 they have gone up to over 6.0 (Laslett 1977:113).[24]

Sex in any of its forms is not a subject on which the people of Törbel speak easily. They are guarded and rigidly conventional in the views they express, and discussions of illegitimacy, even a century ago, are embarrassing. The fact that until recently fewer than 2 births in every 100 took place before marriage indicates the marked effects of such internalized attitudes and community sanctions on behavior. Combined with the enduringly high average age at marriage, this low illegitimacy rate supports the contention that there is no "necessary positive connection between sexual deprivation and the procreation of children outside marriage" (Laslett 1977:127).

Premarital pregnancy, though also considered shameful for the parents and the guilty partners, did not have the serious repercussions of illegitimacy. When a marriage ceremony had been held, perhaps at the urging of the priest, some months before delivery of a child, gossip tended to die down, and even the bride's mother could wipe away her private tears and feel that no permanent harm had been done. Live births occurring less than 9 months after marriage (Table 6.16) have averaged 17 percent of all first births, reaching a peak of 25 percent during 1700–49.[25] When the average age of female marriage declined in 1750–99, so did the incidence of prenuptial pregnancy, and both advanced together in the following 50-year periods. It is impossible to tell when conception was an accidental result of long and increasingly onerous engagements and when a couple deliberately used pregnancy to precipitate a marriage that their elders were delaying. It is interesting to note, however, that such pregnancies were not concentrated among younger women below 25 years of age; they also occurred with considerable frequency among women near and above the average marital age (Table 6.16). It seems possible that most such conceptions took place in the course of socially recognized courtship and that they involved both couples who were merely anticipating a marriage date already set and others who may have wanted to hasten or make inevitable a marriage that went contrary to the wishes of their parents. Instances of promiscuous sexual behavior or of attempting to "trap" a partner into marriage appear less likely, but lack of evidence makes it difficult to accept or reject such explanations.[26] There was, however, no such thing in Törbel as a trial marriage. Once the match had been solemnized, divorce in the eyes

Table 6.16. *Premarital pregnancies: numbers and percentages of first live births less than 9 months after marriage*[a]

Period	Wife younger than 25 years at marriage		Wife aged 25–34 years at marriage		Wife older than 35 years at marriage		Total	
	No.	%	No.	%	No.	%	No.	%
1700–49	4	19	7	27	3	38	14	25
1750–99	2	7	3	10	0	0	5	8
1800–49	4	10	6	10	2	29	12	11
1850–99	11	28	15	19	1	6	27	20
1900–49	18	31	9	10	4	19	31	19
All cohorts	39	21	40	14	10	18	89	17

[a]Tabulation by Cambridge Group for the History of Population and Social Structure.

of church and community could not occur, and there is no evidence for either divorced people or common-law marriage among village residents now or in the past.

Marriage duration

Because marriage in Törbel was traditionally for life and almost all children were born to married couples, changes in marital fertility might be due to a change in the period during which the marriage coincided with a woman's fertile years. Table 6.14 shows that there was no pronounced decrease in female age at marriage. Another possibility for explaining the increased fertility after 1700–49 is that people were living longer and fewer marriages were interrupted by the death of a spouse. It is true that a husband's death did not prevent a younger woman from remarrying. It is said that in the past, the division of labor and especially the care of children required a prompt remarriage. Nevertheless, high mortality, especially of married women in the approximately 15-year period when their children were being born, could certainly decrease fertility.[27] Average total duration of marriage was noticeably shorter during 1700–49, but the number of fertile years spent in marriage was only 1.7 less than in the following period (Table 6.17). Increased mortality shortened marriages but decreased the actual years of fertility by less than 2 years. At most this would have brought total fertility down by 0.43 birth per mother, again less than the average difference of 0.85 birth per mother in 1700–49, as compared with 1750–99. Fertility

Table 6.17. *Duration of marriage*

Period	Sample A[a]		Sample B[b]	
	Number of marriages	Average duration (yr)	Number of marriages	Duration of fertile years
1700–49	47	22.4	64	14.9
1750–99	63	27.3	80	16.6
1800–49	112	28.0	122	16.6
1850–99	143	27.4	144	16.2
1900–49	78	24.3	127	16.5

[a]Sample A is based on tabulations of the Cambridge Group that omitted cases where the wife's date of birth was unknown or estimated dates were used. The duration gives the length of marriage from marriage to death of either partner.
[b]Sample B is based on tabulations done at the University of Arizona giving the average number of fertile years in marriage. The duration gives the length of marriage from marriage year to wife's death, husband's death, or wife's reaching age 48, whichever comes first.

continued to climb, going up by an average 0.38 birth per mother from 1750–99 to 1850–99, but both marriage duration and the period of fertile years of married women remained extremely stable. Declines in female mortality allowing a longer duration of marriage contributed something to growing fertility in the eighteenth century, but they could account for only half the observed increase, and they were not instrumental in the further increase in fertility during the nineteenth century.

Family limitation

Family composition in terms of total number, spacing of births, and even sex of surviving offspring can be controlled in several ways. Within marriage, pregnancy can be avoided through abstinence, the practice of coitus interruptus, or the use of various mechanical or pharmaceutical contraceptive means. Once conception has taken place, abortion can forestall a live birth, or infanticide can remove unwanted infants. There is considerable doubt that induced abortion was widely practiced in preindustrial Europe, both because of adamant religious opposition and because of laws imposing severe punishments.[28] Systematic conscious infanticide was less prevalent than in other peasant societies such as Japan (Smith 1977), although the widespread use of nurses and foundling homes in eighteenth-century England and France (Wrigley 1969:125–7; Langer 1972) certainly increased infant mortality. It is possible that some small children died of neglect or suffocation that may have been more or less accidental. We have no means of measuring the frequency of such occurrences in Törbel, but they were universally considered sinful and evil, contrary both to Catholic dogma and to personal desires for a large family. Because a household was established only when the peasant holding was adequate to sustain a family, people believed they might be poor but would always have enough to feed their families.

Was fertility limited by abstention from intercourse once a desired family size had been reached or by coitus interruptus that could cause births to come further apart? Either of these methods would leave evidence in an altered pattern of age-specific marital fertility and in other statistical measures. If family limitation was a factor in Törbel, we should be able to detect signs of its practice, especially in the 1700–49 period of distinctly lower average fertility. There is a precedent for the appearance of birth control in parts of eighteenth-century rural France (Ganiage 1963; Goubert 1968:593) and in Colyton during the late seventeenth and early eighteenth centuries (Wrigley 1966a:104–5). The abrupt decreases in births during French population crises have been interpreted as reflecting a considerable amount of birth control or abortion (Heilleiner 1958). The lack of evidence for other contraceptive methods suggests, largely by default, that coitus interruptus was being practiced, and 60 percent of the reduction in fertility in the Colyton case has been attributed to conscious control (Crafts and Ireland 1976). Some authorities assume that the many celibates in European populations could not have been chaste and that sterile practices such as coitus interruptus spread from the aristocratic classes and prostitutes to rural married couples (Flandrin 1975).[29]

If married people were artificially halting reproduction before the wife's fertile period was over, there should be a visible lowering of the mother's age at the birth of the last child. In the Bavarian village of Massenhausen, the average age of a woman at her last birth event went steadily downward from 40.6 years in 1750–9 to 36.7 years in 1790–9: "This radical limitation of the possible legitimate period of fertility was a conscious method for desired birth control" (Lee 1975:328), and it coincided with a long decline in population.[30] For completed families in Törbel, no such change in the mother's age at last birth is detectable (Table 6.18). On the contrary, this age of about 42 years was remarkably constant for 250 years, and this suggests a consistent approach to physiological limits of conception. Women stopped having children not because they decided to but because their fecundity declined as they neared menopause. Another test of family limitation is a growing difference between penultimate and ultimate birth intervals, indicating that couples have reached an intended final family size and much later, through accident or a desire to replace a child who has died, reverse this

Table 6.18. *Negative evidence of family limitation*[a]

	1700–49	1750–99	1800–49	1850–99	1900–49
Number of completed families[b]	30	45	87	103	57
Mean number of births	5.3	6.0	5.9	5.8	4.8
Standard deviation	3.4	3.6	3.7	3.6	3.7
Percentage of completed families with nine or more births	28	22	24	23	21
Percentage of completed families with no births	13	9	13	13	19
Average age of mother at birth of last child (years)	42.39	42.74	41.69	42.24	42.18
Penultimate birth interval (months)	34.6	39.6	31.3	30.3	24.9
Ultimate birth interval (months)	40.7	44.7	38.5	38.0	31.9
Difference between ultimate and penultimate (months)	6.1	5.1	7.2	7.7	7.0

[a]The quantitative measures of family limitation in this table were applied and explained by Wrigley (1966a). Tabulations were by the Cambridge Group for the History of Population and Social Structure.
[b]Completed families are those in which the wife reaches age 45 during marriage or in which the marriage is known to have lasted 30 years or more.

decision (Wrigley 1966a:94). Whereas Colyton shows a shift from 7.4 months to 18.6 months and back to 7.7 months in this difference of intervals, the Törbel data show only minor changes (Table 6.18), with nothing suggesting planned restrictions on fertility. There also were no major alterations in the proportion of childless completed families until this century.[31] The continued desirability of large families is shown by the 21 to 28 percent of all completed families who had nine or more births. The mean numbers of births in completed families show less marked changes than the average births per family between 1700–49 and 1750–99, but this may reflect only that there was a larger proportion of uncompleted families due to earlier parental deaths and that vital statistics were less complete in the 1700–49 period.

Where family limitation is a general practice, age-specific marital fertility rates not only decline but do so progressively with rising age. A graphic representation of these rates for Colyton shows a high curve with a convex upper side for the period 1560–1629, whereas the curve for 1647–1719 is distinctly lower and concave (Figure 6.5). The concavity indicates fertility limitation because couples are concentrating their reproductive effort into the earlier parts of the wife's fertile period, whereas the later age groups show a growing shortfall from the full fertility potential of the woman (Wrigley 1966a:91). The contrast is not evident in Törbel fertility rates for either 1700–49 or 1800–49 (Figure

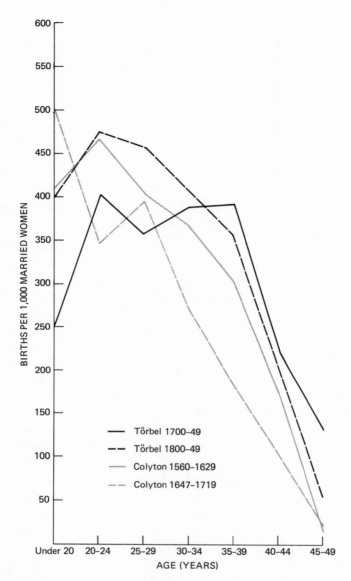

Figure 6.5. Age-specific marital fertility rates for Colyton (1560–1629 and 1647–1719) and for Törbel (1700–49 and 1800–49).

6.5). Although the rates for the later period are higher than those for the earlier one, there is no sign of fertility being purposely limited by older married women. Indeed, the Törbel rates exceed those of Colyton for every age group from 30 years upward, and there is no visible concavity in that part of the curve. None of the indicators developed by historical

Table 6.19. *Age-specific marital fertility rates*

Group	Period	Age < 20	20–4	25–9	30–4	35–9	40–4	45–9
Törbel Swiss	1700–49	250	403	358	390	392	224	131
	1750–99	200	327	369	378	309	196	154
	1800–49	400	475	458	407	356	205	66
	1850–99	444	509	484	442	371	236	35
	1900–49	556	566	551	487	418	219	20
Törbel Swiss	1655–1789	238	359	358	369	288	209	130
	1790–1914	375	483	486	442	373	230	53
Anhausen Germans[a]	1692–1799		472	496	450	355	173	37
	1800–99		482	525	525	362	148	12
Colyton English[b]	1560–1629	412	467	403	369	302	174	18
	1647–1719	500	346	395	272	182	104	20
	1770–1837	500	441	361	347	270	152	22
Crulai French[b]	1674–1742	320	419	429	355	292	142	10
Casal-vecchio Italians[c]	1711–50	238	370	404	337	296	235	88
Pitigliano Italians[c]	1807–66	323	471	370	354	281	177	14
Hutterites[d]	1921–30		550	502	447	406	222	61

[a]Rates for this Bavarian village are from Knodel (1970).
[b]Rates for Colyton are from Wrigley (1966a), and he took the comparative figures for Crulai from Gautier and Henry (1958).
[c]Italian rates from Livi-Bacci (1977:14).
[d]Hutterite rates from Knodel (1970) and from Henry (1961).

demographers to infer the presence of conscious birth control give positive indications of the practice in Törbel.

The opposite of controlled fertility, in which a couple aims for a particular target family size, is natural fertility. "Behavior which affects the level of fertility but is independent of parity, such as breast feeding, abstinence associated with lactation, or periods of separation due to seasonal migration of one of the spouses is not considered a contradiction of natural fertility" (Knodel 1977:219). A population's age-specific fertility can be compared to a standard natural fertility schedule, and an index of fertility control can be derived to indicate the deviation from natural fertility and the amount of fertility control implied. This measure, developed by Coale and Trussell, is based on the observation that "levels of natural fertility vary widely, but provided the factors responsible for the difference in overall levels are independent of age and parity they should not affect the shape of the fertility curve over the reproductive life span which . . . is determined by the decline of fertility

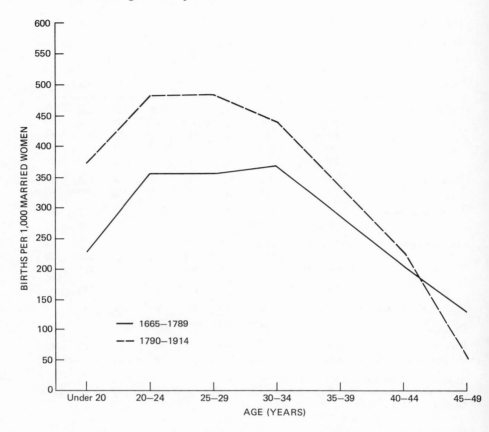

Figure 6.6. Age-specific marital fertility rates for Törbel (1665–1789 and 1790–1914). Tabulation by the Cambridge Group for the History of Population and Social Structure.

with age" (Knodel 1977). A calculation of the index of fertility control m gave values below 0.2, and close to zero, for Törbel in each 50-year time period from 1700 to 1949 and for each age-specific marital fertility rate, demonstrating little or no fertility control.[32] Where family limitation is practiced, as in the United States today, comparable m values are all above 0.5. Observed patterns in Törbel bear some resemblance to the uncontrolled fertility of seventeenth-century Quebec, seventeenth- and eighteenth-century Germany, and Pakistan in 1963–65 (Knodel 1977, Table 1).

When compared with historical marital fertility rates for other European communities, the Törbel figures appear plausible (Table 6.19). For the eighteenth century the Törbel figures hover around the same general levels as those for Colyton and Crulai. The rates are lower for the group

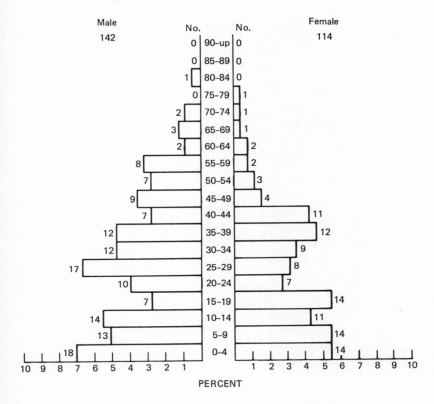

Figure 6.7. Age-sex distribution of population of Törbel (1750).

under 20 years of age because of the paucity of teenage marriages and perhaps also because of adolescent subfecundity (Wrigley 1966a:88). The Törbel age at marriage was higher than those for the other communities, possibly resulting in lower fertility rates for those in their 20s and somewhat higher rates in the later years of marriage. For the 1800s, the Törbel schedules parallel those for the German peasant village of Anhausen during 1692–1799.[33] By the twentieth century, all fertility rates from age 20 through 39 years exceed those for the Hutterites.[34] The total number of births is, of course, smaller than that for the German-speaking North American farming group, but that is due solely to the later age of marriage in Switzerland. Within marriage, Törbel women by this time show high and apparently uncontrolled levels of reproduction.

Birth spacing

If age at marriage, marriage duration, and the cessation of family limitation practices are all inadequate to explain changes in Törbel

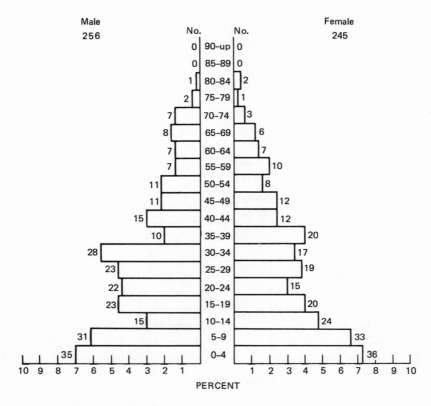

Figure 6.8. Age-sex distribution of population of Törbel (1850).

fertility, what other factors may be involved? That there are real differences in marital fertility for almost every age level is apparent from comparing the eighteenth- and nineteenth-century rates (Table 6.19). Somewhat longer time series present the contrast even more graphically (Figure 6.6). Births per thousand married women rose substantially during the prime fertile years from age 20 through 35 years.

It does not seem likely that the members of the Törbel community were either consciously limiting or increasing their fertility. The changes taking place in average numbers of children, survival of children, and adult life expectancy were probably too gradual and too variable in the short term to be observed by any means other than statistical methods. The structure of the total population also changed very little. The age-sex pyramids (Figures 6.7 and 6.8) continue through time to show the verticality characteristic of stationary or slowly growing populations. The proportions of those in the lowest age classes from 0 to 14 years remained fixed at about 32.5 percent during the late eighteenth century and rose

Table 6.20. *Mean birth intervals in months for Törbel women*

Period	Parity Marriage-1[a]	1-2	2-3	3-4	4-5 and all higher intervals	All intervals
1700-49	23.9 (41)[b]	27.9 (47)	29.2 (42)	30.4 (37)	32.5 (97)	29.3 (264)
1750-99	24.5 (60)	29.9 (58)	28.9 (48)	31.5 (38)	34.1 (135)	30.7 (339)
1800-49	15.3[c] (99)	23.9[c] (99)	25.9 (94)	29.1 (83)	29.9[c] (275)	26.1 (650)
1850-99	15.8 (107)	25.8 (123)	25.7 (115)	27.3 (99)	29.2 (300)	25.9 (744)
1900-49	17.7 (136)	19.9 (148)	22.0 (133)	26.4 (117)	25.4 (401)	23.1 (935)

[a]Births occurring 8 months or sooner after marriage are not included in this calculation.
[b]Numbers of births in parentheses.
[c]The 1800-49 mean birth intervals are significantly different from the 1750-99 intervals: $p < 0.001$, < 0.02, < 0.01, respectively, using the t test.

to only 34.7 percent in 1850. Although the composition of the population showed no marked fluctuations, the total numbers expanded, indicating an even and general growth.

If women were having more offspring without a lowered age at marriage or the relaxation of conscious restrictions on family size, births must necessarily have been coming closer together. Strong support for this hypothesis exists in a comparison of birth intervals in successive 50-year periods (Table 6.20). In every class (namely, between marriage and first birth, first and second births, and so on) the birth intervals before 1800 were longer than those after that date. The differences between 1750-99 and 1800-49 levels are statistically significant in three cases. From an average of about 30 months between births in the 1700s, children were following each other at 26-month intervals in the next century. Between marriage and first birth, the average spacing fell 38 percent, and between first and second births it dropped 20 percent after 1800. Whereas it required a mean period of 12.4 years to have five children during 1750-99, the same number could be born in 10.3 years during 1800-49.[35] There was a further decline in birth interval in most cases in this century. Törbel's eighteenth-century birth intervals cluster at the upper end of the distribution among comparable European populations listed in Table 6.21. The declining birth intervals of the Genevan bourgeoisie after 1600 are paralleled 200 years later in the alpine village, and there is a similar quickening for Colyton around 1720. The range of birth intervals in the French and in the Italian rural villages around 1700 agrees well with the figures from Törbel. The European

Table 6.21. *Comparative birth intervals*

Population	Period	Mean birth interval (mo)				Source
		0–1	1–2	2–3	3–4	
Colyton, Devon.[a]	1560–1646	11.3	25.2	27.4	30.1	Wrigley 1966a:93
	1647–1719	10.3	29.1	32.6	32.1	
	1720–69	11.9	25.1	29.8	32.9	
Cardington, Beds.[a]	1750–80	10.8	25.7	27.4	30.9	Baker 1973:61
French Canada[a]	1700–30	15.8	22.5	21.1	22.6	Henripin 1954:85
Genevan bourgeoisie[a]	before 1600	—	28.5	29.4	27.4	Henry 1956:100
	1600–49	—	23.5	25.4	23.5	
	1650–99	—	19.7	21.6	30.1	
Geneva[a]	1700–72	13.3	18.3	20.1	21.5	Perrenoud 1977:159
Crulai[a]	1674–1742	16.6	22.4	25.3	27.2	Gautier and Henry 1958
Thezels and Saint Sernin[a]	1700–92	—	25.4	30.0	32.2	Valmary 1965:134
Fiesole	1630–60	—	25.9	29.5	30.6	Livi-Bacci 1977:16
Valdibure	1700–1800	—	24.9	29.2	30.7	Livi-Bacci 1977:16
Törbel	1750–99	24.5[b]	29.9	28.9	31.5	
	1800–49	15.3	23.9	25.9	29.1	

[a]Comparative cases from a table from Finlay (1979).
[b]Whereas the Törbel 0–1 cases include only those births occurring at least 9 months after marriage, the other European cases may include prenuptial pregnancies in their averages.

examples give birth-interval series similar to those for Törbel both before and after 1800, and some further demonstrate the possibility of significant across-the-board changes in these intervals over time. Birth spacing must therefore be considered an important potential contributor to marital fertility and eventually to population growth. This raises the fascinating but by no means simple question of the circumstances under which more births can take place in a fixed period of time.

In trying to interpret a change in reproductive behavior, the first tendency of the social scientist is to look for some clear-cut alteration in cultural values and beliefs. Does the population under investigation have a changing division of labor that makes children more economically productive? Does childbearing conflict with new occupations available to women outside of the home? Are attitudes toward sexuality or ideal family size being transformed? Such queries are difficult to answer satisfactorily in contemporary societies, but when applied to an obscure Swiss peasant village of 200 years ago, they become simply impossible.

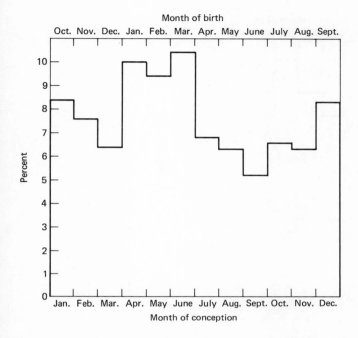

Figure 6.9. Conceptions and births in Törbel (1665–1799).

We have no evidence for radical change in technology or work habits. The documents are silent on both sex and the relations between the sexes. There is some reason to think that residential structures, family organization, religious beliefs, and local political structures showed remarkable continuity and stability in this era. If there was indeed no conscious decision on the part of the Törbel villagers either to limit their families in the early 1700s or to have more children the following century, we are left with the possibility that the increased fertility resulted from biological and physiological changes of which the people were not directly aware.

Birth spacing may be no more than a reflection of coital frequency. "In each 28 day menstrual cycle the time during which it is physiologically possible for copulation to result in conception is quite brief—almost certainly less than two days and possibly less than one. Therefore the probability of conception is related to the frequency of sexual intercourse. The more rarely copulation occurs, the more likely it is that the fertile period will be missed, and then another month must elapse before impregnation is possible again" (Daly and Wilson 1978:287).[36] Could the turn of the eighteenth century have witnessed a measurable upturn in the general level of Törbel libidos? Of course, we have no way of knowing. Yet it is obvious that throughout the period in question there

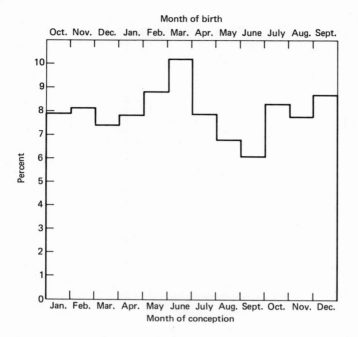

Figure 6.10. Conceptions and births in Törbel (1800–99).

was a pronounced seasonality of births, meaning that conceptions were much more likely in certain months of the year than in others. Before 1800, 30 percent of all conceptions took place in the spring months of April, May, and June, whereas high summer and autumn, from July through November, saw an average of only 6 percent per month (Figure 6.9).

Some of this difference can be referred to first conceptions following marriages, which also peaked in April, May, and especially June, but this would not account for the conceptions of later children, which were also strongly seasonal. Some connection must be posited between the heavy labor demands of summer and the relatively low number of conceptions.[37] The outdoor work of haymaking, irrigating, and grain harvesting kept both sexes busy, often from daybreak until after dark. Tending the vineyards or herding cows and making cheese on the alp might keep men away from their families for a few days or even several months at a time (Papilloud 1973:136). Such seasonal migration has been credited with decisively lowering birth rates among the Italian-Swiss villagers of Ticino (Van de Walle 1975; Menken 1979). On the other hand, when the work schedule was relaxed, people congregated in the village. There was drinking and feasting, as on the spring holiday of

Corpus Christi and to a lesser extent over the Christmas season, and at these times the frequency of conceptions went up. Whether there was more regular intercourse at such times or whether for other reasons there was a greater chance of fertilization and implantation cannot be known. The general fatigue of summer might be complicated for women by a lower level of nutrition resulting in possible suppression of ovulation.[38] Some evidence of preharvest summer malnutrition has been noted in Italian villages (Bell 1979:59), but whether or not the spring abundance of cows' milk followed by the summer dependence on less plentiful goats' milk was a crucial factor in the Törbel diet is not clear. It seems probable, however, that the evident seasonality of conceptions had the effect of lowering general fertility rates.

Longer birth spacing appears to correlate with pronounced seasonal differences in the incidence of conceptions and births (Smith 1977:40–2). Although seasonal fluctuations for Törbel decline somewhat for 1800–1900, a May–June peak and an August–September decline in conceptions are still detectable (Figure 6.10). The demands in time and effort of the heavy agricultural labor, in addition to the possibly lower calorie intake relative to energy expenditure, continue to show correlation with the seasonal conceptions, but the influence on fertility was somewhat more moderate.[39] Whatever the proximate cause of the cyclical peak in conceptions, it produced a corresponding increase in births centering in the months of January, February, and March. In terms of the peasant work schedule, this housebound period of winter allowed the mother to devote full attention to her infant without the competing pressures of work in the fields.

Where the seasonality of births and conceptions has the effect of lengthening birth intervals, the physiological mechanism directly involved may be that of dietary intake and lactation prolonging the period before a nursing mother resumes ovulation. We cannot ignore the possible effects of fatigue and temporary separation on coital frequency, but there seems no good reason to postulate a markedly different work load or scheduling of peasant agricultural activities before and after 1800. Perhaps a more fruitful approach to take in the matter of Törbel birth spacing is to ask whether or not there could have been changes in local nutrition sufficient to affect women's physical condition. It has been known for some time that the period of postpartum amenorrhea while ovulation is suspended in a new mother is prolonged by lactation[40] and may be further inhibited if the maternal diet is inadequate (Solien de Gonzalez 1964; Potter et al. 1965; Jain et al. 1970; Frisch and Revelle 1970; Chen, Ahmed, and Mosley 1974; Kolata 1974). The physiological processes are not well understood, but neural impulses from the teat may affect prolactin hormonal balances (May 1978), and both the frequency and intensity of sucking stimuli may play a part in this reaction (Knodel 1977). The inhibition of ovulation caused by nursing is not perfect and is partially dependent on the mother's nutritional state.

> Even with a fixed duration of lactation, the well-fed mother is likely to resume ovulation earlier than the poorly fed mother. If the child eats supplemental solids and hence suckles less, ovulatory probability goes up. The mechanism is nicely adapted to permit an increasing probability of conception as the chance that resources are adequate for the mother to rear another baby increases. For an undernourished lactating mother to become pregnant might be disastrous— for the nursing infant, for the newly conceived, and for the mother herself. Her reproductive machinery is switched off until nutritive levels indicate that conception is a good risk. The well-fed mother, already weaning her child, is likely to be capable of handling another.   [Daly and Wilson 1978:284]

The evolutionary value of longer birth spacing when food supplies are relatively low is obvious, preventing competition for vital nourishment between one child and the following infant.

There is no question that birth spacings differ significantly from one society to another, but the degree to which "nutrition may be an important determinant of human ovulation" (Delgado et al. 1978) and the relative importance of maternal physical condition and infant supplementary feedings remain matters of considerable debate. Nursing mothers among the well-nourished Hutterites have an average period of postpartum amenorrhea of 6 months, whereas investigations have shown that the period in Taiwan is 11 months (Jain et al. 1970) and in Bangladesh 16 months (Chen, Ahmed, and Mosley 1974). Undernutrition and "hard living," plus the estimated drain of 1,000 calories per day on the nursing mother (Frisch and Revelle 1970; Frisch 1978), may delay conception even in the absence of marked clinical signs of malnutrition.[41] In fact, the reproductive system appears to begin "shutting down" more rapidly than other physiological operations during times of nutritional stress. Amenorrhea caused by wartime famine has been noted among modern European populations, as when a third of all fertile Dutch women ceased ovulating during the food shortages of 1945, and among German city dwellers in 1916–17, when the potato ration was temporarily replaced by rutabagas (Le Roy Ladurie 1975). Women visited their physicians not because of illness but because the cessation of menstruation convinced them that they were pregnant. There is no reason to think that the eighteenth-century Törbel diet was seriously deficient in either protein or calories, and in a generally healthy population a lower calorie intake may result in lower body weight without restricting activity levels or producing permanent damage (Stini 1975:66–

7). If the nutritional level of eighteenth-century Törbel mothers was somewhat below the level of 1800–99, it might account for the difference in average birth interval of 30.161 months, as compared with 25.994 months (Table 6.20). These two figures yield estimates of the period of postpartum amenorrhea of 8.861 and 4.694 months, respectively.[42] Even the initial levels of nearly 9 months do not approach the levels of 10.6 months for Punjab sample villages or 17.7 months for a presumably poorly nourished population in Zaire (Knodel 1977).

As with most factors connected with fertility, the effect of maternal nutrition on the resumption of ovulation is far from clear. One influential hypothesis proposes that a minimal percentage of body weight as fat may be necessary to attain, restore, and maintain menstruation (Frisch and McArthur 1974). A recent study of Bangladesh women in 1970 found that better maternal nutritional status was unlikely to shorten the length of postpartum amenorrhea significantly, but infant food supplementation did lead to decreased frequencies of suckling, and this may have resulted in curtailed durations of amenorrhea and shortened birth intervals (Huffman et al. 1978). Socioeconomic class was also found to be independently related to postpartum amenorrhea; upper-class women in Bangladesh tended to regard breast feeding as less suitable, and they breast-fed less frequently. A seasonality in the return of menstruation was also observed, indicating that women had a greater tendency to begin menstruating in the November rice harvest period than at earlier times, regardless of when in the preceding year they had given birth (Huffman et al. 1978). Critics of the Frisch hypothesis contend on the basis of recent evidence that chronic (as opposed to severe) malnourishment may be responsible for slight differences in the duration of postpartum amenorrhea but that the nutritional level explains very little of the evident variation in fertility among populations (Menken, Trussell, and Watkins 1981:437).

If maternal nutrition is less relevant than duration of lactation and supplementary feeding practices, the change in Törbel birth intervals might be due to historical alterations in attitudes toward breast feeding and corresponding substantial increases in the amount and frequency of solid food in infants' diets.[43] There is no hint that the people of Valais ever adopted the southern Bavarian pattern of feeding small infants on meal pap instead of breast milk. Indeed, the few early references to nursing in the Swiss Alps suggest that it was considered vital to the infant's health and was routinely sustained for several years. Thomas Platter, the great Reformation teacher and scholar who was born in 1499 in Grächen, within sight of Törbel, mentioned in his autobiography that his mother had lacked sufficient breast milk and that he had been given cows' milk in a little horn to suck. "Then they gave the children nothing to eat until they were often four or five years old, but they only got milk to suck" (Platter 1944:24). Citing several reliable sixteenth-century texts from the Bern archives, the folklorist Wackernagel (1959:20) wrote that in the alpine region it was a well-established custom for a child to be fed at the mother's breast up to the fifth year.[44] It is unlikely that children were deprived of all solid food much beyond 1 year of age, but it would appear that the ideal pattern was considered to be relatively long-term lactation. Perhaps nursing, while still the norm, was being reduced in duration around 1800. One tenuous suggestion that this might possibly have been the case comes from the English-language child-rearing literature of the period where "women were being widely recommended to breast feed their infants for an appreciably shorter period in the [middle] and late 18th century than in the 17th and early 18th centuries—an average about twelve months in the former period compared with twenty-one in the latter" (Flinn 1970:36).[45]

No final determination can be made on whether or not there were new attitudes on breast feeding and an earlier time of weaning in the Törbel of 200 years ago. We can legitimately ask, however, whether or not infant food supplementation had become more practical. Until the 1930s nursing bottles were not used in Törbel, and it was frequent for mothers to keep children at the breast for at least 6 months and sometimes 18 months.[46] Some people gave their 4- to 5-month-old infants cows' milk and water (mixed half and half) from a glass and gave them bits of table food such as rye bread soaked in water or potato gruel. The most usual supplement was a kind of pabulum made of white flour cooked in butter and mixed with a little milk. A former village midwife claimed that this pap (*Brei*) was given to children only when they were 1 year old. Commercial baby food appeared in the 1940s.[47] She added that there was no fixed termination for nursing in the past. Women continued to breast-feed either until their first menstruation came or until they felt the stirring of a next child in the womb. Some mothers as recently as 25 years ago were reluctant to give their children any solid food until they were 1 year old "for fear they would choke." Although there was certainly supplementation of the infant diet in this century, opinions differ on whether it usually began before the age of 6 months or after 1 year. Certainly a major part of this extra food was made from white wheat flour, which in earlier times had been rare in the village. The birth interval actually declined noticeably between 1850–99 and 1900–49, perhaps because of increased supplementary feeding and the recent introduction of bottle feeding.[48] Foods available for supplementation around 1800 were probably much less satisfactory. The dry, coarsely ground rye meal would have been difficult to digest, even if the bread had been moistened and chopped up. There was probably no sugar for mixing with milk and a piece of bread wrapped in a cloth for the child to suck on.[49] Because the milk of cows and goats was available is no indication that it was used extensively for infants, and the slight evidence we have suggests that breast feeding was preferred.

Shorter birth spacing after 1800 in Törbel cannot be shown to be linked to revolutionary changes in the seasonality of conceptions, the values associated with childbearing, or the practices of infant care. There is, on the other hand, some biological evidence from other parts of the world for higher fertility associated with declining periods of postpartum amenorrhea and more rapid resumption of ovulation after birth. These complex physiological processes have been related either to improved maternal nutrition or to infant food supplements, allowing less vigorous nursing and earlier weaning. Both of these suggestions are contingent on changes in the amount of food available or the quality of the local diet. Our tentative conclusions are that higher Törbel fertility is best explained by a real increase in the level of nutrition provided by peasant farming and that the resulting rise in female fecundity was neither planned nor expected by the people it affected. It seems likely that the direct effects of poor nutrition, short of real famine conditions, on the female reproductive system may be slight. But contrary to the views of some authorities (Menken, Trussell, and Watkins 1981:440), nutrition and fertility may still show significant though indirect links. Socially mediated biological change could have affected childbearing in Törbel because of an increased frequency of intercourse contingent on better food supplies during seasons of high labor expenditure and because of infant food supplementation decreasing lactation and shortening the infertile period after birth.

CONCLUSION

Births and deaths, when reduced to tables and graphs, then statistically compared and subjected to all manner of emendations and alternative interpretations, are not the stuff of engrossing ethnography or stirring history. Yet with all their quantitative abstraction and cumulative boredom, they provide us with one of the few substantive tools for describing the dynamics of community population and the related regularities in social behavior. The riddle of demographic stability and growth, for all its vast importance to the contemporary world and to our understanding of the past, cannot be solved at one stroke or on the basis of a single case. Yet there is value in the exercise of wringing the parish books of one alpine village for every scrap of evidence they contain, particularly because here the accidents of history left unusually complete and continuous records of vital events.

Not surprisingly, we have concluded that mortality has indeed declined over the last 250 years, but the causes of unusually high death tolls may have changed from the pre-1750 crises caused by harvest failures or plagues to the more recent and milder waves of epidemic disease. A decrease in mortality due to better medical care does not become evident until the current century. The life expectancy for both males and females has gone up, but not in a regular or steady fashion. The Törbel data show that until 1925 the mortality for women between 15 and 45 years of age was higher than that for men at the corresponding ages, suggesting that the dangers of childbearing were significant and accounted for the lower percentage of females in the population. Although falling mortality certainly contributed to population growth, the influence of rising fertility cannot be discounted. Average age at marriage and the celibacy rate climbed as total population went up, but the average number of children per marriage also increased. The number of a woman's fertile years spent in marriage went up only minimally, so that the larger number of children seems unrelated to a longer life span of the married partners. There is no direct or inferential demographic evidence for abortion or contraception limiting family size. However, shorter spacing between births is closely associated with higher average fertility, and the reduced intervals are apparent from about 1800, when population growth was strongest.[50] Both the decline in the death rate and the increase in births may have been associated with environmental and agricultural changes affording a generally higher level of subsistence.

The surplus of births over deaths is evident throughout Europe in an explosive rise in population during this period. Although Törbel participated in this growth, it did so in a rural setting, with little direct influence from mechanical technology, cottage industry, or involvement in trade. The Alps provided no frontier opportunities for expansion, and marriage was not easier or earlier than it had been in the past. It appears that demographic growth took place despite the continued functioning of socioeconomic regulators on population and without degrading the environment or living standards. The expansion of the peasant community, though perhaps stimulated by innovations from without, followed a course of indigenous development peculiar to its own time and place, but reflecting in some measure the forces transforming much of rural Europe.

7

Potatoes and the prevalence of people

The firm evidence we have presented for population growth in Törbel beginning in the late eighteenth century has raised the possibility that there may have been at this time a genuine, perhaps even revolutionary, change in the local environment that in turn directly affected the peasant standard of living. In part, we may be detecting merely a climatic amelioration that made bad harvests and years of crisis mortality less frequent. But there seems also to have been a positive addition to the Törbel subsistence regimen in the form of a new food crop, the potato. We have noted a whole series of demographic indicators, each of which might have responded to improvements in the nutritional status of the resident population. Between 1750 and 1799, mortality began to decline, and marriage duration during a woman's fertile years went up (Tables 6.4 and 6.17). An increase in local food supplies could be expected to make people more resistant to disease, especially to the respiratory illnesses that occur more frequently with malnutrition.[1] As fewer marriages were cut short by the death of one of the partners, total fertility rose (Table 6.11).

Although mortality continued to decline in the nineteenth century, leaving more individuals to swell the village population, an equally important trend was the rising age-specific fertility (Figure 6.3), achieved mainly by shortened birth intervals (Table 6.20). A diet richer in calories may have allowed women to resume ovulation sooner after bearing children. Alternatively, the boiled potato mashed with milk or butter or cooked into a thick soup could have provided an easily prepared and digestible supplement for infant feeding, thereby reducing the length and intensity of breast feeding. We cannot prove that the introduction of a single American food crop had such far-reaching effects on the population dynamics of a Swiss alpine community, but it is clear that the entire local ecosystem was undergoing some important changes at the time of which we speak. Rather than merely to describe what happened demographically, the social scientist's task and the essence of his craft is to attempt explanation, that is, to discern pattern, to postulate cause, and to consider opposing arguments. The "potato hypothesis" is just such a proposition, and the case for a relationship between this food and the growth of population in a self-sufficient peasant economy must be considered on its merits.

Both the probable time of adoption of the potato and the caloric addition it brought to the average diet of mountain people can be specified. The white, or Irish, potato is an American domesticate originating in the Andes of South America. Although it reached Europe as early as 1570 (Salaman 1949:68), its acceptance as a staple crop by peasant cultivators was slow and irregular. It was used as food in seventeenth-century Ireland (Salaman 1949), but as late as the 1770s it had replaced oatmeal, porridge, and wheat bread only in the southwestern part of the country (Cullen 1968:76). Potatoes did not figure in the economy of highland Scotland until after 1750 (Salaman 1949:355). Where a variety of grain crops and good growing conditions were present, as in many parts of England, the potato did not enter the diet significantly until after 1790 (Salaman 1949:494–507). People scorned the potato as a relative of the poisonous nightshade, another member of the *Solanum* family, and blamed it for inducing everything from flatulence to lust (Salaman 1949:104–12). Until bad harvests in Norway were compounded by failures in the herring and cod fisheries and by the blockade of grain imports during the Napoleonic wars around 1800, Norwegian farmers did not take up potato cultivation (Drake 1969:59–61). In Germany it took the famines of 1770, 1801–5, and 1806–17 to compel adoption of the new crop (Abel 1967:313; Teuteberg 1975). Until the potato appeared, there had been no important tuberous plants in northwestern Europe,[2] and both the appearance and behavior of the plant were considered unusual. A German proverb maintains that what the peasant does not know, he will not eat (*Was der Bauer kennt nicht, das isst er nicht*), and sheer unfamiliarity delayed acceptance in an agrarian society where bread was the traditional mainstay. Some members of the landholding establishment also feared that the potato might ruin grain cultivation by lowering prices (Abel 1967:313) or reduce the churchly tithes that were traditionally based in large measure on the grain harvest (Renard and Weulersse 1926). Adam Smith, however, recognized that potato planting would benefit both landlord and tenant (Abel 1967:313), and government policy encouraged its adoption in late eighteenth-century France, Hungary, and Russia (Crosby 1972:184).

There is no single comprehensive history of the diffusion of the potato in Switzerland (Bucher 1974:168), but a series of local and regional monographs (Bielmann 1972; Bucher 1974; Pfister 1975) has recently given a clearer picture of its spread in the second half of the eighteenth century.[3] The initial source may have been Alsatian refugees from the Thirty Years' War, seasonal farm laborers in the eighteenth century, or mercenary soldiers returning from France (Bucher 1974:168). There were early plantings near the lake of Zürich, and the low temperatures and late spring of 1739–40 induced many farmers in the Bern, Glarus, Toggenburg, Appenzell, and Geneva hinterlands to try the crop (Pfister 1975:147). It had been known in the alpine canton of Uri since 1730, but it became a basic element of diet only after 1750 (Bielmann 1972:179). In Emmental it had already almost caught up with bread as an everyday food by 1764 (Pfister 1975:147). Learned men, especially parsons and landowners interested in scientific agricultural improvements, banded together in societies (the so-called Economic Patriots), observed local climates and yields, and disseminated information on promising new crops such as the potato (Bucher 1974; Pfister 1975). The unusually severe winters and heavy precipitation of the years 1768–71 (Pfister 1975:81–3) gave tremendous impetus to potato planting. Contemporaries noted that the failure of the grain crop, the threat of famine in many parts of Europe, and the resulting high prices strongly accelerated the spread of the potato (Pfister 1975:146). The Swiss agriculturalist Samuel Engel combated the widely held view of potato unwholesomeness by citing the strength and fertility of the Irish peasantry, and the great food scarcity of 1772 helped him persuade the people of Nyon on Lake Geneva to adopt the potato as a staple (Salaman 1949:115).

Potatoes are by origin a mountain crop, well adapted to high altitudes and the steep fields that are marginal for grain production.[4] Experiments in the alps above Interlaken showed that grain would not ripen in fields at 1,133 meters, whereas potatoes would grow at 1,488 meters (Bielmann 1972:89). Communities from 750 meters up showed a gradual decline in grain production from 1755 to 1797 (Pfister 1975:145).[5] The potato could be propagated in bad soil as well as good soil, except where dampness was a problem; it could not be damaged by hail that often wiped out standing grain crops, and it could be prepared for eating with the simplest cooking utensils (Bucher 1974:169).[6] A measured, but enthusiastic, appraisal of the potato in Switzerland was offered by Franscini in 1848:

> The cultivation of potatoes that was introduced to us as an invaluable benefit at the beginning of the last century has developed widely in a short time. The high prices of the year 1770, the hardships of 1799 [in the Napoleonic wars], and the famine of 1817 strongly encouraged its adoption. It happened almost everywhere without detriment to cereal cultivation, because the *Erdäpfel* was either planted in meadows that were previously poor and were broken for the first

time for this purpose, or used for improving the production of fallow fields. At
the least, this crop has increased the number of farm households that could
satisfy their own needs and for whom the grain was often insufficient. All of
Switzerland with the population increase that has taken place in the last
century does not have to buy as much foreign grain as previously. The potato is
frequently used by both the rich and the poor who find it tasty and nourishing.
Potatoes are also fed to domestic animals and used in some cantons for brandy.

[Franscini 1848:120]

By the middle of the nineteenth century, Switzerland was producing an
estimated 9 million hectoliters, or 375 liters per inhabitant, from 70,000
hectares (Brugger 1956:39). Because the potato was added to, rather than
substituted for, cereals in most areas, the highland dwellers were freed
from the despotism of the "great winters" and the devastating hail storms
(Pfister 1975:166). The diversification of crops having different seasons
and optimum growing conditions lessened the risk of massive harvest
failure and the ensuing population crises.

The same environmental conditions that made potato cultivation
advantageous in other parts of alpine Switzerland certainly applied to
Törbel and the other villages of upper Valais. Although somewhat more
isolated than the northern slopes of the Alps, the Vispertal was subject to
climatic fluctuations similar to those that endangered the rye crop.
Winter rye, which sprouts in the fall and lies dormant under the snow, is
threatened by a delayed melting and by the fungus *Fusarium nivale*
(*Schneeschimmel*) that develops under these conditions. A wet summer
causes the unripe grain to lodge or fall to the ground. These vagaries of
the weather were not infrequent in Törbel, and it is possible that the
years 1770–1 were especially difficult. There is no direct evidence of
exactly when potatoes were accepted there. They were first listed by
market price in the cantonal capital of Sion in 1800. Stories are still told
of the resistance of villagers to the strange crop. The semilegendary feats
of strength attributed to men of the past were said later to be impossible
"because of the usual eating of potatoes" (Heinzmann n.d.:134). A man
named Peter who lived in the Zen Blatten neighborhood of Törbel is
remembered as defying local convention to grow potatoes. People laughed
at him for harvesting all of three pack baskets full when he had only two
daughters to feed. These occurrences cannot be pinned down in time, but
potatoes were certainly being grown before 1816–17. Bad weather and
great want at that time forced even the valley's largest grain-producing
village, Visperterminen, to adopt the crop. A priest writing in the 1860s
left this account:

This was the time when the potato first came to be rightly honored. Until then
people regarded the potato as a food stuff fit only for swine, and one would have
been embarrassed to put them on the table. Anyone who collected more than a

pack basket (*Tschiffere*) full was the subject of universal derision. In the aforementioned two years (1816, 1817) everyone was delighted to be able to still his hunger with potatoes. . . . Today hundred of families would be hungry if it weren't for potatoes. [Studer, cited by Heinzmann n.d.:120]

This at least provides a terminal date for the general consumption of potatoes, but it is probable that villages such as Törbel, whose rye fields were less extensive and less fortunately situated than those of Vispertermine, had resorted to the new crop somewhat earlier.

Even early trials would have demonstrated the economic potential of potatoes. They can flourish without irrigation, and the dry terraced gardens and fallow grainfields of Törbel were admirably suited to them. Stebler (1922:65) marveled that potatoes could be planted every year in the same Törbel plots without a sign of declining yields. The terraces of Lauiäcker on the way to Embd have never gone out of annual production within human memory. Late frosts or a long summer drought might lessen the harvest, but scattered potato patches at different altitudes could limit that risk. The potato blight did not blacken and rot the tubers until 1852, and even then only about one-third of the crop was lost (Zurbriggen 1960). Wood channels might be used twice a summer to bring some water to potatoes that needed it, but according to a local proverb, "The drier the mountain, the better the potatoes" (Stebler 1914:76). In 1919 potatoes occupied 13.42 hectares within the Törbel village territory, whereas grain was raised on 24.14 hectares (Stebler 1922:58). The heavier production of potatoes, an average 190 kilograms per 100 square meters (Studienwoche 1967:82), as compared with 13 kilograms of rye from the same area (Imboden 1956:38, 51), meant that estimated Törbel annual production would have been 255,000 kilograms of potatoes and 31,400 kilograms of rye. Although raw potatoes contain a good bit of water, they still yield 76 calories per 100 grams, whereas whole-grain rye is equivalent to 334 calories per 100 grams (Watt and Merill 1975). Using the average-yield figures cited earlier, a plot of 100 square meters would produce 144,400 calories of potatoes as against 43,420 calories for rye, a 3.3:1 advantage.

Törbel's conversion to potato cultivation was by no means total. Family holdings still included grain *Aecker,* and a larger area of the choice terrace land was devoted to rye than to potatoes. Household subsistence continued to require dairy products and enough meadows to support a few cows. It seems probable that peasants needed somewhat less land than formerly, but there was no drastic shrinkage in farm size as among the potato-dependent Irish cotters. We may estimate, however, that if the entire area devoted to rye and potatoes in 1919 had produced rye alone, the caloric yield of those 37.56 hectares would have been some

163 million calories. This contrasts with the approximately 296 million calories available from grain and potatoes in the proportions stated earlier. Is it accidental that the increase in carbohydrate calories by a factor of 1.8 closely parallels the 1.8 increase in Törbel population in the major period of growth between 1790 and 1867?

Although potatoes have only about one-sixth the protein of rye, it is probable that protein was not a nutritionally limiting factor where dairy products were consumed year-round. Indeed, the combination of buttermilk and potatoes, so common in pre-famine Ireland, has been judged nutritionally sound (Plaisted n.d.). Thus it would seem that the introduction of potatoes made economic sense in Törbel: The growing of potatoes permitted the use of a wider range of land, including high-altitude, steep, and fallow plots, for food production; potatoes required little or no new investment for cultivating and processing tools; they achieved higher caloric yields per unit of land with perhaps less labor expenditure; they were more dependable than grain in the alpine zone; and they filled a nutritional need. Although it is difficult to infer how rapidly these advantages were realized, it is difficult to believe that the adoption of potatoes did not materially improve the local peasant diet and raise the carrying capacity of their lands.

If the coming of the potato to Törbel in the late eighteenth or early nineteenth century raised living standards sufficiently to alter the old balance of mortality and fertility, we would have to postulate a preexisting diet that was somewhat more limited. Again, the poverty of the records is such that no convincing outline of peasant nutrition in the 1700s can be offered. There are only tantalizing hints on caloric adequacy, seasonal scarcity, and nutritional balance. The general tendencies in European diets as a whole were downward from a peak in the Middle Ages, after the plague had depopulated vast areas and created a surplus of vacant land. The relatively high meat content declined, and meat was increasingly replaced by cereals and vegetable products in succeeding centuries (Braudel 1973:130; Teuteberg 1975). Food prices went up faster than wages, and the buying power of workers declined. A Languedoc peasant of 1590 consumed as many calories as his predecessor of 1480, with average daily rations of almost 2 kilograms of bread and 2 liters of wine for an adult male, but his estimated meat consumption had been cut in half, to 20 kilograms per year, and fat was also deficient in the diet (Le Roy Ladurie 1974:103). Pauperism became a major social problem in Spain, Germany, The Netherlands, and England in the 1530s, and there was widespread hunger (Le Roy Ladurie 1974:142). The food supply remained precarious, and there was no substantial rise in real per-capita incomes until after 1800. Estimated caloric intake per day per person in France went from 1,750 calories in 1781–1800 to 2,000 calories in 1815–24, 2,850 calories in 1855–64, and 3,150 calories in 1895–1900 (Mondot-Bernard 1977:30). Food pensions promised to dependent adults in wills and marriage contracts from a French town in 1754–67 include reference to rye and sometimes barley, cabbage, turnips, salt, lard, cheese, and butter (Bernard 1975). There was provision for at least 500 grams of bread per day, but the rations of dairy products and fats were low. Few of these pensions provided the 2,400 calories per day "needed for moderate work," and several yielded less than 1,500 calories "needed to sustain life." The average of 12 complete pensions was a meager 1,934 calories per day (Bernard 1975).[7]

Until the coming of the potato, Swiss peasants were nourished mainly on bread and cereal porridges, with some beans, fruit, milk, and dairy products. Poorer households had meat only a few times a year (Brugger 1956:13). A cow might give 4 to 5 liters of milk per day, and 15 liters were needed to make 1 kilogram of butter or house cheese (Bielmann 1972:181). A goat might provide about 300 liters of milk per year. Once potato cultivation was adopted in alpine regions, it almost immediately assumed major significance in the diet. From population statistics and a tithe book kept by a country parson from a village near Lucerne in 1782, it appears that already 98 percent of the households were planting potatoes, and only 73 percent continued to grow the former staple grain, barley (Bucher 1974:176). A nutritional analysis for an average family of five, including two adults, two young children, and an adolescent, listed milk and milk products as providing daily 3,711 calories, grains providing 3,611 calories, and potatoes adding 1,927 calories. The total intake of 9,249 calories was 95 percent of the recommended daily dietary allowances for such a household in the United States today. Protein exceeded requirements, and the diet was low only in iron and to a lesser extent in vitamin A (Bucher 1974:178).[8] Because 20 percent of all calories were derived from potatoes, and because this nutritional resource probably exceeded that available in an earlier period from grain alone, as described earlier, it is likely that the new tuber crop brought real quantitative improvement to local peasant diets without undermining the nutritional balance.

An even heavier dependence on the potato may have developed in many Swiss communities over the first few decades of the nineteenth century. Contemporary accounts from Törbel suggest that potatoes were consumed almost every day and might turn up at any or all of the three meals.[9] Potatoes are the main source of carbohydrates in Tristan da Cunha, and a consumption of 1.7 to 2.1 kilograms per person per day is considered adequate (Salaman 1949:546). A traveler in Ireland in

1776–9 estimated that a family of five might eat 127 kilograms of potatoes a week, with grown men averaging in the neighborhood of 5.5 kilograms per day (Salaman 1949:254). Törbel potato use was not on this scale, but the caloric contribution of this single crop to the daily diet was impressive. Estimated production in 1920, minus seed potatoes, would have supplied each person in Törbel with an average 0.94 kilogram of potatoes per day, equal to 673 calories.[10] A family of five would have consumed 3,365 calories per day in potatoes, 75 percent more than that estimated for the Entlebuch village in 1782, as described previously.

We do not know anything about the relative height and weight or the maturation of women in eighteenth-century Swiss villages, but it is a reasonable assumption that their diet was somewhat low in calories, though not usually so deficient as to bring about direct clinical symptoms of malnutrition. Caloric shortfall rather than protein deficiency has been linked with longer periods of postpartum amenorrhea (Mondot-Bernard 1977:7). Not so much a low level of food consumption as a sudden deterioration in the quantity and quality of the diet can show up in temporary cessation of menstruation, as it did when the daily rations in Berlin in 1916 fell from 2,955 to 1,961 calories (Mondot-Bernard 1977:14). Seasonal shortages in pre-potato Törbel might have had a similar effect. A higher level of carbohydrate intake could then directly affect female fertility. Moreover, the potato softened with milk as an infant food supplement would almost certainly have shortened the period of lactation or decreased its intensity, thereby allowing a more rapid resumption of ovulation and shorter birth intervals.[11] Large potato harvests could even increase the supply of protein and fats, because peelings and small tubers were fed to pigs, probably allowing more people to keep these efficient domestic producers of meat and lard. In marginal northern farming areas such as Norway, it is affirmed that potato cultivation did more than anything else to raise the productivity of farms and farm workers and that the decline in the Norwegian death rate after 1815 is attributable to the introduction of the potato (Drake 1969:54, 59).

Despite the imponderables of the exact date of potato adoption in Törbel, the degree to which it increased calories in the peasant diet, and the effect of this nutritional change on mortality and fertility, we have offered a variety of circumstantial evidence linking the historical introduction of a new food resource to demographic changes involving a sustained local population growth. The idea is by no means a new one. Historians, geographers, and demographers have often hypothesized that the coming of American food plants (such as maize, potatoes, sweet potatoes, and peanuts) to the Old World ignited the general population growth visible first in the eighteenth century (Langer 1963; Polgar 1972; Crosby 1972; McKeown 1976; Segraves 1978). Anthropologists have inferred that similar historical processes were at work in Italian, Spanish, Tibetan, and Nepalese localities they have studied.[12] Northern European population expansion is often credited to the effect of the potato in ameliorating the recurrent demographic crises that followed poor grain harvests and thus lowering mortality (Drake 1969:157).[13] Because the potato provided subsistence from a smaller plot of land than that necessary for grain or animal pasturage, an adequate holding was easier to acquire, and peasant children might marry earlier and begin having children. This was evidently the case in Ireland (Blake and Davis 1956:216; Connell 1968:113).[14] The Törbel example, although supporting the notion that the increased food supply may have lowered mortality to some degree, does not show an abrupt decrease in age at marriage or proportion of celibates; rather, it suggests that fertility changes came about because of shorter birth intervals and therefore higher average fecundity among married women.

Tracing major biological and demographic effects to a unique and historically dated innovation may sound suspiciously monocausal, as in those evolutionary schemes in which everything flows from some new technology for capturing energy. However, the acceptance of the potato was not an isolated event of cultural diffusion. The crop had been known in Europe for 200 years, and its adoption was part of a systemic ecological change. Potato cultivation represented a further intensification of mountain mixed farming that already relied on irrigation, manuring, and microadaptations to a number of altitudinal zones. There is presumptive evidence in these agricultural practices, in the attempts to expand the village land base, and in the regulating devices of local land tenure rules and community closure that Törbel had coped with population pressure for hundreds of years. The severe climatic fluctuations and bad grain harvests of the late eighteenth century and early nineteenth century threatened peasant subsistence and forced adoption of a new crop. Population had not suddenly increased, but the means to support it from village lands had dramatically declined, and agricultural intensification followed from the same disequilibrium between population and resources that Ester Boserup (1965) has described. More food production per unit of land and probably a higher total labor input were required, but the change took place only when the availability of the new food crop, filtered through the experience of other Swiss peasants, coincided with a period of severe scarcity.

To preserve their traditional self-sufficiency, the people of Törbel changed, but they changed no more than they had to. They could not know that the means they took to avoid a population crisis would also power sustained population growth. Without altering their rules of land tenure and inheritance, their sanctions associated with marriage, their attitudes toward childbearing, or their cultural values of household economic autonomy, the members of this little Swiss community found themselves experiencing changes in the scale of their social unit and in the nature of their relationship with the environment. The demographic adjustments set in motion by an alteration in diet carried the village along the same course of expansion that cottage industries and new settlement frontiers were producing elsewhere. The results of this growth, such as increased out-migration, economic interdependence, and the breakdown of local isolation and self-determination, were part of a general and basically homogeneous modernization process operating on amazingly diverse original social groups.

8

Prudential checks and balances in inheritance and marriage

Peasant marriage in that great region north of the Mediterranean lands and west of the Slavic countries clearly shows a distinctive European pattern. This has been characterized by Hajnal (1965) as exhibiting two things: a high age at marriage and a high proportion of persons who never marry at all. There is abundant documentation of this pattern in parts of sixteenth-century Western Europe, and its presence has been noted for England during the late fourteenth century (Wrigley 1977). It is possible that a fully evolved European marriage pattern, with most women marrying at age 25 or above, and 10 to 15 percent never marrying, was present everywhere north of the Pyrenees by 1550 (Chaunu 1974; Monter 1979). The classic example of this cultural complex in anthropology is the Irish case of countrymen whose marriages were delayed until late in life and who had a high proportion of celibates (Arensberg and Kimball 1940). Although these social practices may have appeared in such an exaggerated form only after the great mid-nineteenth-century famine, anthropologists have examined them with little reference to either their historical development or their demographic consequences. Instead, late marriage has been functionally related to land scarcity, to the necessity to inherit a farm before establishing a new household, to strong patriarchal control of the estate, to a close mother/son emotional tie, to Irish Catholic sexual prudery, and to the out-migration of noninheriting children.

We cannot deal substantively with the variety of psychological, ethnic, and ideological issues raised by multicausal discussions of age at marriage, but there may be advantages in focusing on a single ethnographic case of interaction between demographic and economic factors. Certainly the economic questions of agricultural land availability, inheritance, farm fragmentation, household labor force, and provision for the elderly have been emphasized by social scientists. "Probably it may be

said with truth that in almost all the more improved countries of modern
Europe, the principal check which at present keeps the population down
to the level of the actual means of subsistence is the prudential restraint
on marriage" (Malthus, quoted by Habakkuk 1971:11). The European
pattern of late marriage and high celibacy, for which Törbel provides
such a classic and continuing example, had been traced to economic
factors even before Malthus. The astronomer Halley concluded from his
study of vital statistics in seventeenth-century Breslau "that the Growth
and Increase of Mankind is not so much stinted by anything in the nature
of the species as it is from the cautious difficulty most people make to
adventure on the state of marriage, from the prospect of the trouble and
charge of providing for a family" (quoted by Habakkuk 1971:11).
Malthus recognized that the fund of food was obviously related to the age
at marriage and that as the pressure of population on food supplies grew,
marriage would be postponed and the procreation of children outside
marriage strictly forbidden (Laslett 1965:108). "Because marriage was
associated with the setting up of a separate household, births were linked
with the availability of resources" (Habakkuk 1971:2).

There is explicit formal recognition of the tie between marriage and
the acquisition of a material foundation for a farm family in very early
legal practices. Although Homans's study (1960) of thirteenth-century
English villagers emphasized the sentiments and values of traditional
village life, the manorial court rolls show stringent controls on marriage.
Not only was the acquisition of rights to land through inheritance or
retirement of a parent necessary before the single heir could gain
permission to marry, but the heir's siblings who remained on the holding
were also compelled to remain single (Homans 1960:137, 149). In other
cases in which primogeniture was the rule, living landholders did not
turn their property over to the heir until written contracts were made out
stipulating in detail the annual amount and type of food, the rights to
gardens and fuel, and the lodging set aside for the retired couple. The
tension that must have been frequent in the relationship between the
unmarried dependent heir and his elderly father is evident in this
Austrian folk song quoted by Berkner (1972a):

> Voda, wann gibst ma denn's Hoamatl,
> Voda, wann loszt ma's vaschreiben?
> s' Dirndl is gwoxen wia's Groamatl,
> Lede wülls a nimmer bleiben.

> Voda, wann gibst ma denn's Hoamatl,
> Voda, wann gibst ma denn's Haus,
> Wann gehst denn amol in dein Stüberl ein,
> Und grobst da bra Eräpfoln aus?

Father, when ya gonna gimme the farm,
Father, w hen ya gonna sign it away?
My girl's been growin every day,
And single no longer wants to stay.

Father, when ya gonna gimme the farm,
Father, when ya gonna gimme the house.
When ya gonna retire to your room out of the way,
And dig up your potatoes all day?

In our discussions of agricultural self-sufficiency, land tenure, marriage, and household formation in Törbel throughout its recent 300-year history, we have assumed that marriage was indeed a prime regulator of demographic growth and that it responded in a systematic fashion to economic factors. We have interpreted the dominance of small-landholder peasant families, the absence of landless laborers, the relatively narrow range of wealth, and the persistence of village family lines as evidence that families continued to have adequate land bases and that marriage was often postponed to protect customary living standards (see Chapters 3 and 4). The decision to marry has been treated as if it were contingent on access to both private and communal agricultural resources in the various environmental zones and to the various domestic animals, implements, and farm buildings needed for a household enter- prise. Because young couples almost never moved in with their parents, finding a vacant apartment (*Wohnung*) or building a new house was a problem in itself. As Malthus noted for eighteenth-century England, "One of the most salutary and least pernicious checks to the frequency of early marriage in this country is the difficulty of procuring a cottage" (quoted by Macfarlane 1976:223). The consistent average of 2.2 children per household who eventually married and the increases in the age at marriage, the proportion of celibates, and the migration that accompanied local population growth all suggest that marriage functioned in a finely calibrated manner to preserve stability and dampen fluctuations in the population/resource system. But the density-dependent mechanisms and feedback loops we describe, although well supported by prevailing opinions in demography, are difficult to demonstrate directly. We have records of marriages and records of the deaths of unmarried adults, but how did individuals evaluate the myriad personal factors that resulted in the choices they made, and what factors produced the statistical regulari- ties we find in their decisions? By looking at the legal and customary constraints and options on property acquisition and at the demographic parameters of individual married partners, we may be able to approxi- mate some of the considerations that affected marriage in Törbel.

Marriage in Törbel created a new household, and a household by definition required its own independent sources of support. Access to the means of peasant livelihood came most often through inheritance of property from relatives of one or both of the new spouses. Inheritance took place at the death or retirement of a parent or of other kin who lacked living offspring as heirs. Alternatively, a household might be financed by the proceeds of wage work, either as continuing income or as an investment in local land and buildings. The rules accompanying the transmission of property from one generation to another both slowed and restricted the circulation of these crucial goods, favoring parents at the expense of children and married village residents over adult but unmarried village residents. In the first place, marriage did not automatically grant either partner some portion of the parental estate. There was no entitlement of a man to share in his father's land so long as the father lived and chose to work it himself. A daughter had no dowry in either real estate or movable wealth conferred on her at the time of marriage. If both parents were alive, they made the decision on when to retire. It was not infrequent to see hale and active Törbel peasant proprietors in their 60s or 70s still working all of their land with the help of grown children who had remained at home. Other sons and daughters were deprived of all support from such estates when they married. Although their eventual shares in the parental property were not affected, they could not benefit from family income until the division took place at death or retirement.[1]

There is no doubt that children who had married or those who wished to marry might put pressure on a father to distribute his wealth, but because most peasants had only enough land to sustain a single household adequately, the father would normally have no desire to reduce his holding while he still had need of it. Economic authority in the household was rooted solidly in the ownership of property, and no one wished to transfer the principal peasant status marker to another and assume a dependent role. Even a widow might remain as the head of the household while her children were young and perhaps for many years after if some of these offspring stayed single. The older generation retained control even over those of their offspring who worked for cash outside of the community. Until perhaps 30 years ago, all the earnings of a young person, except what was needed for bare subsistence, were voluntarily sent back to the parents. There are many tales of people who worked for years in other parts of Switzerland but married with only a few francs in their pockets. Such remittances ceased after marriage, but it was a point of pride that the employed person acted as a full supporting member of his natal household and did not put money away for his own future family.

When advanced age or illness finally persuaded a parent to retire, the shares of the estate might still be too small for the maintenance of separate households. Although Swiss law allows a stated fraction of an estate to be disposed of by testament, with the rest going in equal portions to the heirs, wills are rare in Törbel.[2] The custom of partible inheritance is so strong that it is taken for granted. Heirs themselves agree on the composition of these equivalent shares some weeks before drawing lots for them. In practice, the names of parcels and associated buildings making up each share are written on sheets of paper and drawn from a hat. Drawing is by age, from youngest child to oldest child. A father may have a voice in compiling the shares, but the heirs must agree on the fairness of the division. If an heir is a minor, his interests are protected by a community-appointed guardian. The efficacy of this deliberate and unhurried process of division is indicated by the almost total absence of inheritance disputes.[3] In the past, heirs always had direct experience with the character and potential productivity of each parcel of land, and they arrived at share equivalence without measuring the land or using tax valuations to estimate its monetary value. Nevertheless, calculations of several estate divisions in this century have shown a close approach to equal worth in francs of each heir's portion. Where village records have shown some obvious departure from strict partibility, further inquiry has always revealed that a stated (but not written) transfer of cash from one shareholder to another had righted the balance.[4] Special requirements may be met by the division, as when a lame brother is given land near his village home, but a real equivalence of shares appears to be a cultural ideal that is generally achieved in practice. There are no measurable differences in inheritance based on sex, birth rank, or marital status of the heirs, and even mentally incompetent individuals receive shares held in trust for them.

Parental control over the timing of retirement and inheritance, the absence of marriage portions, the continued residence and support of celibate children in their parental household, and the careful, equitable sharing of the estate when it is eventually divided all militated against early access to property and thus marriage by young adults. The system was, of course, not entirely inflexible. Where a family had extensive lands, use rights (*Nutzungsrecht*) in particular plots might be given to married children, but the land was included with all the rest for the final division by lot. Parents often retired by degrees, arranging one division in which the most distant and least valuable parcels were given out and a second division 6 or 8 years later in which all but a choice garden or meadow and the village house were passed on to the heirs. Vineyards might be apportioned in a separate drawing. After an initial division, the younger children might still keep their livestock with their father's.

Parents assured their own support in old age by retaining a little agricultural land and lifelong rights in a house. Children might, in return for their inheritance, agree to give the old couple a stipulated sum every month. In some cases this retirement fund was a bank deposit that had been accumulated from the children's earnings.[5] Adult single children often lived with their elderly parents or a widowed parent, and such celibate siblings might keep their inherited shares together as a corporate holding (*Erbgemeinschaft*). Old uncles or aunts without children of their own might take their meals with a niece or nephew, having agreed to will the niece or nephew an apartment or a desirable bit of property.

A number of essentially chance factors could affect the possibility of marriage. Property might be more readily available in a wealthier family or in a family in which the parents or celibate kin died early or where there was only one inheriting child. Wages from outside labor might be sufficient to found a household, and a lucky match to a rich spouse might allow a portionless youngster to marry at an age below the average. A young man might rent land and a cow or sharecrop some fields, supplementing his small income with day labor or craft work while he awaited a property division. Although marriage was possible under such circumstances, it was a hand-to-mouth affair, and as Anneler (1917:251) has noted for turn-of-the-century Lötschental, such a couple had to fight for their bread even when their parents were wealthy. Unpredictable demographic or economic circumstances might combine to further delay marriage. A large number of siblings who remained in the village might restrict the size of shares regardless of when they were allocated. Fragmentation of an estate might be wiped out only in a succeeding generation when shares belonging to celibates and childless siblings were recombined in the holdings of their married siblings' children. Debts were also heritable, and if the heirs were too young to assume them, their property might be sold promptly to pay the encumbrances. In such a situation even kin as close as a brother might be unwilling to accept his dead sibling's debts and protect his minor nephews and nieces from loss of property.

The legal framework of inheritance that often delayed and restricted property acquisition, the moral order of a community that required a peasant household to be economically viable, and the limited opportunities for an independent livelihood outside of agriculture combined to limit and channel the possibilities for marriage in traditional Törbel. To discuss the quality of romantic love, the individual dreams and disappointments that accompanied this pairing down through the years, is not possible; the blunt tools of social science cannot fashion an imaginative reconstruction of how people felt. But we can look for regularities gleaned statistically from a multitude of marriages, asking what demographic variables rendered early marriage as opposed to late marriage more probable, how sex and birth rank and marriage order and migration influenced this decision. We must assume that marriage for Törbjers entailed a great deal of very practical forethought and that it was not generally a hasty or precipitate action. There can be little doubt that marriage in a peasant society was a matter in which serious economic considerations often took precedence over emotional attachments and in which parents as well as potential spouses were deeply involved. Although parental preferences were often expressed in Törbel and certain partners were judged unsuitable because of relative wealth or membership in a rival political party, it does not appear that formal matchmaking was important. Because all families were small landholders and there were few, if any, permanently landless laborers, the risks of "marrying down" were not great, and the need for close parental supervision was correspondingly small (Löfgren 1974). There was ample opportunity for the young people, their parents, and, indeed, the community as a whole to decide on the prospects for a marriage during the long courtship. This period of acquaintance or *Bekanntschaft* involved public walking together and Sunday visits to the girl's home. It often went on for 5 to 10 years. The pair had probably known each other from childhood, because until this century 85 percent of those people who remained in Törbel married endogamously (Hagaman, Elias, and Netting 1978). All of a family's knowledge was brought to bear on matters of marriage. As a man from Lötschental shrewdly put it, "If one marries, one must darn well pay attention, so that one doesn't get hooked up with the lower type of people. Many people think that the main thing is to marry money. Pfui! I wouldn't say that. Sure it's good when a man has his little possessions. Everyone knows that. But just to look out for such things does no one any good."

In Törbel the story is told with relish of five brothers who worked together for years as muleteers operating the famous *Maultierpost* and conveying guests and supplies to Saas-Fee in the summer. As the custom was until recently, they turned all of their earnings over without question to their father. The savings were used at the end of World War I to erect an imposing many-story house in the village. Then on a single day in 1921, the brothers all married and moved into their new apartments. They were at the time 39, 37, 34, 32, and 29 years old (Netting 1972). With an average age at first marriage for men of 30.0 and for women of 28.6, it is obvious that Törbel people married only after mature reflection, and a significant number of them never married at all. For purposes of this analysis we shall be using data on the marriages of 885 men and

Table 8.1. *Numbers and cumulative percentages of males and females marrying at different ages*

Age at mar- riage	Males		Females		Age at mar- riage	Males		Females	
	Num- ber	Cumu- lative per- centage	Num- ber	Cumu- lative per- centage		Num- ber	Cumu- lative per- centage	Num- ber	Cumu- lative per- centage
16			2	0	41	8	94	12	97
17	5	1	6	1	42	10	95	8	98
18	3	1	13	2	43	5	96	3	98
19	2	1	20	5	44	5	96	5	99
20	11	2	41	9	45	1	96	1	99
21	13	4	41	14	46	4	97	3	99
22	34	8	57	20	47	6	98		
23	44	13	54	26	48	6	98		
24	56	19	66	33	49	1	98	1	99
25	53	25	64	41	50	1	99	2	99
26	82	34	46	46	51	2	99	1	100
27	64	41	59	52	52	1	99	1	100
28	51	47	132	67	53				
29	57	54	47	72	54	1	99	2	100
30	43	59	39	77	55	2	99		
31	92	69	32	80	56	1	99		
32	45	74	26	83	57	1	99		
33	33	78	19	85	58				
34	26	81	16	87	59	1	100		
35	21	83	18	89	60				
36	21	85	21	91	65	2	100		
37	20	88	7	92	66	1	100		
38	25	91	12	94	68	1	100		
39	17	92	11	95	70			1	100
40	7	93	7	96					

896 women over the period 1667 to 1974.[6] By examining departures from this average age of marriage and the factors correlated with it in the experience of individuals, we may be able to uncover the calculations that swayed this complex and personally critical life choice.

The consistent difference of 2.5 to 3 years between the average ages of males and females at first marriage (Table 8.1) and the fact that these ages tend to rise and fall together suggest that cultural expectations of marriage and the appropriate roles of the sexes did not change a great deal in the time being considered. Although both males and females could own property, men were voting citizens in the closed corporate communi- ty, and communal rights in the village alp and forest were passed down through the male line. Men were at least nominal household heads and

Table 8.2. *Influence of birth rank and marriage rank on marriage age*

	Male (mean age 30.04)		Female (mean age 27.53)	
	Number	Deviation from mean	Number	Deviation from mean
Siblings alive at ego's marriage				
None	246	−1.06	274	−1.45
One or more	640	0.41	623	0.64
Birth rank				
1	178	0.68	171	−0.21
2	146	−0.62	144	1.10
3	110	0.44	126	0.56
4	123	−0.47	106	−0.17
5	89	1.05	95	0.10
6	71	−0.43	67	−1.04
7	53	−0.70	54	0.54
8 or more	96	−0.47	121	−1.19
Marriage rank				
1	322	−2.03	373	−1.77
2	202	0.13	226	−0.25
3	143	1.69	125	2.07
4	95	1.88	77	2.02
5 or more	106	1.95	83	3.62

had the major responsibility for ensuring the family's adequate subsistence. With advancing age, the chances increased that they would have access to sufficient property and could initiate a marriage. Women could presumably marry somewhat earlier because they could find older men able to support them. There are, however, interesting exceptions to this rule that we shall take up later. Because male fertility has a longer span than that of females, males could also marry later and expect to raise a family. About 6 percent of first marriages for males took place after age 45, but only 2 percent of females married late in life for the first time (Table 8.1). By age 31, 80 percent of the women had married, compared with 69 percent of the men. The most frequent age of marriage was 31 for males and 28 for females. The fact that 132 women married at age 28 suggests a cultural preference for this degree of maturity. Almost no one married before age 16, and there were only 10 teenage marriages among men and 41 among women.

If inheritance and rights to property are indeed an important determinant of marriage age, the factor of whether an individual is an only child or has siblings with whom the estate must be shared may be significant. Village consultants told me that most relatively wealthy individuals were so because of the luck of an undivided inheritance. A

Table 8.3. *Relationship between birth rank and marriage status*[a]

	Birth rank								Row total
	1	2	3	4	5	6	7	8+	
Male[b]									
Percent celibate	25.2	25.1	28.1	24.5	23.3	24.5	27.4	25.8	25.4
Percent married	74.8	74.9	71.9	75.5	76.7	75.5	72.6	74.2	74.6
Total number	238	195	153	163	116	94	73	132	1,164
Female[c]									
Percent celibate	20.1	19.2	25.4	22.6	20.2	21.4	27.0	18.8	21.5
Percent married	79.9	80.8	74.6	77.4	79.8	78.6	73.0	81.2	78.5
Total number	214	177	169	137	119	84	74	149	1,123

[a]Married: those individuals married between 1667 and 1974. Celibate: those individuals who reached at least age 15 and who never married.
[b]χ^2 = 1.14688; significance = 0.9932.
[c]χ^2 = 4.57918; significance = 0.7112.

family with only one surviving adult son might encourage that son to marry in order to bring another pair of hands into the household and increase its labor force. A girl who was a sole heiress was especially desirable as a marriage partner, and men often planned and schemed in order to win her. Men with no living siblings married, on the average, 1.5 years earlier than others, and the difference was 2.1 years for such women (Table 8.2). Birth rank showed no consistent relationship with age at marriage, fluctuating up and down at successive birth ranks (Table 8.2). Although there was no primogeniture or ultimogeniture in Törbel, it might well be hypothesized that children early in the birth order would be called on to look after their younger siblings and would therefore have less chance of marrying at all. If partible inheritance in actuality gave some advantage to a first child, a higher proportion of that rank might marry. This was definitely not the case. Table 8.3 shows that about 25.4 percent of males and 21.5 percent of females remained celibate and that the proportion who never married stayed remarkably constant across all birth ranks. Indeed, the figures for men prove the null hypothesis by showing a less than 1 percent probability that the choice of whether or not to marry was influenced by birth order.

Birth order was, however, correlated with marriage rank, explaining 37 percent of the variation in marriage rank among men and 31 percent among women. This suggests that there was at least a tendency for siblings to marry in order of their birth.[7] The relationship is not stronger because siblings at various ranks of the birth order died before reaching marriageable age and because women married, on the average, younger

Table 8.4. *Relationship between marriage rank and average age at marriage*

	Marriage rank				
	1	2	3	4	5 and over
Average marriage age (males)	28.01	30.17	31.73	31.92	31.99
Average marriage age (females)	25.76	27.28	29.60	29.55	31.15

than men. Females married first in their sibling groups 53 percent of the time and males 47 percent.

The order in which successive siblings married was, unlike birth rank, an important factor in marriage age. The analysis of variation in Table 8.4 shows that the average age at marriage for those who married first among a group of siblings was lowered by 2.03 years for men and 1.77 years for women. Although marriage rank contributed most to the explained variance of age at marriage, it also interacted with birth rank to produce a greater range of variation from the mean. If children early in the birth order married first and at lower average ages, and the marriages of those farther down the list were delayed, the numbers of unmarried and married siblings present should also show a relationship to age at marriage. Indeed, there was a clear tendency for the presence of one or more unmarried siblings to decrease marriage age and for one or more married siblings to increase it (Table 8.5). One or two unmarried siblings lowered the marriage age only slightly in the sample that pooled the sexes. Three or more single and presumably younger siblings still at home lowered marriage age by 1.5 years. There was an even stronger progressive tendency for the presence of married siblings to delay the marriage of an individual. If three such siblings founded their own households and moved out of the parental family (there is generally a very small percentage of multiple families in Törbel), a remaining sibling would marry 2.17 years later than normal, whereas with four or more married siblings the delay would average 4.97 years.

In a family with several children, it appears that the first to marry could often do so at a relatively young age. With several single siblings still in the household, the agricultural labor force would not suffer from the loss of one able-bodied member. Because Törbel holdings were generally large enough to support a family, but with few resources for extra adults, an older child could be spared, and his departure would mean that there would be one less mouth to feed. Succeeding marriages might be more difficult because the parental couple would be less willing to part with the remaining children who were taking over an increasing

Table 8.5. *Effects of unmarried and married siblings on marriage age (both sexes)*

	Number	Deviation from mean marriage age of 29.36
Unmarried siblings		
All married	200	3.38
1	366	−0.21
2	250	−0.24
3	173	−1.29
4	93	−1.41
5 or more	94	−1.96
Married siblings		
All unmarried	545	−1.86
1	360	1.03
2	162	1.84
3	70	2.17
4 or more	39	4.97

part of the farm'work. Younger children would have the same chances of marriage as their older siblings in the long run, but it is possible that their parents increasingly sought to keep them at home for support in their old age. This also kept the peasant farmstead together and resisted pressures from married children for the retirement of the older couple and division of the estate. This was particularly evident when all siblings were married (category "All married" in Table 8.5) and marriage came almost 3.4 years later than average. Although an older daughter would evidently not be retained in the household to help with the care of smaller children, a younger daughter might well have acted as housekeeper and nurse for aging or widowed parents. The correlation between age at marriage and the number of married siblings was higher for women ($r = 0.33$) than for men ($r = 0.19$). To this day it is common for a daughter to accept the obligation to look after an elderly parent after the other children have married and left home. When siblings have migrated out of the village, a remaining child has the dual burden of caring for surviving kin and keeping the family land in cultivation. When such duties delay or even prevent marriage, their acceptance is often accompanied by a strong strain of only partially suppressed resentment.

The argument that children who married first tended to marry young seems to run counter to the contention that inheritance of property was necessary to found a new household. Those marrying ahead of and younger than their siblings would frequently be setting out on their own while the parental couple was still young. If, indeed, the estate had been

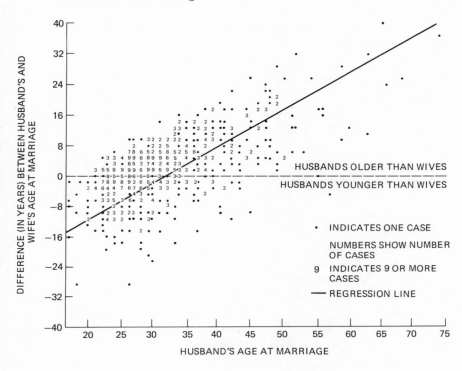

Figure 8.1. Age differences between spouses in Törbel.

divided, children later in the marriage order would have had the chance to marry more promptly than their siblings, rather than waiting as they obviously did. A possible way out of this enigma is to consider what means other than inheritance there were for setting up a new peasant household. A younger adult without immediate prospects for property could always marry by finding a well-endowed mate. In Törbel the chances were high that such a person would be older and thus already in possession of an inheritance or a farmstead left by a deceased spouse.[8] This pattern actually prevailed, as is seen when we plot age at marriage against the difference in the ages of the spouses (Figure 8.1). Twenty-eight percent of all men were younger than their wives at marriage, and up to age 25 the majority of men took older spouses. Beyond age 45, practically no men married women older than themselves. By this age they had almost certainly acquired property of their own, and they could afford to marry a woman many years their junior.[9] The correlation is strong and consistent, with 40 percent of the variation in male age at marriage being explained by the age difference of the spouses; it is also evident, although less consistent, among women, where age difference accounts for 17 percent of the variation. Swiss alpine peasants recognize the romantic attractions of youth and a pretty face, but they are eminently practical about obtaining the economic wherewithal to sustain a new household. When asked why someone married a stolid matronly woman, they replied with the proverb *Sie het Härd am Füdle* (she has earth on her bottom).

If succession to landholdings, livestock, and farm buildings was such an important part of the developmental cycle in peasant households, how often was marriage contingent on the death or retirement of a parent? With a tradition of late marriage, a son would, on the average, not establish his own farm until his father was in his 60s and perhaps ready to retire and divide up his meadows. This pattern would seem to be one in which successive generations replaced each other on the land, rather than overlapping and having the families of parents and the families of their children compete for the same land. "Given that late marriage was normal, the rule that each couple on marriage should establish themselves in a separate household could easily be maintained if there was a rough coincidence between the death of a generation of fathers and the marriage of a generation of sons" (Wrigley 1978). Indeed, 44 percent of all males married after the deaths of their fathers, and a total of 68 percent married when their fathers were either dead or more than 64 years old. Because of their somewhat lower age at marriage, 62 percent of women who married had deceased or aging fathers. There was an obvious positive correlation between age at marriage and parents' ages, but this demographic artifact of limited years of reproduction tells us little about why some children married earlier than others. The death of the father, who controlled the estate, was more important than that of the mother alone in allowing the son to marry. Törbel married adults had a fairly good life expectancy. Of those born between 1800 and 1849, a man at age 30 would live, on the average, to 66 and a woman to 62 (Netting and Elias 1980). If a man was 35 or older when he married, it was more than likely that both his parents were dead. Individuals who had delayed their own marriages to care for older parents would also fall into this category. Only men who married when their fathers were dead or older than 69 showed an average increase of 2.2 years in age at marriage. All others had lower-than-average ages at marriage.

Although numerous Törbel residents engaged in seasonal migration as agricultural laborers, domestic servants, and more recently tourist-trade employees, we count as migrants only those who left the community permanently (Netting 1979*a*). Migration may have been one answer to the problem of waiting for an inheritance and delaying marriage in the village. Males who married under age 25 produced a higher-than-

Table 8.6. *Relationship between migration and age at marriage*

Age at marriage	Male			Female		
	Nonmigrant	Migrant	Number	Nonmigrant	Migrant	Number
Under 25	70.8%	29.2%	168	60.1%	39.9%	301
25–29	75.6%	24.4%	307	67.5%	32.5%	348
30–34	72.4%	27.6%	239	81.8%	18.2%	132
35 or over	83.1%	16.9%	172	85.3%	14.7%	116
Total (%)	75.3%	24.7%		69.5%	30.5%	
Total (No.)	667	219	886	623	274	897

expected frequency of migrants, whereas those marrying at age 35 or older tended to be stay-at-homes (Table 8.6). The cash income of the migrant wage laborer allowed earlier formation of a household, whereas the acquisition of farm property in Törbel and duties to the natal family delayed marriage. About one-quarter of married men were migrants, as were more than 30 percent of women. Females might marry and live out of the village with no particular economic problems, but until this century an emigrant male left behind his citizenship rights to the communal alp and forest, and he lost the opportunity to manage his inherited property. Marriage rank also influenced migration. The first son to marry had a strong tendency to remain in the village. Children from large families who married in the fourth or fifth rank had a tendency to migrate.[10] Although they would be entitled to equal shares in the inheritance, it would be obvious to these younger children that their siblings who were already married needed and wanted the property. A later child would probably have felt some pressure either to sell out and leave (his siblings would be offered first chance to buy land from the parental estate) or to remain on in a celibate and eventually dependent role. Migration may have appeared in these circumstances both a better economic opportunity and a quicker route to marriage. Although migration had a significant effect on marriage age, lowering the average age of out-migrant males by 1.06 years and raising that for men who remained in Törbel by 0.43 year, it was a less important source of variation than whether parents were alive or dead and what the marriage rank of the individual was (Table 8.7). Migration and marriage rank were interrelated factors, but they appear to have been independent of parents' death status. Both marriage rank and migration had greater effects on marriage age for women than for men (Table 8.7), whereas the life or death of parents was more highly associated with age at marriage for men. It would appear that there was a higher cost in delay of marriage for younger daughters whose siblings had

Table 8.7. *Influence of parents' deaths, marriage rank, and migration on marriage age*

	Male (mean age 30.12)		Female (mean age 27.10)	
	Number	Deviation from mean	Number	Deviation from mean
Parents' death status				
Both alive	293	−2.17	342	−1.49
Father dead	165	−0.09	148	−0.02
Mother dead	102	−0.44	112	0.49
Both dead	143	4.85	121	3.80
Marriage rank				
1	231	−2.33	300	−1.94
2	165	−0.09	176	−0.46
3	122	1.56	111	2.36
4	84	1.98	58	1.97
5 or over	101	1.96	78	3.65
Migration				
Nonmigrant	502	0.43	495	0.76
Migrant	201	−1.06	228	−1.65

married and on whom the duties of the parental household were more obligatory than on a man. On the other hand, a woman who left the village to work or who married an outsider had less to lose than a male migrant, and she was enabled to marry somewhat younger.

When the contributions of a number of factors to age at marriage are compared (Table 8.7), and the factors of father's age and mother's age at ego's marriage are entered as covariates, only 18 to 22 percent of the total variation is accounted for. Father's and mother's ages are not significant in themselves, but they add to the explanatory power of parents' death status. Marriage rank goes in a similar direction, especially in the case of women. Although the factor of age difference has not yet been analyzed in conjunction with the other variables, it is possible to give a provisional picture of certain influences on marriage age in Törbel. The best chances of marriage below the average age were for only children or those with several unmarried siblings still at home. Because these individuals tended to be early in the birth order, their parents were often still alive. To compensate for a lack of inherited property, they often sought older spouses whose holdings were sufficient to support a household. They tended to remain in the village. Later children, whose parents were older and some of whose siblings were married, frequently had their own marriages delayed, perhaps by demands for care or continued farm labor by the aging relatives. Although marriage was not eliminated as a possibility in these cases, it came later in life, when the parents were either dead or sufficiently enfeebled to retire from control of the farm. Women were more subject to the problem of late marriage rank than men. An escape from the constraints of the peasant family was migration, which provided a source of income as an alternative to inheritance and freed the individual to marry at an earlier age than the average.

The continuing vitality of the prudential check as it affected marriage in Törbel is indicated not only by the sustained high average age at first marriage in the community for both men and women but also by the manner in which individuals deviated from this mean. The necessity for agricultural resources to maintain a household and the incentives to secure an inheritance that came only at the death or voluntary retirement of parents kept most people from marrying until long after physical maturity. Celibacy and continued participation in the parental household constituted an attractive economic alternative in many cases. Local rules and customs favored established families over newly created household groups.[11] Partible inheritance equalized opportunities (or limita-tions)among siblings and put a premium on combining properties through marriage, inheritance, and purchase to build a viable peasant enterprise. Birth order did not affect the relative chance of marriage or celibacy. Factors having to do with the division of labor, differential fertility spans for males and females, and the inheritance of citizenship rights in the male line made gender an important determinant of marital age. The evidence that marriage rank and whether or not siblings were married affected average marriage age suggests that older children who could be spared from the family work force often married young, whereas their siblings who remained at home had their marriages delayed by the need to help out and care for aging parents. Early marriage, often before a property division had taken place, was possible if one found a spouse who already had the necessary land, either as an only child heir or as an older person already possessed of an inheritance or a farm from a first marriage. The economic constraints of peasant landholding were relaxed by migration and the alternative resource of wage labor. As expected, migration acted to lower marriage age. The statistical outcomes of many marriage choices have pointed out the unavoidable economic realities that confronted Törbel adults and the consistent strategic marital choices made in response to them.

9

Familienpolitik: alliance in
a closed corporate community

Our discussion of marriage has emphasized functional, perhaps even mechanical, relationships between the repetitive social act of pairing a man and woman, setting up an economic and reproductive unit that is the peasant household, and such more general systemic features as the regulation of population growth and the orderly allocation of agricultural resources. Examinations and comparisons of elements of behavior in terms of the probabilities of marriage or celibacy or of marriage at various ages have resulted in what Lévi-Strauss (1953:528) called "statistical models" using averages and frequencies. But we have also attempted to specify the laws of inheritance and the shared beliefs about proper and improper marriages that provide "mechanical models" and ideal templates affecting marriage practices in Törbel. Although the two approaches can be analytically distinguished, both perspectives are needed to explain an essentially unitary phenomenon. In ecological terms, we need both an "operational" understanding of how the system works from the standpoint of a detached "scientific" observer and the native's point of view, an emic or "cognitive model," representing the culturally valid motives and conscious values of the actor (Rappaport 1971a). The practical, calculating, economically rational activities that absorb so much of the Törbjers' time and effort do not exist in a separate sphere from the likes and dislikes, the personal rivalries and alliances that provide the stuff of an active and vibrant emotional life. Political opposition and struggle may at some level reflect conflict over scarce economic resources, but they are screened by the mind into images of kin supporters and unrelated enemies, of marriageable and prohibited potential spouses, and of parties that fight for power.

Shortly after we arrived in Törbel, we began to hear people talk about kinship and local political organization in ways that suggested a pervasive connection: "Political affiliation tends to be inherited from father to son. A. was elected to the community council because his six brothers were all still here then, so they and their friends voted for him." "Seldom do a man and his wife belong to separate parties. When there is a marriage across political lines, people joke about it as miscegenation (*Rassenmischung*)." It is an anthropological truism that kin and marital ties are often both the basis for and the means of altering political alliances.[1] Such relationships may be easy to discern among unilineal descent groups or in systems of preferential marriage with sections designated as wife-givers and wife-receivers. In a European peasant village with bilateral kinship, free political association, and democratic election of public officials, the informal links that unite a political interest group are usually thought of as temporary and opportunistic (as in factions) or personalistic and hierarchical (as in patron-client or leader-follower arrangements). Yet both documentary and interview sources strongly support the characterization of Törbel as a closed corporate peasant community with (1) remarkable diachronic continuity of resident patrilines, (2) political competition by groups recruited on the basis of family membership, and (3) considerable interaction of marital alliance and political affiliation. These factors exist in a clearly bilateral social organization without corporate descent groups[2] and in the context of intense and pervasive political rivalry, an ancient tradition of grass-roots democracy and significant local autonomy, and frequent shifts in both power and individual political allegiance. It is the persistence of kinship ties and the flexibility of political alignments that provide a basic tension and dynamism to village life.

The seeming paradox of the traditional little community with a socially homogeneous, uniformly pious, economically self-sufficient population that is at the same time riven by feuding and poisoned by malicious gossip is a staple of our anthropological literature (Foster 1965; Bailey 1971*a*). Nevertheless, the living proof of fundamental interpersonal cooperation and the survival intact of late medieval village institutions in an atmosphere of bitter factional strife and searing interpersonal *Neid und Hass* (envy and hate) can generate considerable perplexity in the observer. The man who repairs an avalanche-damaged wall on the alp and shares a drink of wine from a wooden flask with his neighbor will speak in private of humiliations suffered by his great-grandfather at the hands of that same neighbor's ancestor well over a century ago and of the implacable political hostility that still absorbs their respective descendants.

The political institutions prevailing within the clearly defined territory of the Törbel commune are characterized by political principles that seem to have remained relatively constant through the centuries. Local sovereignty resided in the assembly (*Gemeindeversammlung*) of adult male citizens. Matters of local concern were freely discussed in the open forum of a village meeting that often took place after mass on Sunday mornings. Today, vigorous debate on important issues is followed by secret balloting and public announcement of the results. Meetings are held in the *Gemeindestube,* a room dedicated to this purpose in 1646 in a building that also housed the parish priest and the *Gemeindekeller,* where community wine and tools were stored. An inscription on the beam of the *Gemeindestube* lists the names of 11 village resident leaders, including the priest, the district magistrate (*Castelan*) of Visp, the churchwarden, and the current and former mayors (Stebler 1922:114). It is probable that a representative elected council, the *Gemeinderat,* has always handled the day-to-day government of the community. In recent times it has consisted of seven members serving 4-year terms. A president and vice-president are chosen from among the *Rat* members by a second election, and the council then allocates internally the positions of secretary, treasurer, forest commissioner, school commissioner, orphans' commissioner, and others. Councilmen are noted in nineteenth-century census lists as *Vorsteher* or supervisors. Formerly the community was headed by a *Gewalthaber* (power holder) who acted as chief executive and accounted for village finances in an annual report presented to the assembly at Christmas. This post had a term of only 1 year, and few incumbents seem to have been reelected. Any adult male citizen was eligible for election to civic office, and there is little evidence of leadership being monopolized by specific individuals or families for long periods of time. Appointed administrative jobs such as village judge (*Gemeinderichter*), registrar of vital statistics, and real estate registrar are often held by experienced local public servants for many years. Because everyone must deal with them at some time or other, the degree of skill and responsibility they bring to their duties is a matter of public knowledge. The compensation they receive and the limited powers they wield do not provoke envy in their peers.

Authority was also diffused in a variety of special-purpose organizations. The communal alp was administered by its own commission subject to a general assembly of all citizens (*Burgerschaft*). Associations of irrigators maintained canals and collecting ponds and controlled the distribution of water (Netting 1974). A volunteer fire department, a fife-and-drum corps, a church choir, and a number of religious groups (the Rosary Solidality, the Brotherhood of the Good Death) also traditionally managed their own affairs with elected officers. Today, many of these groups function under written constitutions, and they have been joined by such new associations as a brass band,[3] the Red Cross (*Samariterverband*), a community savings and loan, cattle and sheep breeders' groups, a rifle club, a church women's association (*Mütterverein*), and many others.

Government in the past dealt largely with the administration of communal resources and the provision of public services. Roads and paths were maintained by obligatory communal labor (*Gemeinwerk*) supervised by the *Gewalthaber* (Niederer 1956). The council annually marked trees in the village forest that could be cut for fuel and managed the drawing of lots for individual timber shares. Work in the community vineyards and rye fields was scheduled, and the resulting wine and bread were dispensed at calendrical feasts. The council also had charge of the church building and the support of the parish priest. External relations, including disputes with neighboring villages over land and water rights and obligations to civil and religious authorities for tithes, special taxes, and military service, were also within the purview of the council. The community, acting through its elected representatives, was also the major financial agency for its members. As early as the fourteenth century, documents mention mortgages granted by the village on the land of individuals, and transactions between the corporate body and its members for property and loans were frequent. The achievements of recent councils most often mentioned are the renovation of the Augstbord irrigation system, the building of a new church, new dairy facilities on the alp, extension of roads, and the installation of electric, water, and sewer networks. To this day, local tax revenues are used chiefly within the community, and canton and Swiss confederation shares are smaller. Indeed, the first cantonal taxation law of 1851 was rejected by Törbel's neighbors Bürchen, Unterbäch, and Eischoll, and a show of armed force was necessary to compel compliance (Fux 1978:65). Increasingly, however, governmental bodies at the cantonal and national levels have begun to influence local decisions, especially as they subsidize major public works and social welfare projects, including schooling, health, and land-use planning.

Viewed from the outside, the political structure of the Swiss community resembled that of a model republic in microcosm. Membership was defined by statute as well as custom, with citizenship giving rights to valuable communal resources and prescribing duties of cooperation. Participation in government was both direct in village assemblies and through representatives elected by universal suffrage among adult males. Frequent changes in governmental leadership and the existence of organized economic, social, and religious interest groups allowed checks and balances on any illegitimate exercise of power by part of the community. Members of the face-to-face little community shared a common language and culture; in addition, they had almost all grown up together, they all depended on agriculture for a major part of their subsistence, and they lacked the extremes of landless poverty and lordly wealth that stratify many peasant communities. All the ingredients of an indigenous classic agrarian democracy appeared to be present. But an enduring and effective political mechanism is not equivalent to social harmony.[4] Politics deals in essence with conflicting interests, and political decisions allocate valued things among two or more individuals or groups (Easton 1959). Despite the romantic ideal of *Gemeinschaft,* a community is not one big happy family.[5]

When describing their politics, the residents of Törbel have frequent recourse to two words: *Spaltung,* meaning split, and *Reiberei,* referring to constant friction or provocation. Indeed, their village is bitterly divided on most local issues of policy, and elections are hotly contested. For practical purposes, political rivalry is channeled into two parties, each of which puts forward candidates for the council and presidency in the voting every 4 years. Although the parties are identified by name and emblematic color with political parties at the cantonal and national levels, most people claim that the labels conservative and Christian social do not represent a clear philosophical stance or allegiance to a defined program among local adherents. Rather, the party split is merely the current embodiment dating from the 1920s of a long-standing polarization of the village.[6] One is born into a party. Household units linked by kinship form the blocs. Many patronyms are identified today as in the past with one side or the other. Segmentary opposition follows family lines.

No one approves of *Familienpolitik,* claiming that it sets neighbors at loggerheads and stymies progress, but both the Törbjers and the residents of surrounding communities admit its existence: "The people here have closed minds. They vote the straight ticket and don't consider the merits of the candidates." As is perhaps always the case in the small arena of the village, disagreements on legislation and administration cannot be divorced from personality, the sort of moral judgments that Bailey (1971*b*:2) has called the politics of reputation. One goes easily from individual character traits to family to party and back again. With some familiarity even the novice can predict the praise or blame evoked by an individual's name and whether a given family will figure in laudatory or disreputable anecdotes, depending on the party of the speaker. The intelligence and energy of prominent individuals from the opposition may be grudgingly admitted, but they are also regularly stigmatized as *schlau* (cunning or sly) and *nicht sehr beliebt* (not very popular).

Where hostility and suspicion characterize the relationships between families, the confrontations and humiliations of long-dead ancestors are narrated as if they had taken place yesterday. The story is told of the first man in the village who wore an overcoat to church, perhaps around the middle of the last century. He sat with the community elders in the choir loft, and after the service another man publicly blew his nose onto the

The fife and drum corps (Alte Musik) coming up the road from the village square.

coat. Whether this gesture was an expression of disdain for an ostentatious claim to undeserved status or an incident in a continuing political competition is not clear.[7] The shamefulness of such an act in the precincts of the church, the single local institution that is explicitly neutral and in which foes worship side by side, is vividly recalled. The families involved were opposed to each other at the time of the *Sonderbundskrieg,* a brief Swiss civil war in 1847, and the distinguished son of the overcoat wearer eventually left Törbel with his family to settle in the French-speaking part of Valais. Descendants of the two families continue their political animosity into the present.

Although party feeling becomes fevered at election time, it is never far from the surface. Teachers from outside the village remark on the disagreements between elementary school students during history lessons and playground fights, both of which follow party lines. At various times the two inns have been identified with opposing political groups, as have the *Alte Musik* (fife-and-drum corps) and *Neue Musik* (brass band) (Weinberg 1976). Competing grocery stores bear party labels. A young man told of his father cautioning him to read only the newspaper of the appropriate political persuasion because "people are known by such signs." The omnipresent gossip revolves around near neighbors or occupants of apartments in the same chalet refusing each other common courtesy and rejecting small gifts of food or milk that might involve them in an obligation to repay. A study of another upper Valais community noted that every occasion of public avoidance and failure to exchange greetings by men in the town square observed over a period of 70 days could be traced to differing party membership (Muehlbauer and Muehlbauer n.d.). A slide show that I presented in Törbel was criticized because there were too many pictures of people from one side of the political fence.

It is perhaps not accurate to term such pervasive political strife factional. Groupings do appear to have a kind of permanence and historical continuity, even though they may in the past have lacked the corporateness of an institutional party (Nicholas 1965:28). Moreover, members are not so much recruited by a leader on diverse principles as continuing an affiliation inherited from their fathers and their patrilines. Political careers are often built on a nucleus of brothers, especially those from a large sibling group who can support one of their number for office and mobilize others through ties of affinity and friendship. Sibling unity and patriarchal authority were especially marked in the past, when unmarried sons lived at home and either worked the family holding together or contributed their earnings from outside jobs to the head of the household. While the members delayed their own marriages, such a "sibling corporation" might cooperate to build a house together with separate apartments for each of the new households. Because no one inherited until the parent either died or voluntarily retired, groups of brothers might have many years during which both economic advantage and filial piety moved them to act in concert. Even after their primary responsibilities shifted to their own families of procreation, it was expected that brothers would form a united front politically. Such bonds could be naturally extended to paternal cousins, and because the majority of Törbel patrilines seldom had more than three to six adult males living contemporaneously (Netting 1979*b*), it is understandable that patrikin were likely to vote together and take similar stands on civic issues.

An emphasis on the importance of descent for political alignments should not be allowed to obscure the latitude for maneuver and shifting alliances within the system. If individuals and families rigidly adhered to a party under any circumstances, meaningful competition would disappear, and demographic chance would determine the majority. Stressing party recruitment along so-called clan lines (Windisch 1976) overschematizes an often fluid political situation. Törbjers tell of numerous instances in which a family has changed sides, in which sons have deserted the cause of their father (though usually after his death), and in which brothers have quarreled and gone their separate ways. A superficial perusal of party membership shows a good number of family names occurring on both sides. This is due in part to the fact that separate patrilines, as many as four, bearing the same surname were already genealogically distinct by 1700 (see Chapter 4), and early political segmentation is quite possible. Families that switch sides politically may lose some respect, but it is recognized that a small group can gain in power by throwing its weight to a minority in such a way that majority status is achieved. Individual soreheads or opportunistic turncoats may be denigrated, but people merely shake their heads and say *Politik ist eine Hure* (politics is a whore).

Monolithic kin-based party loyalty is also undermined by the strong bilaterality of Törbel society. Postmarital residence is and has been for at least 150 years neolocal (Netting 1979*a*). Multiple-family and stem-family households are rare, both because of space constraints in the average dwelling and because of an expressed preference for independent establishments. Because the creation of a viable peasant holding often requires the inheritance of land, the head of a new household no longer shares in the ownership and operation of his siblings' estates. The retired parental couple, even if they have retained a cow and a few meadows, no longer have authority over the economic activities of married offspring. Even when brothers remain in apartments under the same roof, their lands are scattered, they seldom work together, and they do not appear to seek out each other's company. Although inheritance is amicably arranged, with shares carefully made equivalent by the heirs themselves and then allocated by lot, it is possible that latent rivalry among brothers may introduce a measure of formality and distance into their later relationships.

Brothers are further separated by the countervailing attachments to their wives and in-laws after marriage. Strict partible inheritance means that the man and woman both bring important property to the foundation of a new household, and marriage may be delayed or even prevented altogether unless both partners can make substantial contributions (see Chapter 8). In like manner, any child will owe part of his eventual holding to his mother. A woman's portion was in the same mix of fields and buildings as a man's and it could not be legally inferior.[8] Anyone who moved from Törbel might sell inherited property, and siblings were given first option to buy, but there was no direct compulsion to leave. Customary usages reiterated the bilateral theme. Women retained their maiden surnames in many official records. The parish genealogy book allows equally precise tracings of descent through males and females, and the prohibited degrees of marriage applied to both matrikin and patrikin. Wedding guests came equally from the next of kin on both sides, and formerly they were given identical gifts by the groom. Invitations to a funeral were scrupulously conveyed to all members of a kindred, consisting of father's and mother's relatives. Preferred godparents at a baptism were the father's sister and mother's brother.

Balanced bilaterality is further enhanced by the affective and voluntary qualities of the affinal relationship, as opposed to the ascribed, jural aspects of descent. It is as if the mother-daughter and sister-sister ties weather marriage better than the corresponding male links. A young married woman spends considerable time with her mother, accompanies her to Mass, and receives help in child rearing. It is said to be much more comfortable for a bride to live with her parents than with the groom's parents because a girl and her mother "have the same disposition." Sisters maintain active agricultural cooperation even when they occupy separate households. When a group raking hay together is obviously larger than a single resident family, it is usually composed of a core of sisters, their children, and their husbands. A man may have a close relationship with his wife's brother or his sister's husband, both of whom are referred to as *Schwager*. They may exchange favors, as when one loans the other a mule and receives a day's labor in return.[9] A man is more apt to ask for help in this direction than to approach his own brother. Brothers-in-law also often enjoy each other's company, sharing a bottle of wine or chatting informally. Sisters-in-law, on the other hand, are thought to be "jealous of each other." Another warm affinal bond exists between men and their sons-in-law, called *Schwiegersohn* or more colloquially *Tochtermann*. A young husband feels an obligation to help his wife's father in mowing and other agricultural tasks. They often exchange skilled labor, such as masonry for carpentering. A son told me that his parents depended more on their son-in-law than on him. A frequent convivial group around a table in the inn on Sunday is that of a man and his sons-in-law. Family gatherings at the parental home or group outings may also feature married daughters, grandchildren, and satellite sons-in-law, with sons often conspicuous by their absence.

An extended excursion into kinship behavior has been necessary to suggest one of the bases for political flexibility and some alternative principles for mobilizing support. If, indeed, one's agnates could generally be relied on for backing in political conflict, influence could perhaps be most effectively expanded through the affinal network of brothers-in-law, sons-in-law, and ultimately their immediate patrikin.[10] The corollary to such a strategy would seem to be that marriage of a sister or daughter outside the party would sacrifice potential advantage. Marriages beyond the pale were viewed askance by most Törbel observers, as the quotation earlier in this chapter suggests. The political outcome of such a match could not be predicted. A woman who married into the opposite party could merely keep her own counsel (until 1971 women did not have the franchise either nationally or locally), but the children might lean in contrary directions. A wife who wholeheartedly joined her husband might bring over her parents and brothers. A more frequent occurrence, however, seems to have been the estrangement of a man from his brothers by a wife who drew him toward the party of her paternal group. Successful political alliance among patrilines is often traced by the Törbel cognoscenti to marital alliances in preceding generations.[11] In one case, three daughters of a powerful leader married and lived in three apartments of a house that came to them through their mother. Their husbands, as co-resident sons-in-law, acted as staunch supporters of their father-in-law in politics. They were joined, as well, by the affines of the leader's son and the leader's sister's daughter's husband, to whom the leader was also godfather. Five major families formed early in this century were thus knitted together into an alliance that still unites their numerous descendants.

Certainly families opposed matches for reasons other than politics. Many aging parents encouraged children to remain at home with them as celibate companions. A marriage between a rich heir and a much poorer spouse was considered inappropriate. And sometimes parents warned of possible genetic defects in the family of a proposed mate. But marriage across party lines remained socially difficult and correspondingly piquant. Many are the stories of ardor suddenly cooled or promises mysteriously breached. Those who flouted village conventions are said to have been impractical, headstrong, even violent, and passionately moved by exceptional beauty. Of such stuff are romances made, and the West has reverberated with them from Romeo and Juliet[12] to the Hatfields and the McCoys.

Where political fission rather than fusion within a patriline is evident in recent generations, it can often be traced to the diverging marital choices of a group of siblings. One ancestral line that underwent considerable expansion beginning in the second half of the nineteenth century originated from a returned mercenary soldier who may have possessed some wealth and who married a woman from outside the village. Although this man's three sisters apparently married within a particular group of families probably allied with their father politically, the soldier's unusually large family of four sons and three daughters chose a variety of spouses. In the 1880s and 1890s one son married into the patriline's traditional grouping, where his sons also remained. The marriage partners and offspring of the three other sons show a predominance of affiliation with the opposing party, and their three sisters married men of the same persuasion. It is not possible to decide whether this split originated from a decision by the returned soldier or disagreements among his offspring. It is tempting, however, to identify the locus of segmentation as the large sibling group with its possible internal rivalries. Whatever the cause of the breach, it accurately predicted both the political party membership and the marital preferences of the very numerous living descendants of a single individual five generations or more removed from members of the current Törbel population.

Although quite comprehensive data have been collected on the political affiliation of villagers in this century, and behavioral information on the relationships of agnates and affines has functionally supported the folk model of marrying within one's own party, there is no means to demonstrate conclusively the connection between political alliance and marital alliance in the more distant past. However, we may reasonably speculate that a well-defined dualistic opposition has historically been a characteristic of the political process in this highly autonomous closed corporate community. Certainly the structure of its government and local laws, the economic base of the population, and the genealogical continuity of resident patrilines all show remarkable persistence within an unchanging physical environment and integral territory. If, indeed, marital choices have been influenced by the positions of individuals in political "moieties" and if change in party adherence has been signaled by or even instigated by an unconventional marriage, there should be a pattern of marriage preference and avoidance among the various patrilines that would statistically preserve the traces of fossil political alignments. To test such a hypothesis, my colleagues and I cross-tabulated the patriline memberships of the male and female partners in 515 marriages extending in time from 1703 to 1950. The cases were necessarily limited to those marriages in which both spouses were Törbel natives and were unambiguously attached to a secure genealogy.

A preliminary attempt to graphically link all named patrilines whose members had married each other at a rate greater than would have resulted from chance showed a confusing network of ties, resembling nothing so much as a ball of string. Clusters of families always showed cross-cutting ties to other families, and no neat bipolar opposition merged. It dawned on us only gradually that Törbjers had never spoken of specific marital preferences or even of a social institution for matchmaking or arranged marriages. Their observations had in every case referred to *disvaluation* and active disapproval of marriages in the opposite party. By charting avoidances with less than the expected number of marriages between patrilines, a more consistent picture appeared. Two groupings emerged, in each of which the constituent patrilines seldom avoided marriage with each other but frequently discriminated against patrilines from the other side. These polar groupings, termed A and B for convenience, give an impression of enduring internal marital unity and external discontinuity that accords well with the political contraposition of their contemporary representatives. The A group includes five patrilines, and group B includes four.

A larger group of six patrilines, lumped here as the Xs, show less regularity. Individual X patrilines both avoid and are avoided by members of both A and B. In most cases there are also internal avoidances, with certain X patrilines significantly underrepresented in marriages with other X families. No accounts of village politics mention third parties or influential splinter factions, and it would seem that the Xs do not form a group for any practical purposes. Rather, these families are part of a category including the politically mobile members of the community whose alterations in allegiance create the dynamics of political competition. X patrilines are "swing" groups that may cross over, thereby upsetting the balance between parties, bringing into being a new majority, and claiming for themselves an advantage disproportionate to their numbers (Barth 1959). The intermediate patrilines in almost every case are known today for having members in both parties, often traceable to a historical internal fracture or segmentation. On the theory that such divisions are more likely to occur with the stresses of a growing membership, it is interesting to note that five of six X patrilines show marked demographic expansion through time, whereas the constituent A and B families are stable or increasing at a slow rate (see Chapter 4). Recent cases of individual shifts across party lines and of brothers taking positions contrary to the customary affiliations of their fathers, their siblings, or their cousins almost all come from the more volatile X category. A number of recent village council presidents have also come from X patrilines, suggesting the possibilities for welding together alliances founded on large patrilines and ad hoc coalitions. Bolting the party can also promote a leader into the role of a power broker.

Once patrilines have been divided into A, B, and X groupings and another category has been set up for the small patrilines (those in which there is a total of 10 marriages or less), the patterns of preference as well as avoidance become more striking (Table 9.1). Those in the A group married other As, and Xs married other Xs, at a rate well above what one would expect on the basis of chance. Bs also showed some preference for Bs. Small patrilines' members exhibited a positive marital valence toward each other and avoided alliance with females and especially males of the X category. In this instance, wealth considerations may have been dominant, since small patrilines tended to have either substantially more or markedly less wealth than average. Rich individual families may prefer to find spouses in patrilines whose numbers are relatively stable instead of in expanding lines where the growing numbers of heirs in each generation somewhat reduce the amount of property that each can claim. Small poor families (based on the share of village wealth controlled in the late nineteenth century) were often those in the process of dying out, and their remaining members were frequently elderly bachelors and spinsters.

Personal discussions of political alignments and the webs of marital alliances that create and perpetuate them often suggest a wealth differential or even class differential that characterizes the family parties in the recent past.[13] The A patrilines and their most notable supporters from the small patrilines are criticized for their pretensions to being *Bauernaristokraten* (peasant aristocrats) and wielding illegitimate power as a kind of *Patriziertum* (patrician establishment). A comparison of average family household assessed property value by patriline suggested some tendency in this direction, but no pronounced correlation of socioeconomic strata and political affiliations. A, B, and X groupings each had one patriline in which average family wealth was high, but both A and B also had families at the low end of the scale. In each grouping, the modal family wealth fell into the average category. The most prosperous individual families came from a wide variety of patrilines, and wealth was subject to considerable fluctuations over the course of a few generations (Wiegandt 1977b). Given the checks that universal peasant land ownership, partible inheritance, and democratically dispersed power place on the monopoly of goods and authority in such a community, it is not surprising that a party of the rich has not consolidated itself. No single patriline can be

Table 9.1. *Törbel marriage-group preferences and avoidances*[a]

Husband's marriage group	Wife's marriage group							
	Small		A		X		B	
	Ex-pected	Ob-served	Ex-pected	Ob-served	Ex-pected	Ob-served	Ex-pected	Ob-served
Small	7.5	15	14.6	16	22.4	16	9.4	7
A	21.0	21	40.5	53	62.3	58	22.6	18
X	30.9	20	59.6	46	91.8	111	38.6	44
B	12.6	16	24.3	24	37.4	29	15.7	21

[a]The possibility of achieving this distribution of marriage choices by chance, as indicated by a raw χ^2 of 33.01230 with nine degrees of freedom, is 0.0001.

politically dominant, and it is in the interest of wealthy families to join with more numerous, if somewhat poorer, groups to ensure the necessary voting strength on issues. Wealth alone does not automatically yield power. The council members and president are always substantial citizens, but very seldom are they the village's richest members. Indeed, in the past, well-to-do and accomplished men of smaller-than-average patrilines have sometimes been forced to emigrate and even sell their property cheaply, perhaps because they lacked the political support to protect their positions against rival groups. Although one of the parties may have been identified with a somewhat more conservative policy and with the protection of certain privileges, the evidence does not bear out the existence of stable, well-defined economic differences between the pragmatic patriline coalitions.

A further equilibrating mechanism shows up in the contrasting marital choices of men and women in each of our marital groups (Figure 9.1). Although As, Bs, and Xs all show a first preference for members of other patrilines in the same group, the sexes divide in terms of second priority. Males of the A group choose X females at a rate approximating the chance rate, but A females show a random frequency of marriage with B males, whereas X males are underrepresented. In the same manner, B men prefer A women to X women, whereas B women take husbands from the X group more than from among the As. Using the postulated political antagonism between As and Bs, with Xs as a fluid intermediate category, one might expect that both As and Bs would make Xs the second choice for spouses and strictly avoid each other. Such is not the case, however, and the essentially chance-level matings follow a circular pattern. Wives move from As to Bs, from Bs to Xs, and from Xs to As.

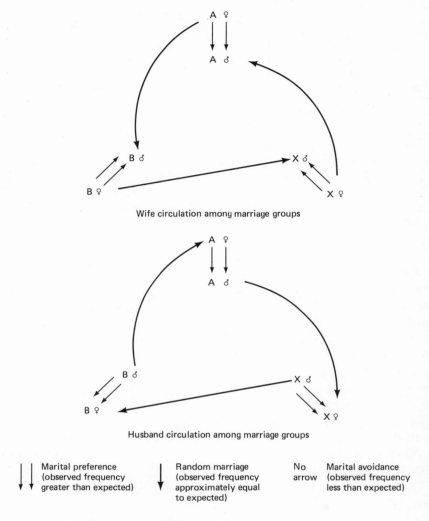

Wife circulation among marriage groups

Husband circulation among marriage groups

↓↓ Marital preference (observed frequency greater than expected)	↓ Random marriage (observed frequency approximately equal to expected)	No arrow — Marital avoidance (observed frequency less than expected)

Figure 9.1. Frequencies of marital preferences in Törbel.

From the female point of view, husbands flow in an opposite or clockwise direction.

Needless to say, there is no folk model of a circulating connubium in the Canton of Valais, nor are status differences ordinarily attached to wife-givers and wife-takers in such a structurally egalitarian society. Yet, over time, the slight statistical directionality of marriages that are not obviously enjoined but are also not proscribed may knit together patri-lines that might otherwise become increasingly discrete. Kinship links between A and B are never severed, stochastic demographic fluctuations in a single generation can be assimilated, and organizational pathways for political alliance may be tested. In the little community, even the stoutest of political dams does not create two separate genetic pools (Ellis and Starmer 1978).

It is important to remember that the marital preferences and avoidances among groups of patrilines appearing in our records are statistical norms rather than the expression of conscious models arising from shared concepts of descent-group corporateness or prescriptive alliance. No one avers that party membership has consisted of the same patrilines for generations or that marriage outside the group was always effectively proscribed. The regularities that emerge from treating all marriages over almost 300 years in a common simplified framework cannot be so apparent to a local observer, concerned as he is with individual cases where idiosyncratic motives, temporary expediency, and political strategy leave the most lasting impression. It is only because of the stability of the local economy and habitat, the enduring institutional framework, and the physical continuity of a single cultural population that quantitative consistencies of marital choice become apparent. The alpine community of Törbel may be unrepresentative because its circumstances so neatly approach the *ceteris paribus* conditions that social science seeks and seldom finds. Nevertheless, it may be that one variant of bilateral peasant society combines the elements of jural patrilineality and calculated marital alliance in the long-term maintenance of balanced political opposition. With *Familienpolitik*, the segmentary split is constant, but the name of the game is alliance.

10

The household:
flexibility within limits

The basic social unit for production, control of agricultural resources, and consumption in peasant Törbel was the household. The formation of this group through marriage and the acquisition of property, its organization of labor, the food and capital goods it needed to survive, and its dissolution through death, retirement, and division of the farm have been the subjects of earlier chapters. Research is still in progress on the comparative wealth of households and the degree of economic stratification in the village. But household form or structure can also be characterized demographically, and changes in its composition through time can reveal the interplay between enduring cultural preferences and the shifting demands of subsistence and biology. Households in nineteenth-century Törbel also provide a point of comparative reference for the growing volume of studies on European and Asian rural households.

Recent historical studies of household size and composition have shown considerable progress in refining typologies of household organization (Laslett 1972; Hammel and Laslett 1974), clearing away stereotypes of the ubiquitous large, complex peasant family (Laslett 1965:90), and indicating the degree of cross-cultural variability in proportions of single-family, extended-family, and multiple-family households within Europe (Berkner 1972b; Plakans 1973; Hammel 1972). Detailed lists of households compiled at regular intervals from the same village, along with supplementary information on the age, sex, and genealogical relationships of household members, are now becoming available. Such data allow both fine-grained descriptions of household composition and inferences as to the varied functions of households in particular social and economic circumstances. We can now ask questions concerning the rate, direction, and possible causes of changes in (1) numbers and sizes of households, (2) retention of adult offspring within the group, (3) extension of household membership to kin and servants outside the nuclear family, and (4) creation of stem families.[1]

Although manuscript lists of named persons arranged in blocks recognizable as reflecting household units have been found and tabulated in considerable numbers (Laslett 1969), relationships of individuals both within and outside of the nuclear family must often be inferred. Family reconstitution (Fleury and Henry 1965), where possible, may partially remedy this lack, but the absence of village genealogies and the extent of in- and out-migration typical of French (Ganiage 1963:42; Valmary 1965:73), English (Hollingsworth 1970; Schofield 1970), and German (Sabean 1970) villages or parishes inevitably result in a number of indeterminate kin links within and among households. Records often lack the maiden names of wives (Berkner 1975), and the question whether "some or many of the servants were kin in economic disguise" (Laslett 1969) is particularly intractable. Although significant temporal changes in proportions of multiple-family households, as opposed to single-family households, have been noted in societies in the Pacific (Sahlins 1957), West Africa (Netting 1965), India (Kessinger n.d.), and medieval France (Le Roy Ladurie 1974), processes of relatively short-term family extension and contraction are more difficult to isolate. Not only are regular and comparable nominative censuses necessary, but the repetitive effects of the developmental cycle and the chance demographic fluctuations characterizing small populations must be separated from real, cumulative trends. "For all their precision, the statistics on mean household size and distribution of household types are only the beginning of an understanding of household structures, an understanding which must recognize the fluidity of structure, the impermanence of boundaries, and the existence of kin relations which continue beyond it" (Wheaton 1975). If, indeed, flexibility of household composition can be demonstrated, causes of such alterations must be sought in the environmental, economic, technological, and sociopolitical options and constraints confronting the local human population.

A variety of demographic sources allow the accurate reconstruction of nineteenth-century household composition in Törbel. Although a national census of Switzerland was first conducted in 1798, only the original enumerator's books for the years 1829, 1837, 1846, 1850, 1870, and 1880 group village members by household.[2] In order to better describe household memberships, census data were compared with a file of all known Törbel residents living from 1665 to 1974 that had previously been compiled from an unbroken series of church registries of baptism, marriage, and death, civil records of the same vital statistics for all citizens kept by local officials (*Zivilstandsbeamten*) from 1875 onward, and a genealogy book begun by a priest before 1850 that listed most families along with systematic tracing of their descent through males

Table 10.1. *Törbel households and children*

	1829	1837	1850	1870	1880
Total resident population	439[a]	442[a]	508	547	544
Number of households	91	92	98	106	120
Mean number of members per household	4.67	4.80	5.18	5.16	4.53
Number of unmarried children of household head	231	226	273	310	276
Proportion of households with children (%)	73.6	71.7	78.6	80.2	75.0
Children per household	2.54	2.46	2.79	2.92	2.30
Unmarried children age 20 and above	37	50	69	82	82
Unmarried children 20 and above per household	0.41	0.54	0.70	0.77	0.68
Households with unmarried children 20 and above	22	27	28	41	40
Proportion of households with children 20 and above (%)	24.2	29.3	28.6	38.7	33.3

[a]Published census figures include nonresident village citizens.

and females from the late seventeenth century through the early twentieth century.

HOUSEHOLD SIZE

In its gross characteristics the Törbel household showed few pronounced changes in the 51 years between 1829 and 1880 (Table 10.1). The average number of members per household climbed gradually from 4.67 to 5.18, remained almost stable over the next 20 years, and then fell to 4.53 in 1880. The abrupt drop of 0.63 between 1870 and 1880 is almost exactly paralleled by a decline of 0.60 in the average number of unmarried children per household. New households were obviously being formed at an accelerated rate during this period, since 14 appeared in the final 10 years, as compared with a net gain of only 15 in the preceding 41 years. It is also apparent that the growth in household size from 1829 to 1850 was due to several factors, in addition to the factor of a larger number of resident children, which by itself accounted for only 62 percent of the increase.

The modal number of household members was either 4 or 5 throughout the period, with the higher figure occurring only in 1837 and 1850 (Figure 10.1). Larger households were less well represented at the beginning and end of the series. Households with 9 or more members went from 5 in 1829 and 2 in 1837 to 10 in 1850, 8 in 1870, and 5 in

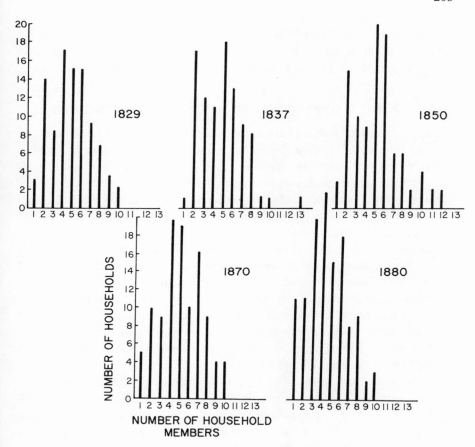

Figure 10.1. Numbers of members of households at successive censuses in Tör-bel (1829–80)

1880. Only in 1837 and 1850 do households with more than 10 residents occur. At the other end of the scale, family households of 1 to 3 members vary only between 24 and 30 until 1880, when their number rises precipitously to 42, largely because of major increases in 1-person and 3-person units. For reasons that will be discussed later, the option of living alone and the option of forming a new independent household became somewhat more viable after 1870.

The nineteenth-century evidence points to continued predominance of 4- to 8-member households in Törbel. These always represented 61 to 70 percent of all households and 67 to 77 percent of the entire population. With the exception of 1850, when an unusual number of large house-holds were recorded, a proportion of the population very closely approximating three-quarters (74–77 percent) resided in 4- to 8-member households. Central tendencies of mean or mode in isolation give little information about household dynamics and indeed can obscure significant variation at the ends of the spectrum, where changes in size and composition of constituent elements may be occurring (Berkner 1975).

ADULT OFFSPRING AS HOUSEHOLD MEMBERS

It appears unlikely that changes in either nineteenth-century household size or number of resident children are traceable directly to differences in female fertility rates or survival rates of offspring. For households founded by marriage during the years 1800–49, the average number of children born was 4.92. In the following half-century this number increased negligibly to 5.07. The number of children surviving to age 20 in the same time periods went from 3.08 to 3.26, showing a small relative improvement in health. The growing number of resident children per household appears to be the result not of more children being born or of decreased childhood mortality but of longer residence by children within their parental households. Table 10.1 supports this interpretation. The average number of resident unmarried children per household increased steadily until 1870. The number of households with mature children almost doubled in 41 years, and the proportion of such households within the village went from 24.2 to 38.7 percent.

Who were the stay-at-homes whose continued presence swelled their natal households? They were, in part, men and women whose own marriages had been postponed. Mean age at marriage for both sexes, always high in Törbel, went from 29.5 during the 1800–24 period to 30.9 in the years 1850–74. Increasing numbers of children who remained with one or both of their aging parents never married. By the first half of the nineteenth century the number of children per family who remained celibate averaged 0.82, and between 1850 and 1899 this reached 1.06. Almost one of every three Törbel children reaching age 20 stayed out of the matrimonial market altogether. Some formed their own independent households, either continuing to live with an unmarried sibling after the death of both parents or living alone, but the numbers of such households showed no marked changes until the single-person household increased sharply in 1880 (Table 10.7). Even with the high age at marriage and frequent celibacy, the number of adult children per household might have declined during the century if migration had been high. Our data are not sufficiently detailed to show short-term or seasonal labor migration, but the average number of children per household who left the community permanently increased only from 0.80 in 1800–49 to 0.96 in 1850–99. These numbers show a considerable jump over the comparable eigh-

Table 10.2. *Life expectancy of married adults: average number of years yet to be lived by those reaching specified age*[a]

Year of marriage	Males aged				Females aged			
	25–9	30–4	35–9	40–4	25–9	30–4	35–9	40–4
1800–49	40.8	36.4	31.6	27.5	35.7	32.3	29.6	26.2
1850–99	41.6	38.7	34.2	30.1	37.9	35.0	30.7	27.5

[a]Tabulation by Cambridge Group for the History of Population and Social Structure.

teenth-century figures, but they remain less than 40 percent of the average per-household migration from 1900 to 1949. It appears likely that out-migration alone did not effectively decrease the number of adult offspring resident in the household until the present century.

FACTORS RESTRICTING AND PROMOTING HOUSEHOLD FORMATION

If the marriage age, celibacy rate, and migration of children all rose gradually from 1800 to 1900, other demographic indices showed more marked fluctuations. Family size may be directly affected by mortality among its members (Wheaton 1975:610, 615). Increasing life expectancy would mean that parents would have a better chance of completing their reproductive years and maintaining for a longer period the household they had founded. Although Törbel households did not grow markedly, the pronounced increase in households that had resident adult unmarried children suggests that parents were indeed living longer. A comparison of the average years remaining to be lived by married adults during the nineteenth century (Table 10.2) shows an increase of 0.8 to 2.6 years for men 25 to 44 years of age and 1.1 to 2.7 years for women in the same age categories. The improved life expectancy was general but not dramatic. Greater longevity of parents would both prevent dissolution of their own households and delay the formation of new families by their children, who usually had to wait until they inherited a share of the family property before they could marry and create self-sufficient, economically viable households (see Chapter 8). The realistic image of limited goods amid a growing and aging population tended to prevent land fragmentation and the formation of new households that would be economically marginal. By remaining single and at home, children assured themselves of an adequate subsistence, whereas those marrying before parental retirement or death could not count on access to necessary resources.

The sudden increase in the total number of households between 1870 and 1880 may reflect relaxation of those factors that restrained household formation. We discussed in Chapter 5 the permanent migration of 1865–76, when at least 63 people left Törbel for South America. Land and apartments left vacant opened niches for new households in the village. At the same time, seasonal wage-labor opportunities became available that did not require moving away from the community. Public works aimed at correcting the courses of the Vispa and Rhone rivers, in order to minimize flood damage and drain swamps, were begun during the 1870s (Zurbriggen 1960). The Gotthard tunnel was completed in 1882. Mountain climbing and summer tourism in Zermatt and Saas-Fee had appeared by 1850. Muleteers from Törbel carried passengers, supplies, and the mail to both resorts in ever-increasing numbers. Agricultural income could therefore be supplemented by new sources of cash, making young men somewhat less dependent on inheritance for the establishment of a household.

The average age of household heads was rising toward the end of the century (Table 10.3), indicating both increased longevity and a tendency of elderly parents to maintain their positions. Although adult children and other relatives may have been supplying a major part of the farm labor, the older man or woman was usually listed as titular head, and there was no indication of retirement. In the 1829 census, a few individuals under age 28 were household heads. Although this was somewhat modified in later years, the late age at marriage and the economic problems of forming an independent household kept the numbers in this category below 10 percent. The decline in the number of household heads in the 38- to 47-year age groups in the 1880 census may reflect the effects of emigration during the 1863–72 period, when this cohort would normally have married.

Household size has been convincingly correlated with wealth and high status in many parts of Europe (Laslett 1965:64; Klapisch 1972; Wheaton 1975). On the other hand, a declining proportion of stem families in peasant communities may result from growing numbers of cottagers and landless laborers who are unable to support more than a single married couple within the household (Berkner 1972a). Economic differences undoubtedly existed among Törbel households in the nineteenth century, but the extremes of poverty represented by agricultural day laborers, weavers and craftsmen in other cottage industries, or unattached paupers are not mentioned in the lists. Ownership of land and dairy cows appears to have been characteristic for most households (see Chapter 3), but there is no evidence for the existence of gentlemen farmers or absentee landlords who were not directly involved in agricultural production.

Table 10.3. *Ages of household heads in Törbel*

Year	Average age	18–27		28–37		38–47		48–57		58–90		Total
		No.	%	No.	%	No.	%	No.	%	No.	%	
1829	47.65	2	2	18	20	24	26	30	33	17	19	91
1850	47.34	9	9	24	25	21	21	15	15	29	30	98
1880	49.63	8	7	25	21	19	16	27	22	41	34	120

The first three censuses listed a total of 21 unpaid citizen officials, including community council members (*Vorsteher*), judges (*Kastlane* or *Richter*), and bailiffs (*Weibel*), but their average household size of 4.86 put them only slightly above the mean for these periods (Table 10.1). Craftsmen were certainly all self-employed and probably plied their trades on a part-time basis in response to local demand.[3] Usually the village had a cooper, a smith, a cheesemaker, several carpenters, and a tailor or two, and occasional mention is made of a glazier, a sculptor, a wood turner, a miller, a butcher, a teacher, and a shoemaker. From 1850 onward, about half of these men were single, a few living alone, but most in households with their parents or siblings. The households of all 30 craftsmen averaged 5.27 members, reflecting perhaps some minimal financial advantage of these subsidiary occupations over those of strictly agricultural families. On the basis of existing information it is not possible to prove a direct correlation between household size and socioeconomic level.

KIN IN THE HOUSEHOLD

Emigration and wage labor may have temporarily lessened some of the constraints on family formation, but they did not abolish them. If there were difficulties for offspring in supporting themselves outside of a household that had access to the full range of necessary resources, there were even greater problems for the young and the old whose families were incomplete. In a society without well-developed social services for dependent individuals, the existing households had to accommodate them somehow. By counting all kin who were not part of the nuclear family of the head of the household, we can gain some impression of the extension of household membership to more distantly related individuals. The results summarized in Table 10.4 show a steady increase (from 19 to 36) in the number of Törbel households with kin. As a percentage of all village households, these rose from 21 percent in 1829 to 31 percent in

Table 10.4. *Kin resident in Törbel households*[a]

	1829	1837	1850	1870	1880
Total number of resident kin	41	63	60	45	57
Households with kin	19	24	30	31	36
Mean number of kin per household with kin	2.16	2.63	2.00	1.45	1.58
Proportion of households with resident kin (%)	21	26	31	29	30
Proportion kin in population (%)	9.3	14.3	11.8	8.2	10.5

[a]Kin are defined as resident relatives connected by blood or marriage to the head of the household, his or her spouse, or their socially recognized children. For comparable cases, see the work of Laslett (1972:83, 149) and Anderson (1972a:220).

1850, remaining near that level through 1880.[4] The actual number of kin per household varied irregularly from 0.44 to 0.65, representing some 10.6 percent of the membership of the average village household. Perhaps more useful is the observation that in those households that had resident kin members, the average number went from a high of 2.5 to a low of 1.47, with some suggestion of a decline through time. It appears, then, that a substantial proportion of Törbel household units included kin beyond the nuclear family, but as the numbers of such households rose, the average number of kin in each showed some tendency to go down. Kin membership became less concentrated and more general through time as the number of extended families approached one-third of all households.[5]

The nature of kin relationships within the domestic group is of particular interest to the anthropologist. Törbel genealogies allow the reconstruction of kinship linkages for individuals listed as household members, although relationships beyond the nuclear family were usually unspecified in the censuses. Kin may be divided according to the directionality and distance of their relationships to members of the nuclear conjugal family. Lineal relatives (Table 10.5) include those consanguines ancestral to or descendant from members of the nuclear family, such as the father and mother of the husband and his wife and the offspring of their sons and daughters. Collateral relatives are reckoned by their sibling ties to lineals, such as brothers and sisters of the husband and wife, siblings of an unmarried head, or siblings of the parents of the married pair at the head of the household. At greater distances are those relatives linked through a combination of collateral and lineal ties, such as the husband's brother's son or the wife's mother's brother's daughter. Affinal connections can also be traced to the spouses of children or grandchildren and the spouses of collateral relatives of the husband and

Table 10.5. *Kin types in Törbel households*

Kin type	1829	1837	1850	1870	1880
Lineals and near collaterals	23	26	39	31	34
Other collaterals	11	13	9	11	16
Affines	7	5	8	1	3
Distant and presumed kin	0	19	4	2	4
Total	41	63	60	45	57

wife. All of these linkages may be further subdivided according to whether the primary tie to the nuclear family is through a man (husband, unmarried male head, or son) or a woman (wife, unmarried female head, or daughter). Some very distant relatives of husband or wife may be specifiable (e.g., husband's father's half-sister's daughter's daughter's child) or merely suspected, as when the household member bears the same surname as one of the spouses. The various resident kin types have been listed in detail by census year elsewhere (Netting 1979a:48–9), but only a summary of major kin classifications is presented here (Table 10.5).

The centrality of the nuclear family in Törbel households and the degree to which the memberships of other kin diminish directly with their genealogical distance from this core are seen when kin types are compared (Table 10.5). In every census the largest group of kin is composed of lineal relatives from the first ascending generation above the household head or the first descending generation below his children, plus immediate collaterals (siblings of the household head and spouse or siblings of an unmarried head). More distant collaterals range between one-quarter and one-half of this number, resident affines are even less numerous, and more distant kin are barely represented. The only marked exception to this pattern is the 1837 census, with its abnormally large number of distant kin. These were, for the most part, children below the age of 19, with one or both parents dead, who were living with a family having the same surname as their own but who were either distantly related or not demonstrably related to the head. The situation appears to be anomalous.

In the 51 years covered by census data, the proportion of kin related to the nuclear family through females, as opposed to males, underwent an interesting shift. In the earlier part of the century, all or almost all kin showed connections with the husband of the household, as his parent, sibling, son's child, or one of their collaterals (Table 10.6).[6] Only after

Table 10.6. *Relationships through males and females of kin in Törbel households*

	1829		1837		1850		1870		1880	
Kin type	M	F	M	F	M	F	M	F	M	F
Lineals and near collaterals	23	0	25	1	34	5	11	20	18	16
Other collaterals	11	0	11	2	9	0	10	1	6	10
Affines	7	0	3	2	8	0	0	1	2	1
Distant and presumed kin	0	0	19	0	4	0	1	1	4	0
Total	41	0	58	5	55	5	22	23	30	27

1850 did this weighting begin to alter, with a growing inclusion of wife's relatives and daughter's children. The patrilineal bias so evident in 1829 had been swamped by 1870, and the extension of kinship assumed an aspect of balanced bilaterality. So far as we know, no external changes in the legal status of spouses, in partible inheritance rules, or in the economic opportunities available for women could account for this tendency. It is possible that wives of men absent from the village as seasonal wage laborers took a larger role in the farm enterprise and acquired the freedom to seek the labor and companionship of their own relatives. That changes in the direction of kin relationships can take place without decisively altering the number of kin living in households or the proportion of households with kin suggests the flexibility of the institution. Although the change does not appear to be an artifact of varying data quality or chance statistical fluctuation, its explanation is not readily apparent.

SERVANTS AND KIN

A major reason for the fact that numbers of kin members in the household appear inflated, whereas the proportions of servants are much smaller than those for comparable English cases (Laslett 1972:83), is the counting of most individuals designated as servants in the appropriate kin classifications. When the Swiss censustakers listed the status of household members not in the nuclear family, their practice was obviously not standardized. Terms for servants were sometimes applied to near relatives. In 1829 a 21-year-old man headed a household in which his 25-year-old sister was called *Jungfrau* (virgin or housekeeper) and his 11-year-old sister was called *Töchterlein* (in Swiss usage, little girl or servant). The word *Magd* (maid) was applied to a 59-year-old sister in

1850, and *Dienstmagd* (serving maid) was often used for a distantly related or unrelated woman. Boys not closely related to the head of the household were termed *Knabe* or *Knäblein* in a way that distinguished them from sons. Herd boys and hired hands are still known by the appellation *Knecht*. In 1870, most of the kin apart from the nuclear family were labeled help (*Hilfe*), but the same word referred to a girl in the priest's household who assisted the housekeeper. By 1880, both elderly relatives and young cousins and nephews were being called guests (*Gäste*). The servant term declined in favor over time and was never applied consistently (Netting 1979b:50). The chances were always greater, however, that it would designate relatives other than the circle of lineal and close collateral kin (Plakans 1977). Affines were never referred to as servants, whereas very distant kin or merely presumed kin frequently bore the term.

The nature of labor on the peasant farmstead probably prevented any regular distinction between parents and children or employers and wage laborers in the tasks performed. Even in families noted for their wealth, a hired girl might merely fill in for her mistress in the haymaking or milking until such time as the wife or children of the household could handle agricultural chores. Young men and women who worked for others either inside the community or in nearby villages often founded their own families in later life, seemingly suffering no social disadvantages because of their years as servants. The fact that, with few exceptions, servants were also kin suggests that the arrangement may have been as much a way of caring for orphaned or otherwise dependent relatives as of adding to the household labor force.[7] Few Törbel families have ever had the capital or the inclination to hire outsiders. In 1829 there were four servants from outside the village, and in 1846 there were only eight.[8] The lack of cash in the local subsistence economy probably prevented the offering of competitive wages. However, Törbjers did seek service (*Dienst*) in neighboring villages, with a few going as far as the French-speaking towns of lower Valais or the Italian settlements just across the Alps. Fourteen men and 5 women were servants elsewhere in 1829, and there were 8 men and 8 women in 1837 and 10 men and 14 women in 1846. These figures do not include mercenary soldiers, occasional craftsmen, and farmers who lived away from the village. Servants tended to be young and unmarried (average ages in 1829 were males 23.1 and females 22.2; in 1837, males 21.6, females 27.8). A period spent as a servant during adolescence or early adulthood was probably a normal option, although it occurred somewhat less frequently than in rural England and Scandinavia (Löfgren 1974:23–57). Within Törbel, both temporary inequalities in labor availability and the **needs of**

Table 10.7. *Structures of Törbel households*

Household type	1829	1837	1850	1870	1880
Solitaries					
Widowed	1	1	1	0	1
Single	2	0	2	5	10
No family					
Co-resident siblings	4	6	4	2	4
Co-resident relatives	1	2	0	1	0
Persons not related	1	2	1	1	0
Simple family households					
Married couples alone	10	8	8	6	9
Married couples with children	49	44	39	45	50
Widowers with children	7	10	7	10	6
Widows with children	2	2	10	8	8
Extended-family households					
Extended upward	2	4	6	3	8
Extended downward	2	5	3	8	9
Extended laterally	5	5	7	10	7
Combinations	2	1	2	5	4
Multiple-family households					
Stem families					
Secondary unit down	3	1	3	1	2
Secondary unit up	0	0	1	1	2
Frereches	0	0	4	0	0
Indeterminate	0	1	0	0	0
Total	91	92	98	106	120

dependent individuals for support and care were met by shifts of personnel from one household to another, usually following lines of kinship.

HOUSEHOLD TYPES

Our structural classification of Törbel households involves a typology standardized by Laslett (1972:28–34). The number of extended-family households[9] may appear somewhat larger than in other contemporary European cases for two reasons: Kinship relationships among household members have been determined with a fair degree of accuracy; servants have been classified as kin where the relationship is proven or probable. The classification in Table 10.7 points up several patterns. Single-member households were generally rare, with unmarried solitaries increasing only in the last censuses and widowed individuals seldom represented. It appears that widows and widowers usually lived either with their unmarried children in independent households or with

Table 10.8. *Summary of structures of Törbel households*

Household type	1829 N	%	1837 N	%	1850 N	%	1870 N	%	1880 N	%
Solitaries	3	3.3	1	1.1	3	3.1	5	4.7	11	9.2
No family	6	6.6	10	10.9	5	5.1	4	3.8	4	3.3
Simple family households	68	74.7	64	69.5	64	65.3	69	65.1	73	60.8
Extended-family households	11	12.1	15	16.3	18	18.4	26	24.5	28	23.4
Multiple-family households	3	3.3	1	1.1	8	8.1	2	1.9	4	3.3
Indeterminate	0		1	1.1	0		0		0	
Total	91	100	92	100	98	100	106	100	120	100

married children and/or other relatives in extended-family households. Although male and female tasks were to some degree interchangeable, the sometimes conflicting demands of dairying, haying, irrigation, gardening, and cooking must have made life alone rather difficult. Units consisting of co-resident unmarried siblings were present at every time period, and they remain a well-recognized and accepted household type in Törbel today. In the nineteenth century they never exceeded 9.5 percent of all households.[10] Groupings of other co-resident relatives and of unrelated persons were infrequent.

Among simple family households, married couples alone appeared in relatively constant numbers but not large numbers. By far the predominant family form was that of married couples with children, although these did not increase regularly in proportion to total number of households or total village population. There seems to have been no absolute requirement that a widower with children either remarry quickly or bring in a female relative to help him provide for his family. Such households were represented with fair constancy. There was a tendency, however, for the number of widow-headed households to increase through time, perhaps reflecting the increasing life expectancy for females (Table 10.2). All types of extended-family households were continuously present, although lateral extension to a sibling or cousin of the head or his spouse was somewhat more popular. Stem families were also in evidence, although never more than four at one time were recorded in the village. What appears to be a peculiar aberration, but may in reality be a censustaker's mistake, is the listing of four households in 1850 as being made up of married brothers. The "frereche," if it existed at that time, was certainly not maintained into later periods. Although we know of both contemporary and historical cases in which brothers cooperated in

216   *Balancing on an Alp*

the building of a house, it is always stated that they occupied separate apartments and maintained distinct units of production.

When household types are grouped under major headings (Table 10.8), one trend becomes apparent: Extended-family households made up an ever-increasing proportion, almost a quarter of all village households by 1870. Although the total number of households was rising during this period, the percentages of households with children over 20 years of age (Table 10.1), households with kin (Table 10.4), and households with the extended-family structure (Table 10.8) were all going up even faster. These changes in composition are only imperfectly mirrored by alterations in average household size. A reciprocal downward tendency is seen in the proportion of simple family households declining by approximately 14 percent in 51 years. The apparent departure of Törbel households from a conjugal family model runs counter to nuclearizing and isolating tendencies elsewhere in Europe (Blayo 1972). Although the probability of an extended-family type was increasing, this does not necessarily reflect any change in preference or a conscious awareness of altered household constitution. Rather, the extended phase through which many households passed in their normal developmental cycle was lasting longer; this was because of the longer life spans of parents and the increasingly delayed or deferred marriages of their offspring.[11]

With population expansion, the needs of both celibate offspring and dependent or unattached relatives could most easily be met within existing household units. Adult children may well have contributed significantly to household labor needs, whereas kin were often younger or elderly individuals. Of 37 resident kin in 1870, 16 were 20 years of age or less, and 13 were over 50 years of age (Table 10.9). In 1880, only 14 of 43 kin were in their prime years (age 21–49), and most of these were women. Some elderly relatives and a few aged non-kin were specifically labeled boarders (*Kostgänger*), thus suggesting that they paid for room and lodging or that the duty of providing these services was undertaken for indigents by all community households in rotation. Although children and teenagers as well as bachelor uncles and maiden aunts certainly helped with household chores, their presence in the family reflected primarily the social responsibility of caring for relatives who lacked functioning families of their own (Kertzer 1977:345, 347).

Household composition may also be seen as changing in response to physical constraints limiting the formation of new households. With the relative inflexibility of the agricultural land base, secure economic support for a household probably became increasingly difficult to achieve. Even more immediate was the problem of shelter. The multistory, log-wall, slate-roof houses in Törbel were constructed to last for centu-

Table 10.9. *Ages of resident kin in extended-family households in Törbel*

	1870				1880			
	0–20	21–49	50+	N	0–20	21–49	50+	N
Males	6	3	7	16	10	3	8	21
Females	10	5	6	21	2	11	9	22
Total	16	8	13	37	12	14	17	43

ries, and in the past they represented a major investment of resources and labor. By the nineteenth century, timbers of sufficient size were obtainable only outside the community territory, and the capital to purchase them required long accumulation through seasonal wage labor. With lengthening life spans, fewer dwellings were vacated. The closely packed houses, separated only by narrow paths threading the precipitous slopes, could not easily be enlarged. Family apartments, individually bought and sold, commanded high prices. They generally included a single sitting room/bedroom (*Wohnstube*), a dark kitchen with open hearth, and perhaps a narrow unheated bedroom used by older children. The large bedstead was shared by parents and small children, and extra sleeping space was provided by a trundle bed. Little privacy was available for additional married couples or for kin, and large families must have experienced a certain unavoidable crowding. Although many households owned one or more small dwellings in outlying hamlets or on the *Voralp*, these were used several times each year in the course of local herding activities and were not available to others for permanent residence.

THE STEM FAMILY HOUSEHOLD

Multiple-family households, especially the so-called stem-family household, have been of particular interest to European sociologists since the time of LePlay. Although any single household list may show only a limited number of such units, a periodic enumeration may show the developmental cycle through which families pass as children grow up, bring spouses into their natal households, and reproduce. Because of mortality in the senior generation, even societies in which the stem family is a culturally valued institution may achieve co-residence of two married couples in as few as 12 percent of all households (Berkner 1972a). An incidence of multiple-family households as low as 1 in 20 has been judged a significant frequency of the type "if there is evidence from other sources indicating that this type is of particular importance in the broader system of kin relations of the society and if it embodies kinds of relationships which the society particularly values" (Wheaton 1975:611). In only one census did multiple-family households exceed 3.3 percent in Törbel (Table 10.8), and several kinds of information suggest that the stem family was never a normative pattern.

The household developmental cycle noted by Berkner (1972a:406) in one eighteenth-century Austrian peasant district was not present in Törbel. Younger men showed no marked tendency to head extended households that included their retired parents or celibate siblings. The few multiple-family households did not cluster at the upper age levels. A comparison of three nineteenth-century censuses shows that in 1829 more household heads of simple families and extended families came from the 48- to 57-year age groups, but by 1880 the modal age was 58 to 90 years for the same types. Although extended-family households occurred with heads belonging to each age group, they were increasingly led by individuals of 58 to 90 years. This may mean that long-established households were sheltering grandchildren and celibate or widowed siblings. In a number of cases, one or both of the head couple were perhaps under the care of a married child or a servant-relative.

The late average age at marriage in nineteenth-century Törbel might have been expected to restrict the creation of upward or downward secondary units. Among 14 stem families recorded in the five censuses, the average age of the eldest males was 67.9 years, and that of their spouses was 59.1 years. The younger secondary families had males averaging 32.9 years and females with a mean age of 30.3 years. Grandchildren were present in 11 cases. In four households the senior couples were listed in a subordinate position and appeared to be retired. The linking relationship was that of parents-son in nine instances and of parents-daughter in five.

There are some indications that the stem-family household may have been seen as a temporary arrangement by Törbjers. The younger couples had been married an average of 6.5 years, and in 9 of 14 cases the period was 5 years or less. A certain man and wife appeared in 1850 living with a newly married son and in 1880 with a different son and his bride of 5 years. A married man living in a frereche with his brother in 1850 had a married son in his household in 1880. In only a single case did the same multiple-family household appear in two successive censuses. It has been suggested (Laslett 1972:67–78) that the stem family may be perpetuated by offspring who have themselves been brought up in this environment; for a criticism of this approach, see the work of Berkner (1975). One Törbel wife of a junior branch in a stem family was descended from parents who had also lived in such a household. In another case a man who was a senior stem member had a daughter who lived for some years in a frereche. Two brothers became senior members of separate stem families existing simultaneously, but it is not known if they had themselves been socialized in such a household. The evidence for continuity of stem families through learning is tantalizing but inconclusive. Somewhat more striking is the fact that 8 of 32 Törbel marriages in which multiple-family co-residence has been documented involved women from outside the community. Such exogamous mates suffer social disadvantages in a small closed community whose members all have intricate kinship connections and a lifetime of common experience. It is possible that women unfamiliar with Törbel and lacking the support of their own kin could be sustained emotionally and integrated into the round of agricultural activities more effectively in the multiple-family household. In-migrant wives also had no inherited rights to houses in Törbel, and it would have been more difficult for such couples to find dwellings.

The existence of stem-family households has often been linked to peasant inheritance practices emphasizing primogeniture. In contrast, Törbel belongs to a western alpine tradition of old, dense settlement in which partible inheritance had long been the rule (Cole 1972).[12] Moreover, the identifiable multiple-family households in the nineteenth century showed few regularities that might relate their occurrence to the circumstances of inheritance. Of the male partners in secondary family units, 7 were middle children among living siblings, whereas 3 were first children, 2 were last children, and 1 was an only child. Their spouses showed a similar range in birth rank. It might happen that one child was allowed to marry and remain in the parental household, whereas his siblings were discouraged by social or economic pressures from taking the same step. In 13 cases of males as junior members of stem families, 12 of them had nonresident married siblings ($\overline{X} = 2.6$), and 5 also had single siblings. It appears that co-residence in a single household may actually have been encouraged by the fact that resources did not allow the setting up of further independent nuclear families on the basis of shares in an already fragmented estate.

Törbjers today are decidedly negative in their evaluation of multiple-family households. Women expect to encounter friction in any co-residential contact with their mothers-in-law, and even a spouse's widowed parent or maiden aunt may cause conflict. The proverbial wisdom holds that having two married women in a household is like having two heating stoves (*Steinöfen*), with the implication that such an arrangement is both unnecessary and uncomfortable.[13] Married brothers may occupy apartments in the same large house, but their daily contact and cooperation may be no more than that of unrelated dwellers in adjoining apartments. The cooperation between married sisters and the frequent warm friendship and labor reciprocity among brothers-in-law (see Chapter 9) do not result in co-residence or a merger of their households.

CONCLUSIONS

If a social ideal of household composition is present in contemporary Törbel, it is clearly that of the economically independent and residentially distinct nuclear family. Because the attitudes of older informants were shaped around the turn of the century, it is probable that the cultural model of a desirable residential group was not radically different in the period covered by this chapter. The quantitative information also indicates few significant alterations in household composition. Multiple families were rare and transient. Household extension was frequent, but apparently the result of duty and necessity rather than preference. Autonomy and self-sufficiency were not readily given up, but kinship carried with it the responsibility of giving aid to those in a temporary or permanent state of dependency. Those referred to as servants were generally kin, but the dual functions of providing supplementary labor and at the same time receiving support and protection blur any consistent distinctions between the categories of relative and servant.

Within the limits of a relatively static agrarian economy with scarce and fully utilized resources and an inelastic supply of housing, the household was perhaps the most flexible and responsive social grouping.[14] Its composition could change to accommodate increasing numbers of adult children and kin outside the nuclear family when increased life expectancy and diminished opportunities for new household formation produced changed demographic conditions. With equal facility the household could contract in size and increase in total numbers when emigration opened slots in the village and wage labor provided new means of external support. None of these adjustments required structural changes or conscious modification of social norms. Nor does it seem likely that psychological relationships among members were crucially altered, although the introduction of affinal kin may have diluted a certain patrilineal bias present early in the century. Although gross contrasts in household organization may exist between world culture areas and major structural changes may be correlated with revolutionary historical processes such as industrialization, the Törbel statistics suggest that the family household is sensitive to minor, short-term fluctuations in the socioeconomic environment and a prime means by which individuals adapt to the subtle shifts in opportunities and constraints that confront them.

11

Overviews and postscripts: ecology, population, and peasants

To portray more adequately an operating, tightly integrated ecological system that was also forced to adjust to varying conditions, this book has adopted three major perspectives: that of geographical and technological description, followed by an analysis of historical demography, and then commentary on the social groupings most immediately involved in these processes. The first three chapters sketched in the most significant physical features of upper Valais Canton and the site of Törbel village in the Visp valley. Altitude, topography, temperatures, precipitation, and soils were discussed in conjunction with an ancient subsistence mode based on self-sufficient dairy and cereal production. An attempt was made to quantify the land use, crops, and domestic animals necessary for family survival. A further consideration of the agricultural strategies of intensification, expansion, and regulation reviewed the history of land use as seen in archival records beginning in the thirteenth century and documented the persistence of communal as well as private landholdings.

Chapters 4, 5, and 6 examined village population. The remarkable continuity of many local family lines, with complete genealogies from before 1700, is related to rules of village citizenship and accompanying property rights. A reconstruction of total village population annually for the last 270 years revealed trends in fertility and mortality. The major contentions of this section were that (1) substantial demographic growth took place between 1775 and 1868, (2) this growth was only in part due to declining mortality resulting from fewer poor harvests or less epidemic disease, and (3) higher female fertility and shorter birth spacing were significant growth factors. In Chapter 7, nutritional change based on adoption of the potato in the late eighteenth century was suggested as instrumental in triggering the village population increase.

Features of social organization were analyzed in Chapters 8, 9, and 10. These features are not solely the results of economic and material causes, nor are they autonomous variables unconditioned by the ecological situation. Characteristically, north European late marriage and high rates of celibacy, along with partible inheritance rules, act to allocate scarce land and regulate population growth, but these institutions were not caused by environmental constraints. Similarly, the independent corporate community of peasant proprietors so typical of mountain Valais has historical roots in the early medieval period, but it differs from other alpine societies as well as from the more familiar feudal economy of the plains. Political competition within Törbel both contradicts the stereotype of peasant village harmony and clarifies the role of marriage alliances in maintaining balanced opposition between parties. The household, as mirrored in nineteenth-century censuses, provides a core unit for food production and human reproduction while adjusting its size and membership to changing economic conditions.

ECOLOGICAL MODELS AND EQUILIBRIUM

Any study that purports to describe and analyze the cultural ecology of a single human community and to consider processes of change and stability over the last 300 years is bound to sound overambitious and logically incomplete. By venturing away from the standard ethnographic account of a preliterate community where the anthropologist reigns unchallenged, I have overlapped the more specialized areas of the geographer, the sociological demographer, the rural economist, and the social historian of Europe. Yet in the absence of an ecological perspective, the connections linking environment, subsistence, physiology, and social organization can be glimpsed only indistinctly, if at all. Even given the limitations of the single observer, it is important to emphasize here the centrality of the ecosystemic view of society, the key role of population dynamics, and the departures of this case from the ideal/typical stereotype of a static peasantry.

It might be wise to indicate that this account of Törbel is quite different in format and aim from many ecological studies. The "system" is never formalized into an information-theory diagram, nor are the energy transfers that are so precisely measured by biological ecologists ever modeled. Quantitative data on field size, hay production, and hours of labor are offered but are not exhaustively developed in Chapter 2, and the caloric productions of rye and potatoes are compared in Chapter 7, but nowhere has this information been schematized in input-output models in the manner of Lee (1969), Rappaport (1971b), or Little and Morren (1976). This was a conscious choice on my part, arising from my trepidation about the advisability and utility of accurately measuring energy flows (especially in the past), a sense of the difficulties of applying strictly defined concepts such as carrying capacity (Street 1969; Brush

1975) or niche (Hardesty 1975; Bennett 1976) to the material, and a conviction that the anthropologist's major concern is with distinctively cultural behavior: kinship and marriage, the division of labor, rights and duties in the household, access to resources, political conflict and coopera- tion. These are the activities I wish to better interpret, and to do this it is not necessary to physically inventory the alpine biome or to anatomize factors in milk yield or the movements necessary to wield a sickle. I think that this is what Julian Steward understood his "cultural ecology" to be about. Murphy summed it up neatly when he wrote the following:

> It is the social organization of labor, and not the tools and resources themselves, that are the proper subjects of our study, for it is only through the process of labor that nature and technique play their parts in molding society. . . .
>
> Cultural ecology is oriented directly and specifically to the analyses of social structure and culture and is concerned with the environment only to the extent that it impinges exactly upon social action. Moreover, when the approach is used in an historic context it does not lead to a theory of evolution but to a more general investigation of social change. In short, it neither shares the interests of biological ecology and evolution nor does it speak in its language.
>
> [Murphy 1970:157, 163]

A more limited, even tentative, investigation of this kind seeks functional relationships and attempts to support its findings with quanti- tative evidence, but it seldom claims invariant patterns or inclusive paradigms. Sequences of change can be observed and causation postu- lated in empirical data, but a thoroughgoing and reductionist materialism that traces ideas and institutions directly to economic forces obscures the diversity and adaptive creativity of even the smallest human group. It is one thing to link the fragmentation of Törbel fields to the need to exploit different altitudinal zones and to schedule the labor of mowing hay with a scythe, but it is quite another to proclaim the existence of a unique kind of political freedom in the Alps because "the steepest places have been at all times the asylum of liberty" and hills are a refuge for democracy and peasant republics (Braudel 1972:40). We can indeed document the fact that feudalism found little foothold in the lean meadows and isolated settlements of upland Valais (see Chapter 3), but high mountains are also consistent with the organized religiosity of a Tibetan lamasery and the bureaucratic control and economic specialization of the Inca empire in the Andes. Nor does the geography explain why modern French alpine villages are deserted, whereas the Swiss government resolutely encour- ages its people to remain there by basing health insurance supplements and other subsidies on the elevation of a community above sea level.

Significant elements of communal land tenure, political structures, and rules governing marriage owe their existence to an interplay of subsistence exigencies, ethnic background and migration, and external legal and military constraints operating through time. Determinism in any clear, unmitigated sense can seldom be discerned among the tangled threads of history. The notion that ecology is a search for origins is misguided and simplistically misleading. I have argued in Chapter 7 that the adoption of the potato in the canton of Valais may have facilitated population increase, but what precipitated its sudden success, how exactly the altered nutrition affected mortality and fertility, and what influenced individual decisions to grow the new crop remain matters of merely plausible speculation. Even marriage is less the outcome of a few cultural rules with preferences and proscriptions that proper peasants follow than a series of linked choices in which age, death of parents, position in sibling set, wealth, migration, political affiliation, and even romantic personal attraction (see Chapters 8 and 9) all play their parts. Patterns there are, and even some statistical inferences on the importance of various factors in behavior are evident, but nothing that fully "determines" or "explains" or "predicts." Attempts at explanation that are dogmatically cultural-materialist or are focused on the genetic roots of behavior in the manner of sociobiology are not wrong but merely restricted, inconclusive, and abstract. When we reach questions of local character and folk assertions, such as "the people of Törbel are more contentious in politics than the inhabitants of Visperterminen," our evaluations of both the evidence and the possible reasons for it cannot even pretend to science. It is enough to say that our provisional ecological regularities are grounded in the ways in which particular people got their food and clothing and shelter in a specific environment over a definable span of years but that these same people neither appeared in the Alps as clean cultural slates or developed there in island isolation. Each wave of settlers came with a full load of cultural baggage and survived in the face of unpredictable shocks from the surrounding natural and social worlds. Such middle-range theorizing from a restricted range of observations may not prove anything. The ethnographic case is of necessity particularistic, but to the extent that the social institutions and modes of change and adaptation can support controlled comparisons, it is the stuff of generalizing. The problem of population increase where resources and available technology set limits on growth is a recurrent practical issue that invokes universal ecological principles. It can be approached through the mundane microcosm of a Swiss peasant village or through the world system. To the degree that this book suggests an intelligible process and some systematic interactions in a framework of ecological anthropology, it will have its uses.

From the structural functionalism of British social anthropology to the equilibrium models of biological ecology, a central difficulty has been the adequate treatment of change. Despite (or perhaps because of) the fact that modern civilization is grounded on growth and rapid change, technologically simpler societies have conventionally been viewed as static and conservative, adjusted once and for all until the plough or the trading schooner or the factory rudely invades their harmonious solitude. It is true that social forms may show remarkable persistence, exceeded only by the tendency of most peoples to claim antiquity, stability, and a measure of distinctiveness for their own customs. By choosing a subject community for study in terms of its historical continuity and the documented persistence of a traditional agricultural system, I consciously maximized these aspects of my research. The local ecosystem seemed to strike a complex balance with its alpine environment and means of production, sustaining life without the threat of want, but with few luxuries, while protecting and carefully harvesting renewable resources. This equilibrium was not the result of natural forces, as the wilderness of the American Rockies might be. Rather, it was created and maintained by intensive human effort for the physical benefits it could confer. The green slopes would not be heavy with hay if people neglected their irrigation or manuring. Fodder in the barn and cheese in the cellar demand unceasing forethought and unfailing thrift. Most significant are the ingenious social devices of regulation (see Chapter 3) that guard community lands from outsiders, prevent overgrazing of the alp and wasteful cutting of the forest, and transfer the necessary peasant property from one generation of stewards to the next. Private good and gain are weighed against village well-being and security, with the checks of democratic, conflict-ridden civil government (see Chapter 9) and the mediating religious observances of the church.

POPULATION AS A FACTOR IN CHANGE

The variable most neglected by students of human ecology and perhaps most vital to equilibrium or its counter in deviation-amplifying mechanisms is population. The effort devoted in Chapters 5 and 6 to the reconstruction of village population and the analysis of demographic trends was based on the proposition that population was indeed subject to a complex of physiological and social regulators, but that their balancing functions could be disrupted, allowing real growth and decisively changing man/land relations. Lacking dependable historical records, anthropologists from Steward through Vayda and Rappaport have been unable to chart population patterns in the past and have seen demographic increase chiefly as the result rather than the cause of other changes in the system. More recent studies of hunter-gatherers (Howell 1979) and shifting cultivators (Chagnon 1975) have shown highly variable rates of fertility and mortality, as well as mobility from group to group much in excess of that found among sedentary peasants. The extreme stability of family lines in Törbel has been shown in Chapter 4 to be due to rules controlling the inheritance of scarce productive property, to the resulting village endogamy, and to codified law restricting migration and granting the advantages of village citizenship only to descendants in the male line. Rapid change in population size was prevented by high mortality, especially of infants and children, and by the European cultural conventions of late marriage and frequent celibacy. The timing of marriage was certainly affected by the death or retirement of parents, which made available resources sufficient to found a new farming household. Thus inheritance formed the crucial feedback link from the land supply to the reproductive potential of the people. Moral values fostered by the Roman Catholic religion contributed to the system by severely condemning premarital sex and illegitimacy and honoring permanent chastity. Social practices and shared beliefs thereby allocated rights to fields, livestock, and buildings on which the peasant family depended and kept fertility well below maximum physiological potential.

At no point did this web of individual decisions and actions depend on knowledge of their latent functions or on knowledge of how the local ecosystem worked. There is no indication that the people of Törbel ever worried about exceeding environmental carrying capacity or consciously attempted to limit internal population growth. Rather, their intentions were built on perfectly understandable desires to acquire property, produce food, find a mate, raise children, and keep the respect and cooperation of their neighbors. Although there was a range of acceptable strategies for pursuing these aims, they were congruent with the potential for continuing exploitation of a demanding alpine environment. The sensitive cybernetic controls of the mountain ecosystem did not arise from the commands of an all-wise steersman.

When local mortality began to decline, perhaps because of a moderating of epidemic disease or an improved diet, local population began to increase. This was part of a great groundswell of new people that began to roll over Europe in the eighteenth and early nineteenth centuries. It no longer seems possible to credit this growth to medical advances and public health measures (McKeown 1976), because it started too early, nor to the Industrial Revolution, because the rise was equally evident in rural areas. There could not have been much evidence of modernization in Törbel around 1800; yet the population was on its way to doubling, life expectancy was going up, and so, strangely enough, was fertility. Birth intervals declined statistically, although this cannot be traced definitively to better nutrition allowing women to conceive sooner after the last pregnancy, to a change in the duration of nursing, or to an increase in sexual activity during the strenuous months of summer agricultural work (see Chapters 6 and 7). But it is obvious that a buildup of population within the village plus the pull of new opportunities for outside wage labor and migration to the New World increased the permanent outflow of people from Törbel after 1850. Migration, rather than mortality and fertility, became the chief factor in regulating community population levels. Small but numerically detectable changes in household composition and the proportions of different household types described in Chapter 10 show the ability of this fundamental social grouping to assimilate and adjust to the products of socioeconomic change during the latter part of the nineteenth century.

PEASANT PATTERNS

Both the ecological and political distinctiveness of Swiss alpine villages in this part of Valais and the historical changes associated with demographic dynamics and economic shifts serve to blur any tidy categorization of Törbel with the archetypal peasants of anthropological literature. If for no other reason than the controversies over the definition of peasantry and the contrasting types of band and tribal societies, townsmen, proletarians, farmers, and post-peasants, I should perhaps have avoided the term altogether. Today's Törbel residents have industrial jobs, and even those who still work the land call themselves *Landwirt* (farmer) and not *Bauer* (peasant). Yet for many centuries the village has been rural and made up almost completely of generally self-sufficient small landholders. At least since the early Middle Ages it has been part of a larger state, although never firmly subjected to outside landlords or nobles who required major payments of rent or taxes from the villagers. The Swiss have been singled out as the one peasantry who successfully defied the feudal class of Europe (Anderson 1974). The degree of autonomy and self-determination reflected in thirteenth-century tithe disputes and the elaborate alp charters of the fifteenth and sixteenth centuries (see Chapter 3) suggest that the people of Törbel had much more control over their own destiny than was the norm for lowland communities in Italy or France or England. Even today there is no police post or other permanent representative of the central government in Törbel, and most bureaucratic chores are handled by local appointees. Although they are sufficiently homogeneous, pious, and geographically isolated to fit any folk model, for generations the Törbjers have seen the world as mercenary soldiers, have traded through the passes down into Italy, and have seized every opportunity to earn a few francs in the tourist industry, mining, or construction. Any view of peasants as "a homogeneous group carrying a homogeneous body of conventional understandings will conceal the fluid, dynamic reality of daily life—and the possibilities both for keeping things as they are, and for making them change" (Mintz 1973).

The closed corporate community is another designation often understood as emphasizing the apartness and distinctiveness of the peasant socioeconomic adaptation. Certainly Törbel, with its ancient, firmly defined boundaries, its historical identity involving jural citizenship, and its obvious legal status in contracts, loans, and property disputes, qualifies as a corporate body. The characteristics assigned to the corporate community by Wolf (1955) apply in almost every case: Törbel was located on ecologically marginal land utilized by a traditional labor-intensive technology. It held jurisdiction over free disposal of land. Its members sought cash through wage work in the outside world, and the basic unit of production and consumption was the nuclear family. But the closure of the community was not so much against incursions by the state as it was a device to protect the patrimonies of its members from outsiders and prevent new settlers from competing for existing resources. Communal property was not a survival from some ideal *Gemeinschaft* of primitive tribal brotherhood but a utilitarian mechanism for administering valuable but diffuse and relatively less productive alpine and forest resources. The commons existed contemporaneously and symbiotically with tight-fisted private rights in meadows and vineyards, cows and barns and houses (see Chapter 3).

Törbel as a community was selectively closed but not impervious; it was communal but internally differentiated and competitive; it was self-sufficient but economically integrated in an international cash economy. Women could marry into the community, but the priest was always an outsider, and foreign men could not easily acquire the rights of citizenship. Anyone who wished could leave the village, and migration has always been appreciable, but no native or his descendants in the male line could lose his membership. Organized cooperative work, communal property, the community-wide observance of ceremonial rituals, and life-crisis rites function vigorously alongside individual acquisitiveness and party strife over political power. Land and cattle have always had a market price, and the cash for manufactured goods has always come in large part from external employment. Some families have had more money than others, and contrary to Wolf's strictures (1955), there seem to have been no explicit community redistribution mechanisms to prevent the accumulation of wealth. Yet the outcome of intense economic and political competition has not been polarization of classes but a system in which every family has had its own small holding, and no group of lifelong landless laborers or artisans has ever emerged. It is apparent that "peasant" is a label of convenience and that reasons must be offered at every point for why Törbel fits and departs from the standard classification.

I have never yet encountered a scholar who relished writing the summary and conclusions chapter in a monograph. The facts, the author feels, have been so laboriously gathered, sifted, and analyzed that they speak for themselves. Writers resent the slight to their efforts implied by the casual reader who starts with the summary in order to determine what, if anything, in the work is worthy of closer attention. Moreover, it seems a shade presumptuous to offer one's findings, with the inevitable lacunae, misinterpretations, and telltale signs of bad fieldwork, as a finished testament and a witness against the established views of other colleagues. Endings, however, are salutary, and the reader deserves some blessedly brief remarks by the author concerning what he has done and what he believes it means. Ten years is a long period of gestation, even for an ecological ethnography of a community as endlessly interesting as Törbel. Research continues, but I am glad that this portion of the task is finished.

Appendix: Mortality in Törbel

The major difficulty in interpreting Törbel infant mortality is in deciding whether children for whom we have birth or baptismal records but no further mention (the so-called uncomputables) represent persons who died early or persons who migrated before either marriage or death put them in the record and thus escaped the village registries completely. The trends in age-specific mortality for children 1 to 4, 5 to 9, and 10 to 14 appear reasonable in our tables, with stability or gradual declines for males and somewhat more marked decreases for females. Despite the emphasis on baptism described earlier and the listing of some stillbirths as N.N. (not named), the marked increase after 1850 in the number of infants listed as dead at birth or dead in the first day suggests previous undercounting. "An infant mortality rate of under 100 is very low for any period before the twentieth century, and it is entirely reasonable to be deeply suspicious of rates as low as this" (Schofield and Wrigley 1979). There is also an abrupt jump after 1800 in the proportions of infants 1 day to 1 year of age who are reported as dying. If we make the assumption that the average rates of deaths in the entire first year of life were at least 14.2 percent for males and 8.8 percent for females (averages of the period 1850–1949), the mortality for the years 1650–1849 is considerably revised (Table A.1). These estimates bring the pre-1850 and post-1850 rates for males and females into a reasonable relationship, eliminating both the implausible 1750–99 drop and the sharp increase in infant mortality after 1850. The real improvement in the infant death rate occurred after 1950, when hospitalization for childbirth and better postpartum medical care would lead us to expect it. The earlier Törbel revised rates bear comparison with those compiled for eight English communities for 1600–49 (Schofield and Wrigley 1979); there the first-year rates for males were as follows: range 91 to 243 and mean 136; for females, range 70 to 204 and mean 117.

We can only speculate about the reasons for listing early Törbel baptisms and omitting burials. Perhaps baptism was considered a more significant ritual by parents, and perhaps the priest was not summoned when an infant died. Infants did not receive the sacrament of extreme unction, and it is possible that some burials occurred without the assistance of a priest (Knodel 1970:359). It may have been that the village priest neglected to note these frequent deaths or merely scribbled a cross near the birth record (Knodel 1970, note 9). Also, families may have been unwilling to come back from an outlying hamlet or to pay burial expenses for young infants. Whatever the reason, omission of infant deaths was an unpredictable and seemingly idiosyncratic element in the Törbel registry. In some

Table A.1. *Infant mortality adjustments*

Period	Total births	Percentage uncomputable	Percentage dead 0–1 yr	Adjusted % dead 0–1 yr using years 1850–1949 as base (male 14.2, female 8.8)	Original rate/1,000	Revised rate/1,000
Males						
1650–99	147	29.9	4.1	+10.1	41	178
1700–49	258	33.7	6.6	+ 7.6	99	193
1750–99	242	23.6	4.1	+10.1	54	162
1800–49	323	22.6	8.3	+ 5.9	108	174
1850–99	392	21.9	12.7		163	
1900–49	301	15.9	15.6		186	
1950–74	142	5.6	3.5		37	
Females						
1650–99	117	23.1	5.1	+ 3.7	51	106
1700–49	238	31.5	6.7	+ 2.1	98	125
1750–99	234	26.9	3.5	+ 5.3	47	114
1800–49	331	26.6	6.9	+ 1.9	95	116
1850–99	344	18.6	8.4		104	
1900–49	263	14.1	9.2		106	
1950–74	146	4.8	3.1		22	

instances it affects birth records among siblings who are fully documented. Parents were permanent village residents, with no history of in- or out-migration. Uncomputable offspring occurred sporadically throughout the population, rather than being clustered in certain families or family lives. They diminished through time but never entirely disappeared.

If the uncomputable cases are assigned in part to unrecorded infant deaths, as suggested in Table A.1, the remaining pool of births unaccounted for may have been out-migrants. This would mean that from 1650 to 1849, something between 13 percent and 26 percent of males born in Törbel left the village before marriage. In the same period, the corresponding figures for emigrant females would have been 20 percent to 29 percent. Such proportions appear at least possible when compared with the documented 25 percent of married males and 31 percent of married females who migrated (Table 8.6). Such a supposition would give greater weight than did Chapter 6 to the influence of migration on regulating village population in the eighteenth century.

It is only the generally high quality of recording and the completeness of reconstituted families that throw the problem of missing deaths and migrations into high relief. Knodel's (1970) reconstruction of the population of Anhausen in Bavaria listed 47.6 percent of all births during 1692–1749 as infants "whose fate is unknown," and succeeding 50-year periods had 20.5 to 31 percent in the same category. Although the absence of some death records and the resulting indeterminacy of infant mortality in Törbel are regrettable, they should not be taken to invalidate the remaining demographic statistics or cast doubt on the mutually consistent population trends that appear in the data.

Table A.2. *Mortality rates in Törbel (1650–99)*

Age	Male			Female		
	Risk	Dying	Rate	Risk	Dying	Rate
0–1	103	6	58	90	6	67
1–4	97	9	92	84	7	83
5–9	88	5	57	77	4	52
10–14	83	3	36	73	3	41
15–19	80	4	50	70	3	43
20–24	76	2	26	67	5	76
25–29	74	2	27	62	10	161
30–34	72	1	14	52	3	58
35–39	71	3	42	49	5	102
40–44	68	7	103	44	8	182
45–49	61	4	66	36	4	111
50–54	57	5	88	32	9	281
55–59	52	7	135	23	4	174
60–64	45	12	267	19	6	316
65–69	33	8	242	13	6	462
70–74	25	12	480	7	4	571
75–79	13	7	538	3	3	1,000
80–84	6	3	500	0	0	
85+	3	3	1,000	0	0	

Table A.3. *Mortality rates in Törbel (1700–49)*

Age	Male			Female		
	Risk	Dying	Rate	Risk	Dying	Rate
0–1	171	17	99	163	16	98
1–4	154	14	91	147	17	80
5–9	140	8	57	130	13	100
10–14	132	5	38	117	7	60
15–19	127	3	27	110	5	45
20–24	124	4	33	105	6	57
25–29	120	7	58	99	4	40
30–34	113	7	62	95	7	74
35–39	106	6	57	88	8	91
40–44	100	9	90	80	9	113
45–49	91	9	99	71	5	70
50–54	82	14	171	66	7	106
55–59	68	9	132	59	10	169
60–64	59	9	153	49	8	163
65–69	50	15	300	41	9	220
70–74	35	5	143	32	7	219
75–79	30	12	400	25	10	400
80–84	18	11	611	15	10	667
85+	7	7	1,000	5	5	1,000

Table A.4. *Mortality rates in Törbel (1750–99)*

Age	Male			Female		
	Risk	Dying	Rate	Risk	Dying	Rate
0–1	185	10	54	171	8	47
1–4	175	12	69	163	15	92
5–9	163	9	55	148	10	68
10–14	154	5	32	138	2	14
15–19	149	5	34	136	5	37
20–24	144	3	21	131	5	38
25–29	141	4	28	126	7	56
30–34	137	5	36	119	6	50
35–39	132	9	68	113	10	88
40–44	123	8	65	103	9	87
45–49	115	10	87	94	8	77
50–54	105	14	133	86	12	140
55–59	91	14	154	74	9	122
60–64	77	12	156	65	14	215
65–69	65	16	246	51	11	216
70–74	49	20	408	40	16	400
75–79	29	15	517	24	14	583
80–84	14	7	500	10	6	600
85+	7	7	1,000	4	4	1,000

Table A.5. *Mortality rates in Törbel (1800–49)*

Age	Male			Female		
	Risk	Dying	Rate	Risk	Dying	Rate
0–1	250	27	108	243	23	95
1–4	223	15	67	220	16	73
5–9	208	10	48	204	8	39
10–14	198	6	30	196	4	20
15–19	192	1	5	192	6	31
20–24	191	7	37	186	4	22
25–29	184	13	71	182	9	49
30–34	171	10	58	173	7	40
35–39	161	6	37	166	9	54
40–44	155	7	45	157	13	83
45–49	148	9	61	144	10	69
50–54	139	10	72	134	11	82
55–59	129	15	116	123	14	114
60–64	114	8	70	109	20	183
65–69	106	19	179	89	25	281
70–74	87	25	287	64	30	469
75–79	62	29	468	34	14	412
80–84	33	15	455	20	13	650
85+	18	18	1,000	7	7	1,000

Table A.6. *Mortality rates in Törbel (1850–99)*

Age	Male			Female		
	Risk	Dying	Rate	Risk	Dying	Rate
0–1	306	50	163	280	29	104
1–4	256	18	70	251	15	60
5–9	238	14	59	236	11	47
10–14	224	7	31	225	3	13
15–19	217	3	14	222	6	27
20–24	214	10	47	216	5	23
25–29	204	2	10	211	9	43
30–34	202	7	35	202	10	50
35–39	195	4	21	192	11	57
40–44	191	8	42	181	14	77
45–49	183	8	44	167	9	54
50–54	175	13	74	158	11	70
55–59	162	12	74	147	8	54
60–64	150	16	107	139	14	101
65–69	134	24	179	125	14	112
70–74	110	28	255	111	26	234
75–79	82	28	341	85	24	382
80–84	54	23	426	61	22	361
85+	31	17	1,000	39	17	1,000
Living	14			22		

Table A.7. *Mortality rates in Törbel (1900–49)*

Age	Male			Female		
	Risk	Dying	Rate	Risk	Dying	Rate
0–1	253	47	186	226	24	106
1–4	206	11	53	202	8	40
5–9	195	10	51	194	5	26
10–14	185	2	11	189	6	32
15–19	183	2	11	183	4	22
20–24	181	7	39	179	6	34
25–29	174	4	23	173	1	6
30–34	170	8	47	172	5	29
35–39	162	4	25	167	1	6
40–44	158	7	44	166	4	24
45–49	151	7	46	162	3	19
50–54	144	6	42	159	2	13
55–59	138	1	7	157	1	6
60–64	137	2		156	3	
65–69	135	3		153	4	
70–74				149	1	
75–79						
80–84						
85+						
Living	132			148		

Tables A.2 through A.7 show mortality rates, by age, for 50-year periods from 1650 to 1949. The numbers at risk are births recorded for which later evidence of date of death is present. This is equivalent to total births as listed in Table A.1 minus uncomputables. Age-specific mortality refers to the cohort born during the specified 50-year time period. No tables are provided for the individuals born from 1950 to 1974 because their mortality experience is in most cases still ahead of them.

Notes

FOREWORD

1   See Wachter, Hammel, and Laslett, 1978, as cited by Netting. His persistence rate is higher than the two others subsequently known, that of the Japanese *Samurai* in Tokugawa times and that of Dutch bourgeois families settled in the countryside. It has to be said that there are difficulties in accepting the identity of each of the cases. Netting believes that the rules of succession, heirs male of the body, was the same in Törbel as among the English baronets. But these rules are nowhere stated by him, and no disputed cases are discussed. Only the absence of known examples seems to stand in the way of what is called "patriline repair," so common among the English gentry and in all such circumstances, except where it was legally forbidden, as with baronets. Patriline repair means the acceptance in the succession of an in-marrying male who changes his name to that of the patriline of which his wife is the only known (or socially recognized) representative.

2   It may be statistical because the numbers of patrilines at risk were so much smaller at Törbel than with the baronets (38 as against 203) and so were liable to much greater fluctuation in their statistics. In any case, we do not know the sampling distribution of patriline persistence, however defined. It may be demographic in that heirship is a function of the intrinsic growth rate of the population at risk, and it is known from Netting's figures and those available at Cambridge that the intrinsic growth of his village population was greater than that of the English population at large, both at the relevant times.

CHAPTER 1.   A PLACE IN THE ALPS WITH A PAST

1   The major Törbel summer grazing ground, Moosalp, is part of the headland overlooking the place where the Vispa meets the westward-flowing Rhone. When both valleys carried huge glaciers, this right-angle meeting bent the tributary Visp ice river from its northerly course, grinding off the valley corner where Törbel and Zeneggen now lie (Gutersohn 1961:52). The gently rolling alp with its open and fairly level pasture clearings lacks the steep gradients of most of the village territory.

2   A description of a scene in Valais used as a guide in a Swiss picture-drawing contest mentioned such traditional elements as a suspended aqueduct, a log granary, a window-less kitchen glimpsed through an open door, the six manure piles allowing one to count the owners of barns, the sparse little grainfields, and the mule train carrying mail. The popular impression of rural Valais is a few houses and barns around a white church (Bellwald 1960).

3   "When a windstream is forced to rise over a range of hills or mountains, being

reduced to its saturation temperature (dew point) and shedding moisture as drizzle and rain during its ascent over the windward side, the latent heat of condensation is converted into feelable heat and results in higher temperatures in the air descending to the same level on the leeward side" (Lamb 1972:381).

4   The junction of the Visp valley's inverted Y, where the Saastal joins the Mattertal (or, as it is still called on some maps, the Nikolaital), gives a certain lateral expansion to the valley just in the vicinity of Törbel. The deep V-shaped Visp valley system is throughout most of its length a textbook example of glacial action (Gutersohn 1961:52).

5   On the lower slopes, and as high as Goldbiel on Moosalp, the dominant tree is the Scotch pine (*Kiefer, Pinus silvestris*). Törbel's southern exposure encourages the sun-loving larch (*Lärche, Larix europoea*), whereas more shaded locations have the spruce (*Rottanne, Picea abies*). The stone pine (*Arve, Pinus cembra*) grows at the highest forest level near the timberline (Stebler 1922:95).

6   "The essential rural economy of what was to become historical Europe has roots which strike very deep in prehistoric antiquity. Mixed farming – the growing of a cereal crop and the concurrent breeding of stock for meat and milk, fleece and hide – begins in Europe probably in the sixth, certainly in the fifth millennium B.C." (Piggott 1965:258).

7   Pollen cores from the Böhnigersee, a little swampy lake above Törbel at 2,095 meters, show a destruction of the pine forest in the Subboreal period around 2,700 B.C. (Markgraf 1969). The charcoal strata appear to result from fires set by Neolithic man rather than from periodic blazes due to lightning. At that time the forest was replaced by spruce (*Picea abies*), with clearings that became even more sizable in the Subatlantic period, and this vegetation has continued to characterize the alp, with minor interruptions, up to the present day.

8   Staub, in a 1944 newspaper article, aptly summarized these conditions for early settlement in the Visp valley.

9   The Keltic tribe inhabiting upper Wallis at the time of Caesar's wars in 56 B.C. were the Uberi. Other Keltic place-names from the region include Visp, Gspon, Nanz, Lalden, and Baltschieder (Zimmermann 1968).

10   European woodland clearance went on at a steady pace during the late Bronze Age. Occupation, which may have been only seasonal, moved into the high lands of the Alps, Pyrenees, and the eastern Massif Central. The climate was drier than it is today, at least before 800 B.C., and along Swiss lakes and rivers there was rapid spread of log-built settlements (Coles and Harding 1979:428). Along with defensive works on promontories, there was a great increase in weaponry. The tomb of a young male at the site Le Petit-Chasseur in Sion contained an elongated flanged axe, a metal-hilted dagger, pins, and necklaces of metal and amber pendants (Coles and Harding 1979:188). First-millennium settlements in northern Switzerland show evidence of bronze casting, pottery, wood carving, and weaving, with large numbers of woodworking and metalworking tools. The frequency of adult cattle bones suggests that techniques for overwintering livestock had been developed (Higham 1969; Coles and Harding 1979:432). The highly developed states of herding and cheese manufacture were documented by Greek and Roman authors. Although archeological dating of high alpine settlements has just begun (Meyer 1979), the practice of annual migration from valley locations to mountain pastures above the timberline was already ancient in Carolingian times.

11   Archeologists suggest that the general European pattern of settlement from Neo-lithic to late La Tène times was the village or agglomerated settlement of several households in rectangular buildings with barns and byres (Piggott 1965:236).

CHAPTER 2.   MAKING A LIVING IN THE MOUNTAINS

1   A great many place names in Vispertal are compounds that include the root *Ried,* meaning manmade clearing for cultivation (Zimmermann 1968:46).

2   Homespun woolen cloth called *Landtuch* or later *Drillch* was used for most garments until the end of the nineteenth century. Then store-bought coats and brightly colored hatbands began to appear on Sundays, and a local priest complained of luxury and conspicuous consumption driving out the traditional peasant fabrics (Heinzmann, n.d:73–4).

3   It is remembered that local people resisted the adoption of metal plows, claiming that they would damage the soil and that they were too heavy for oxen to pull. Both objections proved to be groundless, and the new plows went rapidly into service.

4   In Lötschental, a formerly very isolated valley north of the Rhone, it was thought unwise to give children whole milk because it would make them lavish and wasteful (Anneler 1917:142).

5   It is difficult to determine the contribution of food bought for cash in the Törbel diet of the past. Some families, but not all, bought rye in Visperterminen. Cornmeal for making polenta was shipped in from Italy, but this seems to have functioned as a staple only after 1900. Imported white bread, coffee, and fruit were infrequent luxuries. Only salt purchased from state or cantonal monopolies was an absolute requisite. In 1848, salt use in Switzerland was estimated at 13.5 kilograms per person, the highest in Europe (Franscini 1848:137). Most of the salt went to the livestock or to the processing of cheese, and the ordinary household with cattle was said to consume 70 kilograms per year. Because the government taxed salt at a lower rate than other countries, such as France, the cost of even this amount was reckoned at only 17 to 18 francs (Franscini 1848:139). In the more distant past, salt came up the valley of the Rhone from southern France or across the Simplon and Theodul passes from Italy. There are records of a representative from Törbel in the sixteenth century taking a supply of one wagonload (about 500 kilograms) of salt to the village (Dubois 1965:309).

6   This calculation is based on 106 cattle owners in 1901 (Table 2.3) and a total meadow area of 1,624,600 square meters in use about 1929 (Imboden 1967:19). Not all landowners had cows (Table 2.1), but those with cows would have had access to the hay production of the entire meadow area through other household members with land rights, as well as by renting meadows or purchasing hay supplies.

CHAPTER 3.   STRATEGIES OF ALPINE LAND USE

1   One account mentions that Törbel paid the sodality of the Jungfrau von Grossberg (Virgin of Grossberg) some alp cheese, some dried meat, and several liters of wine. Many times after this, the community of Saint Niklaus attempted to abrogate the sale, but Törbel was able to prove the validity of the bill of sale (Rietschin and Sahli 1966:96). Another source refers to the new ditch as following the course of a more ancient channel (alte Suon) from Jungtal that served five villages and was built by the count of Visp. Although the origin of the system is unclear, documents indicate that it was independently controlled by an association of Törbel and Zeneggen citizens in 1343 (Stebler 1922:71–2). Conflicts with Embd over water rights and further purchases of water from Saint Niklaus are documented for 1400 and 1530 (Stebler 1922:72).

2   Records of milk production in 1780 from a lower-altitude village in the Luzern hinterland show an average of over 5 liters per cow per day (Bucher 1974:176).

3   Other portions of upper Valais were under more direct forms of feudal control. Zermatt, for instance, belonged to a succession of lords from Raron, Leuk, and Visp. The

families in that community purchased their freedom beginning in 1538 (Lehner 1957:9). Even where concepts of freedom and villeinage prevailed, as on early fourteenth-century English manors, historians now consider personal legal status "irrelevant" to the social and economic realities that obtained in the village community (Britton 1977:167). Viewed from within the community, the people of Törbel do not appear as an undifferentiated mass of exploited serfs. They exercised some rights to their means of production and participated in important corporate decision making. Swiss villagers may be exceptional only in terms of a legalistic model of the Middle Ages. "For historians of liberty, as well as for Marxists, the medieval village has been little more than a shabby hostelry on the road to their mutually exclusive utopias. However, one must view with some irony the extent to which historians of such widely divergent persuasions have agreed that the medieval villager was isolated, backward, and above all downtrodden" (Britton 1977:166).

4 Originally, mercenary service consisted of individual voluntary enlistments for a period of several months, amounting to a seasonal emigration. After the Burgundian wars in 1477, foreign military arrangements were made with the cantons of the Swiss confederation as a whole. Stipulated payments or pensions were given to Swiss authorities, who agreed to furnish specified numbers of troops for permanent regiments (Mayer 1952). Officers received a fixed sum to pay their men. Pensions paid by foreign governments directly to individuals or into community and cantonal treasuries were a major source of income through the eighteenth century (Bickel 1947:93). The export of mercenaries was considered a useful outlet for population pressure, "especially for the chronically overpopulated Alpine valleys" (Mayer 1952:18).

5 From Valais Canton as a whole, substantial mercenary contingents were frequently organized. In 1641, Ambuel levied 2,000 men for service in France, and 2,400 went into French service in 1690. Valaisan troops recruited for Sardinia in 1743 numbered 1,400 (Bridel 1820).

6 The typical seventeenth-century mercenary soldier came from a smaller alpine village rather than from one of the valley-floor commercial towns, and lists show 165 men from upper Valais alone in the period 1632–78 (Steffen 1975:230). As Steffen pointed out, the motive for going into such a military unit might be as much social as economic. Citing Foster's image of the limited good (1965), he noted that envy and mistrust limited opportunities for gaining wealth in the closed agricultural village. A soldier's life gave access to an external system in which one could become rich without threatening the livelihood of one's peasant neighbors. The risk of death in battle gave a certain legitimacy to the occasional veteran who returned home with a fortune. Although officers might profit substantially in this way, the average soldier may have been pushed into a regiment by economic adversity. Recruiting was usually done in the January to March season, when the peasant had little work and when in bad years his hay was beginning to run out (Steffen 1975:235).

7 The tithe or *Zehnte* in medieval times was for church purposes, the support of clergy, church buildings, and the poor. In the course of centuries it passed into secular hands, including private individuals, and toward the end of the eighteenth century it took on the character of a public legal tax. The tithe came from the cultivator of a piece of land as one-tenth of the raw produce of an ordinary quality (Brugger 1956:188). Various tithes covered grain, wine, pulses, hay, fruits, and nuts, but where portions of the Törbel tithe were transferred among various owners, mention was made only of measures of grain and cash. Feudal dues such as those collected in the central Swiss cereal-producing area were scarcely known in alpine regions, and a 1798 law forbade land encumbrances, interest, and feudal services that could not be redeemed by payment (Brugger 1956:189). Faint

echoes of a period in which tithes and perhaps also feudal dues were paid remain in the Törbel place-names *Zehntstadel* (tithe granary) and *Lehmannigenstadel* (fiefholder's granary). Compulsory labor (*Frondienste*) was already being commuted in return for cash payments by the Savoyard lords of lower Valais in the thirteenth century (Niederer 1956:26). Upper Valais with its relatively unfruitful land and climate and its Allemanic heritage has no documentary evidence for feudal labor services owed to manorial lords (Niederer 1956:29).

8   A court of arbitration held in Visperterminen just across the valley from Törbel referred to *Geburenzunfte* (peasant guilds or corporations) in 1304, and there are written charters for 27 village groups of this kind in upper Valais from the sixteenth century (Kämpfen 1942:25).

9   A later resolution (1531) exacted certain payments from outsiders holding Törbel property. For every 20 pounds worth of individually owned land, 1 pound was due, and for every 100 pounds of valuation after the first 100, a Rhenish gulden was required. A foreign husband residing on his wife's property paid at the rate of 2 percent rather than 5 percent. It is not clear whether these sums admitted the noncitizen to full community memberships with rights in the commons or merely permitted him to use and occupy land. Any citizen who sold all his property in Törbel was also penalized, giving 1 pound to the community on the feast day of its patron saint (TGA B4). Selling or even giving wood to a noncitizen was grounds for a fine, a Rhenish gulden for "every stick and every twig."

10   A resolution of this kind specifically required a two-thirds majority (TGA B4).

11   It is not important whether the major legal influences on community political structures were those of Allemanic or Burgundian ethnic groups or of even earlier Keltic settlements. It is clear that the idea of a corporate group or *Geteilschaft* for managing such economic resources as alp pastures, irrigation water, and forests was present among the Germanic tribes (Kämpfen 1942:20). Some authorities have discerned major elements of a free peasantry present in the seventh and eighth centuries: "Germanic society rested on a body of free men. The right to bear arms, to follow the war-leader on expeditions undertaken each spring, and so to share in the eventual profits of war, all constituted the basic criteria of liberty. Freedom also implied the duty of assembling at regular intervals to declare the law and do justice. Finally it gave men a voice in the collective exploitation of patches of wasteland and in decisions on whether or not to welcome newcomers to the community of 'neighbours' (*vicini*)" (Duby 1974:33).

Community independence of feudal lords was gained particularly early in Valais. When a knight in 1277 inquired what rights the people of the Goms village of Biel had, they answered that they had been autonomous and independent *(selbstständig und unabhängig)* for the last 40 years (Kämpfen 1942:14). Although the bishop of Sion had been the nominal overlord of the area since 999 (Fux 1978:7), he may well have conceded increasing liberty to the mountain communes in return for military support in his conflicts with Savoy and with the powerful noblemen of the valleys (Kämpfen 1942:14).

12   The long history of European common rights in pasture land, forest, and water suggests that there was very early recognition of the dangers of overuse. Small landholders supplemented their agricultural production with the keeping of a few domestic animals, fishing, harvesting of reeds, and gathering of nuts (Spufford 1974; Jones 1974). Such economic rights were a key feature of community membership, and attempts to alter them by alienation or enclosure stimulated great political opposition. If any common resource was threatened by overuse, local custom, frequently embodied in legal statutes, limited access to it. A traditional restriction on the number of animals a householder could graze on the open fields was termed a "stint" in medieval England and was usually in proportion to the quantity of arable land occupied (McCloskey 1975).

13   A probable transition in Germanic tribal land tenure was noted by Engels; to account for the change from collective ownership of land by the gens and later by communistic family households, he cited the increasing pressure of population on land resources and the lack of sufficient territory to sustain shifting cultivation. Under such circumstances, disputes over land would interfere with the cooperative economy. However, not all types of productive resources became private. "The arable and meadowlands which had hitherto been common were divided in the manner familiar to us, first temporarily and then permanently among the single households which were now coming into being, while forest, pasture land, and water remained common" (Engels 1972:202). In the Swiss case, the Allemanic invaders did not divide all the land they occupied into farmsteads. "Allmende belonged to the community as a whole, and all had grazing rights on it. Majority decision governed all matters affecting the common land, such as rights of way, the use of streams, and the construction of bridges; and the common good took precedence over private interest" (Thürer 1970:19). The cleared, cultivated land and house sites originally claimed by households could be inherited and transferred by individuals, but they remained under group regulations (*Flurzwang*) and reversionary rights that put limits on the exercise of private property rights (Kämpfen 1942:21).

CHAPTER 4.   FAMILY-LINE CONTINUITY IN A CLOSED CORPORATE COMMUNITY

1   The following discussion appeared in somewhat different form as "Eine lange Ahnenreihe: Die Fortdauer von Patrilinien über mehr als drei Jahrhunderte in einem schweizerischen Bergdorf" in the *Schweizerische Zeitschrift für Geschichte* 29:194–215. I would like to thank Prof. Dr. Arnold Niederer for his fine translation of the original article into German and also to express my appreciation to Prof. Dr. Jean-François Bergier, who edited the symposium on the history of the Alps and organized the *National Historikertag* presentations.

2   Records of genealogy were evidently not a mandatory part of parish record keeping, and I have been told that they occur only sporadically in other Valaisan villages. Published versions called *Familienstatistik* exist for Saas (Zurbriggen 1960), Täsch (Zurbriggen 1952), Zermatt (Kronig 1927), and Saint Niklaus (Summermatter 1975). They were evidently based on the registers of baptism (*Taufbücher*) and marriage (*Ehebücher*) kept by the resident priests, but the frequent identity of surnames and the paucity of given names meant that possible confusion in genealogical links could be resolved only with the help of older natives who remembered these relationships among village families. Father Ruppen, who compiled the Saint Niklaus genealogy in the 1860s, acknowledged the help of a man born in 1777 (Summermatter 1975:7). Changes from the fine italic hand in which the original Törbel genealogy is set down suggest that it was written before 1860. The purpose of such a genealogy is not clear, but it may well have combined antiquarian interests in local history by priests (who were usually long-term village pastors, though not natives of their parishes) with an effort to disentangle kinship links for better judging the relationships of prospective spouses. Although the church generally forbade first-cousin marriage, more distant degrees of kin were permitted to marry when a dispensation had been properly requested and paid for.

3   The Kibworth data (Howell 1976) are based on a reading of Figure 1 (p. 124) rather than on the somewhat confusing tabulations for 40-year periods in Table 1 (p. 131).

4   Household composition is discussed in detail in Chapter 10, and Chapter 8 describes rules for the inheritance of property.

5   Törbel orphans or those who lost a parent early in life might be brought up in the households of relatives or sent away seasonally to work in other farm households. Such

foster children inherited only the property of their natural parents or shares in the land of kin who died without heirs. They did not take the name of foster parents, and adoption was not practiced. The records give absolutely no indication of recognized adoption within the community. Fosterage appears to have been rare in medieval England, and full adoption was legally impossible (Macfarlane 1978:150). The Swiss and English cases stand in strong contrast to such peasant societies as India, China, and Russia, where a family with no male heirs would routinely adopt sons (Macfarlane 1978:150).

6   Linear-regression lines fitted to the cumulative extinctions of Törbel patrilines and to a preliminary graph of English baronetcy extinctions give clearly different slopes of 0.09035 and 0.78250, respectively, with intercepts of -1.2479 and -2.4000. The relative consistency of extinctions in both cases is indicated by r^2 values of 0.96168 for Törbel and 0.99525 for the English cases.

7   The relevant Latin section of the original 1483 document (TGA B2) reads as follows: "Sine haberet in ipso monte sive non, quod cum huius modi bonis non possit vendere aliqua jura in ipsorum connumibus alpibus allmeniis nec incisionibus lignorum sive pascuis communibus, sed solum modo substantiam propriam sine aliquibus juribus communibus salva tamen semper gratia ipsorum pro illis qui nunc habent bona in ipso monte et quarterio illos seu aliquem cum hujus modi bonis quae altius emerent in ipso quarterio in hujus modi ipsorum alpibus, et almeniis accipientes vel non. Hoc tamen stare debet semper in gratia ipsius communitatis et indemnitatis presentis instrumenti. Salvo etiam quod ipsi montani et eorum successores possint alter alteri cum bonis ipsorum si quae venderent alter alteri justa ratam spectantem vendere alpagium, almenium et hujus modi jura communia nihil aliud juris actionis rationis, petitionis vel proprietatis impremissis retinendo."

8   Births were not added to the patriline population when there were no further records of the individual's marriage, migration, death, or presence in the community. Emigrants who were no longer resident in the village were subtracted from the resident population at the date of migration (if known), at the date of marriage with an outsider (if that results in the documented establishment of a household elsewhere), or arbitrarily at the 20th birthday for a single migrant who was known to have died outside Törbel.

CHAPTER 5. THE VILLAGE POPULATION: GROWTH, DECLINE, AND STABILITY

1   Because of the lack of both local and regional demographic data before approximately 1650, we must be content with speculation on the earlier population changes in Swiss alpine areas. The economic structure of the mountain cantons was built up in the twelfth and thirteenth centuries and had changed little until the 1700s. Bickel (1947) wrote of Swiss population growth between 1450 and 1500 being halted by wars and resuming in the long period of peace after 1532. Swiss peasants were not subject to the plunder of civil wars that wracked France and Germany. Alpine areas may not have increased significantly in population between 1400 and 1700, but their economic situation possibly improved with the growth in mercenary enlistments and pensions, as well as the pass traffic promoting the export of cattle and milk products to northern Italy, France, and Germany (Bickel 1947:46).

2   Children who died at birth or shortly after birth were baptized and named. Some obvious stillbirths were also listed as N.N., indicating that they had not been named, and there is often reference to the sex of the dead infant. However, it is probably not possible to distinguish definitively between stillbirths and those children who died during the first day of life.

3   Wrigley (1966*b*:96) estimated that a parish of 1,000 inhabitants over three centuries requires about 1,500 hours for family reconstitution. Elaborate and expensive attempts to establish record linkage of this kind by computer means are still going on, but they have encountered formidable obstacles.

4   Knodel (1970) has made similar use of the collected genealogies (*Ortsippen-bücher*) of Bavarian communities.

5   There were, for instance, 38 distinct individuals over a 300-year period who bore the name Maria Carlen. This does not include the numerous Maria Katherinas, Anna Marias, and Maria Katherina Christinas whose baptismal names might be shortened in later written references to the simpler Maria.

6   The first report on Swiss population was ordered by the Minister of the Interior of the Helvetican Republic in 1798. It was not a census in the modern sense but an abstract from parish registers, and it was taken at a time of confusion caused by the Napoleonic wars (Bickel 1947:50). The Törbel document is a list of names with no divisions indicating kinship or household membership. European censuses were first conducted relatively recently. Fairly reliable population estimates exist for the Scandinavian countries in the second half of the eighteenth century, whereas the first censuses were taken for the United States in 1790, for Great Britain and France in 1801, and for Austria-Hungary around 1754 (Glass and Grebenik 1963:56).

7   The "permanent" population growth that began to be noticed in England after 1740 led within two generations to the fear of overpopulation and the investigations of Malthus (Eversley 1977).

8   The population increase in Törbel does not appear exceptional when compared with a sample of Swiss communities and regions for which figures for 1700 and 1850 exist. Using the population of 1700 as a base indexed to 100, the 1850 average population for nine alpine herding areas was 186 (range 74–294); that for four cottage-industry areas in eastern Switzerland was 195 (range 108–267), and that for four cities and grain-producing *Mittelland* areas was 254 (range 217–311) (Reusch 1979:165). Over the same time period, Törbel reached an index of 211, and this doubling of population places it in the middle of the distribution, somewhat above the average for mountain pastoral regions.

9   As mentioned in Chapter 4, the continuity and good documentation of family lines, the distinctive surnames of in-marrying women, and the civil records of citizens who left the community make possible a better control of migration data than that for more open rural communities. However, accounting for the amount and timing of changes in migratory flows remains highly speculative. As Hollingsworth (1977) pointed out, "the greatest weakness of all in historical demography today undoubtedly concerns migration. It is the most irritating of all demographic phenomena, since it seems to be affected by almost anything one thinks of yet is not overwhelmingly influenced by any one variable."

10   It is interesting that the small number of nonnative wives who settled in Törbel contributed disproportionately to the village gene pool. Although the fertility of in-migrants was lower than that for endogamous marriages, the fertility of their grand-children was considerably higher. Thus in-migrants, who figured in only 14% of village marriages, account for nearly 38% of the current genetic constitution of the community. It is apparent from a quantitative analysis of in-migrant genealogies (Hagaman, Elias, and Netting 1978) that a low rate of immigration does not produce the expected genetic isolate.

11   During the 1920s, many families in Embd, right next to Törbel, sold their property and went to other parts of German Switzerland. They could not withstand the Depression

and often had to return completely impoverished to the home community (Imboden 1956:24).

12   This change from migration that releases excess population without greatly affecting local socioeconomic relationships to a modern exodus that decisively alters community expectations and population has been called the shift from institutional migration to transformational migration (Brandes 1975:14).

13   Really massive movements from the village into manufacturing and service industries seem to have been much more recent in Valais than in other European rural areas. Golde (1975) reported that internal migration became important in some German communities in the 1880s and that farmers' sons got jobs as streetcar conductors or jobs with government-run postal and railroad services. Such jobs were attractive, he speculated, because along with the uniform and its authority came a certain amount of job security (Golde 1975:69).

14   Embd, adjacent to Törbel but smaller in population and with a less favorable agricultural situation, had a much higher rate of urban migration. In 1955 there were 104 Embd-born individuals resident in Zürich alone (Imboden 1956:24).

CHAPTER 6.   THE BALANCE OF BIRTHS AND DEATHS

1   At risk of inappropriately comparing a single village to the much larger universes of England and Western Europe as a whole, it might be mentioned that a marked change from a static population to a growing population is a frequently inferred characteristic of the eighteenth century. Tucker pointed to a period of stagnation for English population between 1710 and 1740, with rebounding growth becoming apparent around 1750, whereas Ohlin mentioned abnormally low growth caused by high mortality that did not begin a long-term decline until 1780 (cited by Flinn 1970:21–2). Laslett (1977:125) noted sustained growth only after 1750. Helleiner suggested that the upswing of the eighteenth century merely repeated earlier waves of growth in the Western Europe of the middle eleventh to late thirteenth centuries and the middle fifteenth to the end of the sixteenth centuries (cited by Flinn 1970:22). For England and Wales, there seem to be clearly defined population plateaus from about 1650 to 1750 (Wrigley 1969:78), with Colyton reflecting this stability or even decline by means of a surplus of burials over baptisms from 1645 to the mid-1730s, followed by a surplus of baptisms in the 1780s (Wrigley 1969:82).

2   For a brief outline of transition theory and the criticisms leveled against it, see the work of Kunstadter (1971), AAAS (1974), Macfarlane (1976:303–7), and Swedlund and Armelagos (1976:14–16).

3   This sociable grooming activity was frequent in the medieval French village of Montaillou portrayed by Le Roy Ladurie (1978).

4   Geneva burned several Jews in 1568 as plague-bringers. The one effective measure for restricting the spread of the Black Death was to quarantine whole regions of Switzerland and punish anyone attempting to maintain foreign commerce (Bickel 1947:83).

5   If the newborn child could be baptized before its death, pious belief had it that the infant would become an angel in heaven (*Englein im Himmel*) who could intercede for its parents and siblings. At the burial of such an infant, the mother and godmother wore the gold-embroidered hats appropriate to a festival. In some parts of Valais, the corpses of unbaptized infants were carried to certain pilgrimage churches where prayers were offered for any sign of life so that the children might come into the sight of God (Bellwald 1960:43).

6   Those relatives expected to attend a funeral, in order of their mention by a consultant, are (1) next of kin (*nächsten Verwandten*) (parents, siblings, children, and grandchildren); (2) in-laws (*Schwäger*) (siblings' spouses and spouse's siblings with their husbands or wives); (3) siblings' children (nephews and nieces); (4) first cousins (*Base, Vetter*) and first cousins once removed (*Grossbase, Grossvetter*), although the latter were formerly not specially invited.

7   Even the serious death toll of an epidemic might be rapidly made up by an increasing frequency of new marriages and births. The eighteenth-century writer Waser commented, "A loss of life in the plague can be replaced in ten years. . . . When an epidemic is past, those who remain alive are more vigorous and happy; the dead have opened up new places and left behind their inheritances, and for this reason everyone marries who can" (Bickel 1947:72).

8   After 1710 for France and 1740 for Sweden there is little apparent correlation between years of great scarcity and particularly high mortality. There were no devastating subsistence crises in England after 1700, perhaps because of the relatively advanced state of English agriculture, the existence of grain surpluses in normal years, and the effective system of bulk transportation by water (Flinn 1970:47). More recent explosive population growth in many Third-World countries may be due principally to the elimination of "the periodic crisis caused by bad weather, pests, or other phenomena which might reverse a generation's population increase in one year" (Macfarlane 1976:308).

9   There was a generally bad harvest in Germany in 1771, and its effects were worsened by the spread of bilious and putrid fever. Grain prices went up 50 percent in Munich. Yet population development in two areas of Bavaria that have been investigated was not affected (Lee 1975:321).

10   Langer (1972) estimated that before the development of inoculation, only 4 of every 100 people failed to contract smallpox. It was fatal in 1 of every 7 cases and was the cause of perhaps 10% of all European deaths in the latter part of the eighteenth century.

11   Iodized salt accounted for only 33% of Swiss salt consumption in 1924, but it had reached 100% by 1934. In Valais alone, 11.6% of all army recruits were fully or partially deferred because of goiter in 1900, and when all iodine-deficiency conditions are included, this increases to 23.6% (Schaub 1949:31).

12   The crude death rate for the Swiss nation as a whole varied between 20.3 and 23.1 per 1,000 in the years 1841 to 1890. After 1896 there was a steady decline from 18.1 to 12.5 in 1921 (Glass and Grebenik 1963:68). Törbel rates parallel the national average, but with the decline lagging almost 50 years in the more isolated community. By 1950, Törbel's rate of 13 per 1,000 was still somewhat above the nation's rate of 10.1. Changes in mortality before the 1840s in Europe remain rather shadowy. "Though the fall in the death rate between the mid-eighteenth and mid-nineteenth centuries is rather probable, it is as yet insufficiently documented. And whatever fall occurred is not likely—save as regards smallpox—to have been in any major degree the result of improvements in medical knowledge or practices but rather of more changes in the environment, changes which would in any case have applied to a large part of the population" (Glass and Grebenik 1963:73).

13   My earlier attempts at deriving life expectancy were based on computer analysis of the Törbel data by the Cambridge Group for the Study of Population and Social Structure. These programs were designed to handle infant and child mortality separately from adult married mortality. Rules designed to accommodate observations to fully reconstituted families eliminated some of the Törbel cases, and the combination of late

marriage and high celibacy meant that significant numbers of nonmarried adults were excluded from the Törbel mortality rates. Adolescents and young adults who changed residence while working as servants or who changed residence at marriage obviously escaped the parish death registries, and it is understandable that the Cambridge Group should limit its calculations of adult mortality to married people who remained in observation. As indicated in Chapter 4, this problem is less severe for Törbel. Retabulations using a larger number of individual cases have raised and rendered less erratic our calculations of infant and adult mortality (Netting and Elias 1980, Table 3) and modified the adult mortality rates upward, especially in the younger age groups.

One difficulty in bringing together the mortality data for the very young and for married adults is that the infant-child rates seemed, in general, too high for the adult rates as represented on model life tables. They also united the experience of a birth cohort with the coterminous marriage cohort. Efforts to "splice" the two sets of information suggested either that the raw data were insufficient or that the model life tables did not adequately represent mortality in preindustrial rural Europe. A somewhat better fit was achieved when we based our sample on the more complete Törbel sample using birth cohorts alone (Netting and Elias 1980, Table 4). To arrive at appropriate comparisons, we selected the nearest North and West model life tables for each age-specific mortality rate by sex and then looked for continuous clusterings of these numbered tables. The cluster is denoted by the model life tables listed in Table 6.9 and usually included 11 or 12 of the 18 age categories, and it provided a range of possible life expectancies at birth. The single estimate is derived from the mean for the clustered model life tables.

14   Our lower original life-expectancy estimates for 1900–49 males (Netting and Elias 1980, Table 4) were based on males married during the period rather than born during the period, and they excluded a number of men known to be still living. This skewed totals in favor of those individuals who died early.

15   A proverb from Lötschental emphasizes the natural aspect of reproduction: *Ein Ehestand ohne Kinderschrei gleicht einer Henne ohne Ei!* (a marriage without a baby's cry is like a hen without eggs) (Anneler 1917:252).

16   Anneler (1917:251) wrote of a Lötschental woman who said she wanted only children who would be 8 years old when they were born. Others said of her that if she had no children, she and her husband would have to leave all their possessions to be inherited by relatives, and that would really be their punishment. There was also a story of a woman from Sion who waited a long time to marry because she wanted to avoid children: "And how did it go with this sorry spectacle of a wife? At her first confinement she bore eight infants. They took them all to baptism in a flat winnowing tray, and then they all died. She knew then what the Lord God had said to Adam, that he should multiply. If it were not true, He wouldn't have said it."

17   In areas of large farms and impartible inheritance, such as Bavaria and parts of the Tyrol, betrothal represented a kind of license to have sex and bear children before marriage took place, when a man inherited his father's farm. The substantial and tolerated illegitimacy that accompanied this pattern was neither expected nor present in German-speaking Valais, despite late marriage and high celibacy (Shorter 1978).

18   A description of swaddling from Lötschental probably applied as well to Törbel: "The fidgity arms of the infant are stuck in the sleeves of a cotton shirt that encloses the upper body and that is open below. Then one puts the child on a white swaddling cloth. One wraps this from left to right around the arms and body, pulling it down around the legs, and turning it up over the feet. Then the swaddling band (*Fescha*) is quickly

wrapped around the whole package from top to bottom as one bandages a leg. When the baby can't move any of its limbs anymore, one puts on its head a knitted or kerchief cap. Then one wraps up the child in a big piece of cotton cloth until only the face is visible" (Anneler 1916:61).

19   In the Balkans, where the European pattern did not prevail, women usually married at age 20 to 21 years, and practically all of them eventually married. This resulted in crude birth rates around 40 per 1,000 (Sklar 1970).

20   In Scotland in the decades before 1911, the effect of a 1-year delay in marriage was to reduce the average family by one-third child, and the Irish family census showed that a change in the mean age at marriage of 5 years was required to increase the mean number of live births by one (Habakkuk 1971).

21   The alpine peasants in a village are "closely knitted together through common or adjoining properties. One knows another's virtues and better yet his failings. There are no secrets. Each one keeps watch on the others" (Anneler 1917:249).

22   In a Spanish village it has been noted that the physically handicapped and the socially awkward never marry (Price and Price 1966).

23   By 1970 in Switzerland as a whole, 3.8% of all live births were to unmarried mothers. Nearly one–third of these were legitimated when the natural parents married (Lüscher, Ritter, and Gross 1973). The proportions today in Törbel are quite similar.

24   In the late 1890s, Ireland had the lowest national illegitimacy ratio among 15 countries at 2.46, whereas Scotland had 6.81 and Portugal 12.10 (Connell 1968:119).

25   Premarital intercourse appears to have been more common in the English village of Colyton. One-third of all first children were baptized within 8 months of marriage (Wrigley 1969:88). Modern Switzerland has a national average of 1 of 4 firstborn children conceived before marriage (Lüscher, Ritter, and Gross 1973).

26   Making inferences about the emotional life and associated sexual habits of Swiss alpine peasants is both speculative and potentially fraught with error. We can only be certain that illegitimacy was rare and that premarital pregnancy never occurred in more than a quarter of all first births. It is likely that, whatever drives and desires were felt by individuals, the values and strictures of the society were sufficient to keep sexual activity outside of marriage to a minimum. "What we know from the experience of the last few generations is that sexuality is infinitely malleable; that public ideology, whether repressive or permissive, is a poor indication of actuality; that the long, curiously long, period between puberty and marriage does not make for chronic sexual frustration and deprivation, whether copulation is practiced or not" (Plumb 1977).

27   The French historical demographers have reckoned probable fertility of a marriage made at the median age for both husband and wife and lasting for the full period of the wife's fertility to be eight children. Among the peasantry of Crulai and the Beauvais, there were in fact fewer than five children born to an ordinary marriage. The reason for this, according to Laslett (1965:101), "was that so few marriages lasted long enough for the full number of eight births to take place. The others were broken by death."

28   However, abortion may have been widespread in France, and it has been suggested that there were as many abortions as live births in the country (Glass and Grebenik 1963:115).

29   Periods of lowered fertility are, in and of themselves, no evidence of conscious birth control. Some French scholars may prefer explanations of behavior that depend on rational reflection restraining the deleterious effects of human desires, but the effective practice of coitus interruptus is exceedingly difficult to demonstrate scientifically. Such

a concept (or incomplete conception) is perhaps better honored in the breach than in the observance. One might tentatively reserve judgment or even exercise some intellectual withdrawal from such an as yet unconsummated idea. "As a method of birth control [coitus interruptus] was certainly known, but because it was effectively the only known method, historians have tended to assume that changes in fertility must be explicable by changes in its use. There is of course no direct evidence at all about this. . . . The more positive statements about its use in the 17th and 18th centuries should therefore be treated with great caution" (Flinn 1970:36). Low fertility in the southwest of France between 1720 and 1819 was probably not achieved by the practice of coitus interruptus. Flandrin (1979:232) suggested that more or less strict sexual abstinence was used to avoid conception during the nursing stage and prolong average birth intervals to 2.5 or 3 years.

30   There was a decrease from 39.8 to 37.6 years of age at last pregnancy for women marrying under age 30 in Colyton between 1560–1646 and 1647–1719. The change is in the expected direction, but it is not statistically significant (Wrigley 1966a:95–7).

31   During the period of lowered marital fertility in Colyton, marriages that produced no children went up to 18–21% (Wrigley 1966a:98). In eight German parishes between 1750 and 1849, 10.3% of all uninterrupted marriages were childless. The modern average is 10% (Lee 1975:331). Given the high age of marriage in Törbel and the fact that some couples married when the wife was already past menopause, the earlier averages of 9–13% seem little above the expected level of naturally sterile marriages.

32   John Knodel very kindly computed m using a program that fits optimal values by logarithmic regression to the Törbel age-specific fertility rates for each period. He concluded that the values of the index for Törbel are consistent with natural fertility and support the idea that there was little or no fertility control occurring in any period.

33   Levels of fertility below the supposed maximum reproductive potential of the German peasant women have been credited to "postponed marriage rather than voluntary birth control" (Knodel 1970).

34   Questions have been raised about using the Hutterites, a population with the highest natural fertility recorded, for providing a standard fertility schedule (Hollingsworth 1977). There has been little discussion of possibly distinctive genetic, nutritional, or sociopsychological variables at work in this case.

35   In highland Guatemala there has been an increase in live births per mother but no change in spacing. Heightened fertility in this case is due solely to a decline in age at marriage and age at first birth (Scholl, Odell, and Johnston 1976).

36   "In one American study, married women practicing no birth control took an average of 11.0 months to conceive when they reported a coital frequency of less than two per week. Just 7.1 months were required for conception in couples who had coitus twice a week, and 6.6 for those who reported their weekly frequency to be three or more" (Daly and Wilson 1967:288).

37   A similar seasonal occurrence of conception has been noted for both country and town in the neighborhood of Giessen, Germany, for the eighteenth century. "In interpreting these facts for a region that is predominantly agrarian in character, we find that the decrease and increase of sexual activity correspond respectively with the time of hard work during the harvest in August to October, and with the relatively quiet months between planting and harvesting" (Imhof 1977:316).

38   This has been proposed to account for the correlation of lowest body weights and a calorie-deficient diet with seasonally low conceptions among San Bushmen women (Van der Walt, Wilmsen, and Jenkins 1978). It is not yet possible to decide whether frequency

of intercourse or female hormonal factors affecting conception are principally responsible for the seasonal variation in births.

39   There was certainly not a disappearance of seasonality as in the Botswana hospital records of birth when compared with births among Kalahari San hunter-gatherers and Herero pastoralists (Wilmsen 1978).

40   The average birth interval in a Bavarian village where breast feeding was practiced was 2.15 years, whereas in two communities where babies were fed artificially it was 1.64 and 1.49 years (Knodel 1968). A study in Senegal showed that breast feeding of 0 to 11 months corresponded to a birth interval of 25.1 months, whereas a duration of 21 to 23 months produced birth spacing of 32.5 months (Mondot-Bernard 1977:19). A pioneering study in Paris around 1898 gave the following correlation (Mondot-Bernard 1977:25):

Duration of breast feeding (months)	Mean duration of amenorrhea (months)
1–8	3.1
9–14	9.1
15–20	11.0
21–26	15.1

41   Studies of metabolic stresses on women have shown that pregnant women can easily remain in positive nitrogen balance on an intake of 42 grams of protein and 2,100 calories per day, whereas lactating women show an average negative nitrogen balance of 1 gram per day on the same diet. "In societies where food intake is at the margin, the suppression of ovulation during lactation is probably due to a mixture of nutritional and hormonal factors" (May 1978).

42   Potter, cited by Knodel (1977), estimated that under conditions of less than adequate nutrition, the menstruating interval lasts about 10 months, gestation requires about 9 months, and an additional 2 to 3 months on the average are taken up by pregnancy wastage. We subtracted the total of 21.3 months from the average birth intervals computed for 603 and 1,394 births in the eighteenth and nineteenth centuries, respectively, to arrive at estimates of the duration of the expected infertile period.

43   For Somalia, postpartum amenorrhea begins to decline sharply at the 18th month, when the child is given food other than milk. This does not happen with mixed feeding of cows' milk, camels' milk, or goats' milk introduced very early in cases in which mothers do not produce enough breast milk (Mondot-Bernard 1977:28).

44   Dr. Robert Kruker was kind enough to bring this source to my attention.

45   We cannot discount the possibility that eighteenth-century Törbel women were consciously reducing family size by prolonging lactation. Indian villagers know the relationship between lactation and postpartum amenorrhea (Jain et al. 1970), and Italian peasants use nursing to lessen the possibility of pregnancy (Bell 1979).

46   Children born around 1900 were nursed for "at least a year," and one elderly consultant remembered her 3-year-old younger brother being breast-fed.

47   As recently as 1916 it was claimed that some Vispertal housewives did not know how to prepare oat gruel (*Haferschleim*) for their small children (Bellwald 1960:48).

48   One consultant credited her switch to the use of nursing bottles to increased summer work in the fields. When her husband was absent on wage labor, she had all of the farm tasks to do herself and lacked time for nursing. She mentioned that the time of birth

influenced the length of the nursing period. In the winter, a woman was quite content to stay home and breast-feed her infant, but with the competing activities of summer, she nursed less frequently, and her milk would dry up more rapidly.

49   The primitive pacifier of chewed bread or cheese in a bit of linen cloth was called *Nollen* and is mentioned as early as the time of Luther (Bellwald 1960:45).

50   The results of research on a sample of German village populations "are strongly suggestive of a substantial rise in the level of fecundity of married couples between the mid-eighteenth and the end of the nineteenth centuries, a period which interestingly also encompasses the onset of the Fertility Transition. Part of the increase in fecundity appears to be attributable to increased fecundability; some decrease in the nonsusceptible period following childbirth probably also occurred while primary sterility remained in large part unchanged" (Knodel and Wilson in press).

CHAPTER 7.   POTATOES AND THE PREVALENCE OF PEOPLE

1   It is admittedly difficult to demonstrate that a decline in disease is due to better nutrition. A skeptic might agree that we do not know "at what point, if at all, more and better food provides a barrier against infectious disease" (Appleby 1978).

2   One exception might be the turnip, but this was treated as a small-scale garden vegetable rather than a field crop, and it does not appear to have been a dietary staple (Berg 1971).

3   The potato was certainly known as a curiosity and an ornamental much earlier in the royal gardens and botanical collections of central Europe. It is mentioned in the garden catalogues of Basel (1596), Wiesensteig (1598), Annaberg (1605), and Herborn (1621) (Frank J. Lippe, personal communication). There is the obvious possibility that Swiss Guards from Valais could have encountered the potato at a very early date in the papal gardens (Hans Schüpbach, personal communication). Nevertheless, the weight of evidence is strongly in favor of widespread adoption as a staple peasant crop only in the later eighteenth century.

4   It should be noted, however, that the South American native varieties of *Solanum andigenum* brought first to Europe were probably short-day varieties producing a greater crop in the equatorial environment where there were only 12 hours of sunlight. It is known that the potatoes grown in sixteenth-century Europe were all very late to mature and that the process of selection for strains adapted to the long summer days, strains that would mature earlier in the northern latitudes, required considerable time (Salaman 1949:67).

5   The climate of Canton Graubünden is similar in many ways to that of Valais, and villages between 1,000 and 1,600 meters were in the past girdled with grain and potato fields. In well-situated communities with a southern exposure, potatoes were grown up to 1,900 meters, well beyond the effective range for rye and barley (Thomann 1931/32).

6   In mountainous northern regions, the hardiness and productivity of the potato were particularly appreciated. Hamsun's novel (1917:45) of peasant settlement on the inland agricultural frontier of Norway included the following tribute: "What was that about potatoes? Were they just a thing from foreign parts, like coffee; a luxury, an extra? Oh, the potato is a lordly fruit; drought or downpour, it grows and grows all the same. It laughs at the weather, and will stand anything; only deal kindly with it, and it yields fifteen-fold again. Not the blood of a grape, but the flesh of a chestnut, to be boiled or roasted, used in every way. A man may lack corn to make bread, but give him potatoes

and he will not starve. Roast them in the embers, and there is supper; boil them in water and there's a breakfast ready. As for meat, it's little is needed beside. Potatoes can be served with what you please; a dish of milk, a herring, is enough. The rich eat them with butter; poor folk manage with a tiny pinch of salt. Isak could make a feast of them on Sundays, with a mess of cream from Goldenhorns' milk. Poor despised potato—a blessed thing!"

7   "It should be indicated here that the peasant diet in the Gevaudan was considerably improved by the introduction of the potato, which gradually began to be grown from 1815 on, not without encountering a great deal of resistance. In the Velay region, the potato appears in this very type of document [pensions] at the same time and even somewhat earlier" (Bernard 1975).

8   The protein content of potatoes may well be far higher than is generally recognized. An acre of potatoes yields a year's protein requirements for seven people, whereas an acre of navy beans supplies four people with protein, and an acre of wheat only three. "According to the widely accepted protein scale based on the best mix of amino acids and calculated by two UN bodies, eggs rank perfect at 100, and other rankings include pork, 84; beef, 80; potatoes 71; rice, 57; wheat flour, 52; and navy beans, 47" (Martin 1977). Only when the more traditional "primitive diet" of dairy products, rye bread, and potatoes was modified by the increasing use of white bread and sugar did some nutritional deficiencies appear. Dental decay was very infrequent in examinations made in Grächen and Visperterminen in the 1930s, but where modern foods had entered the diet it increased from 2 to 5 caries per 100 teeth to 20 to 30 (Price 1938). A continuation of these trends and the increasingly heavy use of easily prepared pasta brought a *Karieskatastrophe* to upper Valais by 1955 (Roos 1962).

9   The Törbel situation is by no means anomalous. By the 1770s, practically every family in the Shetland Islands was growing potatoes, and for several months of the year they lived on fish and potatoes alone. "Until a generation ago, potatoes were eaten by many people for breakfast, dinner, and supper, especially when the oatmeal and barley meal stocks were sinking low before the new harvest had been cut" (Fenton 1973).

10   The estimate is based on figures for 1919 of 13.42 hectares planted in potatoes (Imboden 1967:19), average Törbel yields of 190 kilograms per ar (Studienwoche 1967:82), and a 1920 census population of 593. The total production of 254,980 kilograms of potatoes would then be an annual 430 kilograms per person. An adult consuming 2,900 calories per day would be deriving 29% of these from potatoes.

11   It is interesting that the birth interval decreased sharply again at around 1900, when another cheap source of carbohydrates (polenta, or maize meal) became available.

12   The potato introduced into the Val de Non of alpine northern Italy in 1799 "caused a sharp rise in population growth in the second half of the nineteenth century" (Cole and Wolf 1974:112). In a Spanish village, the late-eighteenth-century adoption of the potato may have triggered a population rise reflected in increasing numbers of houses, household heads, stores, and mills (Brandes 1975:180). The fragmentation of landholdings, earlier marriage, and higher fertility appear to have resulted from the acceptance of the potato as a staple by the residents of the Limi area in Tibet (Goldstein 1978). The population of Khumbu in Nepal grew from 169 households in 1836 to 596 households in 1957. Fürer-Haimendorf (1964:10) credited this great increase to the spread of the potato: "The improved food-supply is likely to have reduced mortality among the Sherpas themselves, and the availability of a surplus may have attracted immigrants from Tibet."

13   In summarizing the results of several studies of Swiss historical demography done

under his general direction, Professor Mattmüller disagreed with accounts of population growth that emphasized the influence of hygienic improvements, cessation of plague, and innovations in agricultural technology. "Our works have shown, that probably better nourishment in the regions of mixed agriculture along with some cash from cottage industry were the major reasons for a decline in mortality, especially of young adults, and therefore enabled population increase to take place (Mattmüller 1975).

14   The Irish population had risen from 3.2 million in 1754 to 8.2 million in 1845, not including the 1.75 million who emigrated during the period (Crosby 1972:183).

CHAPTER 8.   PRUDENTIAL CHECKS AND BALANCES IN INHERITANCE AND MARRIAGE

1   As one consultant put it, in the case of those who chose to marry before the property division took place, it was *Jeder für sich und Gott für alle* (everyone for himself and God for all).

2   According to the current Swiss Civil Code, all children receive equal shares of three-fourths of the estate. The surviving spouse has title to the remaining one-fourth in ownership or half in usufruct until death, at which time it, too, is divided among the heirs. If a person leaves no offspring or spouse, the property passes to his parents or, in their absence, to their direct descendants. If only a spouse survives, the deceased may leave one-half of his estate to whomever he pleases. If there are descendants but no spouse, one-fourth of the estate may be disposed of in a will (Wiegandt 1977a:144).

3   Changes in the traditional system of peasant land use have recently introduced inequalities that could not have been foreseen years ago when some divisions were made. Grainfields and their accompanying granaries have gone out of use, reducing their value as compared with meadows. With farming increasingly becoming a part-time endeavor, even high-quality lands at a distance have declined in value. Conversely, accessible land and especially potential house sites on the new roads have become much more desirable. In the few instances of dispute over an inheritance, the village judge, aided by assessors from the community, attempts to find an equitable solution.

4   In some cases one heir may buy all or part of a holding from another (often a permanent migrant), but in order to save notary fees and delays in registration, this transaction immediately following the drawing of lots will not be formally recorded. When property such as a dwelling house is not readily divisible, one of the heirs will purchase the shares of others for cash. It is said that the going market rate is used. Heirs of a childless person will sometimes choose to hold a public auction of the property they have acquired and divide the proceeds equally. Tax valuation is the price at which bidding starts. Often individual heirs offer the highest bids, and it is considered understandable that they should wish to keep the land in the family.

5   Since 1948, social security (AHV) payments have been made by the state to retirees. Full support is available only when the farm property has been divided among the heirs and the former owner is legally retired. This provision has certainly hastened the division of many household estates, even in cases in which all the heirs are away from the village and will not themselves cultivate the land.

6   This material was originally presented as a lecture on "Patterns of Marriage in a Swiss Alpine Community" before the *Volkskundliches Seminar* of the University of Zürich. I am grateful to Prof. Dr. Arnold Niederer for the invitation to speak before his class. The analyses of marriage age were performed as part of a project for a class in quantitative methods in history under the direction of Dr. Rudolph Bell. I benefited

greatly from Rudy Bell's patient and imaginative introduction to the world of SPSS and the interpretation of those amazing statistical methods on the printouts. His suggestions on the resulting paper were very helpful, but any errors in my use of these numbers are unfortunately all my own doing.

7   There is no indication, however, that sibling order dictates marriage order as it does in an Andalusian village, where an older sibling must formally yield his prerogative if a younger one wants to marry first (Price and Price 1966).

8   Among the cotter class in Norway, young men often married older servant women, but landowning farmers were often older than their wives (Drake 1969). There were also noteworthy age differences between spouses in England (Wrigley 1966*a*).

9   Widowers and even widows remarried fairly rapidly. In Scandinavia "the high mortality rates made second marriages quite common, and widows and widowers often sought out quite young partners for their second marriage. In many cultures an elderly widow is not a very attractive party, but among Scandinavian peasants the inheritance system gave her control of the farm of her deceased husband and consequently a good bargaining position on the local marriage market" (Löfgren 1974).

10   This contrasts with the practice of a nineteenth-century Italian village where there was a tendency for older children to migrate. "The eldest brother left first and it was the youngest who stayed on the family plot and, in exchange for caring for aging parents, inherited his father's holdings" (Bell 1979). Although the laws required equal inheritance, local custom avoided subdivision of a holding, and surplus sons from landowning families often left the village.

11   The contrasting pulls of the natal family and the new conjugal family are deftly resolved on Tory Island by "natolocal" residence in which the married partners each remain at home with parents and siblings. "The ideal family unit on Tory Island is the conjugal family of father, mother, and children, living under one roof. This is enshrined in the ideal of the Holy Family. It is also universally agreed that old people should be cared for by their children, indigent relatives helped, etc. But this family ideal is not realized, for the very reason that the islanders consider it treasonable to break up this ideal unit. This is the paradox: Marriage, which is needed to found the unit in the first place, is destructive of the unit once formed. If the children of the family marry and leave their parents, then the ideal unit is destroyed; but unless they do this ideal unit cannot be formed" (Fox 1978:156).

CHAPTER 9. FAMILIENPOLITIK: ALLIANCE IN A CLOSED CORPORATE COMMUNITY

1   Fortes (1978:14–15) noted that "human social organization everywhere emerges as some kind of balance, stable or not, between the political order—Aristotle's polis—and the familial or domestic order—the oikos—a balance between polity and kinship. . . . Rights and duties, privileges and claims, can be maintained either on the basis of the mutual trust and amity that are engendered by and through recognized kinship and descent connection or by the force of politically and jurally sanctioned norms. These, of course, are analytical distinctions; in reality the moral imperatives of kinship amity and the jural imperatives of the political order work together in complementary or supplementary association."

2   Cross-cultural comparisons indicate that peasant societies are generally patrilineal and bilateral with respect to rules of descent, inheritance, and residence. Goldschmidt and Kunkel (1971) further emphasized that clans or agnatic groups are infrequent in peasant

communities and that the extended kin groups seldom hold land collectively where intensive agriculture is practiced.

3   For an informative discussion of the role of voluntary associations, such as bands in the politics of a French-speaking Valaisan community, see the work of Weinberg (1976).

4   The closed corporate community is characterized by Wolf (1966*b*) as "solidary towards outsiders and against the outside; it maintains a monopoly of resources—usually land—and defends the first rights of insiders against outside competition. Internally it tends to level differences, evening out both the chances and the risks of life. This does not lead to the warm communal relations sometimes imputed to such a structure. Quite the contrary, we may note that envy and suspicion play an essential part in maintaining the rough equality of life chances."

5   The Swiss scholar Stebler was a first-hand observer and summer resident of Törbel in the early decades of this century, and he also wrote extensively on other villages of upper Valais. Nevertheless, his perspective was colored by the prevailing intellectual idealization of folk life: "Each community is formed in the fashion of a single large family. Each household has the same interest in the well-being of the community; all citizens have the same occupation, the same opportunities, and seek the same goals. They are all participants in like measure in the community property, the alps, the commons, the forest, and the vineyards. All are served by the same public installations (the irrigation system, electrical works, telephone, bake house). All have the same livelihood. They cultivate and use all the land in the same way; they irrigate the earth under the same rules and have a communal canal system. As in every large family, there are in the community different kinds of members, but all strive after the same goal, the welfare of the whole" (Stebler 1922:113).

6   A lawyer born in Törbel but residing in Brig was active in the organization of the Christian social party in Valais during this period. He founded a newspaper, the *Walliser Volksfreund,* in 1920 (Carlen 1974).

7   Hamsun, in his novel *The Growth of the Soil* (1917), described the powerful social effect of a fashionable cloak worn by a peasant woman in a Norwegian village. Novel or urban attire worn by a neighbor in a rural setting was considered a badge of pretentiousness and a symbolic claim for superior and unmerited social rank.

8   It is possible to examine household composition and kinship as irreducible social factors with a sui generis life of their own or in an equally deterministic fashion to see them as resultants of ecological or economic relationships. "The concepts of descent and affinity are expressions of property relations which endure through time. Marriage unifies; inheritance separates, property endures" (Leach 1961:11). Leach's aphorism seems apt here, but it says little about the political network created among local, relatively egalitarian propertyholders or the relative strength and plasticity of strands derived from the unity-cum-competition of siblings and the ties-cum-cleavages of affines. Although the physical constraint of the land and equipment necessary for a viable peasant homestead and the social sanctions against marriage in the absence of proper economic support were omnipresent conditions, they did not dictate the specific marital choices made in Törbel or the association of such decisions to political considerations.

9   Cooperative work-group organization using both agnatic and affinal kin is evident in the recruitment of Tory Island fishing-boat crews described by Fox (1978:136). The core of a crew was likely to be a group of related brothers, fathers and sons, or cousins, but they would often call on affines as much as consanguines to become members: "If a man asked his wife's brother, then this brother would ask his uncle, and if he wanted he would

come in, certainly, and he would ask his daughter's husband, and they would make a crew like that until they had enough." There was keen competition for skilled boatmen, and "this meant that every string had to be pulled, every connection exploited to fill the places with good men—connected men." Fox also pointed out that although most of these Irish islanders could not trace their genealogies back very far or account for the ties among clan members, they all knew of ongoing affinal links through their knowledge of current and recent marriages.

10   Bloch (1973) perceptively distinguished among various kin and non-kin relationships on the basis of whether they were long-term or short-term and the degree to which they were "moral" and thus tolerant of imbalance in their reciprocal aspects: "We commonly find that relationships classed by the actor as political, neighborhood, or friendship have shorter term than those classed as kinship and thus are less moral." The apparent Törbel strategy of making marital and political relationships mutually reinforcing lent added force to an inherited party commitment or, alternatively, gave a moral quality to political maneuver and possible schism. The highly visible reciprocity between *Schwager* suggests that affinity may indeed be a somewhat less moral social commitment than descent, but it allows a great deal of short-term instrumental manipulation and a distinctly wider group of supporters. "In order to maintain a larger pool of cooperators than an individual is using here and now, he must both continually be calling upon and be called upon by cooperators with a less moral relationship, because this is the only way these relationships can be maintained" (Bloch 1973:83).

11   Important local and cantonal leaders in lower Valais have made skillful use of cross-party marriages as a political device, and they point out the advantages of such an alliance to any aspiring power broker (D. Weinberg, personal communication). Although political affiliation remains associated with the family name and descends by rights from the father, there appear to be many "mixed marriages" among the French-speaking Valaisans (Weinberg 1975:74, 100).

12   The overwhelming nature of her passion is acknowledged by Juliet in her assertion: "Prodigious birth of love it is to me/That I must love a loathed enemy" (Act 1, Scene V). Friar Lawrence, in his role as spiritual mediator in the community, saw the love affair as an opportunity for peace between the leading families of Verona: "For this alliance may so happy prove/To turn your households' rancour to pure love" (Act II, Scene III).

13   Where land and labor are restricted, kin groups may maintain defensive coalitions by limiting the marital choices of their members. "To the extent that kinship bonds constitute one set of resources for an individual or a family, the distribution of kinship alliances forms one important criterion for demarcating the classes of a society" (Wolf 1966*b*).

CHAPTER 10.   THE HOUSEHOLD: FLEXIBILITY WITHIN LIMITS

1   A thorough and provocative review of published sources on these issues in the context of household extension has been provided by Wheaton (1975).

2   Individual name, including maiden name for a married woman, was given for each inhabitant. Birth year was listed in 1829 and 1850, and full birth date was added in 1870 and 1880. Mention was often made of occupation or craft, but the large majority of residents were classified in each census as agricultural worker (*Feldarbeiter*) or later as farmer (*Landwirt*), reflecting the continuing dominance of a subsistence mixed-farming economy in the hands of independent, landowning peasants. Community members were

universally Roman Catholic and German-speaking. A division in the lists of names showing household units was not made explicitly until 1850, but notations, such as *Feldarbeiter, Vorsteher* (member of the village council), *Witfrau* (widow), and *Küfer* (cooper), distinguished household heads and marked the cutoff points where new households began (Anderson 1972*b*). Household members were usually designated as wife, son, or daughter, and individuals not part of the nuclear family were called helpers or servants, or their status was merely left blank.

3   Small independent craftsmen have no need for cooperative production techniques or coordinated mercantile enterprises, forms that often provide direct economic incentives to maintain multiple-family organization (Wheaton 1975; Douglass n.d.).

4   The percentage of households with resident kin falls into the same range as that for North Lancashire in 1851 (27%) and Ashworthy (31%–34%). Anderson (1971, Chapters 1 and 6, 1972*a*:220) suggested that these samples were not typical of England as a whole because of the predominance of family farms with few farm laborers in these areas.

5   The proportion of households with resident kin was only 10.1% in a sample of 100 English communities during 1574–1821 (Laslett 1969). The proportion of resident kin in the population, 3.4%, was only one-third of the Törbel figure. Even if the mean number of unidentified persons per household (0.23 in the English sample) is added to the mean number of resident kin (0.16) (Laslett 1972:83), the resulting 0.39 estimate is well below the lowest Törbel figure.

6   For a similar emphasis on patrilaterally extended households in north-central Italy, see the work of Kertzer (1977).

7   Anderson (1972*a*:228) pointed out that a similar system of servant-kin in nineteenth-century urban-industrial Preston "meant that orphans and the children of destitute kin were provided for, and kin were probably easier to sanction, less likely to leave their jobs, and probably, therefore, more reliable."

8   The 1846 census has not been cited in detail because it falls so close in time to the 1850 listing. Where comparable figures on Törbel residents working out of the community were not given, I have used the 1846 tally.

9   The extended-family household is defined here as "a conjugal family unit with the addition of one or more relatives other than offspring, the whole group living together on its own or with servants" (Laslett 1972:29). What is often called an extended or joint family by anthropologists is termed here a multiple-family household.

10   In a German-language village in the Italian Tyrol, a sibling subset could continue on a holding at the death or retirement of a landowning parent. In about 10% of all cases it persisted in this form, with none of the members ever marrying or bringing a spouse onto the estate (Cole and Wolf 1974:238).

11   This rephrasing of the discussion in an earlier article (Netting 1979*a*) owes much to the suggestions of Rudolph Bell.

12   Abundant legal documents from medieval Valais show that the family household was a jural association whose members shared rights over inherited property, movable goods, and acquired wealth (Partsch 1955). The group was not dominated by the father. He could dispose of family property only with the stated agreement of his spouse and children. Women were equal members until they had been given a marriage portion or had participated in the formal division of the estate that finally dissolved the corporate household.

13   *Frauen mehr ins Haus als Oefen, das war zu viel.* A temporary arrangement in which a mother and her married daughter live together is considered more likely to be

successful than the multiple family with a son's mother and her daughter-in-law. Older widowed women also prefer the home of a married daughter to that of a married son, and they find continued housekeeping with a celibate child the most congenial arrangement of all.

14   I would accept Laslett's emphasis on the household as the "fundamental unit in pre-industrial European society" in which "the relationships between parents, children, servants and kin ..., and the interplay of its size and structure with economic and demographic development, make up an intricate adaptive mechanism" (Laslett 1969).

References

AAAS. 1974. *Culture and Population Change*. Washington: American Association for the Advancement of Science.

Abel, Wilhelm. 1967. *Geschichte der deutschen Landwirtschaft vom frühen Mittelalter bis zum 19. Jahrhundert*. Stuttgart: Eugen Ulmer.

Anderson, Michael. 1971. *Family Structure in Nineteenth Century Lancashire*. Cambridge University Press.

   1972a. Household Structure and the Industrial Revolution: Mid-Nineteenth-Century Preston in Comparative Perspective. In *Household and Family in Past Time*, Peter Laslett, ed., pp. 215–36. Cambridge University Press.

   1972b. Standard Tabulation Procedures for Houses, Households, and Other Groups of Residents, in the Enumeration Books of the Censuses of 1851 to 1891. In *Nineteenth Century Society: Essays in the Use of Quantitative Methods for the Study of Social Data*, E. A. Wrigley, ed. Cambridge University Press.

Anderson, Perry. 1974. *Lineages of the Absolutist State*. London: NLB.

Anneler, Hedwig. 1917. *Lötschen*. Bern: Max Dreschel (Reprint 1980 Bern: Haupt).

   1921. Kinderleben im Loetschental. *Pro Juventute 12:* 569–86.

Appleby, A. B. 1978. Disease, Diet, and History. *Journal of Interdisciplinary History* 8:725–35.

Arensberg, Conrad M. 1963. The Old World Peoples. *Anthropological Quarterly* 36:75–99.

Arensberg, Conrad M., and Solon T. Kimball. 1940. *Family and Community in Ireland*. Cambridge, Mass.: Harvard University Press.

Bailey, F. G. 1971a. The Peasant View of the Bad Life. In *Peasants and Peasant Society*, Teodor Shanin, ed., pp. 299–321. Harmondsworth: Penguin.

   1971b. (Ed.) *Gifts and Poison: The Politics of Reputation*. Oxford: Basil Blackwell.

Baker, David. 1973. The Inhabitants of Cardington in 1782. Bedfordshire Historical Record Society 52.

Barber, Benjamin R. 1974. *The Death of Communal Liberty: A History of Freedom in a Swiss Mountain Canton*. Princeton University Press.

Barclay, George W. 1958. *Techniques of Population Analysis*. New York: Wiley.

Barth, Fredrik. 1959. Segmentary Opposition and the Theory of Games: A Study of Pathan Organization. *Journal of the Royal Anthropological Association* 89:5–21.

Bayliss-Smith, Timothy P. 1977. Human Ecology and Island Populations: The Problems of Change. In *Subsistence and Survival: Rural Ecology in the Pacific*, T. P. Bayliss-Smith and R. G. Feachem, eds., pp. 11–20. New York: Academic.

Bell, Rudolph M. 1979. *Fate and Honor, Family and Village: Demographic and Cultural Change in Rural Italy since 1800.* University of Chicago Press.

Bellwald, Joseph. 1960. *Der Erlebnisraum des Gebirgskindes. Arbeiten zur Psychologie, Pädagogik und Heilpädagogik, Band 18.* Freiburg: Universitätsverlag Freiburg.

Bennett, John W. 1976. *The Ecological Transition: Cultural Anthropology and Human Adaptation.* Oxford: Pergamon.

Berg, Gösta. 1971. Die Kartoffel und die Rübe. *Ethnologia Scandinavica* pp. 158–66.

Berkner, Lutz K. 1972a. The Stem Family and the Developmental Cycle of the Peasant Household: An Eighteenth Century Austrian Example. *American Historical Review* 77:398–418.

1972b. Rural Family Organization in Europe: A Problem in Comparative History. *Peasant Studies Newsletter* 1:145–54.

1975. The Use and Misuse of Census Data for the Historical Analysis of Family Structure. *Journal of Interdisciplinary History* 7:721–38.

Bernard, R.-J. 1975. Peasant Diet in Eighteenth Century Gévaudan. In *European Diet from Pre-Industrial to Modern Times,* E. and R. Forster, eds., pp. 19–46. New York: Harper & Row.

Berthoud, Gerald. 1967. *Changements économiques et sociaux de la montagne.* Berne: A. Francke.

Bickel, Wilhelm. 1947. *Bevölkerungsgeschichte und Bevölkerungspolitik der Schweiz.* Zurich: Büchergilde Gutenberg.

Bielander, J. 1940/44. Die Bauernzünfte als Dorfrecht. *Blätter aus der Walliser Geschichte* 9:509–88.

Bielmann, Jürg. 1972. *Die Lebensverhältnisse im Urnerland während des 18. und zu Beginn des 19. Jahrhunderts. Basler Beiträge zur Geschichtswissenschaft, Band 126.* Basel: Helbling und Lichtenhahn.

Blake, Judith, and Kingsley Davis. 1956. Social Structure and Fertility: An Analytic Framework. *Economic Development and Cultural Change* 4:211–35.

Blayo, Yves. 1972. Size and Structure of Households in a Northern French Village between 1836 and 1861. In *Household and Family in Past Time,* Peter Laslett, ed., pp. 255–66. Cambridge University Press.

Bloch, Maurice. 1973. The Long Term and the Short Term: The Economic and Political Significance of the Morality of Kinship. In *The Character of Kinship,* Jack Goody, ed., pp. 75–87. Cambridge University Press.

Boissevain, Jeremy. 1975. Introduction: Towards a Social Anthropology of Europe. In *Beyond the Community: Social Process in Europe,* J. Boissevain and J. Friedl, eds., pp. 9–17. The Hague: Department of Educational Science of The Netherlands.

Borter, L. 1965/66. Vom Wallis der 7 Zenden zum Schweizerkanton 1790–1815. *Blätter aus der Walliser Geschichte* 14:75–120.

Boserup, Ester. 1965. *The Conditions of Agricultural Growth.* Chicago: Aldine.

Bourdieu, P. 1976. Marriage Strategies as Strategies of Social Reproduction. In *Family and Society,* R. Forster and O. Ranum, eds., pp. 117–44. Baltimore: Johns Hopkins University Press.

Brandes, Stanley H. 1975. *Migration, Kinship, and Community: Tradition and Transition in a Spanish Village.* New York: Academic.

Braudel, Fernand. 1972. *The Mediterranean and the Mediterranean World in the Age of*

Philip II, Vol. 1. New York: Harper & Row (French original, 1966).

1973. *Capitalism and Material Life 1400–1800.* New York: Harper & Row.

Braun, Rudolf. 1960. *Industrialisierung und Volksleben.* Erlenbach-Zürich: Eugen Rentsch.

1978. Early Industrialization and Demographic Changes in the Canton of Zürich. In *Historical Studies of Changing Fertility,* Charles Tilly, ed., pp. 289–334. Princeton University Press.

Bridel, Philippe. 1820. *Essai statistique sur le canton du Valais.* Zürich: Orell Fussli.

Britton, Edward. 1977. *The Community of the Vill: A Study in the History of the Family and Village Life in Fourteenth-Century England.* Toronto: Macmillan.

Brugger, Hans. 1956. *Die schweizerische Landwirtschaft in den ersten Hälfte des 19. Jahrhunderts.* Frauenfeld: Huber.

1968. *Statistisches Handbuch der schweizerischen Landwirtschaft.* Bern: Kommissionsverlag.

Brush, Stephen B. 1975. The Concept of Carrying Capacity for Systems of Shifting Cultivation. *American Anthropologist* 77:799–811.

1976. Introduction to Cultural Adaptations to Mountain Ecosystems. *Human Ecology* 4:125–34.

Bucher, Silvio. 1974. *Bevölkerung und Wirtschaft des Amtes Entlebuch im 18. Jahrhundert.* Luzern: Rex Verlag.

Burns, Robert K., Jr. 1961. The Ecological Basis of French Alpine Peasant Communities in the Dauphiné. *Anthropological Quarterly* 34:19–35.

1963. The Circum-Alpine Culture Area: A Preliminary View. *Anthropological Quarterly* 36:130–55.

Carlen, Louis. 1974. *Walliser Politik im 20. Jahrhundert: Dr. Viktor Petrig.* Naters: Verlag Buchdruckerei Oberwallis.

Carniero, Robert L. 1974. A Reappraisal of the Roles of Technology and Organization in the Origin of Civilization. *American Antiquity* 39:179–86.

Carrier, E. H. 1932. *Water and Grass.* London: Christophers.

Chagnon, N. A. 1975. Genealogy, Solidarity, and Relatedness: Limits to Local Group Size and Patterns of Fissioning in an Expanding Population. In *Yearbook of Physical Anthropology, 1975, Vol. 19,* pp. 95–110. Washington: American Association of Physical Anthropologists.

Chappaz, Maurice. 1979. *Lötschental: Die wilde Würde einer verlorenen Talschaft.* Zürich: Suhrkamp.

Chaunu, Pierre. 1974. *Histoire science sociale: Le Durée, l'espace et l'homme à l'époque moderne.* Paris: Societé d'édition d'enseignement supérieur.

Chen, L. C., S. Ahmed, and W. H. Mosley. 1974. A Prospective Study of Birth Interval Dynamics in Rural Bangladesh. *Population Studies* 28:277–97.

Cheyette, Fredric. 1977. The Origins of European Villages and the First European Expansion. *Journal of Economic History* 37:182–206.

Clarkson, Leslie A. 1975. *Death, Disease, and Famine in Pre-Industrial England.* Dublin: Gill and Macmillan.

Clausen, Emil. 1908. Die Pfarrei Mörel. *Zeitschrift für schweizerische Statistik und Volkswirtschaft* 44:5–12.

Coale, Ansley J., and Paul Demeny. 1966. *Regional Model Life Tables and Stable Populations.* Princeton University Press.

Cohen, Mark N. 1977. *The Food Crisis in Prehistory: Overpopulation and the Origins of Agriculture.* New Haven: Yale University Press.

Cole, John. 1972. Cultural Adaptation in the Eastern Alps. *Anthropological Quarterly* 45:158–76.

Cole, John W., and Eric R. Wolf. 1974. *The Hidden Frontier: Ecology and Ethnicity in an Alpine Valley.* New York: Academic.

Coles, J. M., and A. F. Harding. 1979. *The Bronze Age in Europe.* London: Methuen.

Connell, K. H. 1950. *The Population of Ireland: 1750–1845.* Oxford: Clarendon Press.

1968. *Irish Peasant Society.* London: Oxford University Press.

Cowgill, George L. 1975. On Causes and Consequences of Ancient and Modern Population Changes. *American Anthropologist* 77:505–25.

Crafts, N. F. R., and N. J. Ireland. 1976. Family Limitation and the English Demographic Revolution: A Simulation Approach. *Journal of Economic History* 36:599–623.

Crosby, Alfred W. 1972. The Columbian Exchange: Biological and Cultural Consequences of 1492. Westport, Conn.: Greenwood Press.

Cullen, L. M. 1968. Irish History without the Potato. *Past and Present* 40:72–83.

Daly, Martin, and Margo Wilson. 1978. Sex, Evolution and Behavior. North Scituate, Mass.: Duxbury.

Delgado, Hernán, Aaron Lechtig, Reynaldo Martorell, Elena Brineman, and Robert E. Klein. 1978. Nutrition, Lactation and Postpartum Amenorrhea. *American Journal of Clinical Nutrition* 31:322–7.

Devons, Ely, and Max Gluckman. 1964. Conclusion: Modes and Consequences of Limiting a Field of Study. In *Closed Systems and Open Minds: The Limits of Naivety in Social Anthropology,* Max Gluckman, ed., pp. 158–261. Chicago: Aldine.

Douglass, William A. 1980. The South-Italian Family: A Critique. *Journal of Family History* 5:338–59.

Drake, Michael. 1969. *Population and Society in Norway, 1735–1865.* Cambridge University Press.

Dubois, A. 1965. *Die Salzversorgung des Wallis 1500–1610: Wirtschaft und Politik.* Winterthur: P. G. Keller.

Duby, Georges. 1974. *The Early Growth of the European Economy.* Ithaca: Cornell University Press.

Dumond, Don F. 1975. The Limitation of Human Population: A Natural History. *Science* 187:713–21.

Easton, David. 1959. Political Anthropology. In *Biennial Review of Anthropology,* Bernard Siegel, ed., pp. 210–62. Stanford University Press.

Eddy, J. A. 1977. The Case of the Missing Sunspots. *Scientific American* 236:80–92.

Elias, Walter S., and Robert M. Netting. 1977. Methods in the Analysis of European Population History: The Case of Törbel, Canton Valais, Switzerland. Paper read at the annual meeting of the American Anthropological Association.

Ellis, Walter S., and William T. Starmer. 1978. Inbreeding as Measured by Isonymy, Pedigrees, and Population Size in Törbel, Switzerland. *American Journal of Human Genetics* 30:366–376.

Engels, F. 1972. *The Origin of the Family, Private Property, and the State.* New York: International (original 1884).

Eversley, D. E. C. 1977. Review of Population Patterns in the Past. *Demography* 14:539–48.

Febvre, Lucien. 1925. *Geographical Introduction to History.* New York: Knopf.

Fenton, Alexander. 1973. Traditional Elements in the Diet of the Northern Isles of

262   *References*

Scotland. Ethnological Food Research: Reports from the Second International Symposium for Ethnological Food Research, Helsinki, August.

Finlay, Roger A. P. 1979. Population and Fertility in London, 1580–1650. *Journal of Family History* 4:26–38.

Flandrin, Jean-Louis. 1975. Contraception, Marriage, and Sexual Relations in the Christian West. In *Biology of Man in History*, R. Forster and O. Ranum, eds., pp. 23–47. Baltimore: Johns Hopkins University Press.

1977. Repression and Change in the Sexual Life of Young People in Medieval and Early Modern Times. *Journal of Family History* 2:196–210.

1979. *Families in Former Times: Kinship, Household and Sexuality*. Cambridge University Press.

Flannery, Kent V. 1968. Archeological Systems Theory and Early Mesoamerica. In *Anthropological Archaeology in the Americas*, Betty J. Meggers, ed., pp. 67–87. Washington: Anthropological Society of Washington.

Fleury, M., and L. Henry. 1965. Nouveau manuel de dépouillement et d'exploitation de l'etat civil ancien. Paris: Presses Universitaires de France.

Flinn, M. W. 1970. *British Population Growth 1700–1850*. London: Macmillan.

Fortes, Meyer. 1978. An Anthropologist's Apprenticeship. In *Annual Review of Anthropology*, B. J. Siegel, ed., pp. 1–30. Palo Alto: Annual Reviews.

Foster, George M. 1965. Peasant Society and the Image of the Limited Good. *American Anthropologist* 67:293–315.

Fox, Robin. 1978. *The Tory Islanders: A People of the Celtic Fringe*. Cambridge University Press.

Franscini, Stephan. 1848. *Neue Statistik der Schweiz*. Bern: Haller'scheverlagsbuchhandlung.

Friedl, John. 1973. Benefits of Fragmentation in a Traditional Society: A Case from the Swiss Alps. *Human Organization* 32:29–36.

1974. *Kippel: A Changing Valley in the Alps*. New York: Holt, Rinehart and Winston.

1976. Swiss Family Togetherness. *Natural History* 85:44–51.

Frisch, R. E. 1975. Demographic Implications of the Biological Determinants of Female Fecundity. *Social Biology* 22:17–22.

1978. Population, Food Intake, and Fertility. *Science* 199:22–30.

Frisch, R. E., and J. W. McArthur. 1974. Menstrual Cycle: Fatness as a Determinant of Minimum Weight for Height Necessary for Their Maintenance or Onset. *Science* 185:949–51.

Frisch, R. E., and R. Revelle. 1970. Height and Weight at Menarche and a Hypothesis of Critical Body Weights and Adolescent Events. *Science* 169:397–9.

Fürer-Haimendorf, C. V. 1964. *The Sherpas of Nepal*. Berkeley: University of California Press.

Furrer, S. P. 1850. *Geschichte, Statistik und Urkunden-Sammlung über Wallis*. Sitten: Calpini Albertazzi.

Ganiage, Jean. 1963. *Trois Villages d'Ile-de-France au XVIIIe siècle. Publications de l'institut national d'études démographiques*, No. 40. Paris: Presses Universitaires de France.

Gaunt, David. 1977. Pre-Industrial Economy and Population Structure. *Scandinavian Journal of History* 2:183–210.

Gautier, Etienne, and Louis Henry. 1958. *La Population de Crulai Paroisse Normande*.

Cahier de travaux et documents No. 33, Institut national d'études démographiques. Paris: Presses Universitaires de France.

Gerschenkron, Alexander. 1971. The Concept of Continuity in German Anthropology. *Comparative Studies in History and Society 13*:351–7.

Glass, D. V., and E. Grebenik. 1963. World Population, 1800–1950. In *The Cambridge Economic History of Europe*, H. J. Habakkuk and M. Postan, eds., pp. 60–138. Cambridge University Press.

Golde, Günter. 1975. *Catholics and Protestants: Agricultural Modernization in Two German Villages.* New York: Academic.

Goldschmidt, Walter, and Evalyn J. Kunkel. 1971. The Structure of the Peasant Family. *American Anthropologist 73*:1058–76.

Goldstein, Melvyn C. 1978. Pahari and Tibetan Polyandry Revisited. *Ethnology 17*:325–38.

Goubert, Pierre. 1968. Legitimate Fecundity and Infant Mortality in France during the Eighteenth Century: A Comparison. *Daedalus 97*:593–603.

    1971. Historical Demography and the Reinterpretation of Early Modern French History: A Research Review. In *The Family in History*, T. K. Rabb and R. I. Rotberg, eds. New York: Harper & Row.

Greenwood, Davydd J. 1974. Political Economy and Adaptive Processes: A Framework for the Study of Peasant-States. *Peasant Studies Newsletter 3*:1–10.

    1976. *Unrewarding Wealth: The Commercialization and Collapse of Agriculture in a Spanish Basque Town.* Cambridge University Press.

Gremaud, Jean. 1863. *Chartes Sédunoises. Memoires et documents publiés par la société d'histoire de la Suisse romande, Band 18.* Lausanne.

Gutersohn, Heinrich. 1961. *Geographie der Schweiz, Band II, Alpen.* Bern: Kümmerly und Frey.

Habakkuk, H. J. 1971. *Population Growth and Economic Development since 1750.* Leicester University Press.

Hagaman, Roberta, Walter S. Elias, and Robert M. Netting. 1978. The Genetic and Demographic Impact of In-Migrants in a Largely Endogamous Community. *Annals of Human Biology 5*:505–15.

Hajnal, J. 1965. European Marriage Patterns in Perspective. In *Population in History*, D. V. Glass and D. E. C. Eversley, eds., pp. 101–40. Chicago: Aldine.

Hammel, E. A. 1972. The Zadruga as Process. In *Household and Family in Past Time*, Peter Laslett, ed., pp. 335–73. Cambridge University Press.

Hammel, E. A., and Peter Laslett. 1974. Comparing Household Structure over Time and between Cultures. *Comparative Studies in Society and History 16*:73–109.

Hamsun, Knut. 1917. *The Growth of the Soil (Markens Grode).* New York: Knopf.

Hardin, Garrett. 1968. The Tragedy of the Commons. *Science 162*:1243–8.

Hardesty, Donald L. 1975. The Niche Concept: Suggestions for Its Use in Human Ecology. *Human Ecology 3*:71–86.

Hassan, Fekri A. 1978. Demographic Archaeology. In *Advances in Archaeological Method and Theory, Vol. 1*, Michael Schiffer, ed., pp. 49–103. New York: Academic.

Heilleiner, K. F. 1958. New Light on the History of Urban Populations. *Journal of Economic History 18*:60–1.

Heinzmann, Eligius. n.d. Visperterminen wie es einst war. Mimeograph.

264   *References*

Henripin, Jacques. 1954. *La Population Canadienne au début du XVIII*ᵉ *siécle.* Paris: Presses Universitaires de France.
Henry, Louis. 1956. *Anciennes Familles Genevoises.* Paris: Presses Universitaires de France.
    1961. Some Data on Natural Fertility. *Eugenics Quarterly 8:*81–91.
Herlihy, David. 1977. Deaths, Marriages, Births, and the Tuscan Economy (ca. 1300–1500). In *Population Patterns in the Past,* Ronald D. Lee, ed., pp. 135–64. New York: Academic.
Higham, Charles F. W. 1969. Towards an Economic Prehistory of Europe. *Current Anthropology 10:*135–50.
Hobsbawm, E. J. 1967. The Crisis of the Seventeenth Century. In *Crisis in Europe, 1560–1660,* Trevor Aston, ed., pp. 5–58. New York: Basic Books.
Hollingsworth, T. H. 1964. The Demography of the British Peerage. *Population Studies* (special number) *18:*1–108.
    1970. Historical Studies of Migration. *Annales de Demographie Historique* pp. 87–91.
    1977. Review of Population Patterns in the Past. *Demography 14:*548–56.
Homans, George C. 1960. *English Villages of the Thirteenth Century.* New York: Russell and Russell (original 1941).
Howell, Cicely. 1976. Peasant Inheritance Customs in the Midlands, 1280–1700. In *Family and Inheritance: Rural Society in Western Europe, 1200–1800,* J. Goody, J. Thirsk, and E. P. Thompson, eds., pp. 112–55. Cambridge University Press.
Howell, Nancy. 1979. *Demography of the Dobe !Kung.* New York: Academic.
Huffman, Sandra L., A. K. M. Alauddin Chawdhury, J. Chakraborty, and W. Henry Mosley. 1978. Nutrition and Post-Partum Amenorrhoea in Rural Bangladesh. *Population Studies 32:*251–60.
Imboden, Adrian. 1956. *Die Produktions und Lebensverhältnisse der Walliser Hochgebirgsgemeinde Embd und Möglichkeiten zur Verbesserung der gegenwärtigen Lage.* Brugg: Schweizerische Arbeitsgemeinschaft der Bergbauern.
    1967. *Land- und Alpwirtschaftlicher Produktionkataster der Gemeinde Toerbel.* Bern: Eidg. Volkswirtschaftsdepartement, Abteilung für Landwirtschaft.
Imesch, Dionys. 1899. *Die Kämpfe der Walliser gegen die Franzosen 1798–1799.* Sitten.
    1966. *Der Zenden Visp von seinen Anfängen bis 1798. Schriften des Stockalper-Archivs in Brig, Heft 8.*
Imhof, Arthur E. 1977. Historical Demography as Social History: Possibilities in Germany. *Journal of Family History 2:*305–32.
Jain, A. K., T. C. Hsu, R. Freedman, and M. C. Change. 1970. Demographic Aspects of Lactation and Postpartum Amenorrhea. *Demography 7:*255–71.
Jones, E. L. 1974. Environmental Buffers of a Marginal Peasantry in Southern England. *Peasant Studies Newsletter 3:*13–16.
Joris, Elizabeth. 1979. Sozialer Wandel im Oberwallis i der 2. Hälfte des 19. Jahrhunderts. Unpublished licentiate thesis of the History Seminar, University of Zürich.
Jossen, Erwin. 1973. *Die Kirche im Oberwallis am Vorabend des Franzoseneinfalls 1790–1798.* Brig: Tscherrig.
Kämpfen, Peter-Joseph. 1867. *Freiheits Kämpfe der Oberwalliser in den Jahren 1798 und 1799.* Stans.
Kämpfen, Werner. 1942. *Ein Burgerrechtsstreit im Wallis.* Zürich: Grütli.

Kertzer, David I. 1977. European Peasant Household Structure: Some Implications from a Nineteenth Century Italian Community. *Journal of Family History 2*:333–49.

Kessinger, Tom G. n.d. The Peasant Farm in North India, 1848–1968. Presented before the Sixth International Congress on Economic History, Copenhagen, Denmark, August 19–23, 1974.

Klapisch, Christine. 1972. Household and Family in Tuscany in 1427. In *Household and Family in Past Time*, Peter Laslett, ed., pp. 267–82. Cambridge University Press.

Knodel, John. 1968. Infant Mortality and Fertility in Three Bavarian Villages: An Analysis of Family Histories from the Nineteenth Century. *Population Studies 22*:297–318.

————. 1970. Two and a Half Centuries of Demographic History in a Bavarian Village. *Population Studies 24*:353–76.

————. 1977. Breast-Feeding and Population Growth. *Science 198*:1111–5.

Knodel, John, and Chris Wilson. The Secular Increase in Fecundity in German Village Populations: An Analysis of Reproductive Histories of Couples Married 1750–1899. Unpublished manuscript.

Kolata, Gina Bari. 1974. !Kung Hunter-Gatherers: Feminism, Diet, and Birth Control. *Science 185*:932–4.

Kronig, Stanislaus. 1927. *Familien-Statistik und Geschichtliches über die Gemeinde Zermatt*. Ingenbohl: Päpstl. Theodosius-Buchdruckerei.

Kunstadter, Peter. 1971. Natality, Mortality and Migration in Upland and Lowland Populations in Northwestern Thailand. In *Culture and Population*, Steven Polgar, ed., pp. 46–60. Cambridge: Schenkman.

Lamb, H. H. 1972. *Climate: Present, Past and Future, Vol. 1*. London: Methuen.

Langer, William A. 1963. Europe's Initial Population Explosion. *American Historical Review 49*:1–17.

————. 1972. Checks on Population Growth: 1750–1856. *Scientific American 226*:93–9.

Laslett, Peter. 1965. *The World We Have Lost*. New York: Scribner's.

————. 1966. The Study of Social Structure from Listings of Inhabitants. In *An Introduction to English Historical Demography*, E. A. Wrigley, ed. New York: Basic Books.

————. 1969. Size and Structure of the Household in England Over Three Centuries. *Population Studies 23*:199–223.

————. 1971. Age at Menarche in Europe since the Eighteenth Century: Evidence from Belgrade in 1733–4. *Journal of Interdisciplinary History 2*:221–36.

————. 1972. Introduction: The History of the Family. In *Household and Family in Past Time*, Peter Laslett, ed., pp. 1–89. Cambridge University Press.

————. 1977. *Family Life and Illicit Love in Earlier Generations*. Cambridge University Press.

Leach, Edmund. 1961. *Pul Eliya, A Village in Ceylon*. Cambridge University Press.

Lee, Richard B. 1969. !Kung Bushman Subsistence: An Input-Output Analysis. In *Contributions to Anthropology: Ecological Essays*, David Damas, ed., pp. 73–94. Ottawa: National Museum of Canada (bulletin 230).

Lee, Ronald. 1977. (Ed.) *Population Patterns of the Past*. New York: Academic.

Lee, W. Robert. 1975. Zur Bevölkerungsgeschichte Bayerns 1750–1850: Britische Forschungsergebnisse. *Vierteljahrsschrift für Sozial und Wirtschaftsgeschichte 62*:309–38.

Lehner, Karl. 1957. *Kleine Zermatter Chronik*. Zermatt: Wega.

Le Roy Ladurie, Emmanuel. 1971. *Times of Feast, Times of Famine: A History of Climate since the Year 1000*. Garden City: Doubleday.

———. 1974. *The Peasants of Languedoc*. Urbana: University of Illinois Press.

———. 1975. Famine Amenorrhea (Seventeenth–Twentieth Centuries). In *Biology of Man in History*, R. Forster and O. Ranum, eds., pp. 163–8. Baltimore: Johns Hopkins University Press.

———. 1977. Recent Historical "Discoveries." *Daedalus 106*:141–55.

———. 1978. *Montaillou: The Promised Land of Error*. New York: Braziller.

Levine, David. 1977. *Family Formation in an Age of Nascent Capitalism*. New York: Academic.

Levi-Strauss, Claude. 1953. Social Structure. In *Anthropology Today*, A. L. Kroeber, ed., pp. 524–53. University of Chicago Press.

Lewontin, R. C. 1974. *The Genetic Basis of Evolutionary Change*. New York: Columbia University Press.

Little, M. A., and George E. B. Morren, Jr. 1976. *Ecology, Energetics, and Human Variability*. Dubuque: Wm. C. Brown.

Livi-Bacci, Massimo. 1977. *A History of Italian Fertility during the Last Two Centuries*. Princeton University Press.

Löfgren, Orvar. 1974. Family and Household among Scandinavian Peasants: An Exploratory Essay. *Ethnologia Scandinavica* pp. 17–52.

Lorimer, F. 1954. *Culture and Human Fertility*. Paris: UNESCO.

Lüscher, Kurt K., Verena Ritter, and Peter Gross. 1973. *Early Child Care in Switzerland*. London: Gordon & Breach.

Macfarlane, Alan. 1976. *Resources and Population: A Study of the Gurungs of Nepal*. Cambridge University Press.

———. 1978. *The Origins of English Individualism*. Cambridge University Press.

Manley, Gordon. 1966. Problems of the Climatic Optimum: The Contribution of Glaciology. In *Proceedings of the International Symposium on World Climate 800–0 B.C.*, J. S. Sawyer, ed., pp. 34–9. London: Royal Meteorological Society.

Mariétan, Ignace. 1948. Heilige Wasser. *Schweizer Heimatbücher 21/22*. Bern: Paul Haupt.

Markgraf, Vera. 1969. Moorkundliche und vegetationsgeschichtliche Untersuchungen an einem Moorsee an der Waldgrenze im Wallis. *Botanische Jahrbücher 89*:1–63.

Martin, Everett G. 1977. Inca Treasure Lures a Peruvian Scientist to Search the Andes. *Wall Street Journal* February 16, 1977, p. 1.

Mattmüller, Markus. 1975. Demographische Studien am historischen Seminar der Universität Basel. In *Historische Demographie als Sozialgeschichte*, A. E. Imhof, ed., pp. 1059–66. Darmstadt and Marburg: Selbstverlag der Hessischen Historischen Kommission Darmstadt und der Historischen Kommission für Hessen.

May, Robert M. 1978. Human Reproduction Reconsidered. *Nature 272*:491–5.

Mayer, Kurt Berndt. 1952. *The Population of Switzerland*. New York: Columbia University Press.

McCloskey, Donald. 1975. The Persistence of English Common Fields. In *European Peasants and Their Markets: Essays in Agrarian Economic History*, W. N. Parker and Eric L. Jones, eds., pp. 73–119. Princeton University Press.

McKeown, Thomas. 1976. *The Modern Rise of Population*. New York: Academic.

McKeown, T., and R. G. Record. 1962. Reasons for the Decline of Mortality in England and Wales during the 19th Century. *Population Studies 16:*94–122.

Menken, Jane. 1979. Seasonal Migration and Seasonal Variation in Fecundability: Effects on Birth Rates and Birth Intervals. *Demography 16:*103–19.

Menken, Jane, James Trussell, and Susan Watkins. 1981. The Nutrition Fertility Link: An Evaluation of the Evidence. *Journal of Interdisciplinary History 11:*425–41.

Meuvret, J. 1965. Demographic Crisis in France from the Sixteenth to the Eighteenth Century. In *Population in History,* D. V. Glass and D. E. C. Eversley, eds., pp. 507–22. Chicago: Aldine.

Meyer, L. 1907. Les Recensements de la population du canton du Valais de 1798 à 1900. *Zeitschrift für schweizerische Statistik 44:*289–369.

Meyer, Werner. 1979. Wüstungen als Zeugen des mittelalterlichen Alpwesens. *Schweizerischen Zeitschrift für Geschichte 29:*256–64.

Minge-Kalman, Wanda. 1977. On the Theory and Measurement of Domestic Labor Intensity. *American Ethnologist 4:*273–84.

Mintz, Sidney W. 1973. A Note on the Definition of Peasantries. *Journal of Peasant Studies 1:*91–106.

Mondot-Bernard, Jacqueline M. 1977. *Relationships between Fertility, Child Mortality and Nutrition in Africa: Tentative Analysis.* Paris: Development Center of the Organization for Economic Cooperation and Development.

Monter, E. William. 1979. Historical Demography and Religious History in Sixteenth-Century Geneva. *Journal of Interdisciplinary History 9:*399–428.

Morgan, L. H. 1963. *Ancient Society.* Cleveland: World (original 1877).

Muehlbauer, Gene, and Marjorie K. B. Muehlbauer. n.d. Operationalizing Avoidance Behavior Substantiating the Presence of Conflict in an Alpine Community. Unpublished manuscript.

Murphy, Robert F. 1970. Basin Ethnography and Ecological Theory. In *Languages and Cultures of Western North America,* Earl H. Swanson, Jr., ed., pp. 152–71. Pocatello: Idaho State University Press.

Murphy, R. F., and J. H. Steward. 1956. Tappers and Trappers: Parallel Process in Acculturation. *Economic Development and Cultural Change 4:*335–55.

Murra, John V. 1972. El "Control Vertical" de un Maximo de Pisos Ecologicos en la Economia de las Sociedades Andinas. *Visita de la Provincia de Leon de Huanuco (1562) 2:*429–76.

Netting, Robert M. 1965a. A Trial Model of Cultural Ecology. *Anthropological Quarterly 38:*81–96.

——— 1965b. Household Organization and Intensive Agriculture: The Kofyar Case. *Africa 35:*422–9.

——— 1968. *Hill Farmers of Nigeria: Cultural Ecology of the Kofyar of the Jos Plateau.* Seattle: University of Washington Press.

——— 1969. Ecosystems in Process: A Comparative Study of Change in Two West African Societies. In *Contributions to Anthropology: Ecological Essays,* David Damas, ed., pp. 102–12. Ottawa: National Museum of Canada (bulletin 230).

——— 1972. Of Men and Meadows: Strategies of Alpine Land Use. *Anthropological Quarterly 45:*132–44.

——— 1973. Fighting, Forest, and the Fly: Some Demographic Regulators among the Kofyar. *Journal of Anthropological Research 29:*164–79.

1974a. Kofyar Armed Conflict: Social Causes and Consequences. *Journal of Anthropological Research 30*:139–63.

1974b. The System Nobody Knows: Village Irrigation in the Swiss Alps. In *Irrigation's Impact on Society,* T. E. Downing and M. Gibson, eds., pp. 67–75. Tucson: University of Arizona Press.

1976. What Alpine Peasants Have in Common: Observations on Communal Tenure in a Swiss Village. *Human Ecology 4*:135–46.

1977. *Cultural Ecology.* Menlo Park: Cummings.

1979a. Household Dynamics in a Nineteenth Century Swiss Village. *Journal of Family History 4*:39–58.

1979b. Eine lange Ahnenreihe: Die Fortdauer von Patrilinien über mehr als drei Jahrhunderte in einem schweizerischen Bergdorf. *Schweizerischen Zeitschrift für Geschichte 29*:194–215.

in press. The Ecological Perspective: Holism and Scholasticism in Anthropology. Paper to be published in the proceedings of the conference on American Social and Cultural Anthropology Past and Future, Spring Hill Conference Center, Wayzata, Minnesota, 1976.

Netting, Robert M., and Walter S. Elias. 1978. Familienstatistik Törbel. Computer-printed manuscript.

1980. Balancing on an Alp: Population Stability and Change in a Swiss Peasant Village. In *Village Viability in Contemporary Society, AAAS Selected Symposium 34,* Priscilla Copeland Reining and Barbara Lenkerd, eds., pp. 69–108. Washington: American Association for the Advancement of Science.

Nicholas, Ralph W. 1965. Factions: A Comparative Analysis. In *Political Systems and the Distribution of Power,* Michael Banton, ed., pp. 21–61. London: Tavistock.

Niederer, Arnold. 1956. *Gemeinwerk im Wallis. Schriften der Schweizerischen Gesellschaft für Volkskunde, Vol. 37.* Basel: G. Krebs.

Noti, Stanislaus. 1976. Die de Fonte de Torbio. *Pfarrblatt St. Theodul Törbel.*

1977. Pfarreigeschichtliches (III), vom Kirchenzehnt. *Pfarrblatt St. Theodul Törbel.*

Nurge, E. 1970. Birth Rate and Work Load. *American Anthropologist 72*:1434–9.

Papilloud, J. H. 1973. *Histoire démographique de Conthey (Valais) 1680–1830. Études et recherches d'histoire contemporaine 20.* Fribourg: Editions universitaires.

Partsch, Gottfried. 1955. *Das Mitwirkungsrecht der Familiengemeinschaft im älteren Walliserrecht.* Geneva.

Perrenoud, Alfred. 1977. Variables Sociales en démographie historique: l'exemple de Genève au XVIIIe siècle. In *Démographie urbaine: XVe–XXe Siècle,* Maurice Garden, ed. Lyon: Centre d'Histoire Economique et Sociale de la Région Lyonnaise.

Pfister, Christian. 1975. Agrarkonjunktur und Witterungsverlauf im westlichlichen Schweizer Mittelland 1755–1797. Bern: Geographisches Institut der Universität Bern.

Piggott, Stuart. 1965. *Ancient Europe.* Chicago: Aldine.

Plaisted, R. L. n.d. *Imbalance in Nature—The Potato in Ireland.* Unpublished manuscript. Cornell University.

Plakans, Andrejs. 1973. Peasant Families East and West: A Comment on Lutz K. Berkner's "Rural Family Organization in Europe." *Peasant Studies Newsletter 2*:11–16.

1977. Identifying Kinfolk beyond the Household. *Journal of Family History 2*:3–27.

Platter, Thomas. 1944. *Lebensbeschreibung.* Basel: Benno Schwabe.

Plumb, J. H. 1977. The Rise of Love. A review of *The Family,* by Lawrence Stone. *New York Review of Books* Vol. 24, No. 19, November 24, 1977, pp. 30–6.

Polgar, Steven. 1972. Population History and Population Policies from an Anthropological Perspective. *Current Anthropology 13:*203–11.

Post, John D. 1974. A Study in Meteorological and Trade Cycle History: The Economic Crisis following the Napoleonic Wars. *Journal of Economic History 34:*315–49.

Potter, R. G., M. I. New, J. B. Wyon, and J. B. Gordon. 1965. Applications of Field Studies to Research on the Physiology of Human Reproductions: Lactation and Its Effects upon Birth Interval in Eleven Punjab Villages, India. In *Public Health and Population Change,* M. C. Sheps and J. C. Ridley, eds., pp. 377–99. University of Pittsburgh Press.

Price, Richard, and Sally Price. 1966. Noviazgo in an Andalusian Pueblo. *Southwestern Journal of Anthropology 22:*302–22.

Price, Weston A. 1938. *Nutrition and Physical Degeneration.* New York: Hoeber.

Rappaport, Roy A. 1968. *Pigs for the Ancestors: Ritual in the Ecology of a New Guinea People.* New Haven: Yale University Press.

   1971a. Nature, Culture, and Ecological Anthropology. In *Man, Culture, and Society,* H. L. Shapiro, ed., pp. 237–67. London: Oxford University Press.

   1971b. The Flow of Energy in an Agricultural Society. *Scientific American 224:*116–23.

Redfield, Robert. 1955. *The Little Community.* University of Chicago Press.

   1956. *Peasant Society and Culture.* University of Chicago Press.

Renard, G., and G. Weulersse. 1926. *Life and Work in Modern Europe.* London: Routledge and Kegan Paul.

Rhoades, Robert E., and Stephen I. Thompson. 1975. Adaptive Strategies in Alpine Environments: Beyond Cultural Particularism. *American Ethnologist 2:*535–51.

Rietschin, Peter, and Peter Sahli. 1966. Die Wasserfuhren. In *Studienwoche in Törbel,* pp. 96–122. Bern-Hofwil: Staatliches Lehrerseminar.

Roos, Adolf. 1962. *Kulturzerfall und Zahnverderbnis.* Bern: Medizinischer Verlag Hans Huber.

Roten, Hans Anton von. 1945. Hauptmann Peter Wyss und die Kapelle von Burgen (Törbel). *Walliser Jahrbuch, 14:*34–40.

Roten, Peter von. 1940. Untersuchungen über die Verteilung und die rechtlichen Verhältnisse des Grundbesitzes in den Vispertälern im 13. und 14. Jahrhundert. Unpublished dissertation of the University of Bern.

Ruesch, Hanspeter. 1979. Die Demographie der Alpen zwischen 1650 und 1850: Bericht über den heutigen Wissenstand und Fragen an die künftige Forschung. *Schweizerischen Zeitschrift für Geschichte 29:*159–80.

Sabean, David. 1970. Household Formation and Geographical Mobility: A Family Register Study for a Württemberg Village 1760–1900. *Annales de Démographie Historique* pp. 275–301.

Sahlins, M. D. 1957. Land Use and the Extended Family in Moala, Fiji. *American Anthropologist 59:*449–62.

Salaman, Redcliffe N. 1949. *History and Social Influence of the Potato.* Cambridge University Press.

Saugstad, L. F., and O. Odegard. 1977. Predominance of Extreme Geographical

Proximity of the Spouses of Heirs to Independent Farms in a Mountain Valley in Norway between 1600 and 1850. *Annals of Human Genetics 40:*419–30.

Sauter, Marc-R. 1950. Prèhistoire du Valais. *Vallesia 5:*1–165.

Schaub, F. A. 1949. *Ueber Erfolge der Kropfprophylaxe.* Zurich: J. Weiss.

Schmid, Hans. 1935. *Wallis: Ein Wanderbuch.* Frauenfeld: Huber.

Schofield, R. S. 1970. Age-specific Mobility in an Eighteenth Century Rural English Parish. *Annales de Démographie Historique* pp. 261–74.

Schofield, Roger, and E. A. Wrigley. 1979. Infant and Child Mortality in England in the Late Tudor and Early Stuart Period. In *Health, Medicine and Mortality in the Sixteenth Century,* Charles Webster, ed., pp. 61–95. Cambridge University Press.

Scholl, Theresa O., Mary E. Odell, and Francis E. Johnston. 1976. Biological Correlates of Modernization in a Guatemalan Highland Municipio. *Annals of Human Biology 3:*23–32.

Segraves, B. Abbott. 1978. The Malthusian Proposition and Nutritional Stress: Differing Implications for Man and for Society. In *Malnutrition, Behavior, and Social Organization,* L. S. Greene, ed., pp. 173–218. New York: Academic.

Shorter, Edward. 1977. On Writing the History of Rape. *Signs 3:*471–82.

1978. Bastardy in South Germany: A Comment. *Journal of Interdisciplinary History 3:*459–69.

Sklar, June L. 1970. The Role of Marriage Behaviour in the Demographic Transition: The Case of Eastern Europe around 1900. *Population Studies 28:*231–74.

Smith, Daniel Scott. 1977. A Homeostatic Demographic Regime: Patterns in West European Family Reconstitution Studies. In *Population Patterns in the Past,* Ronald D. Lee, ed., pp. 19–52. New York: Academic.

Smith, P. E. L., and T. C. Young. 1972. The Evolution of Early Agriculture and Culture in Greater Mesopotamia: A Trial Model. In *Population Growth: Anthropological Implications,* Brian Spooner, ed., pp. 1–59. Cambridge, Mass.: MIT Press.

Smith, Thomas C. 1977. *Nakahara: Family Farming and Population in a Japanese Village, 1717–1830.* Stanford University Press.

Solien de Gonzalez, N. M. 1964. Lactation and Pregnancy: A Hypothesis. *American Anthropologist 66:*873–8.

Spufford, Margaret. 1974. *Contrasting Communities: English Villagers in the Sixteenth and Seventeenth Centuries.* Cambridge University Press.

Staub, Walter. 1944. Die ältesten Siedlungen im Gebiet der Vispertäler. *Neue Zürcher Zeitung,* Nr. 2052, November 20, 1944.

Stebler, F. G. 1914. *Sonnige Halden am Lötschberg.* Bern: Monographien aus der Schweizeralpen.

1922. *Die Vispertaler Sonnenberge. Jahrbuch des Schweizer Alpenclub. Sechsundfünfzigster Jahrgang.* Bern: Verlag des Schweizer Alpenclub.

Steffen, Hans. 1975. Die Kompanien Kaspar Jodok Stockalpers: Beispiel eines Soldunternehmens im 17. Jahrhundert. *Blätter aus der Walliser Geschichte* Bd. 16, Nr. 2.

Steward, Julian H. 1965. *Theory of Culture Change.* Urbana: University of Illinois Press.

Stini, William A. 1975. *Ecology and Human Adaptation.* Dubuque: Wm. C. Brown.

Street, J. M. 1969. An Evaluation of the Concept of Carrying Capacity. *Professional Geographer 21:*104–7.

Studienwoche in Törbel. 1967. Bern-Hofwil: Staatliches Lehrerseminar.

Summermatter, Viktor. 1975. *St. Niklaus: Familienstatistik und Chronik*. St. Niklaus: Gemeindeverwaltung.

Swedlund, Alan C., and George J. Armelagos. 1976. *Demographic Anthropology*. Dubuque: Wm. C. Brown.

Teuteberg, H. J. 1975. The General Relationship between Diet and Industrialization. In *European Diet from Pre-Industrial to Modern Times*, E. and R. Forster, eds., pp. 63–109. New York: Harper & Row.

TGA. Törbel Gemeinde Archiv.

Thestrup, Poul. 1972. Methodological Problems of a Family Reconstitution Study in a Danish Rural Parish before 1800. *Scandinavian Economic History Review* 20:1–26.

Thomann, H. 1931/32. *Der Kartoffelbau in Graubünden, 35. Jahresbericht der landwirtschaftliche Schule Plantahof*.

Thrupp, Sylvia L. 1975. Comparative Study in the Barnyard. *Journal of Economic History* 35:1–7.

Thürer, Georg. 1970. *Free and Swiss*. London: Oswald Wolf.

Tönnies, Ferdinand. 1961. Gemeinschaft and Gesellschaft. In *Theories of Society*, Talcott Parsons, Edward Shils, Kaspar D. Naegele, and Jesse R. Pitts, eds., pp. 191–201. New York: Free Press of Glencoe.

TPA. Törbel Pfarrei Archiv.

Utterström, G. 1965. Two Essays on Population in Eighteenth-Century Scandinavia. In *Population in History*, D. V. Glass and D. E. C. Eversley, eds., pp. 523–38. Chicago: Aldine.

Valmary, Pierre. 1965. *Familles Paysannes au XVIIIe siècle en Bas-Quercy. Cahier de travaux et documents No. 45. Publications de l'institut national d'études démographiques*. Paris: Presses Universitaires de France.

Van de Walle, Francine. 1975. Migration and Fertility in Ticino. *Population Studies* 29:447–62.

Van der Walt, L. A., E. N. Wilmsen, and T. Jenkins. 1978. Unusual Sex Hormone Patterns among Desert-Dwelling Hunter-Gatherers. *Journal of Clinical Endocrinology and Metabolism* 46:658–63.

Vayda, A. P., and Roy A. Rappaport. 1968. Ecology, Cultural and Non-cultural. In *Introduction to Cultural Anthropology*, J. A. Clifton, ed., pp. 477–87. Boston: Houghton Mifflin.

Wachter, K. W., and P. Laslett. 1978. Measuring Patriline Extinction for Modeling Social Mobility in the Past. In *Statistical Studies of Historical Social Structure*, K. W. Wachter, E. A. Hammel, and P. Laslett, eds., pp. 113–35. New York: Academic.

Wackernagel, Hans Georg. 1959. *Altes Volkstums der Schweiz*. Basel: Krebs.

Watt, B. K., and A. L. Merrill. 1975. *Composition of Foods*. Washington: U.S. Department of Agriculture.

Weinberg, Daniela. 1975. *Peasant Wisdom: Cultural Adaptation in a Swiss Village*. Berkeley: University of California Press.

——— 1976. Bands and Clans: Political Functions of Voluntary Associations in the Swiss Alps. *American Ethnologist* 3:175–89.

Wheaton, Robert. 1975. Family and Kinship in Western Europe: The Problem of the Joint Family Household. *Journal of Interdisciplinary History* 4:601–28.

Wiegandt, Ellen. 1977a. Communalism and Conflict in the Swiss Alps. Unpublished Ph.D. dissertation, University of Michigan.

1977*b*. Inheritance and Demography in the Swiss Alps. *Ethnohistory 24:*133–48.

Wilmsen, Edwin. 1978. Seasonal Effects of Dietary Intake on Kalahari San. *Federation of American Societies for Experimental Biology Proceedings 37:*25–32.

Windisch, Uli. 1976. *Lutte de Clans, lutte de classes: Chermignon, la politique au village.* Lausanne: Editions l'Age d'Homme S.A.

Wolf, Eric R. 1955. Types of Latin American Peasantry: A Preliminary Discussion. *American Anthropologist 57:*452–71.

1957. Closed Corporate Peasant Communities in Mesoamerica and Central Java. *Southwestern Journal of Anthropology 13:*1–18.

1966*a. Peasants.* Englewood Cliffs: Prentice-Hall.

1966*b.* Kinship, Friendship, and Patron-Client Relations in Complex Societies. In *The Social Anthropology of Complex Societies,* Michael Banton, ed., pp. 1–22. London: Tavistock.

Wolf, F. O. n.d. *Die Visperthäler.* Zürich: Orell Füssli.

Wrigley, E. A. 1966*a.* Family Limitation in Pre-Industrial England. *Economic History Review 19:*82–109.

1966*b.* Family Reconstitution. In *An Introduction to English Historical Demography,* E. A. Wrigley, ed. New York: Basic Books.

1968. Mortality in Pre-Industrial England: The Example of Colyton, Devon, over Three Centuries. *Daedalus 97:*546–80.

1969. *Population and History.* New York: McGraw-Hill.

1977. Reflections on the History of the Family. *Daedalus 106:*71–85.

1978. Fertility Strategy for the Individual and the Group. In *Historical Studies of Changing Fertility,* Charles Tilly, ed., pp. 135–54. Princeton University Press.

Zimmermann, Josef. 1968. *Die Orts- und Flurnamem des Vispertales im Wallis.* Zürich: Juris Druck Verlag.

Zurbriggen, Joseph. 1952. *Täsch: Familienstatistik, Chronik und Kirche.* Brig.

1960. *Familienstatistik Saastal.* Visp: Neue Buchdruckerei.

Index

abortion, 141, 141n
adoption, 75
affinal relationship, 194–195, 194n, 195n, 196, 210–212, 220; *see also* kinship
age difference between spouses, 181–182, 181 n8, 181 n9, 184
agriculture, alpine, 56, 222; commercial, 79; cooperation in, 194; *see also* altitude, influence on agriculture and settlement; crop failure; crop rotation; fallowing; gardens; grainfields; irrigation; land use; meadows; pastures; products, farm; tools, agricultural; vineyards
agricultural intensification, xiv, 42, 43–49, 56, 58, 90–91, 167
agricultural prices, 117, 118n, 161–162, 164
Allemanic invasion, 9, 49, 61n, 63n
alliance, marital, 187, 195, 201
alp, summer pasture, 12, 22, 25, 60, 61, 64, 65, 67, 78
alp association, 65, 66, 188
Alp Bifigen, 12, 64
alp enclosures, 22, 64–65
altitude, influence on agriculture and settlement, 1, 7, 8, 10, 12, 14–20, 90, 161, 161n, 164, 167, 223
amenorrhea, famine, 154, 166
amenorrhea, post partum, 153, 153n, 154, 157
Andes, 57, 160, 223
Argentina, migration to, 101–102
associations, *see* alp association; voluntary associations
Augstbordhorn, 1
Ausserberg, 16, 66
Austria, 130, 170
avalanches, 8, 12

Balkans, 134n
Bangladesh, 154
bankruptcy, 54, 104
baptism, 71n, 92–93, 115n, 129, 230
barns, 11, 24–25, 46, 67
beans, 14, 36
Belgium, 54

Berner Alpen, 6
berries, 13–14
bilaterality, 187n, 193, 194, 201, 212
birth control, 112, 130, 141–147, 158; *see also* coitus interruptus; family limitation
birth intervals, 142–143, 147–157, 153n, 158, 159, 166, 166n, 167, 221
birth practices, 130; *see also* midwife
birth rank, 177–180, 185
birth rates, 130–133
Bishop of Sion, 53, 59, 61n, 65
Black Death, 72, 114, 115n, 116–117
boarders, lodgers, 216
Boserup, E., xiv, 47, 167
boundaries, village, 50, 57, 90
bread, 34, 35–36, 37, 38, 39, 60, 157, 165
Brig, 6, 107
Bronze Age, 8n, 58
Brunnen, 3, 8, 10, 56, 72
buildings, 62, 68; *see also* barns; granaries; houses; huts; store houses
buildings, ownership of, 25, 34
buildings, storage, 32–35
Bürchen, 8, 50, 98, 189
Burgen, 3, 58
Burns, R. K., 5, 44
butter, 165

calories, 153n, 154, 154n, 159, 163–166, 166n
carrying capacity (land), 65, 90, 164, 222–223, 226
cattle breeding, 25, 48, 49
cattle disease, 119
cattle trading, 25–28, 56
celibacy, 56, 76, 83, 135, 136–137, 142, 158, 167, 170, 173–174, 178, 195, 207, 209
cellars, 34
census, Swiss, 54, 73, 93, 95, 95n, 203, 203n
chastity, 129, 136, 142, 226
cheese, 24, 34–35, 37, 38, 165
cheese, production of, 65, 165
cheesemaking, methods of, 8n, 24, 25, 38n, 49, 55, 64, 66
childbirth, dangers of, 124–125, 158
children, desire for, 129, 129n

church, 190–191, 225; *see also* religion; Roman
    Catholic church
citizenship, village, 59, 60, 60n, 66, 71, 78–79,
    87, 176, 183, 185, 228
climate, 6n, 6–7, 8n, 13, 15, 17, 65, 67, 117–
    118, 159, 161–163, 167; *see also* environment
coital frequency, 151, 151n, 153, 157
coitus interruptus, 142, 142n
commons, tragedy of, 58, 61
community, corporate, 52, 59, 60, 61, 61n, 63,
    71, 78–79, 92, 187–188, 190n, 196, 228–229
conflict, interpersonal, 103, 187, 190, 192, 224
conservation, 12
Conthey, 123
Corpus Christi Day, 54, 108, 153
corrals, *see* alp enclosures
cottage industry, 134–135, 158, 168
cows, 8n, 18, 24–28, 49, 50, 54, 66, 108, 165
craftsmen, 56, 79, 87, 104, 105, 106, 135, 194,
    209, 209n
crop failure, 17, 113, 116–118, 117n, 121, 128,
    158, 159, 161–163, 167
crop rotation, 36–37, 46
cultivation, shifting, 43
cultural factors, values, xviii, xxiii, 63, 216,
    218, 220, 224
cultural materialism, 224
culture area, alpine, 44
cybernetic factors, 58

Dauphiné, 57
death, average age at, 126–127
death rate, 121–124, 123n, 131
deaths, away from village, 104
deaths, infant, 93n, 115, 119, 122, 124, 127n,
    128, 129, 141–142, 230
deaths, mercenary, 101
deaths, parents', 182–184
democracy, 58, 63, 79, 187, 189–190, 198, 223
demographic transition, theory of, 112, 158n
demography, xv, xxii, xxiii, 109–158, 166, 171
demography, aggregate totals of births and
    deaths, 109–111, 116–117
Denmark, 97
Depression, 38, 54, 55, 104, 104n
developmental cycle of the family, 85–86, 203,
    216, 217
diet, 37–38, 153, 156n, 159, 164–166
Dilger, Caspar, 114–115
disease, *see* cattle disease; epidemic disease;
    goiter; influenza; malaria; pneumonia; scarlet
    fever; silicosis; smallpox; tuberculosis; typhus
divorce, 139–140
Domodossola, 54

earthquake, 119
ecological anthropology, xiv, xvi, xvii, 222–223,
    224
ecology, 63, 69, 76, 187, 221, 222–225

Economic Patriots, 161
ecosystem, xvi, 5, 15, 42, 58, 89, 90–91, 117,
    222, 225, 226
Eischoll, 189
Eisten, 55
Embd, 3, 6, 8, 10, 44n, 50, 52, 98, 104n, 107,
    107n, 118
Embdbach, 44
Emmental, 161
endogamy, x, 76, 93, 100n, 175; *see also*
    marriage
energy, 50, 153, 167
engagement, betrothal, 137, 175
England, 71, 72–76, 77, 93, 97, 111n, 116–117,
    126, 127, 133, 135, 139, 142, 143, 146, 156,
    160, 164, 169, 170, 203, 212, 230
environment, 5, 42, 57, 117, 158, 159, 196, 220
environmental degradation, 58, 158
environmental determinism, 223
epidemic disease, 77, 78, 91, 113, 119–121, 134,
    158, 226
equilibrium, systemic, xvii, 27, 41, 42, 57, 90,
    96, 101, 167, 199, 222–225
erosion, 46, 67
estate, division of, 172–174, 174n, 180–181
European marriage pattern, 169–170, 221
exogamy, 97–100, 100n, 219; *see also* marriage
expansion, 42, 43, 49–56
extended family household, defined, 214n
extinction of family lines, x, xn, 71–76, 82–84

fabrics, *see* textiles
factions, 187
factory work, 48, 49, 55, 103, 105, 106
fallowing, 32, 37, 46, 163
families, completed, 143; *see also* demography
family limitation, absence of, 87–88
family names, 71–73
family politics, 190–193, 201
family reconstitution, 91–93, 93n, 203, 231
famine, 117, 118, 161, 169
farmers, full-time, 49
Febvre, L., 57
fecundity, 142, 147, 158n, 167; *see also* fertility
Feld, 1, 3, 10, 20
fences, electric, 18
fencing, 28
fertility, age-specific, 143–147, 159
fertility, demographic, 83, 88–89, 92, 129–133,
    158, 221, 227
fertility, marital, 132–133, 140–141, 148
fertility, natural, 84, 133, 146n
fertilizer, artificial, 49; *see also* manuring
feudal dues, 59, 59n, 60
feudalism, 53n, 61n
fief, 50
field research, xxi
fines, 61, 62
firewood, fuel, 12, 22, 60, 66, 68, 78
folktale, 114–115